Pan-Germanism and the Austrofascist state, 1933–38

Manchester University Press

Pan-Germanism and the Austrofascist state, 1933–38

Julie Thorpe

Manchester University Press
Manchester and New York

*distributed in the United States exclusively
by Palgrave Macmillan*

Published by Manchester University Press
Oxford Road, Manchester M13 9NR, UK
and Room 400, 175 Fifth Avenue, New York, NY 10010, USA
www.manchesteruniversitypress.co.uk

Distributed in the United States exclusively by
Palgrave Macmillan, 175 Fifth Avenue, New York,
NY 10010, USA

Distributed in Canada exclusively by
UBC Press, University of British Columbia, 2029 West Mall,
Vancouver, BC, Canada V6T 1Z2

British Library Cataloguing-in-Publication Data
A catalogue record for this book is available from the British Library

Library of Congress Cataloging-in-Publication Data applied for

ISBN   978 0 7190 7967 2   hardback

First published 2011

Typeset
by Toppan Best-set Premedia Limited
Printed in Great Britain
by CPI Antony Rowe Ltd, Chippenham, Wiltshire

In memory of
Dr Wilhelm Maier
and
Marjorie Nugent

Contents

Abbreviations

AdR	Archiv der Republik
BKA	Bundeskanzleramt
BPD	Bundespressedienst
FZHM	Forschungszentrum für historische Minderheiten
HD	Heimatdienst
IKG	Israelitische Kultusgemeinde
NSDAP	Nationalsozialistische Deutsche Arbeiterpartei
ÖJV	Österreichisches Jungvolk
ÖKVDA	Österreichische Korrespondenz für volksdeutsche Arbeit
ÖVVA	Österreichischer Verband für volksdeutsche Auslandsarbeit
ÖStA	Österreichische Staatsarchiv
PA	Partei Archiv
VF	Vaterländische Front

Acknowledgements

I am grateful to colleagues, friends and family who have sustained me and this project over nearly a decade since I began my doctoral thesis in 2001 at the University of Adelaide. My *Doktormutter*, Vesna Drapac, was the reason I embarked on a PhD in history and she has continued to guide my career via phone calls, texts, emails and visits in her home and study, which I was only allowed to visit on completion of my thesis! I have read her two books during the time I wrote my thesis and this book. The diverse subjects of the books – religion in German-occupied Paris and the international community's responses to Yugoslavia over more than a century – have shaped my own interpretation of some of the debates surrounding Austria's place in European history and inspired me to find my own voice as a historian.

The writing of this book took place in three different institutions in three cities in Australia and Europe. The original doctoral thesis on which it is based was undertaken at Adelaide, where I was privileged to meet Dick Geary in my first year as a PhD student while he was a Distinguished Scholar in Residence. I remember how daunted I was to have coffee for the first time with such a famous historian at the University Club, but Dick proved to be (and still is) incredibly generous to an aspiring historian, sharing not only his vast knowledge, but also his intellectual curiosity for just about everything. I was privileged also at Adelaide to be part of an active postgraduate research culture and to have opportunities to present my work to fellow students and staff. I thank all those who asked questions and showed interest in a topic that was seemingly outside the mainstream of European history.

My second intellectual home in Canberra, the Australian National University (ANU), provided a multidisciplinary space to discuss my work with other scholars and PhD students at the National Europe Centre. I am grateful to the Centre's former Director, Simon Bronitt, for the investment he made in my career and the congenial atmosphere he created during the three years I spent at the Centre. I thank all the wonderful staff and fellows for their good humour, home-baked cakes, coffees, walks, runs, dinners, lunches, film evenings, parties and staff meetings that made the Centre such a pleasurable distraction from my writing. Finally, the University of Konstanz provided me with a postdoctoral fellowship in 2009 and a stunning location to write. Sven Reichardt welcomed me into the history department and his transnational approach to fascism helped me finally to locate the Austrian case within a broader framework.

Other colleagues in Britain and North America have shown an interest in my work. Tim Kirk helped me to shape the ideas from my thesis into a book and has encouraged me to continue my research in Austrian history. Pieter Judson, Gary Cohen, Jonathan Kwan and Larissa Douglass were my fellow panellists at the 2009 American Historical Association. Their comments and papers helped me to place my arguments about population politics and state building in the Austrofascist state within a longer trajectory of Central European politics. Most recently, Günter Bischof has welcomed the findings of an Australian Austrianist to the larger community of North American and Austrian scholars through the Contemporary Austrian Studies series.

The research for my thesis was supported by an Australian Postgraduate Award scholarship in 2001–4. I also received financial assistance from the University of Adelaide's D.R. Stranks Postgraduate Travelling Fellowship and Research Abroad Scholarship, as well as the History Postgraduate Committee. Additional research for the book was supported by travel grants from the ANU's National Europe Centre.

I am grateful to the librarians at the universities of Vienna, Salzburg and Graz for access to microfilm newspaper collections. I thank also the Archiv der Stadt Salzburg, the Österreichische Staatsarchiv and the Forschungszentrum für historische Minderheiten in Vienna for their helpful assistance in locating files at short notice. In Salzburg, Ernst Hanisch pointed me to the diary of Hans Glaser and, in Vienna, Gernot Heiss generously gave me a copy of his book, *Asylland Wider Willen*. My translations of the newspapers were improved by Lee Kersten's editing at Adelaide.

I owe a special debt of gratitude to Wilhelm Maier, who spent hours reading aloud Glaser's diary so that I could transcribe the old handwriting-style script. I will always remember our *Kaffee und Kuchen* afternoons in Wilhelm and Erna's home in Salzburg as Wilhelm told me his memories as a boy in interwar Austria and, later, a soldier in the Second World War. Wilhelm passed away in 2008 before I could show him the final product of his work. This book is dedicated to his memory. I thank Erna and her daughter, Dorli Reinthaler, for their ongoing interest in my research. Dorli and Günter have been my Austrian parents since I lived in Salzburg in 1996. They have welcomed me into their home and family, corrected my

German, driven me to airports and train stations, taken me on road trips, and shared their lives with me for almost half my life now. Their two daughters, Edith and Claudia, have carried on the Reinthaler hospitality in Salzburg, Vienna, Heidelberg and Leipzig. Werner, Nicolas and Ian have added to the fun and now Nico and Ian are my new German teachers.

My other family in Salzburg – Bernhard, Michaela and Miriam Helminger – provide a full social calendar every time I visit. Bernhard has been my personal tutor in Austrian politics since 1996. My case study of Salzburg was partly inspired by his own 'small town' political and cultural networks, reading Salzburg's newspaper with him on weekends, and his interest in both local and global affairs.

I thank members of my extended family who have welcomed this project into their homes as well. Julie Baker was my study companion in Adelaide for one semester. The Lavery-Jones family – Ruth, Mark, Alex and Eleanor – let me stay in their attic for the final weeks of this book as I relocated to Sydney. My own family have given endless support and healthy doses of reality. Darren and Anj, Sarah and Nathan, Toby, Sophie, Maddie and Hamish have made sure I was in Newcastle at regular intervals throughout this project. My parents have watched on with a mixture of puzzlement and pride as the seventeen-year-old daughter they sent off to Salzburg finally wrote a book about her adopted home. I thank them for everything. I owe the largest debt of gratitude to my beautiful Nan, who passed away in 2010. I lived with her while I was writing my thesis as she became more dependent on us. So much of this book is part of the memory of her and it is to her, in the end, that I dedicate my book.

Introduction

What is this book about?

This book is about the Austrofascist state that was established the year Adolf Hitler came to power in Germany in 1933 and collapsed the day Hitler annexed his homeland to the German Reich in 1938. It argues that Austria matters to this period of European history, not because Hitler was Austrian, but because the processes and events occurring in Austria between 1933 and 1938 intersected with processes and events occurring elsewhere in Europe. The rationale for this book was to place the Austrian case against a wider backdrop of nationalism and fascism in Europe. I contend that the question of whether the regime in Austria was authoritarian or fascist, which contemporary observers and scholars have debated since 1933, cannot be understood without reference to the political ideas circulating elsewhere in Europe and the impact of and reception to those ideas within Austria itself. Similarly nationalism, one of the central tenets of both fascist and authoritarian states in the interwar period, needs to be understood within a framework of beliefs and practices of nationalists in Europe since the mid-nineteenth century. Other specific questions that this book addresses – the role of public institutions like the press; the relationship between minority populations and the state; local and regional variants of nationalism; the place of religion in the state; and the nature of anti-Semitism prior to 1938 – are also directly related to and relevant for broader themes in European history. In asking why Austria matters for understanding nationalism and fascism in Europe, this book finds answers not only within Austria but more often outside it.

What the book is *not* is a story of Austria's road to *Anschluss*: an analysis of the political events, movements, personalities and decisions that led to Austria's annexation with Nazi Germany in March 1938. The history of the Nazi Party in Austria dating back to its pre-1918 origins under the Austro-Hungarian Empire was one of the dominant strands of earlier historical research on Austria. Andrew Whiteside's 1975 study of the pan-German movement led by the radical liberal politician, Georg von Schönerer (1842–1921), was the first major Anglophone study of right-wing national-ism in the empire.[1] Other studies of the Austrian Nazi movement followed, notably Bruce Pauley's 1981 publication, *Hitler and the Forgotten Nazis*, which along with Whiteside is routinely cited in comparative studies of European fascism.[2]

Austria's interwar foreign relations, and the Austro-German agreement of July 1936 in particular, is another subject that has preoccupied histori-ans for decades.[3] My book draws on these existing studies of the domestic and international factors that contributed to Austria's eventual annexation to Germany, while also offering a fresh perspective on the question of Austro-German relations. I argue that Austrofascist politicians were looking elsewhere, notably Italy, Great Britain and Czechoslovakia, for friendly alliances and political patrons in the days leading up to *Anschluss*. The attempts to expand Austrian influence in Europe and to win allies for the cause of Austrofascism were not a desperate eleventh-hour manoeuvre to thwart an inevitable Nazi takeover; rather, the book demonstrates that these efforts followed a consistent policy since 1933 to build an Austrian state in the image of and as a model to other European states.

My book is also *not* a comparative study of fascism, though it does make comparisons and draws on the literature about Italy and Germany in particular. Comparative work on fascism since the 1960s has marginal-ized examples like Austria that do not fit the pedigree of true fascism in Italy and Germany. Various labels ranging from 'reactionary' or 'conserva-tive', to 'authoritarian' and 'radical' have been used to categorize the myriad right-wing European movements, parties and regimes prior to 1945. Stanley Payne's typology in the mid-1990s of 'three faces of authori-tarian nationalism' classified Austria's Christian Social Party and its suc-cessor, the Fatherland Front, as 'conservative right' alongside Hungarian national unionists and Romanian monarchists. The Austrian *Heimwehr* (Home Guard), a loosely unified body made up of several provincial militia groups that formally entered the ranks of government in 1934, repre-sented the 'radical right', while the only 'fascist' face in Austria, according to Payne, was the Nazi Party.[4] Payne's typology is a slight variation on the earlier work of scholars in the 1960s and 1970s like Ludwig Jedlicka and Francis Carsten, who included both the *Heimwehr* and the Nazi Party in their definitions of fascism, though Payne's definition of 'conservative' for the regime itself is consistent with the older scholarship.[5] Another com-parativist scholar, Robert Paxton, also draws his conclusion that the Aus-trian state was a 'Catholic authoritarian regime' from a thin and dated list of works on Austria, including Whiteside's, Carsten's and Pauley's books.[6] The problem is not always in the comparative method, but in the lack of any substantive new English-language contributions to the field since the 1970s and the fact that virtually no new scholarship either in German or English attempts to situate the Austrian case within a broader European context. Austrian scholars write for an Austrian audience, and Anglophone scholars continue to produce syntheses that reproduce old typologies.

My book challenges the conventional wisdom that the Austrofascist state was an authoritarian regime upholding conservative Catholic values against the tyranny of true fascism, National Socialism. This image of 'authoritarian Austria' – self-fashioned by the state itself in the 1930s – is based on a series of claims about the state that make superficial (if any) comparisons with the Italian and German variants of fascism.[7] The first of these claims is based on a misconception that the Christian Social Party was the political arm of the Austrian Catholic Church and, therefore, that the public role of church leaders and Catholic organizations in the Austrofascist state prevented it from becoming fascist. This claim has been put forward by a number of scholars who reject the political label of 'clerical fascism', but it suffers from an insular perspective that fails to take into account relations between church and state in Italy and Germany, for example, or between Catholics and other right-wing European regimes, such as Vichy France.[8] Another rebuttal of the fascist label argues that the Austrian state did not achieve the same level of mass recruitment for its single party organization – the Fatherland Front – as the Italian and German fascist parties did. Nor, it is claimed, did the Austrian state produce a *Duce* or *Führer* in either of the two chancellors, Engelbert Dollfuss or Kurt von Schuschnigg,[9] although one could argue that the posthumous cult of Dollfuss after his assassination in 1934, including monuments, photographs, placards, death masks and songs in his honour, was an attempt to create a cult of a dead leader. Finally, historians who subscribe to the orthodox view that the Austrian state was authoritarian refer to the many features of the regime that imitated fascism in Italy and Germany – the state leisure organization, *Neues Leben* (New Life), mother care programmes and so on – but did not amount to genuine fascism in Austria.[10] Yet the claim that the Austrian state copied fascist regimes is rarely substantiated with reference to the limits of fascistization in Italy and Germany, where mother care and leisure programmes were equally aimed at inculcating patriotic values and keeping the consumers happy.[11] A recent comparative study of Fascist Italy and Nazi Germany makes the 'imitation fascism' argument redundant with the evidence that the German *Kraft durch Freude* (Strength through Joy) was itself a copy of the Italian mass leisure organization, *Opera Nazionale Dopolavoro* (National After Work Agency).[12]

That Austrofascism borrowed much in style and form from Nazi Germany as well as Fascist Italy has been glossed over in the regime's history and, consequently, in most comparative accounts of European fascism, too. Philipp Ther's criticism of comparative histories, that they continue to make the nation-state the unit of comparison, is especially valid for fascism studies. Transnational or 'relational' histories, on the other hand, look for contacts, exchanges and transfers across national and state borders.[13] New scholarship that takes a transnational approach to fascism has demonstrated the many contacts, exchanges and relations that occurred not only between fascist states within Europe, but also between fascist and non-fascist states outside Europe.[14] This recent burst of scholarship that introduces relational comparisons with North America or Australia might tempt the weary (and wary) to do away with fascism as a category of analysis altogether. But the fact that much of this scholarship is emerging from Germany means that scholars would have a difficult task ignoring the sophistication of these analyses that follow more than half a century of German historiography and are situated within the new global historiographies that break from some of the traditions of national histories. A transnational history of fascism is more concerned with the process of creating a fascist state than with the outcome of whether the state was fascist or not. The claim made by comparativist scholars, however, that Austria's Fatherland Front did not recruit as many followers as Italy's Fascist Party or Germany's Nazi Party and therefore was more authoritarian than fascist, refers only to party numbers (outcomes) rather than the modes of recruitment or coercion (processes).[15]

Instead of seeing the Austrian dictatorship as a paler imitation of the Nazi dictatorship, my book offers a new perspective on the period 1933–38, defining the process of creating a fascist state in Austria as a form of fascism itself. Mine is not the first study to argue for a process-oriented approach to fascism. In *The Anatomy of Fascism*, Paxton charts the five stages of fascism from the creation of fascist movements, to their 'rooting' in the political system, to their seizure of power, to the exercise of power, to the final stage when fascist regimes undergo either radicalization or entropy.[16] However, Paxton never applies the same categories to conservatives that he applies to fascists: they remain 'in essence' conservative, and we are left to draw the conclusion that there is an invisible line over which conservatives do not cross.[17] A further problem with Paxton's model is that it works only for Germany and Italy. Consequently, only successful fascism that completes the full five stages of development counts as genuine fascism, thus reducing fascism again to an outcome.[18]

My definition of fascism is closer to the work of Aristotle Kallis and Michael Mann. Kallis has attempted to overcome the distinction between the regime models of fascism and all other interwar and wartime regimes that adopted fascist structures and organizations, which he terms 'para-fascism', by suggesting that the difference between 'fascism' and 'para-fascism' is a difference of degree rather than substance. He argues that fascism should be seen as a process (fascistization) that was unique in every regime because of the circumstances under which traditional elites co-opted fascist groups or fascist 'commodities'. In some cases, notably Italy and Germany, this process led to fascism coming to power as the elites handed over leadership to fascist groups, which Kallis describes as 'fascistization as last resort'. In other cases, fascistization was designed to fortify conservative rule without necessarily forming an alliance with fascist groups, a phenomenon Kallis calls 'voluntary fascism'. A third cat-egory, 'preventive fascism', describes those regimes that attempted to ward off more radical groups, as occurred in Austria under Dollfuss and Schuschnigg against the Social Democratic Party and later the Nazi Party. While Kallis still seems to be making a distinction between the regimes in Italy and Germany and all others, his typology does not reduce the defini-tion of fascism only to the Italian and German cases. Rather, he sees all regimes as a 'distortion' of fascist ideology because each regime adapted it to the perceived needs and conditions in that society. It is more fruitful, in Kallis's opinion, to focus on the trajectory of fascistization in each country in order to assess the nature of the regime.[19]

Similarly, Mann sees fascism as the 'pursuit' of a form of nationalism that seeks radical 'cleansing' solutions, employs paramilitary force and seeks to 'transcend' social divisions through coercion and control.[20] While he makes all the usual observations of the Austrian regime that it borrowed from fascist structures and ideology but lacked a grass-roots fascist party, Mann also presents Austria as a special case of fascism, arguing that Aus-trian fascists were disproportionately greater in numbers than in Germany or Italy despite their not coming to power until after Austria's annexation to Germany.[21] His conclusion is based on figures for former *Heimwehr* men who became Nazis before 1938, suggesting that Mann has simply substi-tuted 'fascists' for 'Nazis'. On the other hand, his definition of fascism as 'organic' and 'cleansing' nationalism, which refers both to ethnic and politi-cal enemies, and his emphasis on 'anti-Semitic fascism', widens consider-ably the ranks of fascists in Austria and highlights the role nationalism played in the creation of an Austrofascist state.

Scholarship has given scant regard to the relationship between national-ism and fascism in Austria or, indeed, in the entire region of Central and Eastern Europe. The tendency of historians of fascism to focus on regime models and sociological theories to explain why some groups were more attracted to fascism than others has meant that our understanding of

nation building in Habsburg Central Europe is divorced from our understanding of those political and social movements that gained popular currency in the successor states during the interwar years. Paxton is a case in
point: his approach suffers from a Western European approach to fascism
and he essentializes the Austrian case by drawing a linear connection
between the pan-Germanism of Schönerer in the 1880s and the Austrian
Nazis in the interwar period.[22] But Paxton is not alone in this tendency:
historians of Western Europe have tended only to draw on the examples
from Central and Eastern Europe when it suits their theoretical juxtapo-
sitioning of fascism, authoritarianism and national extremism, despite the
efforts of historians to revise persistent West–East dichotomies for nationalism and fascism in the successor states.[23] Questions about minorities,
or ethnic and civic practices of defining citizenship, which have long
concerned historians of nationalism, have to date received no attention
in anatomical explanations of the 'rooting' of fascism outside Italy
and Germany.

To summarize, the historiographical and methodological problems that
this book addresses relate not only to Austrian scholarship, but also more
generally to scholarship on European history. I argue that the Austrofascist
state must be placed outside the constraints of Austrian history and instead
be seen as part of a larger European phenomenon. At the same time, I use
the Austrian case to challenge the tradition of writing about European
fascism from the perspective of Western European examples only, including Germany. My case studies of the Austrian press, regional politics,
minorities, citizenship, immigration and anti-Semitism shed light on
broader questions about how public institutions, politicians, legislators,
religious groups and multi-ethnic communities responded and adapted
to the transformations across Europe in the period between the two
world wars.

Some more definitions

Having established my definition of Austrofascism as a process of creating
a fascist state in Austria before 1938, I want to introduce briefly another
term in this book before introducing my sources and case studies. The
book's title includes a term that will already be familiar to scholars of
German and Austrian history – pan-Germanism. Yet as with fascism,
historians have adopted an overly schematic approach that defines pan-
Germanism according to fixed political categories. Whiteside's earlier definition of pan-Germanism as a radical political movement that grew up in
late imperial Austria and came to maturity in the interwar Nazi Party has
become standard usage in Anglophone scholarship on Austria.[24] However,

the ambiguous use of this term obscures the many varieties of Austrian pan-Germanism and fails to explain why competing political camps in Austria often found themselves on the same side of nationalist politics while maintaining partisan lines on other issues such as religion. Historians have not been able to explain why, for instance, all the major parties in interwar Austria used the term 'pan-German' to refer to Austria's unique identity as a German state and to the shared national identity of Austrian Germans and other Germans in Central Europe. I define pan-Germanism as both the particular or unique aspects of Austrian German identity (which are sometimes expressed in local or regional variants such as Tyrolean German, for example), and the universal sense of all Germans belonging in a larger community united by culture and ethnicity. My definition follows recent theoretical approaches to nationalism that regard civic and political constructions of nationhood as inclusive of ethnic and cultural nationalism.[25] I argue that this breadth of pan-Germanism in Austria made it the preferred national identity – and ideology – of a host of competing interest groups in Austria before 1938.

I deal more extensively with the fluid and contested nature of pan-Germanism in Chapter 1. But my definition of pan-Germanism also underpins one of the central arguments of the book, that Nazis and their sympathizers sometimes clashed with Austrofascists, but more often converged in their efforts to build a new state of German citizens. This is an important corrective to the dominance of the *Lager* theory in Austrian historiography, which divides Austria into three competing political camps of conservative Catholics, socialists and German-nationalists. Historian Adam Wandruszka first developed the theory in 1954 when Austria was still under Allied occupation. It gave historical legitimacy to the post-war party of rehabilitated Austrian Nazis, the League of Independents (the precursor to Jörg Haider's Freedom Party of Austria), who reappeared on Austria's political scene in 1949 following the relaxation of de-Nazification laws in 1948.[26] At a time when Austria's post-war socialist politicians were courting voters on the far left, the *Lager* theory blurred the distinctions between social democrats and communists in the socialist 'camp' and overlooked the German-nationalist orientation of the socialist leader and veteran president of the Austrian republic, Karl Renner (1870–1950), who famously voted 'yes' in Hitler's 1938 plebiscite in favour of Austria's annexation to Nazi Germany.[27] The *Lager* theory dispensed with another inconvenient truth of Austria's interwar past by decoupling Christian Socials and German-nationalists in spite of their shared political positions on a range of domestic issues and the fact that they were in coalition government throughout much of the 1920s.[28] Historians have since acknowledged the Nazi sympathies of interwar conservatives and a few socialists, but the

Lager theory established a fixed relationship between the nationalist camp, pan-Germanism and National Socialism that has never seriously been contested. In overlooking the relationship between pan-Germanism and the Austrofascist state, historians have manufactured a popular myth that the 'nationalist' camp supported National Socialism while the 'conservative' camp under Dollfuss and Schuschnigg acted as a bulwark against fascist movements in Austria.[29] This book is an attempt finally to demolish that myth.

Sources

My study of the Austrofascist state is largely an analysis of the German-nationalist press in Austria. This focus is warranted for a few reasons. As other studies of the press have demonstrated, newspapers are not only a rich source of information about social, political, cultural and everyday life, but they also lead us to discover the ways people gave expression to and derived meaning from their sense of national belonging at a time of instability, ideological extremism and psychological fixation on rebuilding or recovering a seemingly lost collective identity. My intention has not been to amass evidence of public opinion by analysing the numbers of articles on certain topics or chronicling daily experiences and encounters between citizens from the pages of the popular press. Rather I read the three German-nationalist newspapers that form the bulk of my analysis as a contemporary reader might have done: skimming the headlines, pausing to digest articles on important topics, re-reading some reports for evidence of double-speak or the censor's heavy hand, checking the cinema schedule, admiring the latest fashions and glancing through the obituaries for a familiar name. I was able to build up a complex and layered picture of the issues most relevant to readers of the German-nationalist press, many of which are covered in the case studies in this book. Later I combined my own reading of the newspapers with the selective reading of Austrofascist press officials, whose marginalia and underlined portions of text in the newspaper articles often gave insight into the political relationship between Austrofascists and German-nationalists.

The focus on the German-nationalist press has added significance for the period 1933–38, coinciding with both the emergence of the Nazi dictatorship in Germany and the creation of an Austrofascist state. After the state banned the Nazi and Communist parties and newspapers in 1933 and then the organs of the Social Democratic Party in 1934, the German-nationalist newspapers were the only remaining non-government organs that were 'coordinated' within the public sphere of the state. They also represented the single largest readership outside Vienna under

Austrofascism, selling up to fifty percent of all weekday newspapers in regional cities.[30] I argue that while German-nationalist editors and their readers may have admired the success of National Socialism in Germany, they did not always support Nazi designs for Austro-German unity and few were prepared to give unconditional allegiance to the Nazis. The newspapers courted both National Socialists and Austrofascists in the hope of keeping alive a pan-German ideology that could eventually bring about the union of Austria and Germany. Moreover, these newspapers and their readers negotiated their belonging to the national community in ways that often overlapped with Austrofascist efforts to construct an official pan-German identity.

Aside from newspapers, I also had access to files from the federal press agency (*Bundespressedienst*) and propaganda bureau (*Heimatdienst*), which amalgamated at the end of 1936 into a single federal press and propaganda office. These files included article clippings from Austrian newspapers on diverse topics ranging from religion to refugees from Nazi Germany, as well as correspondence on Austria from foreign press agencies. Foreign correspondents reporting news on Austria to international readers were of as much interest to Austria's press officials as Austrian journalists writing for domestic audiences. I also looked at files of the Fatherland Front including coverage of a Front delegation's visit to Italy in 1936. Finally, the protocols of the Federal Council for Culture (*Bundeskulturrat*), one of four legislative bodies in the Austrofascist state, contained the ministerial debates and resolutions on the press legislation and immigration and citizenship bills. These primary sources, along with published memoirs and one unpublished diary of a newspaper editor from the period, provide a rich array of material to supplement the newspaper text analysis. They show how the Austrofascist state accommodated multiple versions of pan-Germanism within its ranks and how, in turn, competing interest groups in Austria united with Austrofascists in the shared vision of creating a new German Austrian state.

Case studies

The case studies of the German-nationalist press form part of a larger series of thematic and regional micro studies on the contours of pan-German identity before and after 1918; the role and function of the press from imperial days to the Austrofascist state; relations between local Austrofascist politicians and national activists; state policy towards linguistic minorities in Austria and German-speaking minorities outside Austria; the nature and extent of anti-Semitism in Austria before 1938; and legislation on citizenship and immigration in the Austrofascist state.

The book begins with a survey of pan-Germanism from the time of the 1848–49 national and liberal revolutions to the end of the Austrofascist period. Chapter 1 shows how first the liberals, then the Christian Socials and Social Democrats, the German-nationalists and later the National Socialists, all at different times espoused the political and cultural unity of the German nation and the German identity of the Austrian state. Placed within this *longue durée* of pan-Germanism in Austria, Austrofascists can be regarded as the heirs of a dual tradition of loyalty both to the German nation and to the Austrian state. I argue that they are better understood for what they embraced than for what they opposed.

Chapter 2 examines the role of the press as both an institution and a medium in the Austrofascist state. It compares the Austrian case with Fascist Italy, drawing on recent scholarship on the Italian press to demonstrate that, as in Italy, Austria's press and propaganda was a product of nineteenth-century censorship practices, twentieth-century efforts to modernize and nationalize the press for a domestic audience, and the inspiration of those whose idea of combined modern media and propaganda was one of the forms of exchange and contact between fascist regimes in the 1930s.

The remaining four chapters flesh out the theoretical and methodological framework of the book. Chapter 3 presents a regional case study of the German-nationalist organ in Salzburg, the *Salzburger Volksblatt*, and its owner, Hans Glaser (1877–1960), whose diary reveals the private and public relationships between newspaper editors, journalists, politicians, clergy, censors and local state functionaries. The evidence from both the newspaper and Glaser's diary shows how the particular intellectual and cultural currents in Salzburg drew Austrofascists and German-nationalists together in their interwar construction of pan-German identity and, in this sense, the chapter serves as a microcosm of the book itself.

Chapter 4 offers another local study of a regional German-nationalist newspaper, the *Tagespost* in Graz, but it also compares the Styrian organ with the leading German-nationalist newspaper in Vienna, the *Wiener Neueste Nachrichten*. The newspapers had different editorships and readerships and therefore offer different perspectives on issues including Austro-German relations, acts of Nazi terrorism in Austria, Dollfuss's assassination in 1934, and the place of nationalist politics in the new Austria. The chapter also compares the German-nationalist press with official organs of the Austrofascist state on other topical issues like bilingual schools and public monuments for Slovenian-, Croatian- and Czech-speaking minorities in Austria, and explores how the state's policies towards its non-German minorities as well as German minorities outside

Austria merged with nationalist activism of former Nazis and their fellow travellers in Austria.

In Chapters 5 and 6 I argue that the issues of assimilation, immigration and citizenship in the Austrofascist state were as central to the construction of pan-German identity as the questions of Austro-German unity and German dominance in Central Europe. Chapter 5 shows how the creation of an anti-Semitic stereotype – the *Ostjude* or Eastern Jew – was aligned with the ethnic and civic boundaries of Austria's pan-German identity. The Austrofascist state itself constructed the legal, political, social and racial boundaries that excluded and discriminated against Jews in Austria. Chapter 6 then explores how these exclusionary mechanisms extended to policy on Austria's immigration and citizenship requirements. Here the book returns to Italy as a model of legislation for a foreigner index system in Austria. This final chapter demonstrates the book's overall conclusion that Austrians were just as concerned with the boundaries of their own state as they were with the wider boundaries of the German nation in the years before 1938. They were not only imagining their identity as Germans in the New Europe: they were also imagining their identity as citizens of the New Austria.

Notes

1 Andrew G. Whiteside, *The Socialism of Fools: Georg Ritter von Schönerer and Austrian Pan-Germanism* (Berkeley: University of California Press, 1975).
2 Bruce Pauley, *Hitler and the Forgotten Nazis: A History of Austrian National Socialism* (Chapel Hill: University of North Carolina Press, 1981).
3 Lájos Kerekes, *Abenddämmerung einer Demokratie: Mussolini, Gömbös und die Heimwehr* (Vienna: Europa, 1966); Ludwig Jedlicka and Rudolf Neck (eds), *Das Juliabkommen von 1936: Vorgeschichte, Hintergründe und Folgen* (Vienna: Verlag für Geschichte und Politik, 1977); Alfred D. Low, *The Anschluss Movement, 1931–1938, and the Great Powers* (Boulder: East European Monographs, 1985).
4 See Table I.2: Three Faces of Authoritarian Nationalism, in Stanley G. Payne, *A History of Fascism, 1914–1945* (London: University College London Press, 1995), p. 15, and his more general account of Austria in Chapter 8.
5 See Ludwig Jedlicka's contribution on Austria in the inaugural 1966 issue of the *Journal of Contemporary History*, which was devoted to the topic of fascism. Jedlicka, 'The Austrian Heimwehr', *Journal of Contemporary History* 1, 1 (1966): 127–44. In his introduction to the special issue, Hugh Seton-Watson also concluded that the regime in Austria was 'reactionary' rather than 'fascist'. Seton-Watson, 'Fascism, Right and Left', *Journal of Contemporary History* 1, 1 (1966), p. 191. On both the Nazis and the *Heimwehr*, see also F.L. Carsten,

Fascist Movements in Austria: From Schönerer to Hitler (London: Sage, 1977);
F.L. Carsten, *The Rise of Fascism*, 2nd edn (London: Batsford, 1980), pp. 223–29.
More recently, Gerhard Botz has also defined the Nazis and the *Heimwehr* as
two 'brands' of fascism in Austria: the Nazis, representing 'national fascism'
akin to Germany's National Socialism, and the *Heimwehr*, representing
'*Heimwehr* fascism' closer to the Italian variant. The Christian Social Party and
the Fatherland Front fall outside the Austrian family of fascism in Botz's assessment and after the *Heimwehr* was absorbed into the Fatherland Front in 1936,
he concludes that the *Heimwehr* also ceased to be fascist. See Gerhard Botz,
'Varieties of Fascism in Austria: Introduction', Stein Ugelvik Larsen, Bernt
Hagtvet and Jan Petter Myklebust (eds), *Who Were the Fascists? Social Roots
of European Fascism* (Bergen: Universitetsforlaget, 1980), p. 194. See also his
chapter, 'The Short- and Long-term Effects of the Authoritarian Regime and
of Nazism in Austria: The Burden of a "Second Dictatorship" ', in Jerzy Borejsza
and Klaus Ziemer (eds), *Totalitarian and Authoritarian Regimes in Europe:
Legacies and Lessons from the Twentieth Century* (New York: Berghahn, 2006),
pp. 188–208.
6 Robert Paxton, *The Anatomy of Fascism* (New York: Allen Lane, 2004), p. 115.
   See his bibliographical essay on Austria, pp. 240–41.
7 See my article for an extended discussion of each of these claims. Julie Thorpe,
   'Austrofascism: Revisiting the "Authoritarian State" Forty Years On', *Journal of
   Contemporary History* 45, 2 (2010): 1–29.
8 Ernst Hanisch sees 'clerical fascism' as a political label, not a type of fascism,
   and argues that while the Vatican and the Austrian bishops formally supported
   the regime, they did not help to establish it. He concludes that the Church's
   presence within and support for the state prevented it from becoming fascist.
   Hanisch, 'Der Politische Katholizismus als ideologischer Träger des "Austrofaschismus" ', in Emmerich Tálos and Wolfgang Neugebauer (eds), *Austrofaschismus: Politik–Ökonomie–Kultur 1933–1938*, 5th rev. edn (Vienna: Lit,
   2005), pp. 68–86.
9 For example, Pauley claims that Dollfuss and Schuschnigg were no more than
   'semi-fascist dictators' because they saw themselves only as a temporary buffer
   against socialism and Nazism and held no plans to transform society into a
   new community of fascists. See Pauley, 'Fascism and the *Führerprinzip*: The
   Austrian Example', *Central European History* 12, 3 (1979), pp. 285–86.
10 Pauley refers to this notion of authoritarianism with fascist trappings as 'positive fascism' in *Hitler and the Forgotten Nazis*, p. 162. Hanisch uses the term
   'imitation fascism' in 'Die Salzburger Presse in der Ersten Republik 1918–1938',
   Mitteilungen der Gesellschaft für Salzburger Landeskunde 128 (1988), p. 362.
11 Scholars of Italian Fascism have also questioned the limits of consensus in daily
   life under the Italian dictatorship. See, notably, Victoria de Grazia, *The Culture
   of Consent: Mass Organization of Leisure in Fascist Italy* (Cambridge: Cambridge University Press, 1981) and de Grazia, *How Fascism Ruled Women: Italy,
   1922–1945* (Berkeley: University of California Press, 1992), and more recently
   R.J.B. Bosworth, *Mussolini's Italy: Life under the Dictatorship* (London: Penguin,

2005). Emmerich Tálos has argued that the failure of the Austrian regime to create a fully-fledged fascist state is not sufficient reason to dismiss or play down its intention to become fascist; neither can the breadth of the Austro-fascist project be underestimated. Tálos points to the imitative elements of fascism – the monopoly of the Fatherland Front, the creation of a state leisure organization and a state youth group, and the 'co-ordination' of the press and schools – as evidence that the regime made no distinction between its own goals of transforming Austria and the transformations that had already occurred in Italy and Germany. See Tálos, 'Das austrofaschistische Herrschaftssystem', in Tálos and Neugebauer (eds), *Austrofaschismus*, pp. 394–420.

12 See Daniela Liebscher, 'Faschismus als Modell: Die faschistische *Opera Nazionale Dopolavoro* und die NS-Gemeinschaft "Kraft durch Freude" in der Zwischenkriegszeit', in Sven Reichardt and Armin Nolzen (eds), *Faschismus in Italien und Deutschland: Studien zu Transfer und Vergleich* (Göttingen: Wallstein, 2005), pp. 94–118.

13 Philipp Ther, 'Beyond the Nation: The Relational Basis of a Comparative History of Germany and Europe', *Central European History* 36, 1 (2003): 45–73. See also the contributions in Deborah Cohen and Maureen O'Connor (eds), *Comparison and History: Europe in Cross-National Perspective* (New York: Routledge, 2004).

14 See the contributions in Reichardt and Nolzen (eds), *Faschismus in Italien und Deutschland*.

15 Statistical comparisons can also lack contextual information about the groups targeted for party membership or the methods of coercion used to recruit members. If we compare the Italian *Partito Nazionale Fascista* (PNF) with the Austrian Fatherland Front at the time that each organization emerged, we see that the Fatherland Front was numerically stronger with 500,000 members by the end of 1933 while the PNF had only 300,000 at the end of 1921. But these numbers are based on different modes of recruitment: the PNF coerced factory workers and farm labourers to join as a condition of keeping their jobs, while entire organizations joined the Fatherland Front on a collective basis. See Philip Morgan, *Fascism in Europe, 1919–1945* (London: Routledge, 2003), p. 48, and Emmerich Tálos and Walter Manoschek, 'Aspekte der politischen Struktur des Austrofaschismus', in Tálos and Neugebauer (eds), *Austrofaschismus*, pp. 145–46.

16 Paxton, *The Anatomy of Fascism*.

17 Robert Soucy points out this criticism of Paxton in his essay, 'Fascism in France: Problematizing the Immunity Thesis', in Brian Jenkins (ed.), *France in the Era of Fascism: Essays on the French Authoritarian Right* (New York: Berghahn, 2005), pp. 65–104.

18 See Jenkins's conclusion ibid., pp. 200–18.

19 Aristotle A. Kallis, ' "Fascism", "Para-fascism" and "Fascistization": On the Similarities of Three Conceptual Categories', *European History Quarterly* 33, 2 (2003): 219–49.

20 Michael Mann, *Fascists* (Cambridge: Cambridge University Press, 2004), p. 13.
21 Ibid., pp. 43–48.
22 For a rebuttal of the claim that the Nazis were the offspring of Schönerer's followers, see Robert Hoffmann, 'Gab es ein "Schönerianisches Milieu?" Versuch einer Kollektivbiographie von Mitgliedern des "Vereins der Salzburger Studenten in Wien"', in Ernst Bruckmüller, et al. (eds), *Bürgertum in der Habsburgermonarchie* (Vienna: Böhlau, 1990), pp. 275–98.
23 On Czechoslovakia, for example, see the contributions in Mark Cornwall and R.J.W. Evans (eds), *Czechoslovakia in a Nationalist and Fascist Europe 1918–1948* (Oxford: Oxford University Press, 2007).
24 Whiteside originally took the term 'Pan-Germans' from the translation of *Alldeutsche* (All-Germans), but also used the term in reference to the radical Young Liberals (*Jungliberale*) who supported Schönerer. See Whiteside, 'The Germans as an Integrative Force in Imperial Austria: The Dilemma of Dominance', *Austrian History Yearbook* 3, 1 (1967), p. 175, and Whiteside, *The Socialism of Fools*. The term has since been used variously to describe both radical and moderate liberals, social democrats and National Socialists. See Carl E. Schorske, 'Politics in a New Key: An Austrian Triptych', *Journal of Modern History* 39, 4 (1967): 343–86; William T. Bluhm, *Building an Austrian Nation: The Political Integration of a Western State* (New Haven: Yale University Press, 1973), pp. 12–45; Kurt Tweraser, 'Carl Beurle and the Triumph of German Nationalism in Austria', *German Studies Review* 4, 3 (1981): 403–26; Roger Fletcher, 'Karl Leuthner's Greater Germany: The Pre-1914 Pan-Germanism of an Austrian Socialist', *Canadian Review of Studies in Nationalism* 9, 1 (1982): 57–79.
25 The literature on ethnic and civic nationalisms is vast. For a recent attempt to overcome the dichotomy between ethnic and civic, see Oliver Zimmer, 'Boundary Mechanisms and Symbolic Resources: Towards a Process-Oriented Approach to National Identity', *Nations and Nationalism* 9, 2 (2003): 173–93.
26 Detlef Lehnert, 'Politisch-kulturelle Integrationsmilieus und Orientierungslager in einer polarisierten Massengesellschaft', in Emmerich Tálos, et al. (eds), *Handbuch des politischen Systems Österreichs: Erste Republik 1918–1933* (Vienna: Manz, 1995), p. 431. On the impact of former Nazis on labour and party politics in occupied Austria, see Jill Lewis, *Workers and Politics in Occupied Austria, 1945–55* (Manchester: Manchester University Press, 2007). Adam Wandruszka's 1954 essay, 'Österreichs politische Struktur:– Die Entwicklung der Parteien und politischen Bewegungen', first appeared in Heinrich Benedikt (ed.), *Geschichte der Republik Österreich* (Vienna: Verlag für Geschichte und Politik, 1954). His work on the '*nationale Lager*' in interwar Austria also appeared in Erika Weinzierl and Kurt Skalnik (eds), *Österreich 1918–1938: Geschichte der Ersten Republik*, vol. 1 (Graz: Styria, 1983), pp. 277–315.
27 Renner had also been the first chancellor of the First Austrian Republic from 1918 to 1920.
28 Lehnert, 'Politisch-kulturelle Integrationsmilieus und Orientierungslager', p. 431.

29 Gerald Stourzh has argued that Social Democrats as well as the Austrofascist state helped propagate the idea of Austria as the 'better German state' in opposition to the Nazi concept of German nationhood. See his essay 'Erschütterung und Konsolidierung des Österreichbewusstseins: Vom Zusammenbruch der Monarchie zur Zweiten Republik', in Richard G. Plaschka, Gerald Stourzh and Jan Paul Niederkorn (eds), *Was heisst Österreich? Inhalt und Umfang des Österreichbegriffs vom 10. Jahrhundert bis heute* (Vienna: Verlag der österreichischen Akademie der Wissenschaften, 1995). For a summary of the debate on national identity and the Austrofascist state, see the review article by Laura Gellott, 'Recent Writings on the Ständestaat, 1934–1938', *Austrian History Yearbook* 26 (1995): 207–38. I would add that much of the debate lacks any rigorous definition of the term 'pan-German', and that to date Anton Staudinger and Michael Steinberg have given the most extensive consideration to the pan-German idea within Austrofascist ideology. See Anton Staudinger, 'Austrofaschistische "Österreich"-Ideologie', in Tálos and Neugebauer (eds), *Austrofaschismus*, pp. 28–52; and Michael Steinberg, *The Meaning of the Salzburg Festival: Austria as Theatre and Ideology, 1890–1938* (Ithaca: Cornell University Press, 1990).

30 Chapter 2 analyses the readerships of each of the newspapers in more depth.

1

Pan-Germanism from empire to republic

> Pan-Germanism in its original and most comprehensive sense meant no
> more than the general desire to promote the political and cultural unity of
> all Germans wherever they lived, and to make all Germans realise that to
> work for this unity was their highest mission . . . [It] repudiated the entire
> conventional political spectrum and the ethical, humanitarian, and religious
> principles that underlay the conventional political camps of both the Left
> and the Right . . . It was, in short, a movement that aimed at replacing the
> politics of consensus with the politics of extremism.[1]

Whiteside's 1975 study of pan-Germanism's origins and fluctuating fortunes under the Habsburg monarchy is striking for what it reveals about
the absence of a pan-German movement in Austria. Divided by class,
regional, ethnic, religious and generational differences, Whiteside's 'Pan-
Germans' were neither a camp nor a movement. However, his definition
of pan-Germanism as a belief or 'desire' for German unity and a common
mission is more useful for assessing the breadth of pan-Germanism in
Austria both before and after the monarchy's collapse in 1918. This chapter
presents a survey of the contested and shifting nature of pan-Germanism
from 1848 to 1938 in order to establish one of the book's central arguments
that Austrofascism was directly linked to the preservation and propagation
of a pan-German identity in Austria. Contrary to most interpretations of
the Austrofascist state, that its leaders and its ideology lacked popular
support, I argue that the state's construction of a pan-German identity
drew on widespread support in Austria. Pan-Germanism might better be
understood as an identity matrix in which various camps, movements and
parties followed their own political and cultural agendas as they sought to
orientate their multiple paths within a common national framework. It was
this shared framework that enabled the Austrofascist state to forge alliances with a host of competing interest groups, including church leaders,
the arts, the press, teachers and academics, conservative and nationalist
politicians, and outlawed Nazi terrorists. Far from being a fringe radical

movement, this chapter shows that pan-Germanism was the unifying creed of all Austrians before 1938.

The first section of the chapter traces the growth of pan-Germanism from its original liberal idea of political unity in the German Confederation to the period of ascendant German nationalism in Austria following the dissolution of the Confederation in 1866. It shows how ethnic and civic conceptions of the German nation and the Austrian state underpinned the nascent construction of an Austrian pan-German identity. The second and third sections of the chapter chart the spread of pan-Germanism from university meeting halls in Vienna to taverns, newspaper rooms and school houses in the countryside and, ultimately, back to Vienna via the two emerging mass political movements in the empire: the Christian Socials and Social Democrats. The creation of the Austrofascist state in 1933 marked the final triumph of provincial pan-Germanism over the capital as homeland and religion made their way back into school textbooks, art competitions and music festivals. The final section of the chapter discusses how the long tradition of Austrian pan-Germanism challenges us to rethink assumptions about political culture in interwar Austria. If pan-Germanism was the guiding national principle across the political spectrum between 1848 and 1938, as this chapter demonstrates, then the Austrofascist period must be seen as the culmination of multiple strands of pan-Germanism over the course of nearly a century of national politics. Austrofascist politicians inherited the legacy of previous contests over national politics in Austria and transformed that legacy into a new national awakening for Austrians. Pan-Germanism lent legitimacy to the Austrofascist state's attempt to rebuild Austria as a sovereign, self-determined nation-state in the interwar period.

From liberal ideals to nationalist solutions

Pan-Germanism first emerged in the 1848–49 revolutions as a liberal platform for reforming the Confederate states on the basis of the constitutional freedoms of education, private property and civic equality.[2] However, the competing nationalist programmes of the German and Austrian liberals prevented the goal of German political unity from being realized. In particular the question of Austrian or Prussian leadership divided delegates who gathered at the Frankfurt Assembly to negotiate a constitution for a unified German state. Most German liberals favoured a *kleindeutsche* union that excluded Austrians and set the way clear for Prussian leadership. Austrian liberals, on the other hand, proposed a *grossdeutsche* solution that would incorporate all of German Austria, including the Bohemian and Moravian crown lands, into a Greater German Empire led by the Habsburg emperor in Vienna. This would have satisfied Catholics and radical democrats among the German contingent, who feared Prussian dominance, but it also would have necessitated a constitutional separation from the non-German Habsburg territories and the dismemberment of the monarchy in all except dynastic ties. Neo-absolutism finally defeated both liberal visions after the Prussian king, Frederich Wilhelm IV, rejected the German liberals' offer of the crown of a *kleindeutsche* empire in March 1849. In December 1850, the Austrian Prime Minister, Prince Felix Schwarzenberg, backed by the new Emperor Franz Josef, and supported by Tsar Nicholas I, forced Prussia and the German kingdoms to accept a revived German Confederation under the Habsburg crown, which effectively restored the 1815 Confederation established at the Vienna Congress.[3]

The arguments on each side of the *kleindeutsche–grossdeutsche* debate are significant for what they reveal about the trajectory of pan-Germanism after 1848. If the immediate objective of *kleindeutsche* nationalists was a German state ruled by Prussia, then we can see the construction of a *kleindeutsche* state primarily as a civic pan-German discourse because it deferred to Prussian state interests rather than ethnic arguments. This is evidenced by the proposed *kleindeutsche* solution's inclusion of Danes in the duchies of Schleswig and Holstein and Poles in East Prussia, but the exclusion of Germans in Austria.[4] The German liberal, Varnhagen von Ense, recognized the need for pragmatism when he declared that nationality was 'not the sole, nor even the most important basis on which to form states. Shared laws and freedoms are undoubtedly much more important than ethnic ties, especially when these ties have been broken and obscured.'[5]

In contrast to *kleindeutsche* nationalism, *grossdeutsche* nationalism was characterized by what Whiteside has referred to as the politics of 'ethnocentrism', that is, the subordination of non-Germans to Germans in a German state.[6] Non-German-speakers were numerically stronger than German-speakers in the Habsburg lands and the liberals wished to secure the *Nationalbesitzstand* (national ownership) of Germans over the empire's territory, property and 'cultural capital'.[7] The inclusion of Czechs, Slovenes and Italians in a *grossdeutsche* state was proposed on ethnic grounds to secure German hegemony, rather than on civic arguments about German political or territorial unity. After the liberals' defeat in 1849, Franz Josef and Austria's conservative elites pressured the liberals to support an economic union of the German Confederate states under Habsburg leadership, a plan that became known as Greater Austria (*Grossösterreich*). This conservative design was similar to the original *grossdeutsche* model and would have included all Germans together with Magyars, Czechs, Slovaks, Slovenes, Serbs, Croats, Ruthenes, Romanians and Italians. Britain, France and Russia opposed this 'Empire of Seventy Millions', but it remained at the forefront of Austrian liberal politics until 1866.[8]

The ultimate triumph of *kleindeutsche* nationalism through Austria's defeat in the Austro-Prussian War in 1866 and Germany's unification under Bismarck in 1871 caused a split between Austrian liberals. As we have seen, the moderate majority of Austrian liberals were *grossdeutsche* nationalists who did not wish for the empire to break up. They concentrated instead on domestic liberal reforms that would preserve the privileges of the politically dominant German Austrians in a centralized Habsburg state. However, after 1866, a younger generation of radical liberals led by Schönerer began to advocate the union of 'German Austria' with Germany. The so-called Linz Programme in 1882 formally outlined this solution, which called for the separation of Austria and Hungary in everything except dynastic ties, the union of the German hereditary lands with Bohemia and Moravia, excluding Dalmatia and Galicia, and a constitutional alliance with Germany.[9] Ironically, the radicals' inclusion of Austria in the German Reich was regarded by their opponents as *kleindeutsche* nationalism – the inverse definition of the Prussian model of German unification that excluded Austria.[10] The Austrian inversion of the original Prussian term is a fitting illustration of the multiple constructions and meanings of pan-German identity. While one definition of '*kleindeutsch*' was intended to secure Prussian state interests and exclude millions of ethnic Germans in Austria, the other definition was an attempt by those who felt marginalized by their position outside the territorial boundaries of the German state to restore the borders of that state along ethnic lines. Within one generation, the *kleindeutsche–grossdeutsche* debate had lost its original political meaning as the pan-German idea was reinvented for a new era of nationalist politics in Austria.

The Austrian student movement in the 1870s and 1880s played a decisive role in this shift in pan-German thought. University fraternities (*Burschenschaften*) with Teutonic names, such as Walhalla, Norica, Frankonia and Markomannia, had been founded during the late 1850s after Austrian authorities removed previous restrictions on secret student societies. Fraternity members continued to shroud their activities and memberships in secrecy so that Austrian police authorities could only estimate that out of a total of 6,000 students attending Vienna's higher education institutes between 1880 and 1900, less than 500 were involved in German-nationalist fraternities. Mirroring the factions of the liberals in parliament, the *Burschenschaften* were split into moderate *grossdeutsche* and radical *kleindeutsche* camps. Yet even within the more radical fraternities, few enthusiasts of *kleindeutsche* nationalism seriously considered overthrowing the Austro-Hungarian Empire to achieve their dream of uniting German Austria with

Bismarck's Reich. After the 1879 Dual Alliance between Germany and Austria-Hungary, the majority of *kleindeutsche* students slowly embraced Austrian patriotism, believing that their primary aim had been achieved.[11] Spurred by 'irredentist' politics after 1866, the remaining radical *kleindeutsche* nationalists represented a fringe minority on the far left of the political spectrum.[12] The various proponents of *grossdeutsche* nationalism, including former student radicals after 1879, were only more moderate on the count of their loyalty to the Habsburg emperor. Their chauvinism towards Slavs and Jews would be regarded as right-wing extremism in the twentieth century. But in late nineteenth-century Habsburg politics, they represented the remnants of a left-wing liberal ideology that sought, above all, to ensure that the empire remained a German state ruled by Germans.

Aside from irredentism, the issue that increasingly divided moderate and radical liberals – and ultimately weakened the *kleindeutsche* faction – was anti-Semitism. Many Jewish students had joined the university fraternities out of admiration for Bismarck and because they shared their fellow students' disdain for conservative Habsburg rule. One of these students was the founding leader of the Austrian Social Democratic Party, Victor Adler (1852–1918), who had been a *Burschenschafter* in the 1870s before entering parliament as a radical democrat alongside Schönerer. But by the late 1870s, Jewish students were excluded from membership in the radical fraternities and subjected to physical attacks by their fellow students. Schönerer led the verbal assault on Jews with his truculent speeches in parliament during the 1880s. He eventually split with his former democratic colleagues, including Adler, in 1884 and three years later led a group of breakaway Young Liberals to form the *Deutschnationale Vereinigung* (German Nationalist Association) to press specifically for anti-Semitic laws in the Austrian parliament.[13] Two proposed items of legislation were modelled on the Californian Chinese Exclusion Act of 1882 and sought a moratorium on Jewish immigration from Galicia and Bukowina as well as a quota on Jewish enrolments in universities.[14] Yet while anti-Semitism brought additional strain on the relationship between moderate and radical German-nationalists, already fractured over the issue of Habsburg loyalty, it was not exclusively the ideology of the radical camp. Rather, it became a potent weapon in the hands of so-called moderates, who combined allegiance to the empire with verbal attacks on Jews in their attempt to broaden their base of support.

Schönerer's split with former colleagues in 1887 may also have been intended to avert a no-confidence vote in his leadership. His unwillingness to compromise and his extreme anti-Semitism alienated many of his supporters – often referred to as Schönerianer – throughout the 1880s. One example of Schönerer's growing isolation was the *Deutscher Schulverein*

(German Schools' Association). Established in 1880 as the associational arm of the Austrian liberals, it rapidly grew to over 100,000 members with almost a thousand local chapters. By 1914, it had doubled its membership to 200,000 members. The *Deutscher Schulverein*'s principal function was to raise funds to build German schools in ethnically mixed borderlands, but it also provided subsidies for Jewish schools in German minority areas, such as Bohemia, which represented nearly half of the total membership and chapters of the *Schulverein*.[15] Schönerer's attempts to expel Jewish members by way of an Aryan paragraph in the constitution failed and he resigned from the organisation in 1886, promptly founding his own *Schul-verein für Deutsche* (Schools' Association for Germans). Former *kleindeut-sche* students who had become teachers joined Schönerer's organization and indoctrinated their own pupils through schoolboy fraternities. However, Schönerer's all-or-nothing brand of anti-Semitic *kleindeutsche* nationalism failed to attract more than a handful of loyal deputies, who continued to support him when he spent four months in prison for assault-ing a group of newspaper editors in 1888.[16] Schönerer spent the years after his release in the political wilderness, but his absence from politics did not quash pan-German sentiment. Rather, the core of pan-Germanism had shifted to the empire's borderlands, where ex-fraternity members mobi-lized middle-class support bases in provincial towns through the schools' association movement. As these former students entered affluent society and matured politically, they rejected the authoritarian leadership of their former mentor and a new phenomenon of pan-Germanism emerged: 'Schönerianer-without-Schönerer'.[17]

Pan-Germanism in the provinces

Schönerer's former supporters gained strong followings in ethnically mixed provinces, such as Bohemia and Styria, but they also made inroads in relatively homogeneous areas, such as Salzburg and Upper Austria, where German-nationalists eclipsed the liberal establishment by the turn of the century. In Bohemia, tensions escalated between Czechs and Germans in the 1880s and 1890s as Prime Minister Count Eduard Taaffe (r.1879–93) made several important concessions to Czech-speakers. The most significant concession was the enfranchisement of the lower middle classes in a fourth curia in 1883, which resulted in the Czech parties gaining a majority in the Bohemian parliament and the German deputies subsequently boycotting the parliament. Tensions erupted in April 1897 when Taaffe's successor, Count Kasimir Badeni, attempted to introduce language ordinances that required the entire civil service of Bohemia and Moravia to be fluent in both Czech and German. The Badeni Decrees sparked street riots in Vienna, Graz and throughout Bohemia, while radical and moderate German-nationalist politicians resorted to fistfights and obstructionist tactics in the Austrian parliament, forcing the successive resignations of three prime ministers and preventing any laws from being passed between 1897 and 1900. When Badeni resigned in November 1897, the Czechs held counter-demonstrations in Prague and the Austrian authorities had to impose martial law there in December. German-Czech economic relations in Bohemia were also disrupted as a result of the Badeni crisis: German employers dismissed Czech employees who sent their children to Czech schools and Czech nationalists branded Czech clients of German and German-Jewish owned businesses as traitors.[18] Yet only a small number of Germans in northern Bohemia supported Schönerer and his goal of Austro-German unification. Pan-Germanism was more widespread at the local level in gymnastics associations and other sporting clubs, as well as the influential national workers' unions that represented the interests of German workers against their lower-paid Czech co-labourers.[19] Thus what John Breuilly has called 'communal nationalism' – antagonisms between different ethnic groups in a common environment – was characteristic of the nature of pan-Germanism in ethnically mixed provinces, where economic competition was politicized by a shift in power relations through franchise reform.[20]

In Styria, pan-German sentiments were fuelled by local resentment towards Slovenian-speakers in the borderlands of southern Styria and Carinthia and the neighbouring province of Carniola. Liberals and German-nationalists built schools and established newspapers to reach German-speaking minorities along the linguistic frontier. The Lower Styrian towns of Celje/Cilli and Maribor/Marburg were typical of the disproportion of German-speakers living in a Slovene hinterland with each town having its own German *Gymnasium* and German-language newspaper, the *Cillier Zeitung* and the *Marburger Zeitung*, respectively.[21] During the Taaffe era and the Badeni crisis, Styria's German-language newspapers portrayed ethnic tensions in other parts of the empire as a threat to the German-speakers of Styria. At times they accused Slovenes of having similar political motivations to the Czechs in Bohemia, printing disparaging reports about 'pan-Slavic chauvinism' from the vantage point of Germans in rural communities. Articles in the *Marburger Zeitung* during 1887 referred to local Slovenian newspapers as organs of the 'Slavic press' and the Slovene Credit Union as 'Slavic money'. German antagonism towards Slovenes rose sharply in 1895 after the Austrian parliament approved funding for parallel Slovenian classes in the *Gymnasium* in Celje/Cilli. German-nationalist fraternity students at the University of Graz staged noisy demonstrations and riots on the streets of the Styrian capital and called for funding to be blocked. The Austrian parliament eventually cancelled budgetary funds for the school in January 1897. In the same year, the Badeni crisis attracted growing attention in Styria's German-nationalist press with reports of riots in other Austrian provinces and editorials that praised German courage amid national compromise.[22]

In a relatively homogeneous province like Upper Austria, on the other hand, the strength of pan-Germanism lay in its capacity to build political cohesion between the competing liberal and German-nationalist associations. This was achieved with the creation of a successful German-nationalist party under the leadership of Carl Beurle (1860–1919). As a former *kleindeutsche* student in Vienna and an executive committee member of Schönerer's German Nationalist Association, Beurle belonged to the minority of Schönerianer who had remained loyal to their leader throughout the anti-Semitic campaign of the 1880s. He moved to Linz in 1883 to pursue a legal career and encountered a liberal establishment in the Chamber of Commerce, the city council and the Liberal-Political Association. Beurle sought to overcome the liberals' stronghold by merging the younger generation of German-nationalists with the newly enfranchised class of artisans and shopkeepers to create a popular anti-Semitic party. In 1888, he founded the German Nationalist Association for Upper Austria and Salzburg, an autonomous regional counterpart of Schönerer's German Nationalist Association, which succeeded in ousting a liberal politican from the Upper Austrian parliament in 1890 and went on to win a seat in the liberal-dominated Linz city council.[23] Meanwhile, the old liberal vanguard was gradually being replaced by a younger generation of liberals who were prepared to cooperate with Beurle's party against the growing Christian Social movement. This informal cooperation led in 1896 to an electoral alliance between the liberals and German-nationalists. The closer ties between liberals and German-nationalists were in part also due to Beurle's private disillusionment with Schönerer, whose coarse anti-Semitism had alienated the bulk of his sympathizers. In 1897, Beurle broke publicly with Schönerer and founded the German People's Party for Upper Austria, an alliance of young liberals and German-nationalists under a common programme of anti-clericalism and 'highbrow' anti-Semitism. While Schönerer's racial slurs against Jews in the parliament had lost him supporters, Beurle's anti-Semitism was no less potent than his former leader's, arguing against Jewish assimilation on the grounds of Zionist claims to a Jewish nation and attacking international Jewish financiers. However, Beurle's anti-clericalism differed more substantially from Schönerer's anti-Catholicism. Schönerer's *Los von Rom* (No Bond with Rome) movement in the 1890s had attempted to make conversion to the Lutheran Church a requirement of membership in German-nationalist organizations, but had met with limited success in parts of northern Bohemia only. To German-nationalist Catholics, Schönerer represented another Bismarck and the *Los von Rom* movement another *Kulturkampf* against Austrian Catholics. Beurle, on the other hand, provided a middle road for German-nationalist Catholics who wanted to keep their religion out of politics, but who also did not want to choose between their religion and their nationality.[24]

Beurle's party won spectacular victories in the 1906 Linz city council elections with German-nationalists winning the offices of mayor and both deputy mayors. Many of the other city councillors were also members of the *Deutscher Schulverein* and presided over council funding requests for its projects. This kind of political power contributed to the street bravado of the German-nationalists, who demanded a ban on Czech services in St Martin's Cathedral, disrupted performances of Czech and Hungarian musicians, formed 'language purification' associations to replace foreign words with German words and launched a campaign to boycott Czech businesses and employees, despite the fact that less than a quarter of a per cent of Linz's population spoke Czech or Slovak.[25] Pan-Germanism in Upper Austria was thus a local phenomenon supported primarily by youthful and upwardly mobile professionals in revolt against their liberal predecessors, whose political success was dependent on the rising star of Beurle.[26] Beurle himself represented another kind of generational rebellion against Schönerer, who had once mesmerized his student followers but had become embarrassing and irrelevant to the increasingly confident provincial elites by the turn of the century.

German-nationalists in Salzburg had close ties with their Upper Austrian neighbours but never acquired the political weight of Beurle's party due to the well-established Catholic-conservative majority in Salzburg's provincial government.[27] Pan-German ideas spread to Salzburg during the 1880s and 1890s as a wave of university-educated Bohemian and Moravian Germans fled the economic competition between Czechs and Germans to seek work opportunities in Salzburg in the civil service and teaching professions. As they joined Salzburg's liberal associations, they helped to export a politicized German identity to a region that had been relatively immune to nationalist ideas. Salzburg's leading newspaper, the *Salzburger Volksblatt*, founded in 1870, was representative of the generational gap between the older liberal elites and the younger German-nationalists from the borderlands. During the years of nationalist tensions in the Austro-Hungarian Empire, the *Salzburger Volksblatt* hovered between conservative liberalism and moderate German-nationalism, which meant that there was a noticeable tone of social concern, anti-clericalism and the usual prejudices against Slavic groups. However, anti-Semitism was not a prevalent strain in the newspaper's early history as it would become later in the interwar period.[28] Schönerianer were also active in the associational life of the province: in 1887, Schönerer's deputy in the German Nationalist Association, Anton Langgassner, founded the *Germanenbund* (Germania League) to spread the Teutonic cult through choral groups, sporting clubs and festivals. The aim of these local German-nationalist chapters was to socialize provincial townspeople and peasants into a milieu they would not otherwise have joined, particularly if it was violently opposed to the Catholic Church and the Habsburg emperor.[29] Pan-German nationalism was not a native phenomenon in Salzburg as it was elsewhere. It gained impetus through the careers of Bohemian German émigrés as well as the efforts of a few Schönerianer who appealed to the German pride of middle-class and rural Salzburg.

Despite the inroads German-nationalists appeared to be making in provincial cultural and sporting associations, the liberal press and in public life by the 1880s, it is doubtful whether their efforts amounted to a national movement. To be sure, the Badeni language ordinances became a cause célèbre for German-nationalists in the borderlands, but much of the public sympathy for the Bohemian German minority came from the ranks of a small group of former fraternity students who had graduated to become teachers, lawyers and politicians in a predominantly liberal political culture. Newspaper journalists and editors writing for a wider readership also represented a minority elite and their views cannot be regarded as popular opinion. Radical German-nationalists constituted less than 1 per cent of the adult German population (less than 100,000) with a further 2–3 per cent who joined for a certain time. Another 10 per cent sympathized with much of the movement's aims but rejected the violent extremes.[30] At best, these are generous estimates. The largest non-political association in the empire, the *Deutscher Schulverein*, had between 100,000 and 200,000 members, which represented less than 2 per cent of the German-speaking population in Austria (excluding the Hungarian half of the Dual Monarchy), and suggests that only a small minority of Austrian Germans actively supported the campaign to Germanize the borderlands. Broader sympathies for such aims would be harder to substantiate from the statistical evidence available.

There is also a definitional problem of labelling pan-Germanism a national movement. As we have seen, pan-Germanism comprised both the notion of German hegemony in Austria and the universalist idea promoting unity between Austrian Germans and other Germans in Central Europe, but not necessarily in a unified German state. If pan-Germanism was a belief in German hegemony and universal belonging, then it formed the basis for the collective identity of primarily middle-class Austrian German men and women. Although women were excluded from voting and holding office until after 1918, they had begun to seek greater visibility in many male-dominated associations by the turn of the century. Trouser-wearing women caused a sensation in the gymnastics leagues, where they were known as *'Jahnturnerinnen'* after the founder of the German gymnastics movement, Friedrich Ludwig Jahn (1778–1852). Middle-class women were also active in associations such as the *Deutscher Schulverein.* It was almost certainly a woman who wrote in the *Schulverein* journal in 1884 that 'when the enemy threatens the most precious of natural posses-sions, the holiest legacy of our ancestors, our mother tongue, then a moth-er's heart is also affected'. [31] The rapid growth of women members in the *Schulverein* – 83 separate women's chapters with almost 10,000 members by 1885 – suggests that many women identified strongly with the German consciousness of their husbands, brothers, fathers, sons and political leaders. [32]

Former fraternity students may have succeeded in mobilizing women for their cause, but they failed in all other ways to create a truly cross-class and cross-regional movement. Factions between *kleindeutsche* and *gross-deutsche* nationalists, and between Schönerianer and Schönerianer-without-Schönerer, and the generational gap between liberals and German-nationalists demonstrate the failure of pan-Germanism to coa-lesce into a mass movement. However, their success in promoting a popular belief in a common German mission in the empire may be gauged by the extent to which the mass political movements that emerged at the end of the century campaigned on national issues.

Pan-Germanism in an era of mass politics

The mass political movements arising in the 1890s began to make compet-ing claims on the original liberal and radical nationalist idea of pan-Germanism. After the introduction of universal male suffrage in 1907, the Social Democratic and Christian Social parties overtook the liberal and German-nationalist parties in the imperial assembly and emerged as the two dominant political camps in the First Republic with a combined voting average of 80 per cent in national elections between 1919 and 1930. [33] The extent to which pan-Germanism also infiltrated these parties is important in considering their relationship to German-nationalists, who continued to maintain an intellectual presence through their associations and news-papers in spite of their political divisions. Rather than distinguishing German-nationalists from Christian Socials and Social Democrats as a third political camp, I suggest they are best understood as contestants of pan-German identity whose nationalism competed with and often com-plemented that of Catholics and socialists.

The pan-Germanism of Social Democrats was evident from the outset of the party's inception in the 1880s. As we have seen, the party's founding leader, Adler, was a former colleague of Schönerer. Another ex-Schönerianer, Engelbert Pernerstorfer (1850–1918), joined the Social Democrats amid the controversy over Badeni's language decrees.[34] In the wake of that crisis, the Social Democratic Party officially recognized separate national organizations within the Austrian labour movement at a party congress in Brno/Brünn in 1899, while at the parliamentary level the leadership continued to champion workers' interests and democratic reform. However, the central leadership remained self-consciously German and fought to preserve the privileges of German workers over non-Germans in the empire, eventually forcing the party to split along national lines by 1912.[35]

The defining thinkers of Austro-Marxism, Renner and Otto Bauer (1881–1938), who rose to prominence in the aftermath of the nationalist conflicts in the 1890s, advocated the idea of national autonomy more forcefully than their predecessors had. Renner's book, *Der Kampf der österreichischen Nationen um den Staat* (The Struggle of the Austrian Nations for the State), published under a pseudonym in 1902, described nationalities as modern 'cultural communities', as opposed to primordial ethnic clusters, and argued that individual nations within the multinational state should be given institutional autonomy on a federalist basis. He envisaged the administrative division of Austria-Hungary on national rather than territorial lines, which would allow individuals to 'opt into' national communities regardless of where they lived. Bauer's landmark study, *Die Sozialdemokratie und die Nationalitätenfrage* (The Nationalities Question and Social Democracy), published five years after Renner's book, proposed a similar modernist view that nations were formed by a common language that gave the working classes access to the national culture and distinguished nationalities from one another. He famously defined the nation as 'the totality of men bound together through a common destiny into a community of character' and he saw workers as being more closely linked to the cultural nation than peasants, who identified with their region rather than the national culture. Building on Renner's ideas, Bauer envisaged an international community of socialist nations that could be integrated according to size and strength into the international production of labour. He proposed, theoretically, that a surplus of German workers might be reduced by their migration to southern Russia where a shortage of labour had occurred, but that the German workers would remain culturally autonomous from the Ukrainians. This 'planned colonization' of workers would lead to a socialist society ordered according to nationality with each member of the nation an equal participant in the national culture.[36]

Yet neither Bauer nor Renner could shake their belief in German superiority, and they continued to uphold the revolutionary ideal of German
unity prior to the Second World War and for most of the duration of the
war. After the collapse of the Austro-Hungarian Empire in 1918, the Social
Democrats were the leading advocates of *Anschluss* in Austria. Middle-
class German-nationalists, wary of socialism, and the Christian Social
Party, fearing another *Kulturkampf* against Catholics, initially distanced
themselves from union with Germany. Bauer was the chief architect and
spokesperson of the *Anschluss* idea after he succeeded Adler as party
leader in 1918. Following a brief stint as foreign minister in 1918–19,
Bauer's chief forum until 1934 was the monthly socialist journal, *Der
Kampf*, in which he continued to promote Austro-German relations. He
argued that to reject *Anschluss* would give greater licence to the political
aims of Austrian National Socialists. The party's 1926 Linz Programme
advocated *Anschluss* 'by peaceful means', a statement that remained officially in place in October 1933, although it had not been an active policy
of the party since 1927. However, even after *Anschluss* had been quietly
dropped from the Social Democratic programme, Bauer continued to
support Austro-German unity in the party's underground journal, *Der
sozialistische Kampf*, which he edited during his exile in Czechoslovakia
after 1934 until his death in Paris in July 1938. Three months before he
died, in April 1938, Bauer cautioned his readers not to resist the political
union between Austria and Germany because, he believed, the eventual
defeat of Nazism would ultimately bring about the 'pan-German (*gesamtdeutsche*) revolution' first espoused by Marx in 1848. Not all workers
shared these pan-German sentiments and the left wing of the party did
not support *Anschluss*; nevertheless, the party leadership defended its
position until 1943, in contrast to their socialist counterparts in non-
German states who fought for national independence under fascist
regimes.[37] Bauer never retracted his position that Austrians were simply a
tribe (*Stamm*) within the German nation.[38] Renner went even further than
Bauer: he had already gone on record in 1918 in his address to the Provisional National Assembly of German-Austria by declaring that Austrians
and Germans were 'one tribe [*Stamm*] and one community of destiny'.[39]
Austrian socialists acquiesced in the political unity of Austria and Germany
in 1938, not because they lacked political muscle, but because they believed
that socialism would ultimately triumph and bring about peaceful relations
between Germans and non-Germans in Central Europe. They aspired less
towards German hegemony in Central Europe than towards a German
cultural community that would model socialism to non-German nations.
In this sense of idealised harmony between nationalities, the pan-
Germanism of Social Democrats contrasted with the goal of German

hegemony in Central Europe that both Christian Socials and German-nationalists upheld.

While the Social Democrats embodied every facet of working-class life, the Christian Social Party coexisted with a broader range of Catholic interest groups in Austria. Alongside the Church and lay organizations, the party represented one part of a broader spectrum of political Catholicism that emerged during the late nineteenth century in response to secular liberalism. The different dimensions within political Catholicism were sometimes in tension with one another – over questions about working wives and youth policies in the Austrofascist period, for example – but they overlapped on other issues, particularly on the question of national identity.[40]

The Christian Socials were initially unconcerned with preserving German privileges in the empire, an issue they regarded as the domain of their liberal rivals. Instead they concentrated on gaining a wider support basis among the newly enfranchised artisans and shopkeepers using an anti-Semitic trump card. The founder of the Christian Social Party, Karl Lueger (1844–1910), began his political career as a Liberal but became a left-wing Democrat to defend the 'little people' of the Viennese petty bourgeoisie against their perceived foe of Jewish liberal capitalists. Schönerer had been patron of the anti-Semitic artisans' association that gave momentum to the early Christian Social movement, but split from this group in 1882 after its leaders rejected his irredentist nationalism. Lueger, in contrast to Schönerer, was an Austrian patriot who embraced Pope Leo XIII's appeals for Catholic political unity, although Lueger had not previously been a practising Catholic. His successful blend of anti-Semitism and Catholic populism attracted artisans, the lower clergy, aristocrats and the middle classes, who eventually merged in 1889 to form the Christian Social Party. However, Lueger's firebrand anti-Semitism shocked conservatives, especially the old Catholic vanguard in the various parliamentary clubs of the landed aristocracy and provincial clergy. After Lueger was elected mayor of Vienna in 1895, Franz Josef refused to ratify his election, seeking papal intervention before finally acceding in 1897.[41] In the same year, the party's ethnocentrism was exposed when its leaders joined ranks with the liberals and German-nationalists in parliament during the Badeni crisis. Where their conservative predecessors had professed loyalty to 'God, Emperor and Fatherland', the Christian Socials now defined their mission as 'a German party that would always stand for the protection of the German people's spiritual and material ownership'.[42] This statement in the 1907 party programme resembled the liberals' rhetoric of 'national ownership' during the 1880s and 1890s and showed the appropriation of nationalist ideology that had occurred in the Christian Social Party since 1897.[43]

Pan-German sentiments were also evident in an Austrian-wide revival of Catholic associational life after 1900. Catholic student fraternities, for example, were more conservative and patriotic than those of the previous generation, eschewing political activism in favour of social welfare. The future Austrian chancellor, Dollfuss, taught evening stenography classes to residents of a workers' hostel while a fraternity student in Vienna before the First World War. However, the Austrian patriotism of these students in no way diminished their pan-Germanism. In 1904, students led noisy street demonstrations against an Italian law faculty established at the University of Innsbruck.[44] The pan-Germanism of Christian Social politicians and Catholic student associations after 1897 set the tone for the interwar period, when the idea of a civilizing mission took on new meaning for Austrian Catholics battling against political rivals.

After 1918, Christian Socials were divided on the issues of *Anschluss* and republicanism. Backed by a predominantly agrarian sector that had been drained by the wartime economy, the party's republican wing tended to support *Anschluss* for economic reasons, while anti-republican groups with economic interests in the Habsburg successor states advocated a Danubian Federation.[45] These divisions were far from clear-cut and, as with the Social Democrats, Christian Socials' views on Austro-German relations shifted during the interwar years. For example, the leader of the anti-republican wing, Ignaz Seipel (1876–1932), priest and twice-appointed chancellor of Austria during the 1920s, indicated his personal views on *Anschluss* in correspondence with the Paris representative of the Austrian State Railways in July 1930. Seipel responded candidly to questions about his government's foreign policy by stating that he regarded Austrians as 'big-state people' (*Grossstaatmenschen*), who had previously not done enough to uphold their special mission among the nations of Central Europe. *Anschluss* still remained a plausible solution for cooperating with other Germans to fulfil their Central European role, Seipel believed, explaining that he was not opposed to *Anschluss* in itself, but only to popular 'agitation', which he regarded as a 'superficial and premature' response that avoided due debate on larger political, economic and national considerations.[46] Publicly, however, Seipel and the influential Viennese Christian Socials were more reticent to support *Anschluss*. The party programme of November 1926 stated the party's commitment to the right of self-determination for Germans and its task of 'cultivating German ways' and combating Jewish influence in intellectual and economic spheres. The 1926 programme and Seipel's personal inclination towards Austria's *grossdeutsche* role in Central Europe show the conflicted nature of pan-Germanism in the Christian Social Party. The Christian Socials had eclipsed the liberals and German-nationalists in their commitment to 'German' Austia by the interwar years. However, they lagged behind the

Social Democrats in having a clear policy on Austria's larger place within the German nation and the question of Austro-German unity.[47]

During the 1930s, the Christian Socials adopted a more explicit German-nationalist position in a calculated effort to recruit young right-wing Catholics to the party. In his 1932 commentary to the 1926 party programme, Richard Schmitz (1885–1954), who became mayor of Vienna in the Austrofascist state, interwove references to German cultural unity with statements about Austrian character. He distinguished between '*Volkstum*', which incorporated Austria's history, landscape, religion, customs, dialects, art and music, and '*Deutschtum*', encompassing the common language and culture of all German-speakers. The duty of the Austrian *Volk* was to work towards the progress of all German people by cultivating the Austrian community as a whole, and its right to self-determination, within the German nation. Schmitz also disparaged the National Socialist idea of race by claiming that the true 'national' idea embraced the mind, body and spirit of the people, whereas the '*völkisch*' idea in National Socialism devalued the people by emphasising only their ethnicity, race and natural history.[48] Schmitz's commentary was a deliberate strategy of wedge politics aimed at marginalizing the Nazis by narrowing the terms of pan-Germanism to cultural identity rather than ethnicity. The extent to which this tactic was successful in swaying Catholic German-nationalists away from National Socialism is difficult to gauge given that political parties and elections were banned following the dissolution of parliament in 1933. However, cultural associations continued to act as vehicles for pan-Germanism under the Austrofascist state and, as we will see in Chapter 4, the state was particularly successful in recruiting former Nazis to the cultural propaganda work on behalf of Sudeten Germans in Czechoslovakia, notably.

Pan-German themes of 'blood and soil' and rural purity dominated cultural life under Austrofascism and signalled a shift away from the values of the cosmopolitan centre to those of the provincial periphery. Notably, the popularity of the *Heimat* movement, with its revival of rural art and poetry and local ethnographical exhibitions, also represented a rejection of Vienna's cosmopolitan influence.[49] The government stipulated in a 1934 document that all cultural and leisure activities should reflect the patriotic sensibilities of the Austrian people (*Volkstum*) and promote everything 'that developed out of the German nation and served to cultivate respect for German achievement, work and essence'. Accordingly, the Ministry of Education's annual state prize for literature was awarded to historical novels, war literature and works that emphasized rural and religious themes.[50] Similarly in art, the proponents of the 'new' Austrian expressionism abandoned the modern motifs of Egon Schiele (1890–1918) and Oskar Kokoschka (1886–1980) and reinvented religious and earthy themes in a

bold neobaroque style. The Carinthian painter, Herbert Boeckl (1894–
1966), was the leading figure of the new expressionism and the recipient
of the Austrian State Prize in 1934, which earned him a teaching appointment at the Vienna Academy of Fine Arts.[51]

Another prominent Catholic figure who promoted a pan-German cultural identity was Hans Brečka (1885–1954), Viennese theatre critic and
cultural editor of the Christian Social newspaper, *Reichspost*. In the interwar years, Brečka was director of the party's *Kunststelle für christliche
Volksbildung* (Office for the Arts for Christian National Education), a
government-sponsored theatre agency that subsidized tickets for workers,
employees and students to performances and concerts deemed culturally
appropriate for Catholic audiences.[52] Under the Austrofascist state, Brečka
was given charge of the new *Österreichische Kunststelle* that replaced all
of Austria's theatre agencies, including those of the Social Democrats and
other independent groups. In his new role, Brečka promoted works by lay
Catholic theatre companies as well as folk-dialect dramas, which glorified
rural life and elevated the moral stature of peasants. He also established
links with the Berlin-based *Deutscher Bühnenvolksbund* (German National
Stage Association), an anti-Semitic body that sponsored German folk
theatre works, particularly those by the Catholic amateur drama companies. After 1938, Brečka continued to direct the renamed *Deutschösterreichische Kunststelle* under the auspices of the Nazi Office for Regional
Culture (*Landeskulturamt*). Shortly after *Anschluss*, Brečka wrote in
the *Reichspost* that Vienna's theatres could now showcase 'German
theatre . . . provided by German performers and tied to our cultural duty
to promote German art.'[53] However, Brečka had already expounded this
pan-German mission in his earlier patronage of folk plays and Catholic
theatre groups that combined German-nationalism and religion in a
distinctly Austrian cultural genre.

A return to themes of Austrian patriotism, German culture and religion
also pervaded the new school curriculum in the Austrofascist state. The
Ministry of Education's curriculum plan for 1935 set out its aim of training
Austrian youth 'to feel, think and conduct themselves in a religious-moral,
national, social and patriotic manner.'[54] The printing of new textbooks for
history and German were delayed to save costs, but official pedagogical
journals instructed teachers in the interim to refer only to sections in the
old textbooks that discussed religious and imperial themes and to set their
pupils straight about the more deviant passages on the foundations of the
Austrian republic and the Social Democratic Party.[55] The new textbooks,
published after 1935, emphasized Austria's place in German history and
its special merits in literature and music. Students were to gain 'a love of
the German language and German, *particularly Austrian*, literature',

according to one middle school study plan, and Viennese musical achievements were to be included alongside the great texts of Weimar German
literature. In geography, the new curriculum introduced in 1935 treated
Austria separately from Germany and lessons were designed to draw similarities between Austria and other parts of the world. Austrian children
reading their first words learnt an 'Austrian ABC' in which each letter of
the alphabet corresponded to a patriotic symbol and word, for example,
'C' for *Christentum* (Christianity), 'D' for *Deutschtum* (Germanism) and
'V' for *Vaterland* (Fatherland). Each term also corresponded with a saying:
'*Deutschtum*', for instance, would prompt pupils to remember that 'a good
Austrian is at the same time a good German'. Students were encouraged
to identify with the words of the late Chancellor Dollfuss, 'who died for
our Fatherland', so that they would, like him, 'joyfully acknowledge our
Germanism'.[56] Religious instruction was left to the Church's jurisdiction
under the terms of the 1934 concordat, which made religion classes compulsory for all baptized Catholics and ensured that curricula taught in
other subjects did not contradict church teaching. Instruction in all other
subjects was interested in religion only insofar as it promoted Austria's
'German Christian' heritage and mission in Europe. Elementary and middle
school history curricula included a core topic about Austria's role as a
'bulwark' against the Turks. Religion served only to highlight Austria's
'German' roots: one middle school history textbook stated that 'Austria was
a German land from time immemorial and is inhabited almost exclusively
by Germans.'[57]

The powerful teachers' unions run by provincial German-nationalists
since the 1880s were able to exploit the national rhetoric of Austrofascist
curriculum planners towards their own end of broadening public sympathies for the *Anschluss*. While Catholic teachers instructed pupils that
Austrian Germandom was the heir of the Holy Roman Empire charged
with the historical mission of bringing peace to the nations of Europe, their
German-nationalist counterparts taught that Austria's historical roots in
the German nation demanded its inclusion in a greater-German state. And
where the official pedagogical journals stressed religious and patriotic duty
to the Austrian fatherland, German-nationalist journals asserted that 'true
religiosity' was the identification with the German people.[58] Historians
who draw attention to divisions between a 'conservative' and 'nationalist'
camp claim that the Austrian state was ultimately unsuccessful in its
attempt to inculcate patriotic values in schools. They point to the evidence
that most students and their teachers, especially those in the larger towns
where German-nationalist associations were strongest, remained sceptical
towards the idea of an Austrian fatherland and embraced Germany more
enthusiastically.[59] In fact, as I have already touched upon, the belief that

Austria had a special Germanizing mission in Central Europe and that it was 'from time immemorial' a German land, was at the very core of an Austrian pan-German identity that each of the interwar Austrian parties defined according to their political viewpoint. Pan-Germanism could, therefore, be appropriated by both the state apparatus and German-nationalist interest groups.

Exploiting the rhetoric of pan-Germanism was also an effective strategy for uniting the splintered German-nationalist groups in the interwar years. In contrast to the populist Christian Social Party and the dense party networks of the Social Democrats, electoral success for German-nationalists remained elusive due to their factionalism and regional disunity and they concentrated their energies instead on local activism in schools, municipal councils and the press to win support at the ballot box. Moderate German-nationalists and liberals had amalgamated in 1910 for the first time in the German National Club (*Deutsche Nationalverband*), which had been hastily formed to recover German-nationalist mandates lost in the 1907 election to the Social Democrats. The German Agrarian Party, founded in 1905, and the German Workers' Party, formed in Bohemia in 1904, completed the spectrum of German-nationalist parties in the pre-war period.[60] German-nationalists did not play a major role in the foundation of the First Republic, winning only 26 of 170 seats in the constitutional assembly of February 1919. As a result of this poor performance, seventeen different German-nationalist parties united to form the *Grossdeutsche Volkspartei* (Greater German People's Party) in time for the first national elections in October 1920.[61] Immediately prior to the party's political debut, Greater German leaders convened in Salzburg to formulate a programme opposed to the internationalist influences of Judaism, Marxism and Catholicism.[62] The party performed even more poorly in the 1920 election than it had done in 1919 with its most successful candidates in provincial centres, such as Salzburg (23.6 per cent), Linz (21.1 per cent) and Graz (21 per cent). Electoral support for the Greater Germans fluctuated during the 1920s and the party often inflated its membership figures. German-nationalist voters saw the Greater Germans as the only party that represented their interests. However, once the *Nationalsozialistische Deutsche Arbeiterpartei* (NSDAP) had become an electoral contender after 1930 the Greater Germans' support plummeted in national and regional elections and the party remnants finally disbanded in 1934.[63] Historians now regard the main contribution of the Greater German party as having made National Socialism socially acceptable (*salonfähig*) in middle-class circles.[64]

While pan-Germanism was widespread in Christian Socialist and German-nationalist circles and, to a lesser extent, among the leadership of the Social Democrats, it also had become influential in certain academic quarters by the 1930s. The Viennese historian, Heinrich von Srbik (1878–1951), sought to overcome the Prusso-centric view of German historians and the Austro-Catholic emphasis of much Austrian historical research by pioneering a pan-German historical framework (*Gesamtdeutsche Geschichtsauffassung*). Srbik sought to link the universal German nation, the Central European idea of German unity, and the tradition of German statehood within a common historical framework. His pan-Germanism adopted the Rankean idea of a *Zeitgeist* propelling individuals towards a common destiny that, for Srbik, represented a German national community.[65] As a student, Srbik had belonged to a radical fraternity at the University of Vienna, though he had rejected what he saw in Schönerer's followers as 'the narrow-minded beer-hall politics of the unshaven.'[66] Instead, he preferred to be politically engaged as a scholar, his 1925 biography of Metternich making him a public figure in Austria. In 1929, the Christian Social chancellor, Johannes Schober, appointed Srbik to a one-year term in his cabinet as Minister of Education. He was in demand as a lecturer in Germany, turning down the prestigious offer of a chair at the University of Berlin. In 1936, Schuschnigg mooted him as a possible candidate for vice-chancellor at the University of Vienna to appease growing public sympathies with National Socialism. After the *Anschluss*, Srbik joined the NSDAP and the German Reichstag and was appointed President of the Academy of Sciences in Vienna, remaining in his post until 1945.[67]

Srbik's pan-German historicism is best encapsulated in his second and monumental work, *Deutsche Einheit* (German Unity). Published in four volumes between 1935 and 1942, Srbik's study dealt with the period from the Holy Roman Empire to Austria's defeat by Prussia in 1866. Writing his conclusion four years after Austro-German unity had been realised, Srbik declared that 'Germany has carried her 1000-year mission and role of leadership to the very frontiers of the Western World . . . Not as imperialism, and not on the basis of a humanitarian ideal, but grounded rather in a new idea, that of *Volkstum*, which recognises the personalities of nations and organically attaches the small nations to the leadership of the great *Volk*.' With this statement Srbik summarized his belief that the German people as a whole were destined for greatness in Europe and that National Socialism was the fulfilment of this pan-German idea.[68] In his third and final major work, *Geist und Geschichte vom deutschen Humanismus zur Gegenwart* (The Spirit and History of German Humanism to the Present), published posthumously by his former students, Srbik openly acknowledged that his own historiographical position stood alongside other extreme nationalist theories of the early twentieth century. Although he distanced himself from Nazi barbarity, he defended his historical concept of racial and national unity that was at the core of National Socialism and he urged future generations of German scholars to continue the idealist tradition in the spirit of Ranke and Goethe.[69]

The parallels between Srbik's historical thought and National Socialism raise questions also about the importance of pan-German ideas in other political-cultural milieux. As we have seen, pan-Germanism was present in much of the theory and political rhetoric of leading theorists and public figures within both the Social Democratic and Christian Social parties and it became an all-consuming idea among German-nationalists. Yet historians may need to look beyond the ballot box to explain how pan-Germanism formed the contours of Austria's national identity and allowed 'being German' to govern other political, social, cultural, regional and spiritual forms of identity.

Beyond the *Lager* theory?

With a few exceptions, Austrian historians have glossed over the question of pan-German identity in the interwar period.[70] This lacuna in the historiography of interwar Austria reflects the tendency to interpret Austrian political history according to the *Lager* theory. As I have already argued, the theory is historically flawed and ideologically fraught in its attempt to trace the divisions between Nazis, socialists and conservatives retrospectively. Whiteside's 1975 study of pan-Germanism accepted uncritically Wandruszka's theory that Austria's three political camps were represented by the Social Democratic, Christian Social and German-nationalist parties. In fact, Whiteside inadvertently discredited the *Lager* theory by demonstrating the political fissures and nomenclature of the 'national' camp that was divided into Greater-Germans, Little-Germans, All-Germans, German-Nationalists, German Liberals, German Libertarians, Greater Austrians, and so on.[71] As I have shown here, the German-nationalists were splintered throughout the liberal period and were politically marginalized by the rise of mass politics by the turn of the century.

One critic of the *Lager* approach, Detlef Lehnert, has argued for a reconfiguration of the three-camp structure in terms of 'orientation' and 'integration'. In his comparative work on communal politics and political culture in Weimar Germany and the First Republic, Lehnert does not dispense with the notion of camps altogether, but redefines them in terms of political 'orientation', that is, the party to which an individual gravitated due to political convictions or family tradition, or by association, through membership in a union, for example. However, an 'orientation camp' could include multiple and potentially divergent social and cultural 'integrative milieux' that socialized individuals or groups into a particular local or provincial worldview.[72] A 'camp' could therefore consist of different milieux: militant anti-clericals and Catholic German-nationalists could be found in the same cafes, reading the same newspapers and attending the same meetings. For example, a liberal politician, German-nationalist journalist and Catholic schoolteacher might have attended a village fundraiser for a new German school sponsored by the German Schools' Association in Lower Styria in the 1890s. Evan Burr Bukey has shown a similar pattern for Upper Austria during the 1920s, where a close network of cooperation existed between Social Democratic, Christian Social and German-nationalist politicians, based on shared *Anschluss* sympathies and an informal system of 'consociational democracy' aimed at containing the political ambitions of the *Heimwehr* and NSDAP in the early 1920s. Many of these politicians had held office before 1914 and developed a sense of solidarity during the war that they maintained after 1918. The Upper Austrian governor, Johann Nepomuk Hauser, dubbed the 'Red Prelate' for his relations with Social Democrats in Linz, is an interesting example of a public figure working in a provincial 'political-cultural milieu' within the 'orientation camp' of the Christian Social Party, but whose strained relationship with the ultra-conservative Bishop Johannes Gföllner in Linz also made him an outsider in an Austrian clerical milieu.[73]

A revision of the *Lager* theory might help us understand the similarities and dissimilarities between the identity politics of rival groups. It may explain why civic constructions of pan-Germanism tended to find broader consensus at times of political upheaval in spite of competing ethnic visions of the national identity. For example, after the collapse of the Austro-Hungarian Empire, all of the major political parties in the new Austrian state envisaged pan-German identity in civic terms of a conjoined state of Germans in Germany and Austria, and it was only the Allied objection to this arrangement that prevented its fulfilment. The entry of National Socialism into the contested arena of pan-German identity caused another shift in nationalist discourses. Christian Socials and Social Democrats rejected the prospect of political unity under a National Socialist state and instead espoused an ethnic vision of universal pan-German identity. Nazi sympathizers, on the other hand, embraced the civic project of universal pan-German nationhood under the banner of National Socialism, rejecting the alternative civic vision of Austria as an independent German state.

This chapter has shown how, for nearly a century, Austrian politicians continually debated and appropriated the terms of pan-German identity in the pursuit of their various political projects. Pan-Germanism represented many things to many people in Austria – a constitutional freedom, an economic union, a secular or religious enlightenment, a workers' revolution, a cultural mission, a racial programme or a rural landscape. It was upon this broad and popular support for Austria's pan-German identity that Austrofascist politicians could claim to build the new Austria where their predecessors had allegedly failed to nurture Austria's German character and maintain its leading place in the German nation. By drawing on competing visions of pan-German identity and uniting them under a single slogan of 'German Christian Austria', Austrofascists were able to mobilize recruits from across different political-cultural milieux in order to legitimize their political project of creating a fascist state.

The case studies in this book do not support the *Lager* theory's assumptions that ideological sympathies and political alliances represented clear-cut divisions between political camps in Austria. On the contrary, the book demonstrates that relationships across political-cultural milieux were fluid and flexible under the Austrofascist state and allowed different interest groups to align their views with the official version of pan-Germanism. We will see in the next chapter that while censorship under the Austrofascist regime prevented the German-nationalist press from voicing its sympathies with National Socialism, there was a wide margin in which the newspapers could continue to articulate their pan-Germanism and maintain a considerable degree of editorial autonomy. There was state-sponsored *Gleichschaltung*, but with large doses of pan-German rhetoric to reflect the editors' national politics and retain readers' interest without undermining the Autrofascist vision of 'German Austria'.

Notes

1 Whiteside, *The Socialism of Fools*, pp. 1–3.
2 Hanns Haas, 'Staats- und Landesbewusstsein in der Ersten Republik', in Tálos, et al. (eds), *Handbuch des politischen Systems Österreichs*, p. 474. The liberal notion of civic equality rested on a division of the public and private spheres, in which educated, property-owning, enfranchised males were equals within the public sphere, while women, children, workers and the non-propertied lower classes remained within a hierarchical private sphere. Pieter M. Judson, ' "Not Another Square Foot!" German Liberalism and the Rhetoric of National Ownership in Nineteenth-Century Austria', *Austrian History Yearbook* 26 (1995), p. 89.
3 Robert A. Kann, *A History of the Habsburg Empire 1526–1918* (Berkeley: University of California Press, 1974), pp. 256–62; Dieter Langewiesche, 'Germany and the National Question in 1848', in John Breuilly (ed.), *The State of Germany: The National Idea in the Making, Unmaking and Remaking of a Modern Nation-state* (London: Longman, 1992), p. 75.
4 William Carr, 'The Unification of Germany', in Breuilly (ed.), *The State of Germany*, p. 89.
5 Cited in Langewiesche, 'Germany and the National Question in 1848', p. 65.

6 Whiteside, 'The Germans as an Integrative Force in Imperial Austria', pp. 173–74.

7 Whiteside has defined *Besitzstand* as the dominance of Germans in intellectual life, the civil service, army, Catholic Church and the dynasty. See ibid. More recently Pieter Judson has defined *Nationalbesitzstand* as the 'cultural and intellectual capital of an imaginary German nation [including] not only the achievements of German speakers and their cultural institutions, but also the degree of cultivation and the moral capacity of the larger German community'. Judson, ' "Not Another Square Foot!" ', p. 83.

8 Carr, 'The Unification of Germany', p. 75; Langewiesche, 'Germany and the National Question in 1848', p. 77. The customs union was the brainchild of the Austrian Minister of Commerce, later the Minister of Finance, Karl Friedrich von Bruck, but it was Schwarzenberg, and later the liberal Minister of State, Anton von Schmerling, who proposed this idea as a political entity. A.J.P. Taylor, *The Habsburg Monarchy, 1809–1918: A History of the Austrian Empire and Austria-Hungary*, paperback edn (Chicago: University of Chicago Press, 1967), p. 77ff.

9 Kann, *A History of the Habsburg Empire 1526–1918*, p. 433; Whiteside, *The Socialism of Fools*, pp. 91–92.

10 Whiteside, *The Socialism of Fools*, pp. 13–14.

11 Ibid., pp. 44–51, 62.

12 Haas, 'Staats- und Landesbewusstsein in der Ersten Republik', p. 477.

13 Whiteside, *The Socialism of Fools*, pp. 24–25, 51–52, 61–62, 102–3.

14 Tweraser, 'Carl Beurle and the Triumph of German Nationalism in Austria', pp. 413–14.

15 Judson's figures for 1886 show 107,835 members in 980 chapters, of which there were 44,608 members and 441 branches in Bohemia. Pieter M. Judson, *Exclusive Revolutionaries: Liberal Politics, Social Experience and National Identity in the Austrian Empire* (Ann Arbor: University of Michigan Press, 1996), p. 210.

16 Whiteside, *The Socialism of Fools*, pp. 25, 56, 124–26.

17 Tweraser, 'Carl Beurle and the Triumph of German Nationalism in Austria', p. 418; Whiteside, *The Socialism of Fools*, p. 130 passim.

18 Catherine Albrecht, 'The Bohemian Question', in Mark Cornwall (ed.), *The Last Years of Austria-Hungary: A Multinational Experiment in Early Twentieth-century Europe* (Exeter: University of Exeter Press, 2002), pp. 77–83; Whiteside, *The Socialism of Fools*, p. 219.

19 Carsten, *The Rise of Fascism*, pp. 38, 84; John Breuilly, *Nationalism and the State*, 2nd edn (Manchester: Manchester University Press, 1993), p. 134.

20 Breuilly, *Nationalism and the State*, pp. 40, 71.

21 This disproportion is evident from the 1890 census, which counted 4,452 people in the town of Celje/Cilli who used German on an everyday basis (*Umgangssprache*) and 1,577 who spoke Slovene, while in the surrounding region 36,299 spoke Slovene and only 965 used German. Judson, ' "Not Another Square Foot!" ', p. 87.

22 Jill E. Mayer, ' "By Drip and By Drop": The Discourse of German Nationalism in the Press of Habsburg Austria: Salzburg, Styria, Vienna, 1877–1897' (PhD dissertation, University of Manitoba, 1993), pp. 43, 61, 173–79, 224–31.

23 Tweraser, 'Carl Beurle and the Triumph of German Nationalism in Austria', pp. 409–15.

24 Ibid., pp. 418–21. On the *Los von Rom* movement, see Chapter 10 in Whiteside, *The Socialism of Fools*, pp. 243–62.

25 Helga Embacher, 'Von Liberal zu National: Das Linzer Vereinswesen 1848–1938', *Historisches Jahrbuch der Stadt Linz* (1991), pp. 89, 95–100.

26 This filial revolt was a literal phenomenon in Linz, where the sons of a number of prominent liberal parliamentarians of the 1870s became notorious German-nationalists in their university years. The students were motivated by what they saw as the oppression of the petty bourgeoisie by the upper middle classes, whom they identified as Jews and liberals. Ibid., pp. 73–74; Tweraser, 'Carl Beurle and the Triumph of German Nationalism in Austria', p. 424.

27 After universal male suffrage was introduced in 1907, replacing the previous curial electoral system, the elections for Salzburg's parliament in 1909 resulted in 21 seats for the Christian Socials, 15 seats for the liberals and German-nationalists, and 2 seats for the Social Democrats. Nicole Felder, *Die historische Identität der österreichischen Bundesländer* (Innsbruck: Studien, 2002), p. 116.

28 Ibid., pp. 115–16; Mayer, ' "By Drip and By Drop" ', pp. 76, 122–23, 144–54.

29 Whiteside, *The Socialism of Fools*, pp. 122–23, 127.

30 Ibid., p. 316.

31 Embacher, 'Von Liberal zu National', pp. 42–45.

32 Judson, *Exclusive Revolutionaries*, pp. 212–13.

33 The elections between 1901 and 1911 revealed the growing strength of the Christian Social and Social Democratic parties at the expense of the liberal and German-nationalist parties: in 1901, the German People's Party had 48 seats, the Liberals 32, the Christian Socials 25, the Social Democrats 10, and Schönerer's radical All-Germans, whose constituencies were almost entirely in Bohemia, gained 21 seats (20 in Bohemia alone). In 1907, the Christian Socials became the largest party with 96 seats and the Social Democrats were the second largest with 88. The Social Democrats became the largest party in the imperial parliament after the 1911 elections. In the interwar period, the Christian Socials won 69 seats in the 1919 elections for the national assembly, 85 in 1920, 82 in 1923, 73 in 1927 and 66 in 1930, which represented an average of 40.6 per cent of the electorate, while the Social Democrats won 72 seats in 1919, 69 in 1920, 68 in 1923, 42 in 1927 and 72 in 1930, an average of 39.9 per cent. See Whiteside, *The Socialism of Fools*, pp. 217–18, 282, 292; Weinzierl and Skalnik (eds), *Österreich 1918–1938*, vol. 2, pp. 1092–93.

34 Whiteside, *The Socialism of Fools*, pp. 25, 91, 171.

35 Roger Fletcher, 'Socialist Nationalism in Central Europe before 1914: The Case of Karl Leuthner', *Canadian Journal of History* 17, 1 (1982), p. 38; Oliver Zimmer, *Nationalism in Europe, 1890–1940* (Basingstoke: Palgrave Macmillan, 2003), p. 117.

36 Zimmer, *Nationalism in Europe*, pp. 115–16; Otto Bauer, 'The Nationalities Question and Social Democracy (1907)', in Omar Dahbour and Micheline R. Ishay (eds), *The Nationalism Reader* (Atlantic Highlands: Humanities Press, 1995).

37 'Das "Linzer Programm" der Sozialdemokratischen Arbeiterpartei Österreichs, 1926', in Albert Kadan and Anton Pelinka (eds), *Die Grundsatzprogramme der österreichischen Parteien: Dokumente und Analyse* (St Pölten: Niederösterreichisches Pressehaus, 1979), p. 93; Haas, 'Staats- und Landesbewusstsein in der Ersten Republik', p. 482. The Austrian socialists' active resistance against National Socialism gained impetus after the 1943 Moscow Declaration, which stated Allied intentions to create an independent Austrian state. Alfred D. Low, 'Otto Bauer, Austro-Marxism, and the *Anschluss* Movement 1918–1938', *Canadian Review of Studies in Nationalism* 6, 1 (1979), p. 56.

38 Bauer's description of Austria as a German tribe appeared in an article in *Der sozialistische Kampf* in June 1938, shortly before his death. See Susanne Frölich-Steffen, *Die österreichische Identität im Wandel* (Vienna: Braumüller, 2003), p. 47.

39 Bluhm, *Building an Austrian Nation*, pp. 25, 30.

40 Andreas Lüer, 'Nationalismus in Christlichsozialen Programmen 1918–1933', *Zeitgeschichte* 14, 4 (1987), p. 151; Hanisch, 'Der Politische Katholizismus als Ideologischer Träger des "Austrofaschismus" ', p. 55. On the relationship between the Catholic Church, the Austrofascist state and lay organizations, see Laura Gellott, *The Catholic Church and the Authoritarian Regime in Austria, 1933–1938* (New York: Garland, 1987).

41 Whiteside, *The Socialism of Fools*, pp. 81–90, 124, 146–48; Schorske, 'Politics in a New Key', pp. 355–65. Lueger formally stated his commitment to the Christian Social movement at a golden jubilee celebration of Pope Leo XIII's priesthood in February 1888. See John S. Boyer, *Political Radicalism in Late Imperial Vienna: Origins of the Christian Social Movement 1848–1897* (Chicago: University of Chicago Press, 1981), p. 220. The exact date of the party's inauguration remains unclear due to the gradual expansion of the original party nucleus to include each of the representative groups. A more recent biographer of Lueger points out that Lueger first referred to the 'Christian Social Party' in 1891. See Richard S. Geehr, *Karl Lueger: Mayor of Fin de Siècle Vienna* (Detroit: Wayne State University Press, 1990), p. 341.

42 Whiteside, *The Socialism of Fools*, pp. 170–71; Haas, 'Staats- und Landesbewusstsein in der Ersten Republik', p. 475; Lüer, 'Nationalismus in Christlichsozialen Programmen', p. 152.

43 Judson, ' "Not Another Square Foot!" '

44 Gordon Brook-Shepherd, *The Austrians: A Thousand-Year Odyssey* (London: HarperCollins, 1996), p. 264; Whiteside, *The Socialism of Fools*, pp. 271–74.

45 Lüer, 'Nationalismus in Christlichsozialen Programmen', p. 150.

46 Paul R. Sweet, 'Seipel's Views on *Anschluss* in 1928: An Unpublished Exchange of Letters', *Journal of Modern History* 19, 4 (1947): 320–23; Kurt Skalnik, 'Auf der Suche nach der Identität', in Weinzierl and Skalnik (eds), *Österreich*

1918–1938, vol. 1, p. 15. For a definitive biography of Seipel, see Klemens von Klemperer, *Ignaz Seipel: Christian Statesman in a Time of Crisis* (Princeton: Princeton University Press, 1972).

47   Lüer, 'Nationalismus in Christlichsozialen Programmen', pp. 156–59; 'Das Programm der Christlichsozialen Partei, 1926', in Kadan and Pelinka (eds), *Die Grundsatzprogramme der österreichischen Parteien*, p. 116.

48   Lüer, 'Nationalismus in Christlichsozialen Programmen', pp. 160–62.

49   C.M. Peniston-Bird, 'The Debate on Austrian National Identity in the First Republic, 1918–1938' (PhD dissertation, University of St Andrews, 1996), p. 238. In 1936, an English tourist visited one such *Heimatmuseum* in Kitzbühel, Tyrol, and noted 'the iron cock which was anciently mounted on the tower of the parish church', and the wrought-iron signs that used to hang from Tyrolean inns 'like pencil sketches on the air – sketches of hounds and huntsmen, of deer and elephant and white horse; of bears and dragons and golden roses and eagles; of pewter pots and crowns and wild men and edelweiss'. Nina Murdoch, *Tyrolean June: A Summer Holiday in Austrian Tyrol* (London: Harrap, 1936), p. 61.

50   Peniston-Bird, 'The Debate on Austrian National Identity', pp. 344–47.

51   Among his other religious motifs, Boeckl's still-life works depicted death as part of the life cycle of birth and resurrection. On the interwar expressionists and their distance both from Austrian Secessionism and other contemporary trends in European art (Bauhaus, Dada, Surrealism, Cubism, Neue Sachlichkeit), see Wieland Schmied, 'Die österreichische Malerei in den Zwischenriegsjahren', in Weinzierl and Skalnik (eds), *Österreich 1918–1938*, vol. 2, pp. 685–703. See also Ernst Hanisch, *Der Lange Schatten des Staates: Österreichische Gesellschaftsgeschichte im 20. Jahrhundert* (Vienna: Ueberreuter, 1994), pp. 331–32.

52   For example, the inaugural season programme in 1920 featured performances of Mozart, Beethoven, Haydn and Nestroy, reflecting both patriotic Austrian and classical German choices, as well as works by the contemporary Austrian Catholic playwright, Richard von Kralik, and a series of church concerts and organ recitals.

53   Judith Beniston, 'Cultural Politics in the First Republic: Hans Brečka and the "Kunststelle für christliche Volksbildung" ', in Judith Beniston and Ritchie Robertson (eds), *Catholicism and Austrian Culture* (Edinburgh: Edinburgh University Press, 1999). Italics in original quote.

54   R. John Rath, 'History and Citizenship Training: An Austrian Example', *Journal of Modern History* 21, 3 (1949), p. 230. See also his earlier article, based on more extensive research on the period 1933–1938, 'Training for Citizenship, "Authoritarian" Austrian Style', *Journal of Central European Affairs* 3, 2 (1943): 121–46.

55   Rath, 'History and Citizenship Training'. See also Herbert Dachs, ' "Austrofaschismus" und Schule: Ein Instrumentalisierungsversuch', in Tálos and Neugebauer (eds), *Austrofaschismus*, p. 286.

56 See Carla Esden-Tempska, 'Civic Education in Authoritarian Austria, 1934–38', *History of Education Quarterly* 30, 2 (1990), pp. 203–4, which draws extensively on Rath's earlier work. (Italics in quote given in original.)

57 Ibid., pp. 194, 204.

58 Dachs, ' "Austrofaschismus" und Schule', p. 290.

59 See ibid. Rath also makes this argument in 'Training for Citizenship'.

60 Klaus Berchtold (ed.), *Österreichische Parteiprogramme, 1868–1966* (Vienna: Verlag für Geschichte und Politik, 1967), pp. 82–83; Carsten, *The Rise of Fascism*, p. 38.

61 Friedrich Weissensteiner, *Der ungeliebte Staat: Österreich zwischen 1918 und 1938* (Vienna: ÖBV, 1990), p. 36; Wandruszka, 'Das "nationale" Lager', pp. 277–82.

62 'Das "Salzburger Programm" der Grossdeutschen Volkspartei, 1920', in Berchtold (ed.), *Österreichische Parteiprogramme*.

63 Thomas Dostal, 'Die Grossdeutsche Volkspartei', in Tálos, et al. (eds), *Handbuch des politischen Systems Österreichs*, pp. 198, 204; Herbert Dachs, 'Das Parteiensystem', in Tálos, et al. (eds), *Handbuch des politischen Systems Österreichs*, p. 146. See Weinzierl and Skalnik (eds), *Österreich 1918–1938*, vol. 2, pp. 1,092–93 on figures for national elections. In 1932, the NSDAP won almost 21 per cent in Salzburg's regional elections, compared to less than 2 per cent for the Greater Germans. Ernst Hanisch, 'Salzburg', in Weinzierl and Skalnik (eds), *Österreich 1918–1938*, vol. 2, p. 909. The NSDAP won 4 seats in the federal parliament on the basis of the result in 1932. Gerhard Jagschitz, 'Die Nationalsozialistische Partei', in Tálos, et al. (eds), *Handbuch des politischen Systems Österreichs*, p. 236. Once the Nazi Party came to power in Germany in 1933, the Greater Germans struggled to attract German financial backing because of pressure to align with the Austrian Nazis. The Greater Germans eventually disbanded in 1934 after Germany formally withdrew its financial support. See Low, *The Anschluss Movement*, pp. 114–15.

64 Dostal, 'Die Grossdeutsche Volkspartei', p. 206; Hanisch, 'Salzburg', p. 917.

65 Paul R. Sweet, 'The Historical Writing of Heinrich von Srbik', *History and Theory* 9, 1 (1970), pp. 46–47.

66 Whiteside, *The Socialism of Fools*, p. 143.

67 John Haag, 'Heinrich von Srbik', in Kelly Boyd (ed.), *Encyclopedia of Historians and Historical Writing* (London: Fitzroy Dearborn, 1999), pp. 1,142–43; Sweet, 'The Historical Writing of Heinrich von Srbik', pp. 45, 51.

68 Sweet, 'The Historical Writing of Heinrich von Srbik', pp. 47–48.

69 Haag, 'Heinrich von Srbik', pp. 1,142–43; Sweet, 'The Historical Writing of Heinrich von Srbik', p. 56.

70 The noteworthy exceptions are Staudinger, 'Austrofaschistische "Österreich"-Ideologie', and Steinberg, *The Meaning of the Salzburg Festival*. Steinberg, for example, argues that through their mission to preserve religious belief, German universalism and cosmopolitanism, the Festival organizers and patrons invoked this Austrian pan-German identity as a counterpoint to Nazism specifically,

and to Protestant Prussian German identity more generally. He also makes a crucial and much under-recognized point that the Austrofascist state's attempt to define Austrian identity against Nazism was thwarted by the state's own manufacturing of a pan-German identity.

71 Whiteside, *The Socialism of Fools*, p. 41.
72 Lehnert, 'Politisch-kulturelle Integrationsmilieus und Orientierungslager'.
73 Evan Burr Bukey, *Hitler's Hometown: Linz, Austria, 1908–1945* (Bloomington: Indiana University Press, 1986), pp. 39–74.

2

Creating a fascist press at home and abroad

In the 'Newspaper Reader's Prayer', the German left-wing journalist, Kurt Tucholsky (1890–1935), satirized his generation's insatiable appetite for news, gossip and rumour.[1] The reader's hysteria at not being able to cram all the world's news into one breakfast sitting may have struck Tucholsky in 1927 as the social and moral disorder of Weimar Germany, but Austrian politicians reached a similar diagnosis of mass hysteria among newspaper readers in Austria's First Republic. This chapter shows the responses of Austrofascist press officials to the apparent moral apathy, apolitical tendencies and sensationalism they perceived were the result of representative democracy in post-war Austria. Charting Austria's press revolution from 1848 until the economic collapse of 1929, the chapter examines the expansion of a reading culture from imperial Austria to the tabloid era of the 1920s. It was significant that the first laws enacted by the Austrofascist state in March 1933 were aimed at halting this growth of newspapers and readers in order to reverse the democratization of the Austrian press.

Austrofascist press officials did not stop at censorship laws and penalties for infringing the new press codes. They also sought to recreate the Austrian press in the image of fascism elsewhere, drawing especially on the model of Italy's journalism academy and press chamber. And as Italy followed Germany's example in combining its press and propaganda bodies into one powerful agent of repression and control, Austria also amalgamated its federal press agency with the state propaganda bureau at the end of 1936. Combining reactionary traditions of censorship with modern enterprises of consumerism, cultural diplomacy and tourism, Austrofascism's new press and propaganda office signalled to onlookers at home and abroad that the Austrian state was growing immune to the Nazi menace. In spite of increasing demands from Nazi Germany that Austria align its domestic propaganda with German foreign ambitions in the country, Austrofascist leaders continued to look to Italy and elsewhere in Europe, directing their propaganda efforts towards an international audience to shore up support for the Austrian state. Contrary to most assessments of the Austrian state's lack of resolve and resources to carve out its independence and mission in Europe, this chapter reveals the extent of Austrofascism's achievements in transforming Austria's political culture and reinventing the country's image abroad as a modernizing state and strategic European ally.

Newspapers and readers in Austria

Like caffeine addiction, the apparent disease of press consumerism in postwar Austria remained undetected at first and only when newspapers went out of print or were banned did readers complain about the availability and standard of their preferred choice of newspaper. Austrian newspapers had steadily built up loyal readerships since the growth of liberal politics in the 1860s and 1870s, then mass politics in the 1880s and 1890s, which established public traditions of reading rooms, and coffee house and workplace subscriptions, as well as private traditions of family subscriptions and discussing the news at home. The reading 'revolution' in the Habsburg Monarchy occurred half a century after France's and lagged in momentum behind Germany, where rapid urbanization after unification in 1871 sent newspaper circulations soaring by the end of the century. Nonetheless, it could be said of Austria that the press had come to represent a 'fourth estate' by the First World War.[2]

Urban migration in the late nineteenth century brought new readers into cities all over Europe. Newspapers acted as compasses to these modern urbanites by printing tram schedules, the stock exchange, and advertisements for film and theatre. The new genre of feuilletons reflected the obsession with city living with articles describing chance meetings between strangers, offering advice about whether to stand up for fellow commuters on a tram and other topics of public etiquette. Peter Fritzsche argues that reading a newspaper – or riding a tram for a weekend excursion to the city – belonged to a 'spectator' culture that socialized urban newcomers in Central Europe's growing modern metropoles of Berlin, Cracow and Vienna by the turn of the century.[3]

Vienna's growth from around 400,000 to more than 2 million inhabitants in the second half of the nineteenth century was slightly smaller than Berlin's, whose population septupled to 3.5 million by 1914.[4] Berlin's leading newspaper, the *Berliner Morgenpost*, sold around 400,000 copies daily, or one copy for every nine Berliners. Assuming that young children, non-German-speaking migrants and other socially disadvantaged groups would not have bought or read newspapers, the circulation figures for the *Morgenpost* represent one copy for every family in Berlin. By contrast, Vienna's leading newspapers sold less than a quarter of the copies of the

Morgenpost, and the ratio of readers to newspapers in Vienna was equivalent to that of Bremen, not Berlin. Although this disparity between the imperial capitals can be partially attributed to Berlin's larger population, it also indicates a difference in political taste and consumption in the two cities. The leading newspapers in Berlin were the flagships of the city's major publishing houses – boulevard dailies that peddled sensationalism and consumerism and supported a democratic programme of civic improvement without any real political commitment to social reform. This formula suited Berlin's working population in the main: the *Morgenpost* sold outside factories and was a household item in workers' quarters, while the socialist organ, *Vorwärts*, relied on party members' subscriptions and sold barely an eighth of the total subscriptions of the *Morgenpost*.[5]

A popular aversion to the political content of the party organs would later beset the Viennese press, too, but competition with the tabloids did not enter the newspaper market until after the First World War when an imperial ban on newspaper vendors was lifted in 1922.[6] Prior to 1914, Vienna's leading newspapers were strictly partisan organs. Liberal newspapers were the first to gain mass readerships in the wake of the failed 1848–49 revolutions. The circulation of Austria's premier daily, the *Neue Freie Presse*, established in 1864, climbed steadily to 55,000 in 1901 with a large readership throughout the empire and abroad.[7] Politicians rubbed shoulders with newspaper editors in the liberal clubs and reading circles that emerged in the revolutionary year and, in turn, newspapers educated their readers in these clubs and circles about their civic responsibilities and political rights. Pieter Judson has argued that this voluntary associational model of political participation allowed for the growth and continuity of liberal ideology throughout the era of liberal politics.[8] But while in France the growth in associational life and the press during the nineteenth century strengthened participation in a democratic political culture, the 'exclusive revolutionaries' of Austrian liberalism were constrained by their factionalism and ethnocentrism.[9] Instead, it was the emergence of mass political movements in the late nineteenth century that socialized individuals into political parties and eclipsed both the liberals and German-nationalists on the eve of the First World War.

While the liberal press had facilitated the rise of liberal politics, the newspapers of Austria's mass political movements emerged through the parties themselves. The organ of the Social Democratic Party, the *Arbeiter-Zeitung*, appeared in July 1888 shortly before the party was inaugurated in December 1888. By 1900, the newspaper had a circulation of 24,000 and had climbed to 54,000 by 1914.[10] The Christian Social organ, the *Reichspost*, did not appear until 1893, four years after the party's inauguration in 1889. The delay in publication was due in part to opposition from Austria's bishops and clerical conservatives in the provincial parliamentary clubs, who feared that Austrian Catholics would be led astray by popular reading habits. Consequently, the provincial Catholic press remained in the hands and printing presses of the clergy with a very low circulation. The *Reichspost* went on to become the most widely read Catholic newspaper in Austria with a circulation of 36,000 in 1914.[11]

The relaxation of press restrictions in the first decade of the First Republic allowed Austrian newspapers to cater for almost every intellectual and political preference. Readership had remained high since the First World War, when newspapers had enjoyed increased circulation – in some cases up to 100 per cent higher – and many had published extra editions with daily news from the theatres of war.[12] But the birth of the tabloid era in Austrian journalism saw the cheap boulevard press begin to overtake the political press. In 1925, the most popular tabloid, *Der Abend*, sold 100,000 copies daily while the *Arbeiter-Zeitung* sold 112,000 and the *Neue Freie Presse* and the *Reichspost* sold 75,000 and 50,000 respectively.[13] Nearly all new newspapers founded during the interwar years were tabloids. However, many of the new newspapers folded as quickly as they had sprung up due to lack of funding and a competitive market.[14] As smaller newspapers struggled to get off the ground, the established newspapers also encountered the burdens of high production costs, taxes on advertising and the coffee house custom of providing in-house reading for patrons, which reduced the overall number of subscriptions.[15] In the immediate post-war years, paper and ink shortages and work strikes frequently disrupted publication schedules and newspapers often appeared with fewer pages and illegible ink-print.[16] The low income of workers and farmers also prevented many potential readers from paying the subscription rates of the daily newspapers, making the cheaper weekly press the most popular medium in the interwar period.[17]

One of the innovations of the interwar Austrian press was the *kleine Blatt* (small sheet), a tabloid-size weekly newspaper that functioned as an organ of the major political parties but catered for a mass readership, rather than for an intellectual elite who read the established dailies. However, the *kleine Blätter* distinguished themselves from the gutter journalism of the boulevard press by publishing the preferred topics of the 'little man'. The small sheets covered the major European headlines with minimal political analysis and included an appealing array of local news, sport, travel stories and advertising.[18] The socialist newspaper, *Das Kleine Blatt*, founded in 1927, epitomized the *kleine Blätter* in name and style. In 1929, the Christian Social Party launched its own version, the *Kleine Volksblatt*, in association with its existing flagship, the *Reichspost*. In both cases, the *kleine Blätter* dramatically outsold the established party organs, partly due to the post-Depression slump in newspaper subscriptions but also due to their successful appeal to popular tastes.[19]

A 1933 study of Viennese reading habits by a Swiss sociologist showed that the tabloid formula was overwhelmingly popular among workers. Based on a survey of 400 Viennese (200 workers and 200 professionals), the study showed that only a third of workers surveyed regularly read the *Arbeiter-Zeitung*, whereas half of the professional group read the daily political broadsheets. Workers also tended to read selectively: 62 per cent reported they always read the local news, compared to 71 per cent of the professionals. The travel, sport and cinema sections, court reports and advertisement pages that were the mainstay of the tabloid press all rated higher than the political content of the daily newspapers. And for families on a tight budget, the serial novel and feuilleton sections in the weekly and monthly press were a cheap alternative to buying books.[20]

Women readers were another group newspapers targeted during the interwar period. Columns on fashion and household tips, and the serialized novel in the weekly press aimed to attract women readers through the new tabloid style, but the major parties also introduced monthly magazines specifically targeting women. The publication with the single largest circulation in the interwar period, *Die Frau*, sold 214,000 copies monthly in 1932. The journal was intended to attract women to the Social Democratic Party and was free for party members. Another socialist organ for women, *Die Unzufriedene* (The Discontented), sought to reach women who were not yet party members. By 1931, seven years after it began circulation in 1924, the magazine was selling 150,000 copies monthly.[21] It fared better than its sister publication after the party's ban and, changing its name to *Das Kleine Frauenblatt* in July 1934, it continued to circulate weekly along with the ranks of other government-patronized magazines for women in the Austrofascist state. Given that the average monthly circulation of the socialist press was around 2 million before 1934, women's journals alone accounted for almost a quarter of the total readership, not including the numbers of women who read the daily and weekly party newspapers.[22]

Readership also needs to be more widely interpreted than circulation and included anyone who picked up a newspaper in a cafe or on a tram seat.[23] Estimates of three readers to every newspaper sold are based on patterns of public reading rooms and coffee house subscriptions and do not accurately gauge the extent to which newspapers could be skimmed for political content, browsed for entertainment or scrutinized for editorial bias.[24] At any rate, reading rooms were less representative of the mass political cultures of the 1920s and 1930s than of the rise of party politics in the late nineteenth century. Newspapers were not a popular strategy for appealing to Nazi voters in Weimar Germany, where most Nazi voters had become alienated from mainstream political and associational networks. Only one in twenty Nazi voters read the party newspapers, but were attracted instead by the local political meetings where the party could promote its different agendas to different local constituencies.[25] Nonetheless, for readers of the daily and weekly party organs we can show a correlation between readership and politics. Theodore Zeldin has argued that in France newspapers did not influence French public opinion but merely reinforced it since readers tended to select which newspapers they read – usually those which reflected their own or their family's politics – or they selected which articles in the newspaper they read or recalled later.[26] We have seen that Austrian workers also read selectively, a habit that did not overly concern leaders of Austria's Social Democratic Party who saw the party organs simply as one of the means to socialize workers into a political movement. Party leaders hoped that a person who read the *Arbeiter-Zeitung* even on an irregular basis, or subscribed to the party's more popular small sheet, *Das Kleine Blatt*, might be more inclined to visit a workers' library, turn up to a local meeting of the party or attend a May Day celebration and meet other workers.[27]

We can test this pattern of readership for Vienna, which had the greatest concentration of newspapers and readers per capita than any other city or province in the First Republic. In 1925, the Viennese press sold 1.2 million copies on weekdays while the combined circulation of the provincial newspapers was just 280,000. The renowned Viennese dailies, including the *Neue Freie Presse*, the *Neue Wiener Tagblatt* and the *Reichspost*, continued to circulate the coffee houses of Prague, Zagreb and Budapest, and they were read widely in the new provinces of Burgenland and Lower Austria, which did not yet have their own newspapers.[28] By 1930 Vienna had 22 morning dailies, 3 midday newspapers, 5 evening newspapers, 5 weekly political newspapers, over thirty weekly political journals, and more than a thousand different journals and magazines of varying genres.[29] The Paris correspondent for the *Manchester Guardian*, Robert Dell, attested to the high standard of Vienna's newspapers in 1931. By comparison with the state-monitored press in Italy and Russia, the increasingly monopolized British newspapers and the low standards of the French press (which Dell blamed on meagre journalists' salaries and government-subsidized opinion journals), Dell singled out Austria and Scandinavia as the remaining examples of an independent press in Europe.[30]

Analysis of the numbers of readers and party voters reveals the tight cohesion of the Christian Social, Social Democratic and Communist party networks in Vienna. Taking the daily newspapers, with an average weekday circulation of approximately 1,327,000 in 1930 as an example, we can break down this figure into 553,000 for the liberal press, 471,000 for the Social Democratic press, 206,000 for the Christian Social press, 57,000 for the German-nationalist press (including Greater Germans and National Socialists) and 5,000 for the communist press.[31] If the readership of the party newspapers was at least three times the number of copies sold, then the numbers of party voters in the 1930 national election were on average slightly fewer than the numbers of those who actually read the party press, with the exception of the communist press whose readership corresponded exactly with the number of party voters. However, less than half the number of those who voted for either the Greater Germans or the National Socialists in 1930 actually read the German-nationalist press.[32] As in Weimar Germany, those who voted for the Nazis in Austria were less likely to read the party organs, but were primarily attracted to the dynamic and spontaneous elements of rallies, marches and tavern meetings.

The figures for liberal readers in Vienna also did not correspond with any of the voting patterns for the 1930 election. According to Paupié, the liberal press had more than 1.6 million readers, but even taking into consideration that newspapers like the *Neue Freie Presse* had a circulation outside Vienna, this figure is astounding for a city of two million: every adult and older child would have had to have read one of the liberal flagships. Supporters of other political parties would also have read the liberal press in addition to their own party newspapers. This pattern is corroborated by a close-up profile of the liberal reader. The Klaar family – Ernst, Stella and son, Georg – was middle class, Viennese and Jewish. Ernst worked as an international banker in the Austrian *Länderbank* and Georg went to one of Vienna's best grammar schools. The Klaar family read both the *Neue Freie Presse* and the *Neues Wiener Tagblatt*, yet voted for the Social Democrats. Writing in his 1981 memoir, *Last Waltz in Vienna*, George Clare (he changed his name in 1941 three years after fleeing Austria) explained that nearly all middle-class Jews supported the Social Democrats, not because they were attracted to socialism, but partly because the Social Democrats were the least anti-Semitic party and partly because most liberal Jews were left leaning anyway: 'Their socialist convictions could easily have been knocked down with the feather of liberalism, had a worthwhile liberal party still been in existence.'[33] The absence of a liberal political party in Austria was a crucial factor in what Lehnert describes as the 'structural deficit' of the liberal milieu. Unlike the socialist and Catholic milieux, which had built up a dense network of associational and political ties, a liberal milieu existed only in the sphere of cultural and professional life. It lacked a liberal-republican 'orientation camp' in which the liberal tendencies of such an organ as the *Neue Freie Presse* could find wider political expression and a democratic will.[34] The 'republic without republicans' cliché of Weimar Germany was equally true of Austria. It was not so much the strength of the Social Democrats, Christian Socials and Nazis in the interwar period, but rather, the chauvinism, fragmentation and radicalization of nineteenth-century Austrian liberals and their heirs that undermined the wider reception to democratic ideas in the interwar period.

We can observe a different correlation between readership and politics in the provincial press. Under the Austro-Hungarian Empire German-nationalists had built up a solid support base by educating newspaper readers in their rights and responsibilities in the national community, similar to the strategy of the earlier liberals.[35] In the First Republic the German-nationalist press continued to dominate the provincial public sphere and had even begun to rival the established Viennese newspapers by the end of the 1930s. The most influential provincial German-nationalist newspaper in Austria was the *Grazer Tagespost*, which had a weekday circulation of 35,000, around twice that of the Catholic and social-ist provincial press.[36] The only Styrian newspaper with a higher circulation than the *Tagespost* was the boulevard *Kleine Zeitung*, which was Catholic-owned but strictly non-partisan; at a third of the price of the political newspapers, it was especially popular among workers and the petty bour-geoisie and sold 44,000 copies on weekdays and 82,000 on Sundays in 1935.[37] Thus on weekdays, the *Tagespost* sold four out of every ten news-papers in Styria, making it the widest read local political newspaper.[38] Moreover, selling over half the number of copies as the *Neue Freie Presse* and equal to the *Reichspost* by 1935, the *Tagespost* had become a formidable rival to the leading Viennese political organs by the late interwar years.

In Salzburg, the German-nationalist *Salzburger Volksblatt* also outsold the socialist and Catholic mainstream newspapers. Pitching its content at small-town educated professionals and shop owners, the *Salzburger Volks-blatt* sold around 10,000 copies after 1922, representing more than 50 per cent of the total circulation of Salzburg's weekday press.[39] The next largest newspaper was the Christian Social *Salzburger Chronik* with a circulation of less than 4,000 during the interwar years, despite the Chris-tian Social Party holding a majority in the provincial government and gaining its highest result of 48 per cent in the 1927 regional elections.[40] The statistics show that Catholics in Salzburg voted for the party but did not read the local newspaper. As we will see in the next chapter, editors of the German-nationalist *Volksblatt* were conscious of their readers' Catho-lic sensibilities and small-town politics sometimes meant that German-nationalists were on better terms with rival Catholic elites than with Nazis in their ranks.

In contrast to the provinces, the leading German-nationalist organ in Vienna, the *Wiener Neueste Nachrichten*, had around 2 per cent of Vienna's newspaper market with a circulation of 25,000 in 1935 and 50,000 by 1938.[41] Even if we compare its circulation to that of the other major daily Viennese political newspapers, excluding the more successful *kleine Blätter*, the *Wiener Neueste Nachrichten* still only had between 5 and 10 per cent of the total market share.[42] Nonetheless the newspaper was the most influential organ of the German-nationalists after it became the mouthpiece of the Greater German party in 1925 and began receiving financial backing from the German Foreign Office.[43] We will see in Chapter 4 how editors of the *Wiener Neueste Nachrichten* sought to gain a wider readership outside Vienna by representing Austria as a borderland under siege from Slavs in a continuation of the kind of frontier nationalism that German-nationalists had used before the war to mobilize provincial readers in the empire.

We have seen that Austria's newspaper revolution was not halted by the collapse of the Austro-Hungarian empire, but was accelerated through new genres of journalism that brought greater diversity and market competition to the press during the interwar years. Despite the economic setbacks after the war and again after 1929, which reduced the number of subscribers and made the weekly press a more affordable alternative, the political press still remained the steady diet of a large number of readers. Liberal newspapers and their socialist counterparts were the leading organs of political opinion in Vienna, while the German-nationalist press dominated the countryside. However, reading a newspaper did not always translate into political commitment in the interwar period: many Viennese Jews found intellectual solace in the liberal standards but were otherwise little engaged in political or associational life. German-nationalists comprised the largest group of readers outside Vienna but lacked a mainstream party organ. By 1933 the Nazi Party had become the most viable political option for these provincial readers. Seizing on the pretext of the Nazi threat in 1933, Austrian politicians launched a counter-revolution against the fourth estate bringing to an end the half-century long democratization of Austria's press and embarking on a process that can be compared directly with the fascistization of Italy's press.

Towards an Austrian press and propaganda ministry

Charting the press revolution in Austria from empire to republic also allows us to note similarities between systems of repression and surveillance over a longer period and locate these systems within a larger context of state-controlled regimes that were not fascist. Historians of Fascist Italy have argued that not every aspect of the press, nor indeed of everyday life under Mussolini, can be regarded as fascist.[44] At the same time, I contend that historians need to be cautious about reducing fascism to a set of outcomes. In her study of the press in Fascist Italy, Stefania Galassi has argued for a broader definition of *'fascistizzazione'*, a term used both by contemporaries of the regime and in historiography on Italian Fascism to refer to the process of creating a fascist state. Italian press officials were often confused whether the term referred to the laws and reforms of the press or the intended result of that legislative process, namely the creation of a fascist press (*stampa fascistizzato*). Galassi's contention is that precisely because regime officials and even Mussolini himself did not always know where the process would lead, *fascistizzazione* cannot be defined only as the laws, censorship decrees and bans on the oppositional press, but includes also the appointments of party functionaries to editorial positions, the creation of a Fascist syndicate for journalists, state training colleges and degrees for journalists and the production of state organs to promote the government at home and abroad.[45] As we will see, the fascistization of the Austrian press mirrored Italy's and was almost complete by 1938, a remarkable feat given that Italian press officials had more than a decade's head start on the Austrians.

Like their Italian counterparts, press officials in the Austrofascist state drew on a long tradition of press censorship dating back to the pre-liberal era. Notably under the iron reign of Metternich (1830–1848), strict controls had been imposed on all publishable material including newspapers, books and plays, as well as gravestone inscriptions, memorial cards, tobacco boxes, badges and cuff links. In Metternich's day, a system of pre-publication or 'preventive' censorship (*Vorzensur*) required newspapers to submit their copy to the censor before going to press. The law was abolished in 1867 and replaced with a system of post-publication or 'repressive' censorship. Under the latter system, government authorities censored newspapers immediately prior to their distribution often at great financial and legal risk to the publishers, who stood to lose money and their licence from having the printed newspapers banned from sale if they were found to contain offensive material.[46] The only other European countries to maintain similar regulations for the press up until 1914 were Germany, Hungary, Russia and Bulgaria.[47]

The outbreak of the First World War ushered in a new era of information control. The War Surveillance Office in Vienna, established by the Army High Command and attached to the War Ministry, introduced emergency decrees that banned the publication of subversive information. Offensive material included 'unpatriotic' articles; reports about economic problems or popular protests; 'provocative' ideas related to religion, socialism or nationalism; criticism of the government; rumours and pacifist propaganda. Censorship laws were relaxed under the new Emperor Karl, who reconvened parliament in 1917 and abandoned the emergency decrees, although censors continued to operate with some inconsistency in different parts of the empire. The War Ministry imposed another method of wartime censorship in 1918 through a military press index that restricted circulation of 'unpatriotic' newspapers to soldiers at the front.[48]

The end of war and collapse of the Austro-Hungarian Empire in 1918 invoked unprecedented constitutional freedoms of speech and a new law guaranteeing freedom of the press came into effect on 1 October 1922.[49] But within seven years, the ruling Christian Social Party had already amended the law to ban public criticism of past and present government policy.[50] This first act of censorship in the democratic era was a purely partisan attempt by the Christian Socials to curb the influence of their rival socialist organs. Presumably Christian Social organs such as the *Reichspost* and the *Kleine Volksblatt* were immune to laws that prevented their criticism of Vienna's Social Democratic municipal government. Nonetheless, the 1929 amendments to the original 1922 law were the first step in the interwar years towards state control of the press.

The next step came on 7 March 1933 when Dollfuss invoked the wartime Enabling Act of 1917 and proclaimed his personal rule by emergency decree, three days after he had prorogued parliament following a deadlock in proceedings. The 1917 Enabling Act had been briefly introduced to deal with food shortages and had been abandoned, but was never annulled, after parliament reconvened.[51] Inspired by the wartime censorship measures as well as the 1867 law on post-publication censorship, Dollfuss's emergency press decrees required newspapers to be inspected two hours prior to circulation for any information that might have caused 'injury to the patriotic, religious or cultural sensibility'.[52] If copy was found to have offending material, the section was blanked out or the entire edition of the newspaper was banned from circulation. This practice of banning a newspaper's publication was known as 'confiscation' (*Beschlagnahme*) and incurred penalties for the publisher who stood to lose sales for a day and the waste of expensive ink and paper. Further press laws in April 1933 made it illegal to criticize domestic and foreign governments and heads of state. Communist and National Socialist newspapers were banned in May and June, respectively, and the Social Democratic press was banned following the civil war in February 1934. From July 1933 newspapers known to be sympathetic to National Socialism were obliged to publish official correspondence from the federal press agency (*Bundespressedienst* – hereafter BPD). Foreign newspapers that supported any of the illegal parties were banned in October 1933.[53]

One important feature of the state's control of the press was the appointment of government commissioners to the editorships of

German-nationalist newspapers. These appointments were significant because unlike the Christian Social and liberal newspapers that also remained in circulation after 1934, the German-nationalist press represented the most significant threat to the state's goal of maintaining Austrian independence. As we have seen, the circulation of the German-nationalist press was much higher than that of the Christian Social newspapers in the provinces and was on par with the *Reichspost* in Vienna. The government commissioners appointed to the German-nationalist newspapers were usually local representatives of the *Heimwehr*: in Graz, a *Heimwehr* official was appointed political editor of the *Tagespost* in November 1934.[54] In Salzburg, too, a member of the local *Heimatschutz* (Homeland Defence corps) was appointed political editor of the *Salzburger Volksblatt*.[55] The *Wiener Neueste Nachrichten* was permitted to keep its previous chief editor, Hans Mauthe, although Mauthe was also obliged to appoint a government commissioner to the general editorship.[56] By all appearances the press was under the control of the *Heimwehr*, which effectively became the government's law and order force following the civil war.

Censorship practices tended to be more indiscriminate, however, since responsibility for monitoring press violations fell to local judicial and police authorities, rather than the BPD. Officials appointed to censor individual newspapers were paid a pittance for their efforts and often what was understood as permissible copy varied from province to province, so that an identical article to one appearing in a government organ might be censored in another newspaper known to be an opponent of the government.[57] This was not a unique problem for the Austrofascist state: the Austro-Hungarian War Surveillance Office in the First World War had made similar complaints about the unreliability of imperial censors. Maureen Healy has argued that wartime censors were subject to the same daily material deprivations as ordinary citizens. The rates of absenteeism and threats of strikes by censors meant that while censorship was imposed from above, the day-to-day practice on the ground was not the work of a well-oiled machine but of bureaucrats who wanted public holidays off, sick leave and extra pay for overtime.[58] German-nationalist editors could exploit the loopholes in the system by publishing government correspondence on the front pages, while retaining considerably wide margins throughout the rest of the newspaper in which they could express, uncensored, their pan-Germanism.

Public interest in newspapers waned and subscription rates dropped overall as a result of press restrictions. The *Neue Freie Presse* dropped in circulation from 78,000 to 50,000 and the *Tagespost* lost 6,000 subscriptions.[59] Meanwhile, Swiss-German newspapers grew in popularity at the expense of the Austrian press with more than three-quarters of a million new subscribers by 1935.[60] Mitzi Hartmann, a medical student at the University of Vienna who emigrated to England in 1938, wrote in her memoir, *Austria Still Lives*, that once the socialist press was banned, the government newspapers also lost subscribers as people became disillusioned with the political press and gathered instead in coffee houses to read the international newspapers:

> The result of the suppression of a full news service was that no one believed anything anymore, that people read incredible meanings between the lines, and that Vienna became a city of rumours, political witticisms, and frequenters of cafes. Indeed, a miracle occurred, and we young people, who had always heartily despised sitting in cafes, were now ourselves forced to frequent cafes in order somehow to keep abreast of the times.[61]

While readers like Hartmann and her peers looked for news outside their country to escape the glum world of domestic politics, others, like Tucholsky's sensation-starved reader, may have had less sophisticated tastes and survived on a diet of small-town gossip and celebrity news about opera stars in Salzburg, or the latest serialized novel. Either way, the first two years of Austrofascism had transformed the landscape of the press into a monotonous cycle of world news, government propaganda and local infotainment for readers, and a constant battle ground with authorities for journalists, editors and publishers.

By December 1934 plans were afoot to create a press chamber in Austria as a constituent body of the corporation for the free professions.[62] The head of the BPD, Eduard Ludwig, appointed a working party of the Union for Publishers of Daily Newspapers (*Verband der Herausgeber der Tageszeitungen*) to begin drafting the legislation for a press chamber. However, a 1932 pamphlet on the organization of a German press chamber by Franz Gustav Ronco in the files of the BPD indicates that Ludwig may have considered plans for a press chamber well before 1934, just as Dollfuss himself had been studying the 1917 Enabling Act some time before he introduced the emergency decrees in March 1933.[63] Ronco's study was part of a series published by the Cologne Research Institute for International Press Affairs and was based on a case study of the Rhein-Westphalian press. It argued that the rationale for a press chamber was to harmonize the interests of the people with those of the state, while preserving the freedom of the press and its function as mediator between people and state. Passages throughout the booklet were highlighted by the BPD and phrases such as 'the newspaper's dual character as bearer of the public and private interests' later ended up in drafts of the Austrian legislation for a press chamber.[64] For example, an early version of the press chamber legislation stated in

Article 2 that the incumbent duties of the Austrian press in the corporative state 'were not simply to make a profit or to represent publicly a certain intellectual tendency, but more than that [to act] as bearer of a public mission'.[65] The final version of the legislation later spelt out this public mission to govern and interpret the cultural interests of the state corporations, to promote the state's economic and social interests, and to establish an academic discipline for journalism.[66]

Memoranda from the working party to Minister Ludwig in 1935 and ministerial discussions in the Federal Council for Culture (*Bundeskulturrat*) in 1936 reveal the inspiration behind the legislation was not only the earlier German model, but also, more significantly, Italy as a model of fascist syndicalism and vocational training for journalists. The parallels between the Austrian and Italian press can be seen in their common trajectory from newspaper bans, censorship and editorial surveillance to the creation of an overarching press body that sought to professionalize and regulate the state media as a whole. Following the Austro-German Agreement in July 1936, Austrian press officials also looked to Nazi Germany's model of an integrated press and propaganda ministry in the interests of guarding Austria's independence against ever closer union with Germany. The German parallel can therefore be seen not as much in a common path towards a fascist press and propaganda ministry, as in the relationship between the Austrian and German states that necessitated their common path.

Just as Nazis and socialists remained legal alongside the government organs and bodies of the Christian Social Party in the months following Dollfuss's declaration of his personal rule, the early years of Fascist rule in Italy had also allowed rival political groups to coexist side by side in uneasy tension. And like Dollfuss, who was a close personal friend of the *Duce* and with whom Dollfuss corresponded regularly prior to his assassination, Mussolini was the 'heir of conservatism' who achieved, by radical means, many long-held dreams of Italian conservatives.[67] His early radicalism as a socialist, while placing him squarely outside a conservative tradition, would seem to discount Mussolini from comparison with Austria's mini-Metternich, as Dollfuss's detractors referred to the small-statured Austrian leader. Yet both leaders came to fascism by breaking with old-style party rule and embracing radical demagogic power unchecked by democratic institutions of the parliament or the free press.[68] In both the Italian and Austrian cases, fascistization of the press was not a revolution bringing about a 'new order' as Austrofascist politicians and Italian Fascist deputies themselves claimed. Rather, it belonged to a longer process spanning nineteenth-century liberalism, interwar parliamentary democracy and beyond the fascist era to post-war republicanism.[69] In Austria, the first two years of the Austrofascist press regime owed as much to earlier periods of censorship and surveillance as to the latter-day birth of the tabloid, which dulled readers' senses to the political realities around them at the same time as preventing them from discovering what those realities were. And just as in Austria the first censorship laws were enacted as a more general set of emergency decrees, so in Italy the first bans on the opposition press were issued under the Public Security Law in November 1926, which also banned emigration among other things.[70]

Thus the first successful phase of fascistization in Italy and Austria had eliminated the opposition press and clamped down on the remaining press. The result in both countries was the depoliticization of the press, which, according to contemporary press observers in Italy, was evident both in the editors themselves giving greater prominence to local, cultural, scientific, economic and historical topics, and in the readers' loss of interest in the press causing a dramatic slump in daily newspaper sales to around a third of their pre-1922 circulation.[71] Whereas in Austria the drop in circulation of newspapers like the *Neue Freie Presse* after 1933 could partially be attributed to the economic crisis, in Italy the slump was a direct outcome of Fascist rule. Even the party organs were affected by the new rules: local Fascist deputies who edited and published their own newspapers were no longer free to flex their journalistic muscle, but were now answerable to a higher authority.

The second phase of fascistization brought journalists and other press professions into a common syndicate; this occurred after 1926 in Italy and corresponded with the legislative proposals for a new press chamber in Austria in 1935–36. In Italy, the previously fragmented national, liberal, Catholic and socialist press bodies were amalgamated into a single powerful Fascist National Syndicate of Journalists (NSFG). This was necessary since not all journalists were convinced fascists, even if they had joined the party or were conforming to the new regime. Catholic journalists, for example, had tended to join the NSFG's predecessor, the National Union of the Italian Press (FNSI), which existed alongside the NSFG for the first four years of Fascist rule until it was brought under the NSFG in 1926.[72] This phase of fascistization also coincided with the creation of university journalism degrees as a way of both modernizing and politicizing the profession to create world-class committed Fascist journalists in Italy. At first students took courses on the history of journalism as part of general university degrees, but the curriculum was later expanded with the creation of an institute of journalism to train students across a broad range of subjects in constitutional and international law, economics, geography and foreign languages in a two-year degree: 134 students enrolled in the first intake for the programme in 1929, including 21 women. Only 50 of the original intake of students sat for their final exams in 1931 and only 36 passed before the programme was cancelled in June 1933 for financial and political reasons.[73] Italian Fascists were not always guided by ideology in their preference of curricula or professional standards. Italy's institute of journalism was modelled on Columbia University's School of Journalism, which had opened in 1903, and Italian students (as well as press officials who designed the curriculum) studied the content of leading American newspapers and calculated the proportion of domestic to international news. Broadsheets like the *New York Times* had between 3 and 10 per cent international content, according to Fascist estimates, while smaller American papers had less than 1 per cent.[74] If Americans could read about their own country on the front page and discover the world's news on the back pages, then Italians had all the more reason to refashion their press to suit a domestic agenda.

In Austria, press officials also despaired of the minimal entry requirements into the journalism profession and the lack of real commitment to promoting Austrian content. They envisaged the creation of a Press and Propaganda Circle (*Ring für Presse und Propaganda*) as an arm of the press chamber that would take responsibility for all press initiatives and, in particular, for the vocational training of journalists, publishers, editors and technicians not just for print media but also for radio and film.[75] A memorandum from the working party of newspaper publishers stated that tertiary training for the media including university departments for print and radio journalism existed 'in most countries in the world', which was evidence of the need for Austria also to have its own press laws and organizations in line with international standards and bodies.[76] Though no specific country was mentioned, another memorandum tabling all the inadequacies and failing standards of the Austrian press pointed to the inspiration of the Italian journalism institute. In a section entitled 'What is to be done?', the memo described new entry-level requirements for the profession and ongoing training. Journalist apprenticeships for matriculated school leavers were not entirely scrapped, but applicants would have to sit an entry examination on their general education. After one year as an 'honorary' employee, the candidate would then have to pass a gruelling examination on their editorial knowledge comprising a written test on domestic and international politics, contemporary history, German literature and art, economics, medicine, law, geography, mathematics, physics, chemistry, sport, printing and advertising. In addition to the written test, the candidate had to perform a series of editorial tasks over a week long period, which included filing a court case, reporting a family drama, compiling a foreign news telegram and dictating a local news story. The candidate had to pass each task to the satisfaction of the assessor, who was appointed by the chancellor's office. On top of these entry requirements, the pension age was reduced to sixty years of age to allow for regeneration in the profession.[77] Austria's journalism training was less ambitious than Italy's and the Italian institute's premature closure in 1933 was perhaps a cautionary tale to the Austrian officials to keep the training in-house and separate from tertiary structures. However, given the prevalence of pro-Nazi sympathies among academics and students in Austrian universities, the decision to keep the training of Austrian journalists outside universities was as much for political as well as financial reasons. Nonetheless, the academic requirements set by the working party and the span of knowledge required to pass the two-stage entry to the editorial profession were clearly aimed at modernizing the profession in line with international standards. Moreover, the emphasis on history and German literature was also intended to ensure the cultural orientation of the Austrian profession was embedded in the pan-German identity of the Austrian state.

That the designers of the new journalism training rules were aiming to nationalize the profession by turning out committed Austrian patriots was also evident from the ministerial discussions about the press chamber legislation. The Speaker for the Federal Council for Culture, Dr Rudolf Henz (1897–1987), introduced the draft bill for a press chamber in the Council's 28th session on 26 June 1936. A poet and journalist, Henz was a prominent figure in the government's cultural propaganda work. He was director of the Austrian radio broadcasting corporation, RAVAG (*Österreichische Radio-Verkehrs-Aktiengesellschaft*), and later helped to establish *Neues Leben* on the model of the Italian *Opera Nazionale Dopolavoro*.[78] As Speaker for the Federal Council for Culture, he was elevated to the highest level of policy making in the Austrofascist state. Henz introduced the bill with some preliminary remarks about the importance of the press for both nation and state. Firstly, Austria had witnessed in the immediate post-war years that when given licence to print the views of individual editors, newspapers had the power 'to bring down banks, provoke crises, to besmirch and slander the names of respectable people, and to rule the streets'. Secondly, Henz stated that this 'tyranny of the press' went hand in hand with the tyranny of 'formal democracy' that had allowed parties to rule above the state and nation. Such excessive political freedoms made it possible for 'any writer who just arrived here, mostly people who had only learnt German out of necessity, to influence public opinion and to rule by international political and moral free-bootery'.[79] The reference to non-German writers who arrived uninvited on Austrian soil after the war to spread their cosmopolitan worldviews was a familiar anti-Semitic argument that Austrofascist politicians also made when drafting the immigration legislation, as we will see in Chapter 6. Crediting 'the authoritarian state of Dollfuss-Austria' for finally breaking the hold of these journalist newcomers, Henz expressed gratitude to Chancellor Schuschnigg and Minister Ludwig for having found the solution to the difficult task of rebuilding Austria's press, prompting loud applause from the members of the Council. The solution, Henz explained, was the creation of an institution – the press chamber – that could act as a mediator of both the state and the national interest. Newspapers that were 'Austrian by requirement' rather than by inner commitment were easily identifiable and it would be the task of the press chamber to change this attitude of outward conformism by educating journalists, editors and publishers in their responsibilities to their profession, to the nation and to the state. It was intolerable for a German Christian state, Henz continued, that a newspaper could write patriotic lines on the front page but deviate on the back page from both a Christian and German position in its reporting on divorce and robbery: 'We must always be watchful that the ideas preached at the beginning are not immediately undermined in the feuilleton section.' 'We welcome the chamber', he concluded, 'not only as one that will resolve the corporative concerns for the press, but also as a body of the Christian-German population in Austria.'[80]

Another minister in the Council, Dr Adolf Lenz (1868–1959), expressed his wish for the bill to go further along the lines of other countries' press laws and organizations. Like Henz, Lenz had also been appointed to the Federal Council for Culture on account of his achievements outside politics, in Lenz's case as a criminologist.[81] Lenz did not mention any country specifically, but his comments – which again met with loud applause from the Council members – placed the Austrian state alongside Italy and Germany. Lenz regarded the creation of a press chamber as the first step towards greater state control of the whole of the public sphere and stated that 'the great cultural problem of our times' was how to organize and rule the masses. Newspapers were not the primary means of influencing the population, in his view, but along with the school, the radio, theatre and film, the press represented an 'organ of state culture'. He pointed out that amid the rising production costs for the press and the popular disinterest in the political content of newspapers, film was increasingly an important medium for influencing public opinion given its 'affective' function on the masses. Lenz called for the press chamber to incorporate a separate institution for film, indicating his preference for a press and propaganda ministry along the lines of Goebbels' ministry, although he did not mention Nazi Germany. He also called for the bill to include a professional index (*Berufsregister*) of individual publishers, editors and journalists as well as a special press court comprising members of the press chamber, which he said was in line with other countries but, again, not mentioning which ones.[82] In the end, the Austrian bill did include a *Berufsregister* listing publishers and editors in line with both Italy and Germany, but, unlike the latter, left journalists off the index.[83] The new press chamber also had exclusive voting power over the licences of newspaper publishers, which meant that known detractors or disloyal newspapers such as the German-nationalist press could easily be shut down.[84]

By the time the press chamber began operating in November 1936, however, détente between Austria and Germany had already begun to restrain the Austrofascist state's repression of the German-nationalist press. Under the terms of the July Agreement signed by Schuschnigg and Hitler in July 1936, Germany pledged to stay out of Austria's internal affairs as long as Austria pursued a common foreign policy with her.[85] The two chancellors also signed a confidential 'Gentlemen's Agreement', which bound Schuschnigg to a general amnesty of imprisoned National Socialists, the inclusion of members of the 'national opposition' in the government and the distribution of five newspapers from one country in the other. But almost immediately and in clear violation of the terms of the July Agreement, the German Ministry of Propaganda began publishing critical reports about Austria in the *Essener National Zeitung*, an official party organ of the Nazis that was circulated in Austria after July. The other four German newspapers were instructed not to offend Austrian readers and reports about the show trials of priests and monks in Germany were banned, for example. On the Austrian side, two government organs, the *Wiener Zeitung* and the *Volkszeitung*, a Viennese liberal daily, the *Neue Wiener Journal*, and two German-nationalist organs, the *Linzer Tagespost* and the *Grazer Tagespost*, were allowed access to the German market after July 1936. Under the terms of this propaganda 'truce', the German-nationalist newspapers were able to express their Nazi sympathies as long as they refrained from criticizing the Austrian authorities or openly inciting agitation for *Anschluss*.[86]

Blaming the Austro-German détente for the press chamber's ineffectiveness in shutting down oppositional views, Ludwig resigned as head of the BPD at the end of 1936 but stayed on as president of the new press chamber. He quit before he could be pushed by Schuschnigg, who thought Ludwig was not pro-German enough to keep the truce. He was replaced by Walter Adam, the federal commissioner for propaganda and, from October 1934, secretary of the Fatherland Front.[87] Adam's position as head of Austria's propaganda office was the first new government portfolio that Dollfuss created when he declared his rule by dictatorship. The federal propaganda commission (*Bundeskommissariat für Propaganda*) was established in March 1933 as the propaganda arm of the Fatherland Front with Richard Steidle, leader of the Tyrolean *Heimwehr*, appointed commissioner. In July 1934 Adam was appointed to Steidle's role in conjunction with his position as general secretary of the Fatherland Front.[88] The Austrian propaganda commission was later renamed *Heimatdienst* (Homeland Service) to avoid parallels with the Nazi German Ministry of Propaganda, but by 1936 the comparison with Germany was no longer a cause for unease. When Adam replaced Ludwig, Schuschnigg chose not to replace Adam as *Heimatdienst* commissioner but instead merged the federal offices for press and propaganda to create a single ministry along the same lines as the German and Italian models.[89] The new Austrian press and propaganda ministry was never renamed as such – although I will refer to it as a ministry hereafter – and the two sections continued to function much as they had before merging, but the amalgamation of Austria's press and propaganda was symbolic, nonetheless, of Austrofascism's relationship with other fascist states. Adam explicitly mentioned the comparison with Germany's and Italy's press and propaganda in early 1937,[90] but it had already been implied in the ministerial discussions for a new press chamber in June 1936, one month before détente with Germany took effect.

A year on from the July Agreement, Austria renewed its commitment to a propaganda truce by appointing a government trustee for the German-nationalist press as part of a coordinated strategy to integrate Nazi sympathizers into the ranks of the government.[91] The trustee for the German-nationalist press was Arthur Seyss-Inquart, a former Nazi Party member whom Schuschnigg later appointed to his cabinet as Interior Minister.[92] Seyss-Inquart's responsibility as trustee was to ensure that the German-nationalist newspapers adhered to the terms of the July Agreement by refraining from polemical reporting about either the German or Austrian governments. At the same time, he established a separate news agency for the German-nationalist press under the editorship of a known Nazi, Herbert Friedl, and lobbied the press chamber to lift restrictions against these newspapers.[93]

The government also renewed its own propaganda campaign through the new press and propaganda ministry. In November 1937 a new illustrated monthly publication, *Österreich in Wort und Bild* (Austria in Text and Image) replaced the previous organs of the *Heimatdienst*, which had appeared irregularly since 1934. Under the rubric, 'The Austrian has a fatherland, which he loves and has reason to love', the new magazine covered cultural, economic and political news exclusively in Austria. The only international section was a brief overview of international press reports about Austria. The emphasis was on promoting Austria to Austrians. The inaugural edition featured a report on the new boarding school for boys in the former military academy in Traiskirchen, where there was also a chapel erected in Dollfuss's memory. A special edition on 24

February 1938 commemorating 'the German peace', as the lead article referred to the Berchtesgaden talks between Hitler and Schuschnigg, showed photos of Schuschnigg's speech in the parliament and people listening on radio in the street and at home, as well as extended coverage of international press reports about Schuschnigg's speech. The final edition in March 1938, which went to press before the *Anschluss*, included feature stories on Austrian actresses, ice-skaters and a competition to find Austria's best stenographer.[94]

The *Anschluss* cut short attempts by the press chamber to pass a new press law. Discussions in the Federal Council for Culture on the bill for a press chamber had included calls for a new press law modelled on Italian and German legislation and specifically aimed at tightening up on the rank and file of Austrian journalists, who had escaped the brunt of press reforms since 1933.[95] The professional index of publishers and editors left journalists out, as we saw, and it had been the publishers and editors, not individual journalists, who received penalties for violating codes of conduct. At the opening of a press exhibition on 4 March 1938, the president of the press chamber, Ludwig, referred to the new law, which he described as the third stage of building a press guild in the new corporative state.[96] Visitors to the exhibition were treated to rare archival copies of Austria's oldest newspapers, including a warning in one 1751 publication against the public circulation of untruths and an article by Metternich in 1814 in the government organ, *Wiener Zeitung*, about the pope's return to Rome following Napoleon's defeat.[97] The exhibition was organized by Austria's press and propaganda ministry, which we have seen was directly modelled on Germany and Italy. The references to the Metternich era of censorship in the exhibition were consistent with the Austrofascist press code on censorship introduced in 1933. But now while the message of Austria's press and propaganda officials was still to present themselves as Metternich's heirs intent on preserving the moral and religious fabric of Austrian society, the medium through which they sought to legitimize their function in the state had changed. Faced with a mass readership their methods had extended beyond press codes to encompass a broader strategy of appealing to the masses via popular reading habits and family excursions to an exhibition. Elisabeth El Refaie suggests that the Austrofascist press exhibition amounted to pride before the fall: 'For just over a week, the Austrian Ständestaat was able to present its press in all its glory, before German troops entered Austria and the whole organization was swallowed up into the jaws of the German propaganda system.'[98] El Refaie concludes that all the efforts of the Austrofascist state to create a powerful press and propaganda ministry had been 'swallowed up' by an even more powerful machine under the Nazis.

The Austrian efforts can hardly be classified as a failure. At the beginning of this book, I noted that the history of the Austrofascist state has largely been written out of the history of fascism as an experiment in authoritarian, at best semi-fascist, dictatorship that pales into insignificance next to the fiercer jaws of the Nazi dictatorship. But the comparison with the Nazi state is misleading and distorts the trajectory of fascism in Austria. As I have shown here, Austria's press reforms over the space of five years of fascist rule were comparable to the press reforms achieved in more than a decade of fascism in Italy. Moreover, by the mid-1930s the Italians were also seeking a closer alliance with Goebbels' Ministry of Enlightenment and Propaganda during the third stage of fascistization of the Italian press. In 1934 Mussolini handed over the Italian press bureau to his son-in-law, Galeazzo Ciano, who reshaped it as a secretariat for press and propaganda within the Interior Ministry. By 1935 Ciano had expanded the propaganda section to four portfolios, including portfolios for radio and film, upgraded the secretariat into a ministry for press and propaganda and appointed himself minister. After Ciano's appointment as Foreign Minister in August 1935, his replacement, Dino Alfieri, aligned the ministry for press and propaganda more closely with Goebbels' ministry.[99] Unlike Austria, however, Italy was not engaged in a lopsided propaganda 'truce' against Germany at the same time that it was seeking a closer engagement with Berlin. Yet even at the height of this apparent truce with Germany, Austrofascist functionaries were looking elsewhere – including Italy – for allies and opportunities to project an image of 'German Christian Austria' abroad.

Promoting Austria abroad

A visit of over four hundred delegates of the Fatherland Front to Italy in October 1936 sent a message internationally that the Austrofascist state was intent on keeping up its Italian friendship in the wake of Austro-German détente. At home, the visit would bolster the popular image of the Fatherland Front as the only true fascist group in Austria. Minister without portfolio, Emmerich Czermak, who led the delegation, wrote in his diary that the trip to Italy was 'a political event' insofar as Italy would now regard the Fatherland Front as its ally, rather than the *Heimwehr*, which had been dissolved in May 1936 and brought into the Front's storm troopers.[100] The Fatherland Front's new general secretary, Guido Zernatto, who had replaced Adam following the latter's appointment to head up the Austrian press and propaganda ministry, instructed delegates that their official visit should impress favourable images of Italy and Austria on each country.[101]

Two of the delegates wrote up their impressions after the trip. The first, by the Lower Austrian district leader of the Front in Hubertendorf, Franz Hurdes, had high praise for Italy's rural colonization project in the province of Pontinia, south of Rome, that had built over 2,000 farmhouses, 346 km of roads, 1,370 km of canals and 8,200 km of waste canals, along with the record feat of building the town of Littoria for 5,000 inhabitants in less than nine months. Rome had not been built in a day, and Hurdes had only admiration for Mussolini and the young Fascist mayor who had built Littoria in 265 days. He also wrote a detailed report about the work of the *Opera Nazionale Dopolavoro* (OND) and the *Opera Nazionale Maternità e Infanzia* (ONMI). Both organizations were of special interest to Fatherland Front leaders after they had established their own leisure and mother care organizations on the model of the OND and OMNI. The Fatherland Front's *Mutterschutzwerk* (Motherhood Defence Action) had been founded in March 1934 to promote motherhood as a patriotic duty. It offered summer retreats for mothers and infant-care courses which administered government stipends to families with four or more children, and organized local award ceremonies for mothers of large families.[102] Similarly, the Austrian leisure organization, *Neues Leben*, was founded in early 1936, several months prior to the Fatherland Front delegation's visit to Italy. Like its Italian counterpart, *Neues Leben* offered ski holiday packages and discounted theatre tickets and rail fares, held sporting events, sponsored cultural prizes for art, photography, film, music and plays, and established travelling theatre companies to keep actors in full-time employment.[103] During the October 1936 visit, Fatherland Front delegates visited the headquarters of the OND chapter for railway workers in Rome, the *Dopolavoro Ferroviario in Roma*, which included offices, a theatre with a 1,500 seating capacity, guestrooms, a restaurant, a library and lecture rooms for education courses. Italy's maternalist policies had already been the subject of an earlier study visit of leaders of the Fatherland Front's *Mütterschutzwerk* and on this occasion Hurdes made note of Italy's new marriage laws, including the requirement that all rural deputies be married, thus excluding priests and elevating married farmers and civil servants from rural functions.[104]

Another delegate's report resembled a travelogue that could be broken into serial form for publication in the Front newspaper or one of the approved tabloid sheets. The anonymous delegate was apparently a leader of the Fatherland Front's youth section, the *Österreichisches Jungvolk* (ÖJV), judging from the novice journalistic style and the references to Austria's youth throughout the report. Before the train had even left Vienna, the moment of Schuschnigg's appearance at Vienna's South Railway Station to bid farewell to the delegates 'filled us with excitement' and they sang the youth anthem, 'With Dollfuss into the New Era', as the train departed into the night through 'our Austria'. After travelling the length of Austria from north to south to cross the border to Italy, the realization dawned on this delegate that 'our Austria is not big, but we love this Austria our homeland all the more, and want to preserve and protect this home-land of ours'. Italians evidently shared this love of Austria for on arrival at Florence the delegates were greeted with applause and shouts of '*Eviva il Austria*' not just at the railway station but along the streets as they were taken to their hotel in buses decked out in both the Italian and Austrian flags. After dinner the delegates joined a group of representatives from the Fascist Party to watch a film about the war in Abyssinia, clapping along with the Fascists when Mussolini appeared on screen. 'Like eager pupils' learning from their older Italian cousins, 'this film shows us what a people is capable of after 14 years of work rebuilding'.[105]

The report's description of the audience with Mussolini in the Palazzo Venezia captured the thrill of seeing in person a leader they had only ever seen in newspapers and cinemas. As the *Duce* made a full round of the delegates assembled in a square formation in the room, he (allegedly) looked every one of them in the eye before mounting the podium to assume his characteristic upright pose, head held high, with hands on hips, just like they had seen in photographs and in the cinema, his serious expression, his powerful figure, his voice metallic and droning, even more so when he spoke in German to welcome the delegates. At the end of Mussolini's speech some of the delegates cried out '*Hoch der Duce*' and he returned the delegates' enthusiasm by calling out '*Auf wiedersehen*' as he left the room before returning to the podium, as if for an encore, with a beaming smile on his face and the Roman salute, while the delegates chanted '*Duce, Duce, Duce*'. The audience with Mussolini was significant not only because it was the first encounter with him in person, but also because it was the first time that he had received such a large group of women side by side with men.[106] Zernatto's instructions to the delegates in the booklet they were given indicated that one of the eight sections in the group was for women, predictably called the 'pink' group. Women delegates in this group were not included in official processions and marches during the visit, but they could attend as spectators. On the occasion of the audience with Mussolini, as on other occasions like watching a film with Italian Fascists, they were treated as equals.

Clearly an enthusiast for history and architecture, the anonymous del-egate described many other memorable experiences in Rome like carrying candles into the Colosseum along with expatriate Austrians on the night of the anniversary of Dollfuss's birthday as they sang the Austrian anthem in memory of him and all fallen Austrian soldiers. But an audience with

Pius XI outshone all other experiences of the trip, including the encounter with Mussolini. There had been cheers for the *Duce*, but reverent silence for the Holy Father as '450 Austrians sank to their knees before the head of the church' while he walked to his chair. He spoke in German first to the young delegates of the ÖJV, telling them of their responsibility to build up the Austrian youth in the spirit of the Catholic Church and the legacy of one of its beloved sons, Chancellor Dollfuss. The delegates knelt again to receive the pope's blessing and prayed with him that they would put into action his instructions to them. As he went to leave, one voice began to sing the youth anthem, the song in honour of Dollfuss, and as more voices joined in the pope stayed standing and the delegates knew then that His Holiness 'was thinking with love of the Austrian Chancellor whom he had known well'. The papal audience concluded the official itinerary and over refreshments in the Austrian embassy Zernatto announced a competition for the best amateur sketch from the trip, the best description of the trip, and the best essay on 'Fascism in Italy'.[107] Hurdes' report, based on the trip and his own research before and after the trip, may well have been the prize-winning essay while the anonymous female delegate of the ÖJV presumably won for best overall description.

The visit of the Fatherland Front delegation to Italy in late 1936 was an example of the kind of cultural diplomacy between the two countries that was as much an effort in shaping an image abroad as promoting fascism at home. In March 1935 Chancellor Schuschnigg had opened an Italian cultural institute in Vienna as a symbol of the long political and cultural relationship between Italy and Austria.[108] That the modern Italian state had been founded on the spoils of Austria's territorial losses to Piedmont and then Prussia, was seemingly erased from memory for the sake of cultural diplomacy. We will see in Chapter 5 how Italo-Austrian relations could also be serviced by anti-Semites in the interests of defending Austria's cultural mission of Germanizing Europe without resorting to the racial scientific principles of National Socialism.[109] Another high level exchange between the two countries occurred following the Fatherland Front's visit to Italy. In November 1936 Italian and Hungarian journalists were in Vienna on the occasion of the visit of Italian Foreign Minister Ciano to mark the original signing of the Rome Protocols two years earlier.[110] The fact that Mussolini himself did not attend this meeting but sent Ciano instead indicates the shift in Italy's foreign policy towards Germany. Nonetheless, the significance of the event for Italian journalists, some perhaps graduates of Mussolini's journalism school, and for their Austrian hosts, who may have been studying the Italian training modules in preparation for the new entry-level requirements for Austrian journalism, was in the form of cultural and political exchange that occurred between professional groups in both countries. Fostering exchanges between academics, scientists and students was the purpose of the new cultural institute in Vienna, and its corresponding Austrian institute in Rome that was opened a month earlier in February 1935.[111] But under fascist states, journalists, editors and publishers were also exchanged as official mouth-pieces, supplanting foreign correspondents whose views were tainted by extended periods abroad and could be relied on only for basic reports devoid of editorial content.

Sending journalists abroad was also expensive so the Austrian press and propaganda ministry opened a special cultural-political section to dis-seminate and monitor propaganda about Austrian culture abroad, above all in Britain. A number of correspondences took place in early 1937 between the new section head, Wilhelm Wolf, and the Austrian radio journalist, Berthe Grossbard, in London. In January 1937 Grossbard reported to Wolf that she had requested historical material about Johann Strauss and the 'Blue Danube' waltz to include in her radio programme.[112] Wolf also solicited the help of Grossbard's fellow Austrian expatriate, the caricaturist, Fred Joss, whose cartoons in the *Star* and *News Chronicle* brought his unique perspective on world affairs and leaders. (One of his sketches included in the BDP files, 'Joss in Geneva', was a series of carica-tures of world leaders at the League of Nations' conference in July 1936.) Wolf believed Joss's service to Austria went beyond his illustrations to encompass wider questions of Austrian art and culture, describing him in a letter to Grossbard as 'one of the leading caricaturists of England [who] has shown time and again that he is willing to be of service to every Aus-trian in both speech and action.'[113] Wolf wrote to Joss in February 1937, congratulating him on his work in the *Star* and for being one of Austria's 'shining stars' (*Glanzleuten*) and enquired of Joss whether he might be willing to assist the new cultural-political section of the press and propa-ganda ministry in promoting Austrian culture in the English press.[114] We do not know what Joss made of Wolf's approach; what is interesting, however, is how Austrofascist functionaries courted Jewish émigrés for their efforts in promoting Austria abroad. We will see in Chapter 5 how another prominent Jewish cultural figure in Austria, the theatre director and founder of the Salzburg Festival, Max Reinhardt, was also lauded for putting Austria on the world stage. In Joss's case, his Jewish heritage did not dint his Austrian patriotic credentials if he could be of service to the Austrian state.

Another Austrian cultural ambassador in England, literary historian, Stefan Hock (1877–1947), was also approached by the cultural-political section of the press and propaganda ministry. Hock had worked with Reinhardt at Vienna's Theater an der Josefstadt, and also worked in England before immigrating there in 1938.[115] In April 1937 Erwin

Müller-Karbach wrote to Hock, at the time living in Turnham, England, seeking his advice on which themes would interest English audiences across a range of cultural media in theatre, film, art, books.[116] Hock replied that Hugo von Hofmannsthal's *Salzburger grosse Welttheater* (Salzburg's Great World Theatre), which Hock had directed in Liverpool, had been a great success and 'would represent our homeland well in many respects'. He also confirmed the thoughts of Austrian ministers like Lenz that cinema is nowadays 'the strongest weapon in propaganda' and even the rich people prefer the cinema over the theatre.[117] Later that year Hock referred Müller-Karbach to his article published in the *Contemporary Review*, which was based on a chapter of his manuscript.[118] Hock's article, 'Vienna Life', painted a cheerful picture of Austrians' drinking, eating and leisure pursuits, their carefree nature which could be mistaken for careless behaviour if one believed the musicals and films about Vienna, and above all their loyalty to family, to the poor, and to the arts. Hock's article was not a political appraisal of the Austrian state and he balanced his praise for the municipal housing and education projects of the socialist government (without mentioning the socialists) with reference to the Catholic Church's calendar of festivities as the 'democratic chain that unites the whole country'. He also alluded to Austrian radicalism (without mentioning the Nazis) by speculating that the 'over-long thraldom to the apron-strings' among Austrian youth compared to their English counterparts who lived in nurseries, boarding schools and university residential colleges away from parental influence, was perhaps 'one of the reasons for that unruliness of mind which is responsible for the sudden changes of Austrian politics'.[119] Hock had been unable to find a publisher for his manuscript in part because he did not have illustrations, a comment Müller-Karbach noted and underlined.[120] Collaboration between Austria's press and propaganda ministry and its agents abroad was mutually beneficial as artists like Hock sought patrons for their work and Austrian politicians orchestrated their propaganda efforts abroad by connecting expatriate writers, cartoonists, publishers, photographers and journalists in the service of the Austrian state.

In December 1937 Müller-Karbach contacted E. Hopkinson from *The Times* and Robert Ehrenzweig, the London editor of the *New Freie Presse*, about the possibility of a *Times* Special Number for Austria. Plans for a special edition had been under negotiation between the two newspapers since 1936 and *The Times* had already published special editions on Egypt and Yugoslavia. In the end the cost for such an edition of £350 for the front page and £300 for each subsequent page proved too expensive for Austria, but Müller-Karbach did not rule out those funds becoming available in the future.[121]

The Austrian press and propaganda section apparently saw their potential donors in English royalty and solicited the help of the Austrian ambassador in London, Baron George Franckenstein, who had close connections with the royal family and with Queen Mary in particular. Franckenstein had first met the Queen during the visit of Austria's former chancellor, Johannes Schober, and became acquainted with her art collection at Windsor Castle. Later he was invited to dinner where he discussed Vienna's latest art exhibitions with the Queen. Members of the royal family, including the Queen's first cousin by marriage, Princess Helena Victoria, were frequent visitors at the Austrian embassy's musical recitals with visiting Austrian artists and the whole family turned out for a special exhibition Franckenstein organized, *Austria in London*, at Dorland House in 1934, which displayed Austrian arts and crafts, national costumes and a puppet theatre, and recreated Old Vienna with miniature buildings, churches and monuments by renowned Austrian architect, Clemens von Holzmeister (1886–1983), who had designed the new Salzburg Festival House and many churches in the interwar period. Baron Franckenstein was knighted in 1938 for his efforts in promoting Austria abroad during his eighteen-year term as ambassador in London.[122] In correspondence between Franckenstein and Princess Helena Victoria in January 1938, which was sent back to the press and propaganda office in Vienna, Helena thanked Franckenstein for the 'charming' photographs of Old Vienna which she intended to show the Queen immediately when she went to Sandringham the next day. Two days later, Princess Helena reported that the Queen had 'begged me to ask you w[h]ether you could let her have a set, like the one you so kindly sent me.'[123] Austrofascist functionaries sought patrons on high, drawing on shared dynastic traditions and pandering to elite British tastes to boost their image across the English Channel.

Ironically, given the traditional anti-Habsburg sentiments in Britain, Austria had suddenly become of strategic import to Britain's interests in Central Europe following Italy's invasion of Ethiopia in 1935. British historian and doyen of Central European affairs, Robert Seton-Watson (1879–1951), summed up the changes in Austrian public opinion in a public lecture at Chatham House on 11 February 1936:

> The choice [for Austrians] no longer lay between Germany and Italy, in which everyone preferred Germany in theory and the more reckless were ready to risk it in practice. The choice now lay between Germany and *Austria*: and an independent Austrian national feeling is again raising its head, and is reinforced by the arguments afforded by the bad economic position inside Germany, the distrust roused by excessive armament, and the repressive methods adopted towards the Church, the Socialists and the Jews – in short, there is an argument for everyone.[124]

Seton-Watson's close associate, the British historian and journalist, Henry Wickham Steed (1871–1956), was present at the lecture and responded with an anecdote about an Oxford don friend who had told Wickham Steed of an undergraduate student's claim that the 'wickedness' of the Treaty of Versailles had been responsible for breaking up Austria-Hungary. The don had corrected the student, informing him that the empire had already ceased to exist several months prior to the peace conference. The story was told by Wickham Steed to reinforce how unpopular the Habsburgs had been in Central Europe, even in Austria. He was confident that if a plebiscite were to be held now in Austria to decide between a Habsburg restoration or *Anschluss* with Nazi Germany, Austrians would vote 'over-whelmingly' for Hitler. It was a matter for Britain's foreign interests in Central Europe that a British-led coalition of anti-Nazi states – including Austria – form a buffer against Germany, though Britain must take care not to actively intervene in Central European affairs. Seton-Watson agreed with Steed that 'a firm British policy, allowing no suggestion of *"Einkreis-ung"* ', was necessary to fill the power vacuum created in Central Europe since the collapse of the Habsburg Monarchy. Without Britain's clear leadership, Seton-Watson concluded, 'Great Britain was lost, the League of Nations was lost, the little nations were lost, and Germany would be able to do what she liked with Austria.'[125]

Seton-Watson's observation of Austria's desire for independence was made just prior to the July Agreement in 1936 and the renewed efforts by National Socialists both within and outside Austria's borders to align Austria more closely with Germany. The visit of the Fatherland Front delegation to Italy a few months later in October 1936 showed, contrary to Seton-Watson's pragmatic assessment, that Austria was in fact still looking to Italy, which it continued to do right up until the *Anschluss*. The efforts of the Austrian press and propaganda ministry throughout 1937 and early 1938 to court British publicity also shows that Austria's relationship with Italy and Germany took place within a larger international context of cultural diplomacy. It was this relational process of exchange and contacts with other fascist states, and with non-fascist states, that legitimized the Austrofascist state's radicalizing internal politics. In other words, creating fascism at home relied as much on patrons abroad as on domestic reforms.

Notes

1 Peter Fritzsche, *Reading Berlin 1900* (Cambridge, MA: Harvard University Press, 1996), pp. 55–56.
2 Malcolm Gee and Tim Kirk (eds), *Printed Matters: Printing, Publishing and Urban Culture in Europe in the Modern Period* (Aldershot: Ashgate, 2002),

pp. 4–5. On France's reading 'revolution', which coincided with the French Revolution and corresponded with the growth of booksellers and book printing from the late eighteenth century, see James Smith Allen, *In the Public Eye: A History of Reading in Modern France, 1800–1940* (Princeton: Princeton University Press, 1991), pp. 42–43, 52–53. On Germany, see Fritzsche, *Reading Berlin 1900*.

3 Peter Fritzsche, 'Readers, Browsers, Strangers, Spectators: Narrative Forms and Metropolitan Encounters in Twentieth-Century Berlin', in Gee and Kirk (eds), *Printed Matters*. On the press in fin-de-siècle Cracow, see Nathaniel D. Wood, 'Urban Self-Identification in East Central Europe before the Great War: The Case of Cracow', *East Central Europe/L'Europe du Centre-Est/Eine wissenschaftliche Zeitung* 33, 1–2 (2006): 11–31.

4 Berlin grew from around 400,000 in 1848 to 2 million in 1905 with a further 1.5 million inhabitants of the city living in the suburban belt of Greater Berlin. Fritzsche, *Reading Berlin 1900*, pp. 7–8.

5 Ibid., pp. 7–8, 51–53, 72–78.

6 The ban, which had been in place since the 1870s, licensed the state-owned tobacco agents to sell newspapers, giving them a monopoly on press sales and allowing government officials to issue and revoke licences at will. Mayer, ' "By Drip and By Drop" ', p. 94.

7 Kurt Paupié, *Handbuch der Österreichischen Pressegeschichte, 1848–1959*, vol. 1 (Vienna: Braumüller, 1960), p. 144.

8 Judson, *Exclusive Revolutionaries*, pp. 43–44, 96–97.

9 Philip Nord has argued that the press was central to the formation of French republican political culture. Writing for or reading a newspaper was a way of participating in democratic citizenship in the Third Republic, similar to attending a civil funeral ceremony or visiting the local library. See Philip Nord, *The Republican Moment: Struggles for Democracy in Nineteenth-Century France* (Cambridge, MA: Harvard University Press, 1995).

10 Paupié, *Handbuch der Österreichischen Pressegeschichte*, vol. 1, pp. 83, 88–89, 144.

11 Ibid., pp. 94–101. The *Reichspost* received donations from the ranks of the lower clergy, including monks, but it was the only Catholic newspaper in the monarchy that remained independent of the episcopate. See Boyer, *Political Radicalism in Late Imperial Vienna*, pp. 339–40.

12 Fritz Csoklich, 'Presse und Rundfunk', in Weinzierl and Skalnik (eds), *Österreich 1918–1938*, vol. 2, p. 715.

13 Ibid., p. 718.

14 Paupié, *Handbuch der Österreichischen Pressegeschichte*, vol. 1, pp. 40, 58.

15 Claudia Grillhofer, 'Die Öffentlichkeitsarbeit wird "amtlich": Zur Geschichte der Wiener "Rathaus-Korrespondenz" in der Ersten Republik', in Wolfgang Duchkowitsch, Hannes Haas and Klaus Lojka (eds), *Kreativität aus der Krise: Konzepte zur gesellschaftlichen Kommunikation in der Ersten Republik* (Vienna: Literas, 1991), p. 176.

16 Malcolm Bullock, *Austria 1918–1938: A Study in Failure* (London: Macmillan, 1939), p. 120.

17 Paupié, *Handbuch der Österreichischen Pressegeschichte*, vol. 1, p. 42.
18 See Alexander Potyka, 'Ideologie und Tagesgeschehen für den "kleinen Mann": Das "Kleine Blatt" 1927–1934', in Duchkowitsch, Haas and Lojka (eds), *Kreativität aus der Krise*; Franz Ivan, Helmut W. Lang and Heinz Pürer (eds), *200 Jahre Tageszeitungen in Österreich 1783–1983: Festschrift von Ausstellungskatalog* (Vienna: ÖNB, 1983), p. 415.
19 Paupié, *Handbuch der Österreichischen Pressegeschichte*, vol. 1, pp. 93, 103–4.
20 Dieter Langewiesche, *Zur Freiheit des Arbeiters: Bildungsbestrebungen und Freizeitgestaltung österreichischer Arbeiter im Kaiserreich und in der Ersten Republik* (Stuttgart: Klett-Cotta, 1980), pp. 123–24.
21 Ibid., pp. 120–21.
22 Ibid., p. 119. The figure of 2 million is based on 1926 circulation figures for all daily, weekly and monthly organs as well as the party trade union newsletters.
23 Fritzsche, 'Readers, Browsers, Strangers, Spectators', p. 100.
24 The ratio of 3:1 is based on Kurt Paupié's analysis of the interwar Austrian political press for 1930. See Paupié, 'Das Pressewesen in Österreich 1918–1938', *Österreich in Geschichte und Literatur* 6, 4 (1962), pp. 167–68.
25 In northern Bavaria, for example, the party held 10,000 local meetings prior to the 1930 national elections. See Dick Geary, *Hitler and Nazism*, 2nd edn (London and New York: Routledge, 2000), pp. 26–31. The ratio of Nazi newspaper readers to voters is based on Richard Grunberger's figures of 17 million party voters in the March 1933 election, but a national circulation of Nazi newspapers of only 800,000. See Grunberger, *The 12–Year Reich: A Social History of Nazi Germany, 1933–1945* (New York: Holt, Rinehart, and Winston, 1971), p. 391. The circulation of National Socialist newspapers in Germany rose only after 1933: the *Völkische Beobachter*, the party's main organ, sold 127,500 copies daily in 1933 and 580,000 by late 1938. See Thomas Pegelow, ' "German Jews", "National Jews", "Jewish Volk" or "Racial Jews"? The Constitution and Contestation of "Jewishness" in Newspapers of Nazi Germany, 1933–1938', *Central European History* 35, 2 (2002), p. 197.
26 Theodore Zeldin, *France, 1848–1945*, vol. 2 (Oxford: Clarendon, 1977), pp. 492, 570.
27 Langewiesche, *Zur Freiheit des Arbeiters*, p. 120.
28 Csoklich, 'Presse und Rundfunk', pp. 720, 716. Lower Austria became a separate province from Vienna in 1920.
29 Paupié, 'Das Pressewesen in Österreich 1918–1938', pp. 167–68.
30 Robert Dell, 'The Corruption of the French Press', *Current History* 35 (1931): 193–97.
31 Paupié, 'Das Pressewesen in Österreich 1918–1938', pp. 167–68.
32 According to Paupié's analysis, the Social Democrats had a total readership of 1,413,000 and gained 1,032,000 votes in Vienna in the elections of 1930. The Christian Socials had a readership of 824,000 and 695,000 votes; the Communist Party had equally 15,000 voters and readers, while the Greater Germans and National Socialists had a total of 370,000 votes, compared with 171,000 readers of the German-nationalist press. See ibid., pp. 167–68.

33 George Clare, *Last Waltz in Vienna: The Destruction of a Family 1842–1942* (London: Pan Books, 1982), p. 125.

34 Lehnert, 'Politisch-kulturelle Integrationsmilieus und Orientierungslager', p. 442.

35 See Chapter 1.

36 Csoklich, 'Presse und Rundfunk', p. 720. The major Christian Social daily in Styria, the *Grazer Volksblatt*, sold 5,000 copies on weekdays in 1935, while the socialist organ, the *Arbeiterwille*, sold 20,000 copies daily in 1933 before it was banned in February 1934.

37 Nora Aschacher, 'Die Presse der Steiermark von 1918 – 31 July 1955' (PhD dissertation, University of Vienna, 1972), pp. 13–37.

38 This figure is based on the 1935 total circulation of 84,000 for weekday newspaper sales of each of the main political organs and the *Kleine Zeitung*.

39 Hanisch, 'Die Salzburger Presse in der Ersten Republik 1918–1938', p. 354. The socialist *Salzburger Wacht* sold around 5,000 copies during the 1920s.

40 Hanisch, 'Salzburg', p. 909.

41 Paupié, *Handbuch der Österreichischen Pressegeschichte*, vol. 1, pp. 111–12, 204–5; Gerhard Jagschitz, 'Die Presse in Österreich von 1918 bis 1945', in Heinz Purer, Helmut W. Lang and Wolfgang Duchkowitsch (eds), *Die österreichische Tagespresse: Vergangenheit, Gegenwart, Zukunft. Ein Dokumentation von Vorträgen des Symposions "200 Jahre Tageszeitung in Österreich"* (Salzburg: Kuratorium für Journalistenausbildung, 1983), p. 50.

42 These figures are based on the 1930 survey, in which Vienna's total press circulation was 1,327,000 (see above), and the 1935 estimate for the *Wiener Neueste Nachrichten* of 25,000. The circulation figures of Vienna's daily political press are based on the figures for the *Arbeiter-Zeitung*, *Neue Freie Presse* and the *Reichspost*, cited already in this chapter, and do not include the other major liberal daily, the *Neue Wiener Tagblatt*.

43 The German Foreign Office remained in financial control of the newspaper until *Anschluss*. See Jagschitz, 'Die Presse in Österreich von 1918 bis 1945', p. 50.

44 Notably, R.J.B. Bosworth has argued that for most Italians, 'everyday Mussolinism' did not equate with 'Fascist totalitarianism'. See Bosworth, *Mussolini's Italy*. Bosworth has argued that the history of Mussolini's dictatorship can be written as multiple histories: the history of family, town and region, religion, all overlapping with one another and intersecting at points with the history of fascism.

45 Stefania Galassi, *Pressepolitik im Faschismus: Das Verhältnis von Herrschaft und Presseordnung in Italien zwischen 1922 und 1940* (Stuttgart: Steiner, 2008).

46 James Smith Allen has made this differentiation between 'preventive' and 'repressive' censorship for eighteenth-century France. See Allen, *In the Public Eye*, pp. 84–92.

47 Robert J. Goldstein, 'Freedom of the Press in Europe, 1815–1914', *Journalism Monographs* 80 (1983), pp. 9–11.

48 Mark Cornwall, 'News, Rumour and the Control of Information in Austria-Hungary, 1914–1918', *History* 77, 249 (1992), pp. 52–63; Mark Cornwall, *The Undermining of Austria-Hungary: The Battle for Hearts and Minds* (New York: St Martins, 2000), pp. 29, 286.

49 Jakob Waltraud, *Salzburger Zeitungsgeschichte* (Salzburg: Schriftenreihe des Landespressebüros, 1979), p. 185.

50 Bullock, *Austria 1918–1938*, pp. 120–21.

51 Gerhard Botz, *Gewalt in der Politik: Attentate, Zusammenstösse, Putschversuche, Unruhen in Österreich 1918 bis 1938*, 2nd edn (Munich: Wilhelm Fink, 1983), p. 211; Hanisch, *Der Lange Schatten des Staates*, p. 491; Cornwall, 'News, Rumour and Control', p. 59.

52 Wolfgang Duchowitsch, 'Umgang mit "Schädlingen" und "schädlichen Auswüchsen": Zur Auslöschung der freien Medienstruktur im "Ständestaat"', in Tálos and Neugebauer (eds), *Austrofaschismus*, p. 359.

53 Paupié, *Handbuch der Österreichischen Pressegeschichte*, vol. 1, pp. 47–49.

54 Harald Schmied, ' "D'rum straff angezogen . . . den stahldrähtigen Maulkorb": Presse und Diktatur (1933–1938) am Beispiel der Steiermark' (MA dissertation, Karl-Franzens-University, 1996), pp. 65–66.

55 Waltraud, *Salzburger Zeitungsgeschichte*, p. 191.

56 Paupié, *Handbuch der Österreichischen Pressegeschichte*, vol. 1, pp. 111–12. See also Milan Dubrovic, *Veruntreute Geschichte: Die Wiener Salons und Literatencafes* (Berlin: Aufbau Taschenbuch, 2001 [Vienna: Paul Tsolnay, 1985]), pp. 229–30.

57 Ibid., pp. 51–52.

58 Maureen Healy, *Vienna and the Fall of the Habsburg Empire: Total War and Everyday Life in World War I* (Cambridge: Cambridge University Press, 2004), pp. 133, 139.

59 Paupié, *Handbuch der Österreichischen Pressegeschichte*, vol. 1, p. 144; Schmied, 'Presse und Diktatur', p. 64.

60 Duchowitsch, 'Umgang mit "Schädlingen" und "schädlichen Auswüchsen"', p. 361; Elisabeth El Refaie, 'Keeping the Truce? Austrian Press Politics between the "July Agreement" (1936) and the *Anschluss* (1938)', *German History* 20, 1 (2002), p. 52.

61 Mitzi Hartmann, *Austria Still Lives* (London: Michael Joseph, 1938), pp. 109–10.

62 Along with the six other corporations in the Austrofascist state, the corporation of the free professions did not have legislative power but acted only as a government advisory body. Legislative power rested with a federal diet, composed of members from four legislative councils for state, culture, the economy and the provinces. See Barbara Jelavich, *Modern Austria: Empire to Republic* (Cambridge: Cambridge University Press, 1987), pp. 203–4; John Rath and Carolyn W. Schum, 'The Dollfuss-Schuschnigg Regime: Fascist or Authoritarian?' in Larsen, Hagtvet and Jan Myklebust (eds), *Who Were the Fascists?*, p. 251. The other six corporations represented agriculture and forestry; industry and alpine works; business; trade and exchange; finance, credit and

insurance; and the civil service. See Gerhard Jagschitz, 'Der österreichische Ständestaat 1934–1938', in Weinzierl and Skalnik (eds), *Österreich 1918–1938*, vol. 1, p. 501.

63 Dollfuss had already stated publicly in November 1932 his government's intention to do away with 'parliamentary struggles', ostensibly as a necessary solution to the depressed state economy. Lewis, 'Conservatives and Fascists in Austria, 1918–34', pp. 113–14n.79.

64 ÖStA/AdR, BKA/BPD – Akte, Carton 16, Franz Gustav Ronco, *Zur Organisation der Pressekammer* (Bonn & Köln, 1932).

65 ÖStA/AdR, BKA/BPD – Akte, Carton 16, Bundesgesetz über den Berufsverband der österreichischern Presse (Bundeskammer), n.d.

66 ÖStA/AdR, BKA/BPD – Akte, Carton 16, Satzungen der österreichischen Pressekammer samt dem Wortlaut des Bundesgesetzes über die Errichtung einer Pressekammer, BGBl. Nr. 228/36, und den Durchführungsverordnungen (Vienna, 1937), here Article 4.

67 The quote is from Galassi, *Pressepolitik im Faschismus*, p. 224. Mussolini and Dollfuss's correspondence was originally published in 1949, and republished with additional material by Wolfgang Maderthaner and Michaela Maier (eds), *'Der Führer bin ich selbst': Engelbert Dollfuss-Benito Mussolini Briefwechsel* (Vienna: Löcker, 2004).

68 Dollfuss's posthumous cult can be seen in the lyric of the Fatherland Front anthem: 'A dead man now leads us' (Ein Toter führt uns an). See Wolfgang Maderthaner, 'Legitimationsmuster des Austrofaschismus', in Maderthaner and Maier (eds), *'Der Führer bin ich selbst'*, p. 151.

69 Galassi, *Pressepolitik im Faschismus*, p. 224.

70 Ibid., pp. 41–42. The ban on emigration will be discussed further in Chapter 6.

71 Ibid., p. 335.

72 Ibid., p. 236.

73 Ibid., pp. 348–66, 384. The closure of the journalism institute was ostensibly a financial decision, but its viability had also been compromised by competing political factions with different conceptions of the role of the press in a fascist state.

74 Ibid., pp. 368–70.

75 ÖStA/AdR, BKA/BPD – Akte, Carton 16, Memorandum des Verbandes der Herausgeber der Tageszeitungen, 24 June 1935.

76 ÖStA/AdR, BKA/BPD – Akte, Carton 16, Denkschrift über die berufsständische Organisation der Presse, n.d.

77 ÖStA/AdR, BKA/BPD – Akte, Carton 16, Memorandum über die Verhältnisse in der österreichischen Presse und Vorschläge zur Behebung gewisser Misstände, n.d.

78 John Warren, ' "Weisse Strümpfe oder neue Kutten": Cultural Decline in Vienna in the 1930s', in Deborah Holmes and Lisa Silverman (eds), *Interwar Vienna: Culture Between Tradition and Modernity* (Rochester, NY: Camden House, 2009), pp. 41, 52n.41. See also Viktor Suchy (ed.), *Dichter zwischen*

den Zeiten: Festschrift für Rudolf Henz zum 80. Geburtstag (Vienna: Braumüller, 1977).

79 ÖStA/AdR, Bundeskulturrat Protokolle, Sitzung 28, 26 June 1936.

80 Ibid.

81 On Lenz's criminology work, see Christian Bachhiesl, *Der Fall Josef Streck:
Ein Sträfling, sein Professor und die Erforschung der Persönlichkeit* (Vienna:
Lit, 2006).

82 ÖStA/AdR, Bundeskulturrat Protokolle, Sitzung 28, 26 June 1936.

83 Duchowitsch, 'Umgang mit "Schädlingen" und "schädlichen Auswüchsen" ',
p. 363. The index of Viennese, provincial and foreign press agencies, editors
and publishers was included in miscellaneous files of the *Bundespressedienst*,
ÖStA/AdR, BKA/BPD – Akte, Carton 16.

84 Paupié, *Handbuch der Österreichischen Pressegeschichte*, vol. 1, p. 54.

85 On the terms of the agreement, see Low, *The Anschluss Movement*,
pp. 184–85.

86 El Refaie, 'Keeping the Truce?', pp. 54–57; Kurt Schuschnigg, *Im Kampf gegen
Hitler: Die Überwindung der Anschlussidee* (Vienna: Fritz Molden, 1969),
p. 189.

87 El Refaie, 'Keeping the Truce?', p. 56.

88 Ibid., p. 53. Adam was appointed general secretary of the Fatherland Front
but he retained his post as *Heimatdienst* commissioner. See Irmgard Bärnthaler, 'Geschichte und Organisation der Vaterländische Front: Ein Beitrag
zum Verständnis totalitärer Organisation' (PhD dissertation, University of
Vienna, 1964), pp. 7–8, 95–97.

89 El Refaie, 'Keeping the Truce?', pp. 53, 56.

90 Ibid., p. 56.

91 A trustee was also appointed for the wider Austrian press, Edmund Weber,
director of the official Austrian news agency, *Amtliche Nachrichtenagentur*,
whose job it was to ensure Austria's adherence to more balanced reporting
on Germany. A trustee was also appointed on the German side. See El Refaie,
'Keeping the Truce?', pp. 60–63.

92 Ibid., p. 63. Seyss-Inquart's membership in the NSDAP dated back to his
membership in the Styrian *Heimatschutz*, which merged with the Nazi Party
in April 1933, but party receipts show he had paid his first membership dues
to the NSDAP already in December 1931. On Seyss-Inquart's Nazi connections, see Low, *The Anschluss Movement*, pp. 100–1, 175–76, and John Haag,
'Marginal Men and the Dream of the Reich: Eight Austrian National-Catholic
Intellectuals, 1918–1938', in Larsen, Hagtvet and Myklebust (eds), *Who Were
the Fascists?* Seyss-Inquart was appointed Interior Minister in February 1938
following the Berchtesgaden talks between Hitler and Schuschnigg in February 1938 and eventually replaced Schuschnigg as chancellor on the eve of
Anschluss. After *Anschluss*, Seyss-Inquart was made governor of the newly
incorporated Austrian province, *Ostmark*, of Nazi Germany until May 1939
and the following year he was appointed Reich Commissioner of Nazi-
occupied Holland, where he remained until the end of the war.

 93 El Refaie, 'Keeping the Truce?', p. 63.
 94 ÖStA/AdR, BKA/HD, Carton 12, *Österreich in Wort und Bild*, November 1937 – March 1938.
 95 El Refaie, 'Keeping the Truce?', pp. 64–65.
 96 See report on the exhibition opening in the *Reichspost*, 5 March 1938, p. 2.
 97 *Neue Freie Presse*, 5 March 1938, p. 4.
 98 El Refaie, 'Keeping the Truce?', p. 65.
 99 Galassi, *Pressepolitik im Faschismus*, pp. 411–20.
100 Bärnthaler, 'Geschichte und Organisation der Vaterländische Front', pp. 174–75. Czermak was Christian Social Education Minister and party chairman prior to 1934. After 1934 he had several functions in the Austrofascist state, including a founding role in the Austrian Association for Germandom Work Abroad, which I discuss in Chapter 4.
101 ÖStA/AdR, PA/VF Allg, Carton 41, VF Amtswalter-Romfahrt.
102 On the *Mutterschutzwerk*, see Laura Gellott, 'Defending Catholic Interests in the Christian State: The Role of Catholic Action in Austria, 1933–1938', *Catholic Historical Review* 74, 4 (1988): 571–89; and Laura Gellott and Michael Phayer, 'Dissenting Voices: Catholic Women in Opposition to Fascism', *Journal of Contemporary History* 22, 1 (1987): 91–114.
103 Pauley, *Hitler and the Forgotten Nazis*, p. 162.
104 ÖStA/AdR, PA/VF Allg, Carton 41, VF Amtswalter-Romfahrt, Report by Franz Hurdes, 13 January 1937.
105 ÖStA/AdR, PA/VF Allg, Carton 41, VF Amtswalter-Romfahrt, anonymous report, n.d.
106 Ibid.
107 Ibid.
108 ÖStA/AdR, BKA/HD, Carton 6, *Wiener Neueste Nachrichten*, 22 March 1935.
109 Chapter 5 includes a discussion of the Austrian bishop in Rome, Alois Hudal, whose views of Nazi Germany were famously apologetic in their defence of the virtues of National Socialism and anti-Semitism in particular at the same time as he opposed the 'paganism' of Nazi ideologues like Alfred Rosenberg, whom he claimed was 'Eastern' in origin anyway.
110 ÖStA/AdR, BKA/BPD – Akte, Carton 16, Printed programme of the journalists' visit, 11–12 November 1936.
111 See the reports on the institute in Rome in ÖStA/AdR, BKA/HD, Carton 6, *Reichspost*, 3 February 1935; *Neue Freie Presse*, 6 and 10 February 1935. The *Neues Wiener Tagblatt* reported on the exchange of an Austrian astrophysicist to Florence. See ÖStA/AdR, BKA/HD, Carton 411, *Neues Wiener Tagblatt*, 6 March 1936.
112 ÖStA/AdR, BKA/BPD – Akte, Carton 16, Letter dated 28 January 1937.
113 ÖStA/AdR, BKA/BPD – Akte, Carton 16, Letter dated 26 January 1937.
114 ÖStA/AdR, BKA/BPD – Akte, Carton 16, Letter dated 6 February 1937.
115 'Stefan Hock', AEIOU Encyclopedia (www.aeiou.at/aeiou.encyclop.h/h695876.htm;internal&action=_setlanguage.action?LANGUAGE=en), accessed 30 June 2010.

116 ÖStA/AdR, BKA/BPD – Akte, Carton 16, Letter dated 14 April 1937.

117 ÖStA/AdR, BKA/BPD – Akte, Carton 16, Letter dated 18 April 1937.

118 ÖStA/AdR, BKA/BPD – Akte, Carton 16, Letter dated 17 September 1937.

119 Stefan Hock, 'Vienna Life', *Contemporary Review* 151, 1 (Jan–June 1937), pp. 480, 482.

120 ÖStA/AdR, BKA/BPD – Akte, Carton 16, Letter dated 17 September 1937.

121 ÖStA/AdR, BKA/BPD – Akte, Carton 16, Correspondence throughout December 1937.

122 The anecdotes and photographs of his encounters with the royal family are described in his memoir, Sir George Franckenstein, *Facts and Figures of My Life* (London: Cassell, 1939), which he dedicated to 'the resurrection of Austria'.

123 ÖStA/AdR, BKA/BPD – Akte, Carton 16, Correspondence throughout January 1938. Presumably Princess Helena was referring to Queen Mary, with whom Franckenstein had earlier encounters over Austrian art and culture, rather than Queen Elizabeth whose husband, George VI, had ascended the throne in 1936.

124 R.W. Seton-Watson, 'Europe and the Austrian Problem', *International Affairs* 15, 3 (May–June 1936), p. 340 (italic in original).

125 Ibid., pp. 347, 350.

3

Pan-Germanism and Austrofascism in a small town

In May 1938 the owner of Salzburg's German-nationalist newspaper, Hans Glaser, received a visit from the sister of Salzburg's former governor, Franz Rehrl, asking him to intervene on her brother's behalf after he had been arrested and imprisoned by the Gestapo.[1] Rehrl's sister was a former employee of Glaser's rival, the Catholic *Salzburger Chronik*, and she knew Glaser had connections with local Nazi figures, although he himself was not a party member. She also knew that Glaser and her brother had been on friendly terms prior to the Nazi takeover, even if politically they had not seen eye to eye. Indeed, as the highest functionary of the Austrofascist state in Salzburg, Rehrl was Glaser's political adversary with respect to the penalties handed out by the provincial authorities for violations of the press code. However, Glaser's diary entries reveal that Rehrl often confided in Glaser about the burdens of public life and it may have been Rehrl himself who asked his sister to call on Glaser in 1938. The divisions between political-cultural milieux were less visible in Salzburg than in Vienna. Shaped by the many mutual private and professional contacts that were typical of a provincial elite culture, and fortified by a common commitment to 'German Austria', pan-Germanism in Salzburg drew German-nationalists and Austrofascists closer together in spite of their professed political and ideological differences.

This chapter presents a local case study of pan-Germanism and Austrofascism in Salzburg. We saw in the previous chapter how Austrofascists sought international patrons; here we will see them courting local allies. Whereas federal politicians found legitimacy outside Austria's borders, provincial elites consolidated their position locally through a complex entanglement of cultural, associational, religious and cultural ties. In Vienna, Austrofascist politicians visited, hosted and corresponded with associates abroad, whereas Salzburg's politicians drew on long time acquaintances with editors, journalists, playwrights, priests and even the archbishop. Better the foe you knew and saw every day in the town square than the friend you read about in the newspaper. Or, as we will see in this chapter, better the foe in a rival political camp than the one time friend who had now become a Nazi terrorist.

Moravia comes to Salzburg

The *Salzburger Volksblatt* was representative of a German-nationalist milieu whose cultural and intellectual roots lay in the Bohemian and Moravian lands. Its owner, Hans Glaser (1877–1960), belonged to a generation of young Bohemian and Moravian German-speaking civil servants and educated professionals who migrated to Salzburg in the late nineteenth century during one of the peaks of Czech–German hostilities. As we saw in Chapter 1, the younger German-nationalists infused Salzburg's liberal associational culture with the pan-German ideas they had brought with them from the borderlands.[2] Glaser himself had been born in Šumperk/ Mährisch Schönberg in northern Moravia, which was almost entirely German except for a small Czech enclave that divided northern Moravia from the region around Svitavy/Zwittau.[3] Moravia's German population was smaller than Bohemia's, around 28 per cent of the inhabitants compared to 37 per cent in Bohemia, and the largely agrarian population of Moravia also meant that German-nationalism was more moderate and Catholicism stronger than in Bohemia.[4] Moravian peasants were renowned for their pioneering language exchange programmes, swapping their children for holidays or for an entire school year.[5] It would be fascinating to discover if Glaser was also a beneficiary of the famous *Kindertausche*, but he does not mention his upbringing in his diary. We can only surmise that his early years would have been less tainted by nationalist politics than if he had grown up in Prague. At any rate, his first exposure to German-nationalists was most likely in Salzburg given the penetration there of Bohemian and Moravian German-nationalists in the 1880s and 1890s. Glaser arrived in Salzburg in 1896 at the age of nineteen to take up a position in a publishing company owned by a German émigré from Stuttgart, Reinhold Kiesel, who had established Salzburg's first daily newspaper, the *Salzburger Volksblatt*, in 1870.[6] Glaser married Kiesel's daughter and, after his father-in-law's death, eventually took over the reins of the newspaper in 1907.

Glaser's political connections with German-nationalists in the interwar period tended to be formed through expediency rather than ideology. He joined the Greater German party after its inauguration in Salzburg in 1920, partly because the party leadership informed him that paper quotas would be allocated only to those newspapers that had the patronage of a political party. However, he was keen to extend his newspaper's reputation beyond the Greater Germans, whose Salzburg branch had barely two thousand members, only a fraction of the newspaper's readership. Glaser wrote in his diary on 18 October 1920: 'I want an independent *Volksblatt*, but in a tone and presentation that the supporters of other political parties will also read. The newspaper cannot live off the Greater Germans alone.' He eventually withdrew his party membership in 1929. With the Greater Germans in internal disarray in 1931, he threw his weight behind the National Socialists in whom he believed 'the youth, and so the future lies.'[7] The NSDAP made decisive gains in Salzburg in the regional and municipal elections in 1932 winning just under 21 per cent, well above the national average of 16 per cent.[8] In view of their new-found respectability, National Socialists sought out the *Salzburger Volksblatt* as a potential mouthpiece since they did not have an official organ in Salzburg. However, the relationship was strained and the newspaper's editors were often under pressure to appease the party elite.[9] Glaser met NSDAP leaders in Salzburg in January 1933 and agreed to maintain a more neutral position after the newspaper had publicly fended off what he regarded as 'impertinent' letters from anonymous readers, presumably Nazis challenging the views of the editorship.[10]

On the other hand, Glaser's relationships with prominent Christian Socials in Salzburg were more amicable than one would expect from the owner of a German-nationalist newspaper. He was on friendly terms with the governor of Salzburg, Franz Rehrl, as we have seen, and Glaser's political standing was also high among his colleagues in Austrian press circles. In June 1934, he was elected chair of the Union of Publishers of Daily Newspapers, and he met regularly with the head of the federal press agency, Ludwig, to discuss changes to the press law.[11] After the new Austrofascist press chamber began meeting in November 1936, Glaser travelled regularly to Vienna to participate in chamber sessions.[12]

These examples of both professional and political collaboration with Christian Social and Austrofascist politicians showed that Glaser was more opportunistic than ideological. He associated with colleagues and public figures from a Catholic cultural and political milieu, although Glaser himself was not Catholic. His wife's family were Protestant and Glaser's diary records that his grandchildren had Protestant christenings. Given his upbringing in predominantly Catholic Moravia, Glaser may have converted when he married Kiesel's daughter. Many of Glaser's colleagues at the *Salzburger Volksblatt* may also have been Catholic, even if they were also proponents of the newspaper's German-nationalism. This is significant, as we will see, because the newspaper promoted a form of 'positive Christianity' that sought to persuade readers that national identity transcended religion. Although this tactic was intended to undermine the government's notion of a 'Christian' state, it also demonstrates how

German-nationalists found common ground with Austrofascists in their attempt to construct a pan-German identity. For German-nationalists, as much as for Austrofascists, Christianity was integral to the notion that Austria was a 'German' state.

A priest, an archbishop and a festival

The pan-Germanism of local elites from a Catholic milieu can be seen from the examples of two influential clerical figures in Salzburg: the owner of the *Salzburger Chronik*, Leonhard Steinwender, and Archbishop Ignatius Rieder (1858–1934). It was not unusual that Steinwender presided over the *Salzburger Chronik* at the same time as he carried out his duties as canon of Mattsee monastery. The absence of a lay Catholic intelligentsia in a provincial town like Salzburg meant that priests often had a second vocation as journalist or as a local dignitary of the Christian Social Party. Steinwender was a true believer in Austria's German and Christian identity in the '*Ostmark*', a term that was ubiquitous in the Austrofascist era. For Catholic intellectuals like Steinwender it described Austria's spiritual and cultural mission as bearer and proselyte of German Christianity in Central Europe. He wrote in the *Salzburger Chronik* that 'to be an East Marcher [*Ostmärker*], to be an Austrian' was 'a wonderful pan-German vocation'. In 1934, Steinwender became director of the Fatherland Front's propaganda section in Salzburg and editor of Salzburg's official Front publication, *Die Front in Salzburg*.[13]

As a provincial functionary of the Fatherland Front and devotee of Austria's *Ostmark* heritage, Steinwender was invited in June 1937 to speak at the St Boniface Day celebrations in Vienna. The Boniface Day festivities were organized by the Fatherland Front's auxiliary body for German minorities outside Austria, the *Österreichischer Verband für volksdeutsche Auslandsarbeit* (Austrian Association for Germandom Work Abroad – ÖVVA), which will be discussed further in Chapter 4. In what was possibly the shining moment of his career, Steinwender addressed a distinguished audience that included Cardinal Theodor Innitzer; the Education Minister, Hans Perntner (standing in for Chancellor Schuschnigg who had to cancel his attendance at the last minute); and leaders of the Fatherland Front. He spoke about the legacy of the eighth-century 'Apostle to the Germans' who had united the German nation by converting the German tribes to Christianity and 'opened the door to world history for the German nation' to play a leading role in Western Christendom. But Boniface Day was more than just a day of commemoration; it was a call to renounce those who had made idols out of the German nation instead of following the laws of the 'eternal God'. It was also a call to reclaim Boniface's legacy so that the German nation would not be consigned to a spiritual 'desert' like the Africa of St Augustine, or descend into chaos like the Orient of the saints Chrysostom and Jerome. Steinwender was referring to the persecution of German clergy and Catholic associational life in Nazi Germany although he also mentioned the 'satanic wave of anti-Christ Bolshevism' in his address.[14] We will see in the next chapter that the relationship between 'Germandom' work and National Socialism was far more ambivalent than Steinwender believed and his views on this occasion were not representative of the views of the organizers of the festivities.

Proving he was not another government mouthpiece, Steinwender went on to warn the German people of the danger of modern idolatry in politics. He quoted a former archbishop of Salzburg, Balthasar Kaltner, who had warned Europe on the eve of the Great War in 1914 not to forsake its Christian heritage or it would lose its ruling place in the West. Steinwender paraphrased these 'prophetic words' and called on the German nation to preserve its Christian roots and its leading role in Christendom for if the German nation fell, all of Christendom would fall with it. He ended his remarkable speech, which the audience interrupted several times with enthusiastic applause, by appealing to the German people to follow 'a leader so noble, so courageous, so gloriously good . . . Christ the King, the Son of God and Man, with his cross of redemption and his promise: Have faith, I have overcome the world!'[15]

Steinwender later claimed he had found the 'paths of grace' inside Buchenwald concentration camp where he was incarcerated for two years until his release in November 1940. After the war, he published his reminiscences of Buchenwald including a collection of his homilies he gave in secret to fellow inmates and wrote down only after his release. In both his reminiscences and homilies, Steinwender addressed at length the subject of the Austrian 'homeland' and acknowledged past mistakes in the persecution of Social Democrats and the comparative leniency towards National Socialists. For Steinwender, the German nation lingered on, but now it lay amid the ruins of the 'idol' of the Third Reich 'in the deepest abyss of its history'. He asked all who still loved the German nation 'in spite of everything' to 'pray with deep distress "De profundis", the de profundis of the German nation'. For 'if after the bitter experiences of the last century we are serious in acknowledging that only Christ and his law of justice and love can save a human life, then this call of distress from the depths of depths will not remain a cry of the dead, but will awaken new life'.[16] Steinwender's reflections after Buchenwald serve to illustrate how his belief in Austria's 'Christian' and 'German' spiritual and cultural heritage had blurred with the pan-Germanism of German-nationalists and National

Socialists and only unravelled amid the moral, physical and spiritual deprivation of a Nazi concentration camp.

Archbishop Rieder also saw Austria as custodian of German Christianity in Europe. Appointed archbishop of Salzburg in 1918, succeeding Kaltner before him, Rieder championed a religious renewal movement in the interwar period that included plans to establish both a German Catholic university and an international festival in Salzburg. The idea for a German Catholic university had its roots in the 1848 Catholic associational movement in Germany and Austria, but the Austro-Prussian War and dissolution of the German Confederation had halted plans for such a university and Rieder wanted to revive the idea in the aftermath of military defeat in 1918. Outlining his proposal in an article entitled 'Reflections on a Catholic University of the German People in Salzburg' (*Denkschrift über eine katholische Universität des deutschen Volkstums in Salzburg*), Rieder envisaged the university, which was originally designed to be an extension of the existing theological faculty at the University of Salzburg, as a common intellectual and social 'meeting ground' for Catholics from southern Germany and Austria. Even in the title of his pamphlet, Rieder emphasized the pan-German idea of a common German people and, implicitly, a common German Catholicism, without mention of a separate Austrian Catholic tradition. Prominent Austrian Catholic politicians, including Seipel and Dollfuss, were advocates of the idea, but its opponents, notably German sociologist Max Weber, rejected the proposal on the grounds that religious criteria would count in the appointment of academic positions.[17]

Seeking to renew the spiritual as well as intellectual life of German-speakers in Europe, Rieder lent his support to the founders of the Salzburg Festival, Hugo von Hofmannstahl (1874–1929) and Max Reinhardt (1873–1943). If the Festival's founders were its artistic directors, Rieder was its spiritual guardian especially in the early years after its inauguration in 1920. Hofmannstahl consulted with Rieder in 1922 for final approval of his manuscript for *Das Salzburger grosse Welttheater* (The Salzburg Great World Theatre) in return for permission to stage the play in Salzburg's Baroque Church.[18] Rieder also defended Reinhardt from frequent anti-Semitic attacks from Salzburg's Nazi organs, who objected to a Jew staging Catholic motifs in Salzburg's sacred edifices. In 1924, he gave permission for Reinhardt to perform his play, *Das Mirakel* (The Miracle), in the Collegiate Church, amid a sustained campaign by the Nazi organ in Salzburg, *Der Eiserne Besen*, to prevent Reinhardt from doing so.[19]

While he objected to anti-Semitism where the Festival was concerned, Rieder later lent his support to the National German Working Group of

Austrian Catholics (*Volksdeutsche Arbeitskreis österreichischer Katholiken*). The group published a book to mark the All-German Catholic Congress in September 1933, entitled 'Catholic Faith and the German National Character in Austria' (*Katholischer Glaube und deutsches Volkstum in Österreich*), for which Rieder wrote the foreword. In it he described 1933 as a 'holy year for Germans' because it commemorated the 250th anniversary of the victory over the Turks in 1683.[20] The anniversary was the theme of the 1933 celebrations and Pius XI sent a papal legate to attend the commemorative events in Vienna. But in contemporary publications marking the anniversary the reference stressed a different understanding of a 'holy year' for Germans, one that would lead to a new 'German Christian' defeat of the unholy bolshevist warriors, as we saw in Steinwender's speech, and Jews as we will see in Chapter 5. Rieder died in 1934 and so did not live to see the collapse of such a German Christian Austrian state, nor its nemesis in a National Socialist German *Ostmark*, but he was one of the earliest representatives of an influential Catholic elite who guarded Austria's pan-German heritage throughout the interwar years with religious commitment.

For their part the Festival's founders also wanted to promote German art and culture in Salzburg. Hofmannstahl described Salzburg as the historic heart of the Bavarian-Austrian tribal lands, whose 'instinctively German' folk ethos was the antithesis of Vienna's 'alien' intelligentsia and obsession with novelty.[21] Reinhardt had stipulated in 1918 that 'home-grown' German art would be the essence and the attraction of the Festival, 'the master of the house who chooses to extend the hand of friendship to guests'.[22] A wider elite in Salzburg, including Glaser, who was an avid theatregoer and whose newspaper provided full coverage and reviews of the Festival programmes and performers each year, shared these beliefs about German superiority and hegemony. The Festival symbolized all that Salzburg's elite held sacred and shows how widespread pan-German ideas were in Salzburg in the interwar years.

After the creation of a Nazi state in Germany, Austrofascists distanced themselves from National Socialism and Germany, while German-nationalists openly embraced both the movement and the regime. The latter's only cause for concern was the campaign of violence carried out by Nazis in Austria from 1933 to 1934, although even this anxiety was a pragmatic response to extremism rather than moral objection to the political aims of the movement. The following sections trace these ideological sympathies with National Socialism in the *Salzburger Volksblatt* after 1933. At the same time, the chapter also shows how the newspaper's construction of a pan-German identity during this period converged in many important respects with the pan-Germanism of the Austrofascist state.

'National Socialists are not traitors'

Notwithstanding some tensions between local party officials and the owner of the *Salzburger Volksblatt*, the newspaper's editors had already given their endorsement of the National Socialist Party's programme for *Anschluss* well before Hitler's appointment as German chancellor on 30 January 1933. After Hitler came to power, the newspaper continued to publish notices of rallies, public lectures and radio broadcasts of speeches by Nazi leaders in Germany in a propaganda campaign made respectable by its appearance in an established newspaper.[23] Notices about party events often appeared on the front pages and advertised entry for non-Jews only. The day following the German election on 5 March, the *Salzburger Volksblatt* published a special morning edition with a boldface notice from the NSDAP calling for 'every upright German-Austrian who wants *Anschluss* with the German Reich' to attend the *Anschluss* rally in the Salzburg Festival House the next day.[24] The next day, it reported that the Festival House had been filled to capacity, demonstrating that 'the German will for *Anschluss* had also received powerful momentum in Salzburg'.[25]

For Glaser, however, other priorities larger than the Nazi Party loomed with the news of Dollfuss's dictatorship. His diary entries for March 1933 show that his immediate preoccupation lay not with the German elections, but with his newspaper's prospects in the wake of the new press laws.[26] The *Salzburger Volksblatt* responded initially to the press laws by accusing the government of creating an 'oligarchy' and calling for a return to the 1920 constitution and new elections.[27] Later the newspaper's editors tried to circumvent the government's gag orders by drawing attention to events in Germany without directly mentioning the Nazis.[28] A special report on the May Day celebrations in Germany told stories of men, women and children who expressed pride in their national identity as Germans, rather than their regional identity as Saxons or Bavarians. The journalist asked one boy where Adolf Hitler came from and he replied: 'From Germany'. The journalist corrected him saying that Hitler was in fact an Austrian, to which the boy answered: 'Then he is still a German!' The journalist echoed the boy's expression of pan-German identity: 'I am proud to be an alpine Austrian but I am even prouder to be a real German [*ein ganzer Deutscher*] first and foremost'.[29] The article was left uncensored in the newspaper and did not attract the penalties that subsequent reports did for expressing oppositional views to the Austrian government. It was an early example of the *Salzburger Volksblatt*'s strategy of promoting a universalist pan-German identity under the sometimes loose reins of Austrofascist censorship. These reins tightened, however, whenever the editors were seen to be blatantly disregarding the official propaganda.

By the middle of May, the newspaper's hostile outbursts at the government resulted in four confiscations in swift succession. The edition on 5 May was confiscated following the publication of an article about the government's ban on uniforms, which amounted to incitement according to Paragraph 300 of the penal law code. Five days later, the newspaper was confiscated a second time for a scathing article about the Austrian public service. This time the newspaper's chief editor, August Ramsauer, was also forced to pay a fine of 1,440 schillings for allowing the offending articles to go to print. A third confiscation occurred on 12 May for an article that criticized the Geneva Disarmament Conference and, again, on 7 June, the newspaper was seized for an article attacking the Austrian ambassador to Berlin. On 10 June the government introduced a new decree that gave the chancellor the power to ban newspapers for up to three months if they were confiscated more than twice. Given that it already had four strikes, the *Salzburger Volksblatt* gave notice to its readers that it 'was forced by the new press emergency decrees to exercise the greatest caution from now on in commenting on the political situation in Austria'. The newspaper announced that it would report only 'the bare facts' of Austrian politics and withhold editorial comments, but that it would continue in its capacity as a 'national paper' to represent the interests of the 'national idea'.[30]

For the editors of the *Salzburger Volksblatt* the national idea meant a community in which all Germans were bound together by blood, language and culture. They couched this idea in an ethnic universalist pan-German discourse that resembled the Nazis' vision of a *Volksgemeinschaft* (national community). At the same time, the newspaper also used a civic discourse of universal pan-German identity in support of National Socialists, whom both Glaser and the newspaper's editors regarded as indispensable to the national movement. The editors were at pains to point out that this 'national idea' was not unpatriotic to Austria and defended Austrian Nazis as loyal Austrians, who should be seen first as members of the national community and second as members of a political party. A front-page editorial on 17 June declared that 'National Socialists are not traitors, they love their Austrian homeland, but they want to see it liberated and the whole of its population spoken for, not just one party'.[31]

The editors' support for National Socialists diminished slightly in the wake of a campaign of violence and terror carried out by Austrian Nazis across the country that lasted less than a month in its initial intensity, but did not fully abate until July 1934. The violence began in Innsbruck on 11 June 1933 when a twenty-year-old German Nazi from Berlin attempted to assassinate the leader of the Tyrolean *Heimatwehr* (Homeland Guard), Richard Steidle. Over the next five days, three people were killed in a series of bomb explosions in predominantly Jewish-owned shops, cafes and department stores. The Austrian government believed the perpetrators to be a small band of German Nazi youths and accused party members in Germany of supporting the terror campaign by smuggling propaganda, finances, bomb explosives, weapons and assassins into Austria. The smugglers were in fact several thousand Austrian National Socialists, the so-called 'Austrian Legion', who had fled to Bavaria and were stationed in military camps along the border. Heightened agitation towards the Austrian government, and growing disillusionment with the Nazi authorities who refused to settle them in Germany permanently, contributed to the sense of alienation among these Austrian refugees and fuelled their determination to bring about a violent coup in Austria.[32]

Dollfuss finally banned the Nazi Party on 19 June 1933 after a hand grenade attack in the Lower Austrian town of Krems killed one person and injured thirty others. Austrian Nazis retaliated by embarking on a country-wide campaign of violent attacks and propaganda, painting swastikas in public places, on houses, streets, trees, rocks, on scattered pamphlets and burning swastika signs into hillsides. Dollfuss narrowly escaped an assassin's bullets in the Austrian parliament on 3 October, but this was not the first assassination attempt on a government minister. Vice-chancellor and Minister of Security, Major Emil Fey, had already been the target of several planned or aborted attempts in July and August. Between October 1933 and January 1934, Nazis carried out tear gas attacks in cafes, shops and cinemas and detonated explosives in cars, buildings and streets, using handmade bombs from paper, clay and chlorate when dynamite could not be smuggled in from Germany. By the beginning of 1934, the number of daily bomb explosions had reached 40 and 140 separate incidents were recorded for the beginning of January alone. After a brief ceasefire during the February civil war between Social Democrats and government troops, the violence began to rise again after Hitler's birthday in April 1934.[33]

In Salzburg, bomb explosions in cars and public buildings prompted the editors of the *Salzburger Volksblatt* to issue an impassioned plea to their readers that Austro-German unity be achieved by peaceful means. An editorial on 28 June 1933 sent a stern warning to those responsible for the attacks and likened acts of terror to the assassination of Archduke Franz Ferdinand and his wife on the anniversary of the killings. 'And now to you young ones! You are the hope of the national and liberal movement in Austria. You must not let it happen that foolish pranks get you thrown into jail – and rightly so if you rashly commit crimes! – and therefore excluded from the ranks of national fighters for a long time, perhaps even forever.' Youthful passions could be put to better use if they were channelled towards votes instead of deeds that 'might seem to some to be heroic, but in truth can only be regarded as childish tricks! German youth must not sink to the methods of the assassins of the heir to the throne that with the revolver shots in Sarajevo exactly nineteen years ago unleashed the fateful war, which led to disaster for Austria and Germany.' 'National unity is something that must come to fruition in peace, something that requires a very great deal of patience', the editorial asserted, pointing to the example of Italy's unification. 'You young ones must save yourselves for that time, which we older ones will no longer witness. But you should enter the greater Fatherland with clean hands and hearts, not tainted by innocent blood that you spilled.'[34]

The author of this editorial was the newspaper's long-standing chief editor, Thomas Mayrhofer.[35] A former member of a German-nationalist student fraternity, Mayrhofer had joined the Greater German party in 1920 along with Glaser.[36] The editorial's reference to a 'national and liberal movement in Austria' reflected the pan-Germanism of Mayrhofer's and Glaser's generation for whom National Socialism represented the fulfilment of their youthful pan-German ideals. But the experience of a world war during their lifetime had also caused them to recoil from the violent extremes of the Nazis. While Mayrhofer cautioned restraint in the goal of Austro-German unity, he also argued that National Socialists should be able to participate in Austrian public life. He said that the priority for German-nationalists was to harness the energy of all 'liberal- and national-minded people in Austria' into a national front that could act as a democratic opposition to the Fatherland Front. He was adamant that the government would not be able continue to suppress opposition indefinitely or deny the political rights of those Austrians who did not wish to join the Fatherland Front. Moreover, this opposition front should be free to adopt National Socialist principles of government and ideology within the parameters of the Austrian state as long as Austria remained politically separated from Germany. He endorsed 'all the ideas and methods of Adolf Hitler, which can be used in Austria and do not contravene our laws' if such an opposition were to come into force in Austrian politics. However, he also reminded his readers that the primary goal of such a 'German liberation front in Austria . . . ought to be to bring about normal friendly relations between Austria and Germany'. To that end, the national liberation front would 'pursue Austrian goals until the international resistance against the establishment of Greater Germany can be overcome.'[37]

One reader sent a letter to the editors disagreeing with Mayrhofer that National Socialism was the exclusive path to Austro-German unity. Could not that unity also be achieved under the banner of the Fatherland Front, the reader asked? 'It surely is not acceptable to stamp as second-class Germans all those who reject the swastika as the absolute and exclusive symbol of what is German, particularly if they do not live within the Reich.

No lesser man than Bismarck once said that he was a Prussian first and then a German. Why should this saying, *mutatis mutandis*, not be able to be applied to us Austrians?' The reader also claimed that Austria's annexation to Nazi Germany was inevitable unless German-nationalists could be integrated into the Fatherland Front. 'In the interest of the liberal German national idea in Austria, and so, fundamentally, in the pan-German interest', the writer concluded, 'I would think it absolutely desirable to have the widest possible participation of these groups in order to prevent what would otherwise be inevitable and must be feared.' The *Salzburger Volksblatt* published this letter with only the briefest comment that the points it raised 'could perhaps give cause for a fruitful political discussion.'[38]

The letter from the reader showed that real fears about National Socialism did exist among German-nationalists, if only a minority of them. Yet such reservations did not always amount to ideological or political commitment to the Fatherland Front. As we will see below, Glaser joined the Fatherland Front partly because it was a more expedient option than the *Heimatschutz* and partly because it guaranteed a level of political immunity for his newspaper. Glaser's commitment to the National Socialist Party, on the other hand, extended only as far as his commitment to Austro-German unity. After the government banned the NSDAP, Glaser wrote in his diary that the remaining 'nationalist circles' would have to band together under a new leadership. His personal choice of candidate for the leader of this proposed new national front was Franz Hueber, the former Austrian Justice Minister and Hermann Göring's brother-in-law, who resigned from the leadership of the Salzburg *Heimatschutz* in protest at Dollfuss's anti-German politics.[39] Glaser was less of an ideologue than Mayrhofer, but he was equally steeped in the historic vision of a greater-German nation. We might describe Glaser's response to National Socialism as consent and his participation in the political life of the Austrofascist state as compliance: in other words, he continued to endorse the National Socialist programme of Austro-German unity, while seeking to protect the position of his newspaper in the public sphere of the Austrofascist state. Glaser's stance towards National Socialism and Austrofascism also highlights the shared stake that German-nationalists and Austrofascists held in an Austrian pan-German identity. This identity not only reflected the place of Austria in the German nation and therefore the question of Austro-German unity, but also underscored the national character of the Austrian state itself.

Compliance and consent

The interactions between local functionaries and the editors of a provincial German-nationalist newspaper demonstrate the extent of compliance and consent under the Austrofascist state. By seeing how editors continued to articulate their position within the new constraints on press freedom, we can observe the extent to which German-nationalists promoted their own interests within a public sphere that was constantly monitored by the state. At the same time that they complied with the state's official version of pan-Germanism, they were also able to give consent to their own prefer- ence for a National Socialist vision of a *Volksgemeinschaft*. That the Aus- trofascist vision of a German Austrian state did not clash with the Nazi version of a universal German nation indicates how far such consent went in a dictatorship that ostensibly saw itself as a bulwark against Nazism.

During the course of 1933 the *Salzburger Volksblatt* was under close surveillance and incurred severe penalties, but the editors were forced to concede even greater autonomy in 1934 with the appointment of a local *Heimatschutz* representative to the editorship. On 22 February 1934, Salz- burg's Director of Public Security, Rudolf Scholz, summoned Glaser to inform him that his licence would be revoked if he continued to publish the *Salzburger Volksblatt* under proprietorship of the Kiesel publishing house. The specific offence that prompted this action was the newspaper's report alleging that Tyrolean *Heimatwehr* soldiers in Hallein had violently attacked local residents, behaved in a 'scandalous' manner and should be removed. Two days later Scholz's deputy, Helmut Hirschall, offered Glaser an eleventh-hour compromise: the appointment of a *Heimatschutz* com- missioner, Konstantin Kreuzer, as the *Salzburger Volksblatt*'s political editor in return for the withdrawal of the threat to revoke Glaser's publish- ing licence.[40]

The appointment of a *Heimatschutz* representative did not immediately end hostilities between the newspaper and the provincial authorities. This was partly due to the uneasy alliance between the Fatherland Front and the Salzburg leaders of the *Heimatschutz*. As mentioned above, the head of the *Heimatschutz*, Hueber, stood down in June 1933 because of his loyal- ties to the NSDAP while the remaining leaders declared their allegiance to Dollfuss. On 8 February 1934, the *Heimatschutz* outlined a set of provi- sional demands to Rehrl including the establishment of an advisory committee comprising representatives of the Fatherland Front and the *Heimatschutz*, as well as the appointment of *Heimatschutz* representatives to every district and municipality and to every public office and school.[41] The appointment of Kreuzer as political editor of the *Salzburger Volksblatt* can therefore be seen as a concession by the Fatherland Front authorities to the demands of the *Heimatschutz* leaders. However, Kreuzer's militant language and his admiration for Mussolini were an affront to the Security Director, Scholz, a loyal Christian Social foot soldier who distrusted the *Heimatschutz*. Consequently, the newspaper was again subject to confiscations several times between February and June. On frequent other occasions, the censors simply blacked out whole sections of print.[42]

Under Kreuzer, the *Heimatschutz* press dispatches were particularly belligerent towards Christian Socials. One front-page article on 28 March 1934, entitled 'The Sins of the Parties', claimed that by defeating the Social Democrats in the civil war, the *Heimwehr* had done in three days what the Christian Social Party had been unable to do in fourteen years. To illustrate the party's ineptitude, the article pointed out that the leader of the Christian Social Workers' Movement, Leopold Kunschak, had shaken the hand of Vienna's socialist mayor, Karl Seitz, in the town hall just days before the civil war broke out. The article claimed that 'the new era demanded new men, not just a change in name' and called for 'the whole population and especially the nationalist groups in the population' to work together to eliminate all parties from the 'new state'.[43] The reference to 'nationalist groups' in a dispatch in the *Salzburger Volksblatt* showed that the *Heimatschutz* regarded Kreuzer's appointment as a tactical manoeuvre against the dominant Christian Socials in Salzburg.

Glaser did not view the *Heimatschutz* as an ally against the Christian Socials or the Fatherland Front. In fact, he joined the Fatherland Front in September 1934 to guard against Kreuzer's machinations to make the *Salzburger Volksblatt* an organ of the *Heimatschutz*.[44] His decision may also have been prompted by a wish to distance himself from National Socialists after some of his colleagues were implicated in another wave of Nazi violence in June and July 1934. Editor Franz Krotsch was accused in June 1934 of circulating memos to National Socialists with instructions for carrying out terror attacks. On 28 June 1934, he was arrested and criminal proceedings began against him in July. He returned briefly to the editorship in August, but was discharged from his position at the end of 1934. Without employment opportunities in Austria and with his professional reputation in tatters, Krotsch fled to Germany and only returned to Salzburg after the *Anschluss*.[45] Glaser was horrified by the violence and wrote in his diary on 28 June 1934: 'No sensible person knows where these dangerous acts of terror will lead that cause innocent people to come to grave harm.'[46]

Glaser apparently did not foresee a political assassination on the horizon, unlike his colleague, Mayrhofer, who warned against a repetition of Sarajevo. Nor did he predict that the local uncoordinated efforts of terrorists would climax in an attempted coup in the capital. In fact the Nazi putsch on 25 July 1934 had been a year in the planning. Led by a band of former soldiers who were members of the NSDAP and had been discharged from the Austrian army following the party's ban, the execution of the putsch was clumsy and a couple of key government figures had been forewarned. Still some of the rebels managed to occupy the building of the Austrian radio broadcaster and announce that Dollfuss had resigned, prompting small uprisings by Austrian Nazis in the provinces. The putsch was put down within a few hours by government troops, but not before one of the rebels, Otto Planetta, broke into Dollfuss's office and shot the chancellor, who died of his wounds before medical attention or a priest arrived.[47] On 27 July, two days later, Glaser still seemed more shocked by the audacity of the rebels than by Dollfuss's death at the hands of assassins. He described the coup as 'a crazy undertaking that has neither sense nor purpose and hurries the young people wantonly to their death. They must surely realise that their cause is long lost!'[48] Glaser's reaction to Nazi terrorists, like his decision to join the Fatherland Front, was motivated by fear and alarm at extremist politics, rather than a vote of confidence in the Austrofascist state or a nod of respect to its dead leader.

The *Salzburger Volksblatt* continued to maintain its distance from the Fatherland Front by publishing only government propaganda from the *Heimatdienst* and keeping all other Front notices to a minimum. By 1935, the newspaper had condensed the number of pages in the weekday editions to a dozen, including regular supplements on fashion and cooking.[49] Domesticity, at least, complied with the patriotic jargon of much of the Fatherland Front's propaganda, as evidenced by the myriad notices for local *Mutterschutzwerk* meetings and infant care programmes that were published in the *Salzburger Volksblatt*. However, these were mostly relegated to the back pages.[50] The newspaper also sought to compensate for the monopoly of Fatherland Front news by publishing correspondence from foreign press agencies in Czechoslovakia, Poland, Switzerland, Italy and Germany. In September 1935 it was banned from publishing reports from the radio service of the Nazi press agency, *Deutsches Nachrichten-Bureau* (DNB). The editors managed to evade this latest interdiction by rewording the DNB reports and publishing them as reports from the *Salzburger Volksblatt*'s own correspondents.[51]

The editors continued to promote their agenda for a National Socialist vision of pan-German identity, often by reprinting public lectures by known Nazi sympathizers. An article on 29 January 1936 was an extract of a talk given by former *Heimatschutz* leader, Hueber, to the *Salzburger Turnverein* (gymnastics association) in which Hueber described the German people as ethnically and culturally distinct from other nationalities and pointed to distinctions in folk costume, art and music.[52] Another article in February from a lecture by the German ethnologist, Paul Rohrbach, depicted the nation as a universal community tied by language and culture. The article claimed that there were a total number of 90 million Germans in the world, including 68 million in the German Reich and a further 12 million in countries bordering Germany. The remaining 10 million Germans included emigrants and their descendants abroad, although Rohrbach excluded from this figure second-generation Germans in North America who had lost their ties with the language.[53] The figure of 12 million was especially significant because it made no distinction between Austrian Germans, Baltic Germans or Sudeten Germans. Articles like these represented an ethnic universal discourse that differed from the Austrofascist vision of a resurrected 'Holy Roman Empire of the German Nation', in which Austria would play the leading role in its German Christian mission to the nations of Central Europe. The ethnic discourse of Austrofascists was about religion, not language and blood. But while their universalist visions of pan-Germanism may have diverged, German-nationalists and Austrofascists had much in common when it came to defending their idea of a German Christian Austrian state.

Defending German Christian Austria

The *Salzburger Volksblatt*'s construction of a German Christian identity bore resemblance to the pan-German rhetoric of local Austrofascist functionaries. But whereas German-nationalists elsewhere in Austria sought chiefly to preserve the 'German' character of the state, an aim which converged also with the approach of the Austrofascist state, German-nationalists in Salzburg and local state functionaries were seemingly more concerned with Austria's 'Christian' identity, even if they differed over the definition of a Christian state. The attempts of German-nationalists and Austrofascists to give a spiritual dimension to pan-German identity after 1936 show that religion was the site of least resistance in Salzburg in the pre-*Anschluss* era.

The July Agreement in 1936 mitigated some of the previous restrictions on the *Salzburger Volksblatt*'s editorship. Initially the newspaper welcomed the July Agreement cautiously and reiterated the need for Austria to maintain its sovereignty.[54] Privately, however, Hans Glaser greeted the Austro-German détente with relief, writing in his diary that the agreement between Schuschnigg and Hitler was 'a rather major domestic and foreign political event that we have all desired for a long time'.[55] One important local consequence of the July Agreement was the departure of Kreuzer from the post of political editor. His departure meant that press correspondence from the *Heimatschutz* was relegated to the back pages of the newspaper and he finally left the newspaper altogether in March 1937. A Nazi sympathizer and former diplomatic envoy in Berlin, Adolf Frank, replaced Kreuzer in August 1936. Frank had made many contacts with National Socialists during his diplomatic posting in Germany. One of these contacts was Franz Krotsch, who had come to the *Salzburger Volksblatt* in 1924 on

Frank's recommendation only to flee back to Germany ten years later after he was charged for terrorist attacks.[56] Frank's appointment to the editorship, a direct result of the July Agreement and Austro-German détente, widened considerably the margins in which the *Salzburger Volksblatt* could voice its consent for National Socialism. Throughout the remainder of 1936, the newspaper openly championed political unity with Germany and hoped that the Austrian state would promote the pan-German idea towards this goal.[57]

It was significant, therefore, that a front-page article in November 1936 mentioned the July Agreement in connection with the Srbik school of pan-German history. As we saw in Chapter 1, Srbik developed historical and conceptual links between the universal German nation, the Central European idea of German unity, and the tradition of German statehood. The article in the *Salzburger Volksblatt* in November 1936 lauded his pan-Germanism as the 'spirit' behind the July Agreement and hoped for this spirit to prevail within the historical belief in a common German nation that was 'certain to become the common basis of the new pan-German national reality'. Srbik's historicism gave credence to the National Socialist idea of Austro-German unity in the same way that the *Salzburger Volksblatt* sought to interpret the July Agreement as a step towards this goal. The November article explained that Srbik's pan-Germanism provided a more critical appraisal of the great personalities and feats of Austrian history within the broader framework of German history because it was able to overcome the biases of the separate Prussian and Austrian historical traditions.[58] In fact, it was not Srbik's intention to make such a critical historical judgement when he began work on his magnum opus, *Deutsche Einheit*, in 1935. Rather, his goal was to show how the National Socialist vision of a thousand-year empire was the fulfilment of the previous thousand years of German history. Nonetheless, Frank's attempt to disseminate Srbik's scholarship in the *Salzburger Volksblatt* was tantamount to intellectual consent for National Socialism. That this consent was couched in terms that also made reference to Habsburg history shows how the newspaper could comply with Austrofascist visions of the past, while promoting Nazi ideas under the guise of a universal pan-German historicism.

Frank's Christmas Eve editorial in 1936 showed further the newspaper's affirmation of political unity with Nazi Germany. Frank paid homage to the 'great, glorious German homeland' and claimed that in the Sudeten territories, 'thousands and thousands were . . . denied the peace of Christmas in the German living-space (*Lebensraum*)':

> Hundreds of thousands of our national comrades in the outlying northern Bohemian areas are waging a desperate bitter struggle for a meagre and

paltry existence under the oppressive yoke of an illegitimate foreign power. Countless fathers, mothers and starving children will spend Christmas Eve there in hopeless numb despair.[59]

Frank's intimation that the dispossession of Germans in Czechoslovakia was a national dishonour showed his commitment to Nazi foreign policy aims, in particular to the political unity of all Germans in Central Europe. As we will see in Chapter 4, the Austrofascist state also sought mileage out of the Sudeten issue in its 'Germandom' work, even recruiting former Nazis to its ranks, but here Frank's reference to a German *Lebensraum* was an unequivocal message of support for National Socialism's expansionist racial designs on the East.

Frank also sought to discredit the Austrofascist notion of a 'Christian' state and replace it with a National Socialist version of Christianity. He claimed that Christmas was an ancient German custom, which retained its German character despite its appropriation by the Church. 'This festival', Frank wrote, 'opens up to us like no other the highest mystery of our being in symbolizing joy, love and goodness, as well as our eternal urge and dim yearning for the German homeland.'[60] In elevating pre-Christian traditions to the status of true religion, Frank used similar language to Nazi paganists in Germany, such as Alfred Rosenberg.[61] We do not know from this passage what Frank's religious background or beliefs were, but his claims competed with Austrofascism's orthodox view of Christianity. Where local state functionaries in Salzburg, such as Steinwender, described Austria's spiritual and cultural identity as 'a wonderful pan-German vocation', German-nationalists and Nazi sympathizers, such as Frank, also twinned 'German' and 'Christian' but attached different meanings to those terms so as to undermine the official version of pan-Germanism.

At the same time, Austrofascists were trying to win the hearts and minds of German-nationalists by drawing a distinction between the spiritual and cultural values of Austrian pan-Germanism and the racial principles of National Socialism. One anonymous spokesperson for the Fatherland Front in Salzburg – identified only by the initials 'K.F.G.' – contributed several lengthy essays in the *Salzburger Volksblatt* on topics ranging from charity and the principle of individual freedom, to the nature of fascism and anti-Semitism. The writer forcefully condemned National Socialism as a totalitarian ideology of fanatics and sought to justify Austrofascism against the 'tyranny of the majority'.[62] The author was possibly an academic for in an article in June 1936 he argued that academic research, religious beliefs, marriage and family life must not become subordinate to the state.[63] The editorials by K.F.G. became more prominent on the front pages of the *Salzburger Volksblatt* after 1936. Although these editorials were still grounded in the rhetoric of Austrofascists, they also consciously attempted to engage the newspaper's German-nationalist readership. For example, an editorial on 5 June 1937 distinguished between nationalism that had cultural value to the people and that which only edified the state. The writer illustrated this subordination to the state by arguing that the intellectual and religious icons of nineteenth-century Russian nationalism had disappeared under Bolshevism. In contrast, he argued, the Austrian state should uphold and value the life of the Austrian people and cultivate the collective expression of pan-German nationhood through the 'two-state nature of our German people' (*Zweistaatlichkeit unseres deutschen Volkes*). Such a 'healthy genuine nationalism', the writer concluded, regarded 'the life of the people [to be] worth more than the national costume'.[64] The combination of a universalist discourse ('our German people') with a particularist discourse (the Austrian state) stressed an Austrian pan-German identity that the newspaper's editors had upheld since 1934 and which they continued to promote in the era of Austro-German détente.[65]

A front-page editorial on 9 December 1937 by K.F.G. illustrates further the entangled Austrofascist and German-nationalist notions of pan-German identity. The editorial, entitled 'Fascism and Authority', distinguished between Nazi Germany and the Austrian state on the basis of Austria's claim to be both German and Christian. Fascism was foreign to the German people as a whole, the writer argued, and it had been only out of demographic and geopolitical necessity that 'the Germans on the other side of the border' followed the path of fascism. He contrasted the German experience of fascism with the experience of other Europeans, whom he identified as speakers of Romance languages (*Romanen*) with a psychological and historical predisposition towards fascism:

> It is characteristic that fascism became the destiny of two states, one of which did not yet possess the power that it needed and desired, while the other was in fact robbed utterly of the power, to which it undoubtedly had the most justified claim, by virtue of the essentially undiminished size of its population and territory. The totality principle of the state (*Allstaatlichkeit*), the primacy of the state ahead of the citizen, is more of a foreign concept to the German people, historically, nationally, and even racially, than to speakers of the Romance languages, who instinctively think as collectives.[66]

Thus the writer carefully avoided essentialist arguments about Reich Germans so as not to undermine the universal basis for pan-German unity. The slur against Italy, contrary to official government policy and even more curiously in view of the Italo-German alliance, belied the writer's preference for an exclusive Austro-German alliance without the Italophile tendencies in the ranks of Austrofascists.

The writer also hesitated to label Austria a 'Christian' state, asserting that Austria's claim to be authoritarian, and 'not outrightly fascist', rested on the principle of individual freedom, rather than on the right of the state to enforce its power:

> The Austrian state is neither in practice nor in theory intended to have unfettered power. It recognizes the individual and his rights, in accordance with the Christian belief that the individual person is of highest value, since Christ came as a man to men and not to states.[67]

The statement that Christ had come 'to men and not to states' was a subtle departure from the usual rhetoric about Austria's Christian identity. It was a conscious attempt to engage readers of the *Salzburger Volksblatt* by asserting the primacy of the individual over the state, national belonging over ideology, and faith over dogma. As we will see, National Socialists also used this tactic to discredit Austrofascism and appeal to readers on the basis of national identity, rather than political loyalties. Whoever K.F.G. was, he (or she) was not a mouthpiece of the state in the usual way of providing copy for the press and propaganda ministry. That the views of such a person could also be published in the front pages of a provincial German-nationalist newspaper under the helm of a pro-Nazi editor like Frank indicates the local context of pan-Germanism in Salzburg. Here in a German-nationalist organ was a Catholic academic espousing a universal pan-German identity in ethnic and cultural terms (by distinguishing Italians from Germans, for example) and promoting the particular German credentials of the Austrian people, while sidestepping the question of the state's Christian heritage and mission. All of this chimed well with the pan-Germanism of Nazi sympathizers who objected to the Christian label of the Austrofascist state (except in the racial sense of excluding Jews) but were happy enough to support its 'Germandom' politics.

The appointment of a national political advisor (*Volkspolitischer Referat*) to Salzburg's provincial government in October 1937 gave further impetus to the *Salzburg Volksblatt*'s campaign of consent for National Socialism. The creation of this advisory role at the provincial level followed Schuschnigg's appointment of Seyss-Inquart to the position of trustee of the German-nationalist press in July 1937.[68] The appointee in Salzburg was a lawyer, Albert Reitter. In December 1937 Reitter was instructed by his counterpart in Vienna, Pembauer, to publish a New Year's Eve editorial in the *Salzburger Volksblatt* outlining the aims of the national movement in Austria.[69] Reitter's editorial contended that National Socialism was compatible with Austrofascism's claim to represent an 'independent, Christian and German Austria'. He argued that Austria's independence could be guaranteed only if Austrians were allotted the right of self-determination within the framework of 'a pan-German solution', that is, the right to choose political union with Germany. Secondly, he drew on the Nazi formulation of positive Christianity to demonstrate National Socialism's compatibility with religion.[70] Reitter declared that the Austrofascist state's identification with Christianity 'has nothing to do with a religious confession, but with a political confession of a bourgeois view of the state'. 'This view of the Christian state does not constitute a contradiction of National Socialism', he claimed. 'On the contrary, what it directly expects is more practical Christianity and less learned comment on the Scriptures.' Finally, Reitter argued that National Socialists were the only group in Austria truly committed to making Austria a 'German' state. In contrast to those who seemed more interested in rebuilding the 'old Emperor's house' or the Catholic Church, National Socialists were intent on creating a 'German community of blood as the basis of a common historical destiny for all time' that would build a bridge between Austria and Germany.[71] Reitter sought to persuade readers that by committing themselves to Austria's universal and particular pan-German identity, and by rejecting the place of religious or dynastic traditions within that identity, they, too, would be able to pledge allegiance to National Socialism.

The reaction to Reitter's editorial within senior ranks of the Fatherland Front was swift. Zernatto, the Front general secretary, wanted to remove Reitter from his position as national political advisor in Salzburg, but Pembauer interjected by stating that Reitter's article had been approved by the provincial leader of the Fatherland Front.[72] Pembauer was probably correct in his claim that the local authorities in Salzburg had approved the intention, if not the content, of Reitter's editorial. We have already seen how one anonymous Front functionary had sought to pitch the Austrofascist conception of a German and Christian identity to a German-nationalist readership and, like Reitter, had sought to disentangle Christian beliefs and practices from the status of official religion. To be sure, Reitter's attempt to cast Nazis as the better Christians and more committed Germans struck a different chord from those local elites who sought to integrate German-nationalists within the larger aims of the Austrofascist state. Nonetheless, their common efforts to create a spiritual basis for pan-Germanism can be understood from a local perspective in a town whose Christian and German heritage dating back to Boniface's days was contested and appropriated by different groups in Salzburg all claiming to be the true heirs of the German apostle.

Glaser, for his part, endorsed the National Socialist view of pan-German unity over the Austrofascist concept of Austria as a separate German state. However, as we have seen, his private attitude towards National Socialism was characterized by political, rather than ideological consent. He was never a member or close adherent of the Nazi Party and, even after 1938, did not join the NSDAP.[73] He saw National Socialism as the fulfilment of his generation's pan-German ideals and that his role was to facilitate National Socialism's path to power by endorsing it in his newspaper. At times, he was a critical observer of Nazism and was not afraid to denounce what he regarded as the excesses of National Socialists. For him, violence and terror were unacceptable, but he held no objection to the political and racial aims of the party. He appears not to have shared the Nazis' distaste for 'degenerate' art, however: after visiting the *Entartete Kunst* (Degenerate Art) exhibition in Munich in January 1938, Glaser commented that Oskar Kokoschka's *Old Man* was 'not all that bad after all.'[74] Yet he was overjoyed and relieved with the political developments as they unfolded after the Berchtesgaden talks between Hitler and Schuschnigg in February 1938. 'One cannot put into words', he wrote in his diary six days after *Anschluss*, 'the joy and satisfaction over the historical world event that is the unification of Austria with the Reich – one can only say, thank God we have found home!'[75]

If Glaser gave political consent for National Socialism, we can regard his compliance with the Austrofascist state as professional expedience. His chief concern after 1933 had been the preservation of his publishing rights to the point of exploiting the rivalry between the *Heimatschutz* and local Fatherland Front officials in order to secure political immunity for his newspaper. Even after he handed over the reins of his newspaper to his son, Reinhold, in July 1935, Glaser continued to work in the editorial offices in Salzburg and with press officials in Vienna.[76] He complied with the regime whenever the interests of his newspaper were at stake, and it was only due to his fortuitous professional and personal connections that he advanced to a position of relatively high standing in the Austrofascist press chamber for an owner of a German-nationalist organ in Salzburg.

The relationship between consent and compliance also highlights the extent of collaboration between German-nationalists and Austrofascists, which this book seeks to define. Their relationship was less complex than the relations between state and oppositional groups under regimes where resistance and collaboration were fraught with consequences far worse than censorship or the loss of a publishing licence. The lines of consent for National Socialism can be seen in the *Salzburger Volksblatt*'s universal ethnic and civic identity discourses of pan-Germanism, which underscored the ethnic ties between German-speakers while asserting that National Socialism was the only path towards political union of the German nation. After the ban on the NSDAP editors tended to emphasize only an ethnic discourse of universal German nationhood and a few maintained private reservations about the short-term political strategies of the Nazis, but publicly they continued to adhere to National Socialist doctrines such as *Lebensraum* and positive Christianity. The lines of compliance with Austrofascism, on the other hand, can be seen in the construction of Austria's identity as a 'German Christian' state. Although Austrofascists adhered to an orthodox interpretation of Christian doctrines, while German-nationalists drew on the notion of positive Christianity, both linked Christianity with the belief that Austria was a German state. As we will see in the next chapter, German-nationalists and Austrofascists mined this dual heritage of Germandom and Christendom whenever and wherever the occasion rose to defend it: whether on the linguistic frontier of the *Ostmark* in Carinthia or among German-speaking minorities beyond Austria's borders, the state mobilized its national and religious resources to expand and legitimize its vision of pan-Germanism.

Notes

1 Archiv der Stadt Salzburg, PA 024, Hans Glaser, *Tagebuch* (hereafter Glaser, *Tagebuch*), 29 December 1933; 10 May 1938. Hanisch, 'Die Salzburger Presse', p. 359.

2 Felder, *Die historische Identität der österreichischen Bundesländer*, pp. 115–16.

3 Mark Cornwall, 'The Struggle on the Czech–German Language Border, 1880–1940', *English Historical Review* 109, 433 (1994), pp. 941–42. The following description of Glaser's background and career is drawn from his obituary in the *Mitteilungen der Gesellschaft für Salzburger Landeskunde* 101 (1961), pp. 343–44, and his biographical entry in Adolf Haslinger and Peter Mittermayr (eds), *Salzburger Kulturlexikon* (Salzburg: Residenz, 2001). In addition, Glaser's diary provides biographical details of key personalities at the *Salzburger Volksblatt* and public figures in Salzburg.

4 Robert A. Kann, *The Multinational Empire: Nationalism and National Reform in the Habsburg Monarchy 1848–1918*, vol. 1 (New York: Columbia University Press, 1950), p. 207; Pauley, 'Fascism and the *Führerprinzip*', p. 293.

5 On this practice of *Kindertausch* in the Czech lands, see Erich Zöllner, 'The Germans as an Integrating and Disintegrating Force', *Austrian History Yearbook* 3, 1 (1967), p. 229; Christian Promitzer, 'The South Slavs in the Austrian Imagination: Serbs and Slovenes in the Changing View from German Nationalism to National Socialism', in Nancy M. Wingfield (ed.), *Creating the Other: Ethnic Conflict and Nationalism in Habsburg Central Europe* (New York: Berghahn, 2003), p. 186; Pieter M. Judson, 'Nationalizing Rural Landscapes in Cisleithania, 1880–1914', in Wingfield (ed.), *Creating the Other*, pp. 135, 148n.15. See also Tara Zahra, 'Reclaiming Children for the Nation: Germanization, National Ascription and Democracy in the Bohemian Lands, 1900–1945', *Central European History* 37, 4 (2004): 501–43.

6 Michael Schmolke, 'Das Salzburger Medienwesen', in Heinz Dopsch and Hans Spatzenegger (eds), *Geschichte Salzburgs: Stadt und Land* (Salzburg: Anton Pustet, 1991), p. 1,975.

7 Ernst Hanisch, 'Die Salzburger Presse', pp. 350, 356–57. The Salzburg wing of the Greater German party unofficially dissolved itself in July 1932, thereafter joining ranks with the National Socialists until 1934, when the remaining members formed the obscure German People's Association for the Province of Salzburg (*Deutschen Volksverein für das Land Salzburg*). See Hanisch, 'Salzburg', p. 917.

8 Hanisch, 'Salzburg', p. 909; Morgan, *Fascism in Europe*, p. 72.

9 Hanisch, 'Die Salzburger Presse', p. 357.

10 Glaser, *Tagebuch*, 24 January 1933.

11 Glaser, *Tagebuch*, 22, 23 June 1934.

12 Glaser, *Tagebuch*, 30 October 1936; 29 September 1937.

13 Hanisch, 'Die Salzburger Presse', pp. 359–60; Schmolke, 'Das Salzburger Medienwesen', p. 1,980.

14 ÖStA/AdR, BKA/HD, Carton 10, ÖKVDA, 19 June 1937.

15 Ibid.

16 Leonhard Steinwender, *Christus im Konzentrationslager: Wege der Gnade und Opfers* (Salzburg: Otto Müller, 1946), p. 133.

17 Steinberg, *The Meaning of the Salzburg Festival*, pp. 130–31. On Dollfuss's support for a Catholic university in Salzburg, see Rudolf Ebneth, *Die österreichische Wochenschrift 'Der Christliche Ständestaat': Deutsche Emigration in Österreich 1933–1938* (Mainz: Matthias-Grünewald, 1976), p. 8.

18 Harald Waitzbauer, ' "San die Juden scho' furt?": Salzburg, die Festspiele und das jüdische Publikum', in Robert Kriechbaumer (ed.), *Der Geschmack der Vergänglichkeit: Jüdische Sommerfrische in Salzburg* (Vienna: Böhlau, 2002), p. 256.

19 See Steinberg, *The Meaning of the Salzburg Festival*, pp. 72–74.

20 Staudinger, 'Austrofaschistische "Österreich"-Ideologie', pp. 31–33.

21 Kenneth Segar, 'Austria in the Thirties: Reality and Exemplum', in Kenneth Segar and John Warren (eds), *Austria in the Thirties: Culture and Politics* (Riverside, CA: Ariadne, 1991).

22 Steinberg, *The Meaning of the Salzburg Festival*, p. 48.

23 See, for example, the notice for a public lecture in Salzburg by Ing. Vogl of the NSDAP in Munich. *Salzburger Volksblatt*, 31 January 1933, p. 6.

24 *Salzburger Volksblatt*, 6 March 1933 (Sonderausgabe), p. 2.

25 *Salzburger Volksblatt*, 7 March 1933, p. 6.

26 Glaser, *Tagebuch*, 7 March 1933.

27 *Salzburger Volksblatt*, 10 March 1933, p. 2.

28 See Chapter 2 on press laws.

29 *Salzburger Volksblatt*, 2 May 1933, p. 2.

30 Gerlinde Neureitner, 'Die Geschichte des *Salzburger Volksblattes* von 1870 bis 1942' (PhD dissertation, University of Salzburg, 1985), pp. 201, 207–9. See also *Salzburger Volksblatt*, 14 June 1933, p. 1.

31 *Salzburger Volksblatt*, 17 June 1933, pp. 1–2.

32 Botz, *Gewalt in der Politik*, pp. 215–17, 260–62.

33 Ibid., pp. 219–64; Hanisch, *Der Lange Schatten des Staates*, p. 149.

34 *Salzburger Volksblatt*, 28 June 1933, p. 1.

35 The editorial was written under the initial 'M', but Mayrhofer implied in a later editorial that he had written the editorial of 28 June to condemn acts of violence and also that he had openly and personally expressed his opinion to National Socialists regarding terrorism. See *Salzburger Volksblatt*, 4 January 1935, p. 5.

36 Hanisch, 'Die Salzburger Presse', p. 356.

37 *Salzburger Volksblatt*, 28 June 1933, pp. 1–2.

38 *Salzburger Volksblatt*, 30 June 1933, p. 6.

39 Glaser, *Tagebuch*, 29 June 1933. On Hueber, see C. Earl Edmondson, *The Heimwehr and Austrian Politics, 1918–1936* (Athens: University of Georgia Press, 1978), pp. 112, 114, 266.

40 Neureitner, 'Die Geschichte des *Salzburger Volksblattes* von 1870 bis 1942', pp. 212–13; Glaser, *Tagebuch*, 22 February 1934; 24 February 1934.

41 'Forderungsprogramm der Salzburger Heimwehr vom 8. Februar 1934', in Rudolf G. Ardelt (ed.), *Salzburger Quellenbuch: Von der Monarchie bis zum Anschluss* (Salzburg: Schriftenreihe des Landespressebüros, 1985), pp. 262–64.

42 Glaser, *Tagebuch*, 14 April 1934.

43 *Salzburger Volksblatt*, 28 March 1934, p. 1.

44 Glaser, *Tagebuch*, 20 September 1934.

45 Glaser, *Tagebuch*, 14 June 1934; 28 June 1934; 26 July 1934; 13 August 1934; 26 November 1934; 1 January 1935. See also Hanisch, 'Die Salzburger Presse', p. 363; Waltraud, *Salzburger Zeitungsgeschichte*, pp. 206, 211.

46 Glaser, *Tagebuch*, 28 June 1934.

47 See Jelavich, *Modern Austria*, p. 206; Brook-Shepherd, *The Austrians*, pp. 287–93. For a detailed account of the putsch, see Botz, *Gewalt in der Politik*, pp. 266–75.

48 Glaser, *Tagebuch*, 27 July 1934.

49 Neureitner, 'Die Geschichte des *Salzburger Volksblattes* von 1870 bis 1942', p. 216.

50 See, for example, *Salzburger Volksblatt*, 3 January 1935, p. 8; 14 April 1936, p. 8.

51 Neureitner, 'Die Geschichte des *Salzburger Volksblattes* von 1870 bis 1942', pp. 216–17.

52 *Salzburger Volksblatt*, 29 January 1936, p. 5.

53 *Salzburger Volksblatt*, 8 February 1936, p. 7.

54 *Salzburger Volksblatt*, 13 July 1936, p. 1.

55 Glaser, *Tagebuch*, 12 July 1936.

56 See above.

57 Glaser, *Tagebuch*, 14 May 1936; 31 March 1937. See also Neureitner, 'Die Geschichte des *Salzburger Volksblattes* von 1870 bis 1942', pp. 215, 218.

58 *Salzburger Volksblatt*, 3 November 1936, p. 1.

59 *Salzburger Volksblatt*, 24 December 1936, p. 1.

60 Ibid.

61 On Rosenberg and other Nazi paganists, see Richard Steigmann-Gall, *The Holy Reich: Nazi Conceptions of Christianity, 1919–1945* (Cambridge: Cambridge University Press, 2003).

62 See *Salzburger Volksblatt*, 1 September 1934, p. 2; 1 December 1934, pp. 2–3; 18 May 1936, pp. 1–2.

63 *Salzburger Volksblatt*, 9 June 1936, pp. 1–2.

64 *Salzburger Volksblatt*, 5 June 1937, pp. 2–3.

65 See, for example, *Salzburger Volskblatt*, 25 August 1937, p. 1.

66 *Salzburger Volksblatt*, 9 December 1937, pp. 1–2.

67 Ibid.

68 Hanisch, *Der Lange Schatten des Staates*, p. 321. On Seyss-Inquart's role as trustee, see Chapter 2.

69 Bärnthaler, 'Geschichte und Organisation der Vaterländische Front', pp. 210–12.

70 The Nazi formulation of positive Christianity first appeared in 1920 under Point 24 of the NSDAP's 'Twenty-Five Point Programme'. It emphasized charity in place of theology, esteemed Christ as a model anti-Semite, and sought to develop a new syncretism based on the confessional traditions of both Catholicism and Protestantism, although it relied heavily on a liberal Protestant heritage. See Steigmann-Gall, *The Holy Reich*.

71 *Salzburger Volksblatt*, 31 December 1937, p. 2.

72 Bärnthaler, 'Geschichte und Organisation der Vaterländische Front', pp. 211–14.

73 Ernst Hanisch, *Gau der guten Nerven: Die nationalsozialistische Herrschaft in Salzburg 1938–1945* (Salzburg: Anton Pustet, 1997), p. 31.

74 Glaser, *Tagebuch*, 26 January 1938.

75 Glaser, *Tagebuch*, 18 March 1938.

76 Neureitner, 'Die Geschichte des *Salzburger Volksblattes* von 1870 bis 1942', p. 217. Reinhold Glaser was chief editor of the *Salzburger Volksblatt* from July 1937 to February 1938. See Waltraud, *Salzburger Zeitungsgeschichte*, p. 211.

4

Reich Germans, *Auslandsdeutsche* and minorities

'Long Live the Greater German Empire', the editors of the *Wiener Neueste Nachrichten* heralded the *Anschluss* on 12 March 1938. The next day Hitler's rallying cry to his homeland, 'Long Live National Socialist German Austria', took up half the newspaper's front page.[1] The variation in headlines may have gone unnoticed by the newspaper's jubilant readers, but it is significant for our assessment of pan-Germanism in the 1930s. Was the union of Reich Germans and Austrian Germans in 1938 the fulfilment of German-nationalist aspirations for pan-German unity since 1848, or did it signify a departure from the Austrian imperial idea of a German sphere of influence over non-Germans? In 1933, some German-nationalists expressed caution at the violent extremes of National Socialism, and a few went so far as to denounce National Socialism and curry favour with the Austrofascist regime, but all remained firm in their belief that a genuine nationalist movement, including National Socialists, would ultimately bring about political unity in a greater-German state, one in which German minorities abroad would have a home and non-Germans would be forced to dissimilate from their non-German identities once and for all.

Fortunately for these true believers, Austrofascists also cherished the hope that former National Socialists and their fellow travellers could be rehabilitated into the Fatherland Front. Accordingly, the state sought to harness their talents and experiences on Austria's linguistic frontiers. The merging of state policy and nationalist activism can best be seen in the activities and publications of the Austrian Association for Germandom Work Abroad (ÖVVA), established in 1934 to foster ties with German minorities outside Austria. The intersections between state propaganda and policy on the one hand, and nationalist activism in the coordinated public sphere of the state on the other, show how Austrofascists and German-nationalists each sought to define the particular and universal expressions of Austrian pan-German identity – Austria as a German state and Austria within the German nation – in the years before *Anschluss*.

Austrian Germans and Reich Germans

On the eve of Hitler's appointment to the German chancellorship on 30 January 1933, the *Wiener Neueste Nachrichten* endorsed National Socialism as the path to Austro-German unity and identified opponents of the party as enemies of a future greater-German state. First in line for attack were the Austrian clergy, followed by Catholic voters in Austria and Germany. On 24 January 1933, the newspaper published an excerpt from Bishop Gföllner's pastoral letter, entitled 'On True and False Nationalism', which condemned National Socialism's 'un-Christian' ideology and its racism and emphasized the spiritual and cultural dimensions of 'true' nationalism in contrast to the 'false' nationalism of National Socialism. The dichotomy between true and false nationalism also served as an anti-Semitic platform in the bishop's letter, although the editorial piece accompanying the article did not make reference to it.[2] Instead the editors sought to discredit the bishop's moral authority by claiming that his office had been outspoken about such 'trivial' matters as the fashion industry, swimming after dark and girls' participation in gymnastics. But more significant than their anti-clericalism was the editors' sharp censuring of Gföllner's comments that the Austrian state and not the German nation provided the true identity for Austrians. The editorial warned that the bishop's diminution of German nationhood was offensive to the national sensibilities of Austrians and could unleash a dangerous political struggle in Austria.[3] By invoking such a tone of higher moral authority, the editors sought to undermine the Church's position in the matter of Austria's national interest.

A report about Bavarian voters in the March 1933 German elections revealed a similar attempt to discredit the Catholic Church and Austria's Christian Social Party in particular. The newspaper claimed the National Socialists' success in Germany as an occasion for all Austrians to share in and pointed to the result in Bavaria, where the Nazi vote reached over 900,000, as evidence of the popular support for National Socialism in 'a stronghold of political Catholicism'.[4] The newspaper failed to mention that the Nazis had pressured Bavarian peasants to vote, resulting in higher voter participation figures of up to 95 per cent in some areas, and it was these new voters who provided the biggest increase of votes for the NSDAP in Bavaria, from 30.5 per cent to 43.1 per cent, rather than significant losses by Catholic parties.[5] Warning that the Nazis' electoral success in Germany sent a message to Austria's Christian Social government that nationalism was a more powerful force than 'political Catholicism', the editors declared that religion was no barrier to national ideology. Here the newspaper showed a familiar strategy – used successfully three decades earlier by

Beurle's Upper Austrian German-nationalists – of trying to appeal to a wider audience on the basis of national, rather than confessional loyalties.

The newspaper's derision of 'political Catholicism', and of its representatives in Gföllner and the Christian Social Party, indicates how closely the newspaper stood to National Socialism at this point. National Socialists frequently used the term 'political Catholicism' to attack a range of their opponents; in the first instance, the term referred to Catholics in public life who posed a threat to the political aims of Nazis, but it was also used whenever a church dignitary or organ of the Catholic Church criticized National Socialism or Nazi Germany, as in the case of Gföllner's pastoral letter, and implied that the accused bishop, priest or newspaper was a Vatican agent meddling in state affairs.[6] National Socialists also used the term to denounce their ideological opponents, not necessarily on the grounds of being Catholic.[7] Austrian German-nationalist editors and journalists were mostly predisposed towards this third use of the term since they usually had no particular axe to grind against members of the clergy, except when it came to support for Nazi Germany. As we saw in Salzburg, priests were active in local associations and press circles and attacks against clergy at the provincial level were rare in Austria before 1938. Carinthia's Slovenian-speaking priests were the exception to the rule, as we will see below, and even then their removal from office by German-nationalists was motivated by nationalism rather than anti-clericalism since they were replaced by German-speaking priests.

The editors of the *Wiener Neueste Nachrichten* continued to align themselves with National Socialists after Dollfuss introduced the March emergency decrees. They accused the government of attacking the civil liberties of German-nationalists and National Socialists and called for a German-nationalist opposition front that would prevent the anti-German extremes of the Dollfuss regime and restore Austria's diplomatic standing with Germany.[8] Relations between Austria and Germany finally broke off in May when Hitler retaliated against the Austrian government's decision to expel the Bavarian Justice Minister, Hans Frank, by issuing a 1,000-mark tariff on every German traveller to Austria. The German government eventually lifted the tariff under the terms of the July Agreement in 1936, but in the meantime the travel ban had crippled Austria's tourism industry and this explains partly why the Austrian propaganda ministry sought to promote Austria as a tourist destination for Britons especially, as we saw in Chapter 2. The Viennese editors responded to this latest diplomatic crisis by appealing for a national coalition to rebuild ties with Germany, reiterating their earlier calls for the Austrian government to lift political restrictions against members of the NSDAP.[9] Their overtures for a united coalition of German-nationalist groups in Austria showed that the editors regarded National Socialists as an integral but not exclusive force in the political struggle for Austro-German unity.

The editors' support for National Socialists wavered during the June violence and they were quick to distance their agenda for *Anschluss* from terrorism, describing acts of violence as on the 'periphery' of National Socialism. The explosions outside Nazi headquarters in Leopoldstadt and two parcel bomb explosions that killed two people and injured several bystanders were 'deeds that originate in criminal instinct' and unrelated to politics.[10] A front-page editorial on 13 June supported the Austrian government's response to punish criminals and called for the country's leaders to put in place security measures that would reassure Austrians of the government's commitment to justice and peace.[11] Yet the following day, the editors lashed out at the government's accusations of treason against National Socialists and asserted that a ban on the party violated the 1918 constitution affirming German-Austria as a constituent member of the German Republic.[12] Though declaring their abhorrence of violence, the editors continued to uphold the legitimacy of a greater-German ideology, which they sought to defend from anti-Nazi and anti-German attacks.

The assassination of Chancellor Dollfuss during the failed Nazi putsch on 25 July 1934 was the final nail in the coffin for the editors' hopes of a united nationalist front. The following day, the *Wiener Neueste Nachrichten* condemned the rebels' action and called for an end finally to the violence. 'It is clear that the death of Federal Chancellor Dr Dollfuss will not change anything about Austria's political system and that it will most likely . . . call into play initially a tightened course of action against National Socialism in which international politics will have a strong say.' Resigning themselves to an era where great power diplomacy would determine Austria's fate, the editors acknowledged that National Socialist designs for the immediate future of Austro-German relations were seditious in an age of terrorism. 'What has taken place in the past year in Austria and in the relationship between the two German states belongs to the saddest and most depressing chapter of German history. It is hoped that yesterday's black day will put an end to it. Stop the terrorism!'[13]

The newspaper's change of course from affirming the role of National Socialism in Austrian politics in early 1933 to condemning the party's violent extremes was due also in part to changes in the editorship. The newspaper's key personalities have recently come to light in the memoir of a prominent Austrian liberal journalist, Milan Dubrovic (1903–94), who held editorial posts at the *Wiener Allgemeine Zeitung* and the *Neue Wiener Tagblatt*. In his memoir published in 1985, Dubrovic recalls that the greater-German ideology of the *Wiener Neueste Nachrichten* was made a mockery of in Viennese journalistic witticisms and Dubrovic himself divulges that the newspaper occasionally lapsed into 'a fantasy world of teutonic romance'. Yet Dubrovic writes that at the time 'one distinguished between *grossdeutsch-* and National Socialist-oriented journalists'. Hans Mauthe, the most prominent personality at the *Wiener Neueste Nachrichten* after he became editor-in-chief of the newspaper in July 1933, was according to Dubrovic a 'democratic-greater-German opponent of National Socialism' who believed that the success of Hitler would bring about the destruction of the greater-German idea. The Austrofascist government apparently believed that Mauthe could be useful as an ally in their campaign against National Socialists. After Dollfuss's assassination Schuschnigg appointed Mauthe as government commissioner of the *Wiener Neueste Nachrichten*, a position normally filled by functionaries of the Fatherland Front or the *Heimwehr*. A government representative was appointed to the editorship as well, but Mauthe remained at the helm until 1938. Mauthe's views were anathema to some of his National Socialist colleagues at the newspaper. Alfred Petrou, for example, a former editor of the National Socialist newspaper *Deutschösterreichische Tageszeitung*, was the newspaper's foreign editor from 1929 to 1939. Other colleagues shared Mauthe's opposition to National Socialism, including the feuilleton writer, Arnold Wasserbauer, and the theatre critic, Alois Nagler, who both held only marginal influence next to a senior editorial figure, such as Petrou.[14]

Yet Dubrovic fails to shed light on Mauthe's complicity with National Socialists, a discretion typical of Second Republic political alliances: after 1945 Dubrovic worked alongside Mauthe in the editorship of the liberal *Presse*. Mauthe was one of the members of the 'National Action' group who met Schuschnigg and other government representatives in October 1934 to discuss the integration of Nazis and German-nationalists into the Fatherland Front. Present at the meeting were Schuschnigg; his deputy and leader of the Fatherland Front, Starhemberg; general secretary of the Fatherland Front, Walter Adam; head of the federal press agency, Eduard Ludwig; and the representatives of 'National Action', including the National Socialist leader, Walter Riehl; former Greater German representatives, Hermann Foppa and Franz Langoth; ex-*Heimatschutz* chief in Salzburg and brother-in-law of Hermann Göring, Franz Hueber; as well as Mauthe. Following his appointment to the chancellorship, Schuschnigg had attempted to conciliate National Socialists by supporting the Austrian Refugee Relief Society, which provided aid for the families of Nazis who were in prison or who had fled Austria after the failed putsch. Schuschnigg also advocated for Nazis to join the Fatherland Front, but on an individual basis rather than integrating them as a whole, and he encouraged the formation of a National Unity Front within the Fatherland Front comprising

German-nationalist organizations. The existing leadership structures of these organizations were to be further dismantled by the appointment of prominent German-nationalists to leadership positions in the Unity Front. The meeting on 27 October 1934 between representatives of the government and the 'National Action' group can therefore be seen as part of a selection process of appointing German-nationalists to these roles and evidently Schuschnigg had Mauthe in mind for such an appointment. However, it became clear to Schuschnigg at this meeting that the radical wing of the NSDAP could not be held in check by any leadership of a proposed National Front, so he abandoned this idea and committed instead to a regime of control and coercion inside the Fatherland Front.[15] One of the ways we shall see how this control and coercion was exercised is the recruitment of German-nationalist activists to the Fatherland Front's 'Germandom Work' section. Another method we have already seen was in the appointment of moderate German-nationalists, such as Mauthe in Vienna and Glaser in Salzburg, to senior positions not just in their own newspapers but also in the federal press bodies of the Austrofascist state.

Insofar as its editors were able to redefine their pan-Germanism to suit the new era of Austrian patriotism and anti-Nazi rhetoric, the *Wiener Neueste Nachrichten* was not unlike its Catholic counterpart in Vienna, the *Reichspost*. Known in Austrofascist circles for its National Socialist sympathies, the *Reichspost* was regarded by Dollfuss as a potential threat to his patriotic politics and in 1933 he supported prominent German Catholic refugees to establish a weekly journal, *Der Christliche Ständestaat* (The Christian Corporate State), as an unofficial mouthpiece of the Austrofascist regime and a rival organ to the *Anschluss*-friendly *Reichspost*.[16] Peter Malina's study of the *Reichspost*'s reportage of church politics in Nazi Germany has shown how the newspaper's editors blurred the official anti-Nazi line and an unofficial admiration for what National Socialism had achieved in Germany in stamping out the Church's twin enemies of bolshevism and liberalism.[17] An example of this blurring can be seen in an editorial on 1 October 1934 written by the newspaper's co-editor and former Christian Social politician, Heinrich Mataja (1877–1937). 'We shall promote and support whatever is good and noble and pan-German in National Socialism. When it degenerates into intolerant party politics and an un-German despotism, then we will fight against it. While we welcome every move towards a common understanding, and well beyond that to pan-German brotherhood, as steadfast Austrians we shall oppose all force, all brutality. Long live the German people, Austria for the Austrians!'[18] Mataja's recoil from National Socialism's 'un-German despotism' and the ignoble violence of Nazis was merely a defensive logic against the party's extremes and not against the movement itself. Like the *Wiener Neueste*

Nachrichten editors, who showed only marginally less restraint than the *Reichspost* in endorsing National Socialism, Mataja with his avowal of a 'pan-German brotherhood' indicated the extent of his newspaper's ongoing commitment to Austro-German relations alongside National Socialist designs for unity.

The most prominent personality at the *Reichspost*, Friedrich Funder (1872–1959), was the newspaper's chief editor and a close adviser to both Dollfuss and Schuschnigg on matters of press politics. Funder's position towards National Socialism has been the subject of several studies, but among the more vivid examples of his pan-Germanism were his vitriolic attacks against the sociologist and political writer, Ernst Karl Winter (1895–1959), in late 1936.[19] Winter was a member of a group of centre-left Catholic intellectuals, the so-called 'Austrian Action' circle named for a collection of essays the group published in 1927. Their writings blended pan-European sentiment with the idea of an Austrian nation in the tradition of a *Staatsnation*. While they acknowledged Austria as the 'German-speaking centre of Europe', they rejected a pan-German community in preference for an 'Austrian man' who was ethnically a mix of Slav and German and more concerned with humanity and knowledge than with power and progress. As Austrian patriots still loyal to the empire, they upheld the legitimacy of monarchical states and advocated a 'social monarchy' as a form of government that would 'stand on the right' against democratic liberalism, but 'think with the left' in its support of the proletariat.[20] After the ban on the Social Democrats in February 1934, Dollfuss appointed Winter third deputy mayor of Vienna to appease the workers' movement, but Schuschnigg demoted him in 1936 after the initiative failed to attract workers' support.[21] Winter was also demoted because his book, *Monarchie und Arbeiterschaft* (Monarchy and the Working Class), published after the July Agreement in 1936, criticized Schuschnigg's rapprochement with National Socialists. In a series of editorials in the *Reichspost*, Funder described Winter's idea of a common front of Catholics, socialists, communists, democrats and 'authoritarian-fascists' against National Socialists as a 'trojan horse' and his writings as the 'sentences . . . of an intellectually abnormal literary type'.[22] Funder devoted much copy to attacking Winter's book and it is plausible that his public criticism influenced Schuschnigg's decision to remove Winter from office on 24 October 1936. In an editorial the day prior to his removal, Funder wrote: 'Dr Ernst Karl Winter's dance around the Kremlin has reached the high point of his idiotic frenzy. But it must also be the final point!'[23] The hyperbole with which Funder carried out his own frenzied attacks against an intellectual opponent should not surprise, but what made these attacks emblematic of his pan-Germanism, rather than just personal or professional dislike, was his unwillingness to clutch at even one straw of Winter's arguments about Germans and Slavs or to deconstruct the idea of an 'Austrian man'. What Funder was unwilling to do, in short, was to trample on ground that may have undermined Austria's relationship with Germany. Better to leave alone the political implications of Winter's ideas and attack instead his intellectual credentials. His alacrity in pursuing an opponent of pan-Germanism in the new era of Austro-German détente also explains Funder's vitriole on this occasion.

As well as to mainstream Catholic newspapers, the *Wiener Neueste Nachrichten* can be compared to the provincial German-nationalist press. The *Grazer Tagespost* was Austria's leading regional German-nationalist newspaper, as we saw in Chapter 2, whose beginnings in 1883 corresponded with the expansion of nationalist associations and new forms of provincial activism. By the 1930s it was more closely aligned with National Socialism in its conception of the national community than its Viennese and Salzburg counterparts. An editorial on 4 January 1933 defined the national community as one in which all Germans, despite their political background, worked together in a common community of labour: a conscientious truck driver was just as German as an alpine farmer. The editors' vision of a universal nation bound by blood and soil was implicit in the image of the German alpine farmer in a German 'labour community', but at the same time the reference to a 'conscientious' driver also belied the editors' prejudice against the stereotypical worker, who had a tendency to be less industrious, and perhaps less German, than the alpine farmer.[24] The editors also believed this universal pan-German identity was dependent on the particular expression of what was uniquely Austrian in the German 'Ostmark'. A 'strong sense of what is Austrian [and] a general sense of what is East March German (*Ostmarkdeutschtum*) does not stand in contradiction to pan-German ideas, but is, rather, the necessary pre-requisite'.[25] The reference to an *Ostmarkdeutschtum* appeared repeatedly in *Tagespost* editorials and had a different connotation from the Catholic use of the term as we saw in Chapter 3. Whereas Catholics referred to Austria as the bearer and representative of German Christendom in the East Marches of the old Holy Roman Empire, German-nationalists used the term in reference to Austria's position on the borderlands of the German nation. On 4 July 1933, the editors lamented that the 'unfortunate feud' between the German and Austrian governments 'makes it seemingly impossible for the best person to be a good Austrian and a good German at the same time'. Without a 'synthesis of what is Austrian and German (*Österreichertum und Deutschtum*)', the editorial concluded that there could be no peace in

Austria.[26] Analogous in tone to the earlier editorial in January, this statement reaffirmed the editors' commitment to both a particular and universal pan-German creed.

Coverage of local NSDAP events throughout 1933 showed that the editors saw National Socialism as the only true heir of the *Ostmark*. In April 1933, for example, the newspaper reported on the political agreement between the Styrian *Heimatschutz* and the provincial wing of the NSDAP in the Upper Styrian town of Liezen. The *Heimatschutz* leaders already received financial support from Nazi Germany (though the newspaper did not print that) and by signing the agreement on 22 April they now declared allegiance to Hitler as leader of the German nation, seeking common political goals between the two organizations but affirming their autonomy and separate identities. The sign of unity was to be a swastika armband, which was banned after Dollfuss issued a general prohibition on uniforms in May.[27] A week following the agreement in Liezen, the *Tagespost* reported that the Styrian leaders of the Greater German party had resolved to join the NSDAP-*Heimatschutz* front. The editors stated that the 'Hitlerite movement' had penetrated deep into Styria's conservative middle-class and agrarian circles, effectively ending the Greater Germans' role as a second national front in Austria.[28] These reports showed the editors' loyalty was first to National Socialists, and secondly to other German-nationalists, whom they saw not as equal partners in a united national front, but as fellow 'Hitlerites' under the symbol of the swastika. Readers of the *Tagespost* would have had direct knowledge of these local events, and many were likely to have been personally involved in the formation of the NSDAP-*Heimatschutz*-Greater German pact. They expected of their newspaper not just a faithful account of what had taken place, but also an editorial comment that would affirm their belief in National Socialism. On this occasion, the editors did not leave them disappointed.

Whereas the Vienna editors had tactfully withdrawn their support for political unity with Germany following the Nazi violence, the *Tagespost* editors did not condemn the attacks and opted instead for a more expedient solution. In January 1934, the newspaper's editor-in-chief, Julius Keil, wrote to the director of the federal press agency, Ludwig, to offer his willingness to publish official press releases. The manoeuvre won him high esteem from top ministry officials, including Chancellor Dollfuss, but the *Tagespost* forfeited a significant block of its readership for this backdown from its previous support for National Socialism, losing 6,000 subscriptions over the course of nine months.[29] Keil was forced to make further concessions to the government in June 1934 by appointing a government official as the Viennese correspondent and, after Dollfuss's assassination in July 1934, a *Heimwehr* deputy, Baron Rudolf Kapri, was made political editor of the *Tagespost*.[30] After the July Agreement, the newspaper's chief editor, Keil, exerted pressure on the federal press authorities in Vienna to remove Kapri from the political editorship. He had the support of the Styrian provincial governor, Karl Maria Stepan, and eventually on 4 November 1936, Keil was able to replace Kapri with the previous political editor, Max Zaversky.[31] In addition to these concessions, the *Tagespost* was also one of five Austrian newspapers allowed to circulate in Germany under the terms of the Gentlemen's Agreement, giving the editors licence to comment on Austro-German relations so long as they refrained from criticism of the Austrian government.[32]

Lavish front-page coverage of German Foreign Minister Konstantin von Neurath's visit to Vienna in February 1937 indicated the editorial changes in the *Tagespost* that had taken place following the July Agreement.[33] During his two-day visit, which was marked by Nazi demonstrations on his arrival and a counter-demonstration by the Fatherland Front on his departure, Neurath held discussions with Schuschnigg and demanded, among other things, that German citizens in Austria be allowed to wear the swastika and give the Nazi salute. He also wanted the Austrian government to allow the repatriation of Austrian Nazis who had fled to Germany as refugees after the party's ban in June 1933 and in the wake of Dollfuss's assassination during the failed Nazi coup of July 1934.[34] Neurath's visit sent a warning to Austria's leaders of Germany's intentions in Austria and the *Tagespost* editors were fully aware of its significance for the future of Austro-German relations.

Throughout 1937 the editors threw caution to the wind and vented their exasperation with the Austrian government's continued restrictions on National Socialists. An editorial on 26 November 1937, entitled 'Wishes and Expectations', accused the government of reneging on its commitment to build a 'state of national honour', a phrase the editors lifted directly from a speech by Front secretary, Zernatto. The editors appropriated Zernatto's vocabulary of a state for the young generation, not for 'the disinterested' or 'the reactionaries'. They warned that opposition to the spirit of the July Agreement must indeed be seen as 'reactionary' and, addressing Zernatto himself, it seemed, the editors declared that 'Time has moved on past a person who confuses responsibility and rebuilding with fits of hysteria, only ever wanting to hold demonstrations with outdated slogans or carry out purges and meanwhile fails to notice that he is still embroiled in party rancour and civil war passions; such a person remains consumed by hate and stands as a living memorial to a reactionary past. There is no place for him in a "State of National Honour", which the young generation is to shape.' The editors' veiled references to the Fatherland Front's demonstrations during Neurath's visit to Austria, to the role of the 'young generation', as well as to the government's purges of Nazis, was the newspaper's boldest statement of support for National Socialism since the party's ban in 1933. The editorial ended with a call for National Socialists to be permitted to help shape the new German Austrian state: 'What positive energies full of a fanatic will for rebuilding, activity and joy in the future will have been gained for the state once they know that the state also belongs to them! A new field of action lies before us. If it is pursued and claimed, then only one victor will emerge out of the years of upheaval: German Austria!'[35]

The *Tagespost* did not immediately report the meeting at Berchtesgaden between Hitler and Schuschnigg on 12 February 1938 in accordance with instructions from the press and propaganda ministry warning against premature agitation.[36] The meeting had been less a meeting than a summons to which Schuschnigg had been called to accept Hitler's demands of an alignment with Germany's foreign policy, the immediate appointment of Arthur Seyss-Inquart as Interior Minister and a general amnesty of all imprisoned Austrian Nazis. Hitler made clear his intention to occupy Austria militarily if Schuschnigg did not comply within three days on all of the major demands.[37] The following day, 13 February, the *Tagespost* editors cautiously greeted the news from Berchtesgaden, although the headline story was actually the departure of the German ambassador in Austria, Franz von Papen, who had been recalled to Berlin following the Berchtesgaden talks.[38] Finally, on 16 February a front-page editorial announced with obvious jubilation that 'a happy day' had come to Austria and that the recent developments in Austro-German relations only affirmed what Austrians already believed was their common future with Germany. 'In Austria it has never been questioned that the Austrian people can only pursue their further spiritual, cultural and material development within the framework of pan-German interests.' The editors brushed aside any 'incidents' in the recent past that had seemed contradictory to this view for they had 'not been able to shake the belief that everything would be brought back into line in the near future.'[39]

Following the Berchtesgaden talks, the editors reverted to their pre-1934 vocabulary of a synthesis between '*Österreichertum*' and '*Deutschtum*'. A front-page editorial on 5 March 1938 gave guarded praise for Schuschnigg's speech at the opening of the press exhibition, which we saw in Chapter 2 was organized by the Austrian press and propaganda ministry. The *Tagespost* welcomed the chancellor's choice of 'wise and conciliatory words' that conveyed 'the necessary synthesis of good German and good Austrian'. However, the editors expressed their frustration that government representatives were still 'talking as if "German" and "Austrian" are opposed to one another'. 'Those who support the idea of a fatherland', the editors insisted, 'should not be afraid of saying the word "German" ';

nor should 'the National Socialist feel obliged . . . to avoid mentioning anything Austrian. One must have the courage to admit, without being afraid of losing one's own sense of identity, that on the other side of the border, great and wonderful things are also being done'[40]

In view of these unambiguous motions of support for National Socialism and Austria's inclusion in the Nazi German state, it is surprising that editorial changes were made on the eve of *Anschluss*. Among those editors suddenly deposed by Nazi commissioners was the political editor, Zaversky, who had been replaced earlier by a *Heimwehr* editor in July 1934 and had then been reinstated following the July Agreement in 1936. It is unclear why he was replaced in March 1938 since the fact that Zaversky was forced aside from the political editorship after the failed Nazi putsch and reinstated after the resumption of Austro-German relations is an indication of his political sympathies with National Socialists. Another editor, Oskar Stanglauer, was also replaced on account of his Jewish wife.[41] But in spite of the eleventh-hour intervention from the Nazi authorities, who presumably saw a change in personnel as the only sure means of adherence to the party line, the *Tagespost* editors had remained consistent on all other fronts in promoting a version of pan-Germanism that resembled National Socialist designs for pan-German unity.

Austrian German-nationalists saw the advent of Nazi politics as the catalyst for propelling Austrian Germans and Reich Germans closer together in a universal pan-German community, although some were reticent to acknowledge National Socialism's exclusive ideological ownership over that community. A number of prominent Austrofascist personalities and organs that sympathized with National Socialism also hesitated to disclaim Nazis altogether for fear of selling out the pan-German idea. The common interest of German-nationalists and Austrofascists between 1933 and 1938 rested on this commitment to Austria's place in the German nation. There were points of divergence, to be sure, especially as Nazis turned to terror and Dollfuss's assassination led some who had previously sympathized with them to question their methods. But the July Agreement cast aside many of those doubts and, once again, German-nationalists and Austrofascists went in to bat for the pan-German idea and defended that idea vigorously against those who would seek to dismantle its legitimacy. If rapprochement had not been achieved between Reich Germans and Austrian Germans prior to 1938, it had long been realized between the supporters of pan-Germanism in both 'camps' of Austrian politics.

On the occasion of the *Wiener Neueste Nachrichten*'s tenth anniversary in October 1935, readers wrote to the editors with messages of congratulations.[42] Letters came in from prominent German-nationalists including Richard Bahr, commentator on minority politics in the *Wiener Neueste*

Nachrichten and author of a book on German minorities published in 1933, *Volk jenseits der Grenzen* (The Nation on the Other Side of the Border), as well as representatives from commerce, the civil service union, former Greater German politicians, and German-nationalist women's associations. Paula Kraus wrote to the editors on behalf of the '*Volksgemeinschaft*' League of German Women, declaring that over the past decade the *Wiener Neueste Nachrichten* had been 'a signpost for us that we have gladly and willingly followed'. A few state functionaries were also among the list of well-wishers, including Eduard Ludwig and the chair of the Austrofascist Union of Journalists, Hermann Mailer.[43]

Such an impressive line-up of readers, community leaders and politicians indicates the esteem in which the *Wiener Neueste Nachrichten*'s editorship was held. If there was any further doubt about the newspaper's loyalty to Austria, it was dispelled in an editorial marking the tenth anniversary edition, which professed the editors' steadfast commitment to Austria's interests as a German state and a part of the German nation: 'The *Wiener Neueste Nachrichten* is an Austrian paper. We do not see, as sometimes is the case, cultivating love for our Austrian homeland as opposed to cultivating the pan-German idea, but rather, the one as an extension of the other. The Austrian is a German, and Germany – we differentiate the term Germany from the German Empire – is not possible without Austria.' Apparently thinking they had been commissioned to author the new school textbooks for the Austrofascist Education Ministry, the editors wrote: 'Austria is a German country, and has been from the beginning, according to which, by virtue of its geographical position, its thousand-year history and the particular character of its culture and the nature of its inhabitants, it is allotted its own task within the framework of the German cultural mission in Europe.' They went on to acknowledge the 'tribal' particularity of Austria within the German nation, but warned against any levelling down or distorted representations of Austria's national character, as in the writings of the 'Austrian Action' group. 'One must guard against exaggerations – on both sides. It is just as false to see an Austrian as lazy, sloppy and weak, as it is wrong to regard him as a particular species, "an Austrian man", or see him as part of a particular Austrian nation.' As final evidence of a well-balanced commitment to both the Austrian state and the German nation, the editors pointed to their habit of speaking up for Germans 'whenever a cry for help is heard'.[44] Their activism on behalf of Carinthian German-nationalists and German minorities outside Austria, endorsed by the state, as we will see, showed that it was irrelevant whether the cry for help was genuine or contrived. No small 'exaggeration' was too great for the sake of the national community.

Slovene Austrians or German Slovenes?

Schools and monuments remained the sites of nationalist battles in the Austrian press in the 1930s, just as they had been prior to 1914. But as Pieter Judson has argued, where nationalists before the war constructed the frontier myth in order to legitimize their nationalizing projects in the empire, in the interwar period they sought to remake the state and its entire population writ large into a borderland.[45] The battle for German Austria in the 1930s appropriated the old national discourses and projects, but legitimized them in the new era of state building by rebirthing the Austrian state, palingenetically, on the frontier. Austria was to be reborn through a process of ethnic dissimilation, which meant that inferior groups would be required to assimilate to the German language and culture while gradually detaching from non-German languages and cultures. German-nationalists envisaged their borderland victories in terms of this evolutionary process since true victory came through popular will rather than brute force. They had no patience for short-term political solutions like minority rights, mired as these were in Old Austria, and instead they set their gaze on the horizons of Greater Germany.

German-nationalists disregarded minority rights for practical reasons, too, since the legal provisions for Austria's minorities in the interwar period, set out in the 1920 constitution, had been lifted directly from the 1867 Basic State Law Regarding the General Rights of Citizens. Article 149 of the 1920 constitution, taken from the original Article 19 in the 1867 law, guaranteed Austria's minorities the right to maintain and cultivate their own national identity and language, including every child's entitlement to 'the requisite means for education in its own language without the use of compulsion in regard to learning a second language of the province'. However, this provision on education in bilingual areas was juxtaposed against Article 8 in the 1920 constitution, which stated that 'the German language is the language of the state without affecting adversely the rights conceded by federal law to the linguistic minorities'.[46] German-nationalists exploited this ambiguity at every opportunity to prove that there were no linguistic minorities in Austria since non-German-speakers had willingly embraced the German language and culture in the face of hostile opposition from those who would seek to claim them for irredentist purposes.

The German–Slovene language frontier in Carinthia was proof for German-nationalists of how one group (Slovenes) had already adopted the German language and culture and become thoroughly Germanized. They were not thoroughly German, however. They remained Germanized Slavs, who were in constant danger of being re-Slavicized by Slovene nationalists in Austria and in Yugoslavia. Carinthian German-nationalists propounded their theories on race and assimilation in articles and lectures that were reprinted in the press. Their central claim was that Slovenes could be divided into two groups: Slovene nationalists and assimilated (Germanized) Slovenes, or *Windische*. Derived from the old German word for Slav, *Wend*, the term *Windisch* by the end of the nineteenth century had come to define the linguistic and ethnic separateness of Carinthian Slovenes from ethnic Slovenes, who spoke and wrote in Standard Slovene. Academic specialists on south-eastern Europe in the 1920s and 1930s developed the *Windisch*-theory through their research on assimilated and nationalist Slovenes. Martin Wutte (1876–1948), a local Carinthian historian, archivist and academic adviser to the Austrian delegation at the Paris Peace Conference, was the most well known of these interwar racial experts. He defined *Windische* as those Slovenes who identified culturally and racially with German-speakers through 'natural assimilation', or intermarriage. The imagined ethnic border between Slovenes and *Windische* was seemingly affirmed by the result in the October 1920 plebiscite in Lower Carinthia, in which 59 per cent voted in favour of Austrian rule while 41 per cent voted to join the Kingdom of Serbs, Croats and Slovenes (renamed the Kingdom of Yugoslavia in 1929). Between 10,000 and 12,000 of the more than 22,000 who voted for Austria were Slovenes. Carinthian German-nationalists interpreted that statistic as evidence of a German identity among Slovenes, although Allied observers who visited the region at the time and historians ever since have speculated that Slovenes who identified with Austria did so out of class-consciousness, rather than national loyalty. Later, under National Socialist rule, the *Windisch*-theory became the basis of Aryanization policies in the province under which '*Windische*' were Germanized while 'ethnically conscious' Slovenes were resettled in the Reich. After 1941, however, this distinction was abolished.[47]

Several articles in the *Wiener Neueste Nachrichten* and the *Tagespost* discussed at length the alleged differences between '*Windische*' and 'Slovenes'. In March 1935, the *Wiener Neueste Nachrichten* took as its cue reports in the *Reichspost* that Yugoslavian students were planning to spend the summer with Slovenian families in Carinthia, distributing Slovenian books and newspapers to the families they stayed with as part of a larger irredentist mission in Lower Carinthia. On this occasion the apparent threat of Slovenian irredentism was not the core issue, as it would emerge in reports later that year. The author of the article also chose not to dwell on the long history of complaints by 'radical national Slovenes' of cultural and economic oppression. The evidence of a vibrant Slovene associational life and economy – 'one even hears that more money flows into Slovenian accounts than into German ones!' – could quickly quash any protest of

Slovene nationalists and their advocates on both sides of the Austro-Yugoslav border. Instead the article drew attention to the greatest advantage that the German population in Carinthia held over the 'radical national Slovenes', namely the *Windische* population, who for centuries had assimilated to the German language and culture and resisted Slovene nationalist attempts to force them to attend Slovene schools. Slovene nationalists would do well to note that the Germans and the 'German-friendly Slovenes' together made up a majority in Carinthia and, the article concluded, a 'minority right' could not therefore be imposed on a 'majority population'. Repeated declarations by the Carinthian Slovene press that Slovenes shared the same Austrian patriotism and Catholic faith as the rest of the Austrian population were 'excellent and very gratifying' but 'what has that to do with our problem?' Religion and state had little to do with the 'national problem' in Carinthia and the problem would only be resolved for both sides from the position of national politics, not confessional or state politics.[48] Once again we see in the German-nationalist press a tendency to frame anti-clericalism in terms of nationalism, partly out of compliance with the press laws, but mainly because the battle for German Austria was not against the Church, but against those refusing to become Germanized.

An article in May 1935 noted the efforts of Carinthian Slovenian politicians in lobbying the League of Nations to grant Lower Carinthia the status of an autonomous territory on the grounds that the 1923 and 1934 censuses in Austria had distorted the numbers of Slovenes living in the province. The Slovenian press, for example, had estimated that in addition to the 9,122 Slovenes officially counted in the 1934 census, there were some 21,424 people whom unofficial Slovenian sources could show had been wrongly classified as Germans. The *Wiener Neueste Nachrichten* stuck to its claim that Carinthia had a two-thirds majority German population (this time the newspaper did not mention the 'German-friendly' Slovenes who made up that majority), for whom the territorial integrity of the whole province was a historic and national right. History had already shown that Austria's Slovenian political parties saw territorial autonomy as a path towards the ultimate goal of annexation to Yugoslavia. 'We think of the demands made by Dr [Ante] Trumbic's Yugoslav Committee in London during the world war', the article ran, the same demands behind the words of the Slovenian priest who wrote on the eve of the 1920 plebiscite in the organ of the Carinthian Slovenes, *Koroški slovenec*: 'I . . . do not know any Slovenian priest who would not have sympathized with the Serbs, even if only in their hearts!' 'We also know', the *Wiener Neueste Nachrichten* chimed, 'and that is why we answer . . . no!' But just as the territorial division of Carinthia had been rejected in 'Old Austria', so it would be again in the new Austria since the 'thousand year history continues and in

Carinthia the future will be on the side of Germandom rather than Slavdom.[49] The author's explicit reference to Hitler's proclamation of a thousand-year rule over non-Germans revealed the newspaper's belief that the solution to the province's 'national problem' lay over the German border, not in the Austrofascist state.

Related to the *Windische* question was the issue of bilingual schools in Carinthia. The 'utraquistic' school system that Slovene nationalists had fought for and won in 1848 streamlined Slovene language classes alongside German classes, but Slovene instruction in these schools had been discouraged first by the liberals and then by German-nationalists, who relegated the Slovene language to the status of a remedial tool in the first years of schooling.[50] In the interwar period, German-nationalist activists of the *Südmark* schools' organization, supported by the *Heimatbund* (Homeland League) in the Carinthian government, waged a constant campaign against Slovenian-speaking teachers and priests. Fifty-eight priests were discharged from their clerical duties or transferred, to be replaced by German-speaking priests, and another 58 teachers were expelled from their posts, while private Slovenian schools were shut down and six utraquistic schools were also closed. Meanwhile, the *Südmark* schools' association built German schools and kindergartens in Slovenian-speaking towns with funds from Germany.[51] The influence of the *Heimatbund* began to subside towards the end of 1934, when the Carinthian parliament was finally dissolved and replaced by an Austrofascist administration on 1 November 1934.[52] Nonetheless, both the *Heimatbund* and the *Südmark* continued to exert pressure on local authorities and, as we will see, Austrofascist authorities recruited *Südmark* leaders in the Fatherland Front as much for their wealth of experience in local activism as for the state's efforts to prevent them otherwise going underground with National Socialists.[53]

In May 1935 Slovenian nationalists set out their demands for new bilingual schools. One of the demands included a provision that children be taught in Slovenian for the first four years of school with German to be introduced gradually into the curriculum starting with 2 hours in the first year, 4 in the second, and so on, before switching to German as the principle language of instruction in middle school with Slovenian taught for at least 6 hours a week. They also stipulated that teachers be proficient in both languages and pass a compulsory examination in Slovenian, overseen by a Slovenian school inspector. All these demands were duly noted (and translated into German) for readers of the *Wiener Neueste Nachrichten* in an extract from the Carinthian German-nationalist newspaper, *Freie Stimme*.[54] The response from the side of the Carinthian Germans appeared the following day by an anonymous 'freedom fighter', who explained that the problem with this and many other such articles in the *Koroški slovenec*

was that the newspaper never divulged details about where and to whom
these demands, in this case the bilingual schools, applied. Were such bilingual schools now to be built in areas where a majority German population
lived? 'Out of the question!' And it was equally out of the question for those
Slovenes who identified with the German culture, the author added: 'The
"*Windische*" most certainly will not let themselves be forced into the
Slovenian schools and Slavic cultural circles.'[55]

This was not the only time the newspaper spoke on behalf of Germanized Slovenes. On another occasion the editors published a letter from a
so-called '*Windische*', in which the author implored the editors of the
Wiener Neueste Nachrichten to publicize the struggle of the *Windische* in
their quest to remain independent of the Slovene nationalists in the province. 'Your newspaper has come to our aid on a number of previous occasions [and] we ask again for your help', a request that may also have implied
the Austrian authorities were not doing enough to help. 'We will not allow
ourselves, or our children, to be made into Slovenes, followers of the
Koroški slovenec. We will remain *Windische*. And the more that the *Koroški
slovenec* opposes us . . . the more we will say why we do not want to be
"Slovenes" and what the difference is between "Slovenes" and us "*Wind-
ischen*".' The writer illustrated one of these alleged differences by referring
to the children of Carinthian Slovenes who attended schools in Carniola
(Krain) in Yugoslavia. 'Slovenes are those who send their children to Krain,
so that they will return as fit Slovenian fighters. We *Windische* let our
children attend our Carinthian schools, they are just as good as the schools
in Krain and our children learn to get along with the Germans, with whom
they have to live.'[56] The letter was signed off 'with Carinthian greetings'
from F. Kordesch, which tells us little about the letter's provenance. It is
highly doubtful that the author was a Germanized Slovene who accepted
uncritically the German-nationalist *Windisch*-theory. It is more plausible
that the newspaper used a ghost writer, probably a Carinthian German-
nationalist and quite possibly the anonymous 'freedom fighter', to boast of
its reputation as an organ of the borderlands, whose cause had long been
central to the politics and activism of nationalists in Austria.

The debate in the Slovenian and German press about bilingual schools
coincided with Chancellor Schuschnigg's visit to Carinthia for a Fatherland
Front rally in Villach on 10 June 1935. Around seven thousand members
of youth organizations of the *Heimatschutz* and *Östmärkische Sturmscharen* (East Mark Storm Troops) attended the rally and although
Schuschnigg did not use national labels in addressing his listeners, he
sought to reassure them that the state was still committed to a German
path, which indicates his intention in attending the rally personally was to
appease German-nationalists in the province. At the same time he also

offered cautionary words that the new Austrian state had to be built up according to a new 'ethos', and not a 'myth' of national rebirth. Although Schuschnigg did not mention the Carinthian Slovenes, his call for a new ethos of state building appeared to affirm their loyalty to Austria and the Catholic Church.[57] Schuschnigg's own grandfather had been a Slovenian-speaker and Slovenian nationalists saw Schuschnigg as an advocate in their struggle against German-nationalists in Carinthia. But the chancellor's office adopted a far more ambivalent position, for example rejecting an official Slovenian translation of Austria's national anthem allegedly on the grounds that it was a mistranslation of the original German version. However, a more chauvinistic objection to the Slovenian version can be detected in the lyrics of one verse in the original German: 'earnest and honest German work, tender and warm German love' (deutsche Arbeit, ernst und erhrlich – deutsche Liebe, zart und weich), which was translated into Slovenian as 'a strong people lives here, honesty is at home here' (Ljudstovo krepko tu trebiva, tu postenost je doma).[58] Affirming on the one hand the patriotism and religious commitment of the Slovenes, while forcing them to sing about German labour and German love in the new Austrian state, probably seemed more mythical than ethical to Slovenian-speakers. But the larger point is that not only German-nationalists but also Austrofascist functionaries saw the borderlands as a symbolic 'cradle' in which the new Austria would be reborn.[59] That the rally was held four months before the fifteenth anniversary of the October 1920 plebiscite only emphasizes that memories of past victories in the borderlands, and lingering concerns about irredentism, animated Austrofascists' rhetoric and activism as much as German-nationalists'.

A few months after Schuschnigg's visit to Carinthia, a ceremony unveiling a commemorative prince's stone in the Yugoslavian town of Prävali (Prevalje), close to the border with Austria, provoked swift accusations of irrendentism in the German-nationalist press. The so-called Maria Saaler Prince's Stone, named after the church in Klagenfurt where the coronations of the dukes of Carinthia took place from the fourteenth century, had a contested heritage in Carinthia as Slovenian nationalists traced the prince's stone even further back to the early Middle Ages when the ceremonial installation of the princes of Carantania was celebrated in the Slovenian language, or rather the Slavic patois of the Carantanian population.[60] The original prince's stone remained in Klagenfurt after the partition of Carinthia in October 1920 and the unveiling of a replica stone on the Yugoslavian side of the border fifteen years after the partition incensed German-nationalists, who referred to it as the 'irredentist stone' in the headline of the Wiener Neueste Nachrichten on 21 September 1935.[61] Unlike the Yugoslavian student exchanges, whose irredentist motives were easier to suspect than prove, the staging of an event that traced its origins to a pre-Habsburg rite of royal succession smacked of Slovenian nationalist attempts to reclaim Lower Carinthia for Yugoslavia. The anonymous 'Carinthian freedom fighter' in the *Wiener Neueste Nachrichten* quoted the Slovenian member of Belgrade's parliament, Karl Dobersek, who spoke at the unveiling ceremony and addressed his fellow Slovenes living on the other side of the border in Austria: 'We swear to you that we will never forget you . . . To our brothers and sisters still living in hell, we declare our loyalty to our king and our people and the firmness of our borders.'[62] The author of the article exclaimed over Dobersek's assertion that his fellow Slovenes living in a foreign land had been consigned to a fate worse than death, a claim, if indeed Dobersek had made it, that matched the exaggerated claims and half-truths of the newspaper. But what apparently went over the head of the 'freedom fighter' and the Vienna editors who published the article, was Dobersek's alleged profession of loyalty to King Alexander of Yugoslavia, who had declared a dictatorship in 1929 and clearly was not the focus of the Slovenian nationalist commemoration of the prince's stone. Placing a written charter inside the stone as in a time capsule, blaming the result of the 1920 plebiscite on the hostility of the British and Italian representatives of the Allied commission, the Slovenes at Prevalje vowed to commemorate the ceremony of the prince's stone annually until the 'old right' of the Slovenian people was again restored.[63] German-nationalists may well have read this as an irredentist threat, but they also missed the subtext of the Slovenian declaration, which was more a provocation towards the Serb-dominated parliament and the Serbian king, whose British connections had paved the way for the creation of the Kingdom in 1918, than an ultimatum for Carinthian German-nationalists on the other side of the border.[64]

While Carinthia's southern frontier embodied the larger struggles of the Austrian state in the decade and a half following its border revisions, Carinthia's neighbour, Styria, had in fact lost the greater portion of its pre-war territory and also lost its borderland status in the eyes of German-nationalists. According to the interwar census data, Styria officially retained a Slovenian minority of less than one per cent of the province's population. However, the proportion of Slovenes vis-à-vis Germans in the pre-1918 region of Greater Styria had been substantially higher: more than a third of all Styrians in the pre-war period were Slovenes.[65] Yet unlike Carinthia, the partition of Styria had occurred without a plebiscite and so the national trauma of a borderland under siege was projected on to Carinthia in the lead up to the fifteenth anniversary of the 1920 plebiscite. This transference was evident in the regular feature column on Carinthia that the *Tagespost* published from 1935.[66] The *Tagespost* also published dense coverage of

Yugoslavia during the interwar period and earned a reputation in press circles for flouting the government censors by printing mainly international news while publishing official correspondence in small print.[67] *Salzburger Volksblatt* owner Hans Glaser observed that 'the custom of the *Grazer Tagespost* to push domestic political issues to the side and publish lead articles about Yugoslavia or Japan would no longer be tolerated' by press authorities.[68] It was a bit rich for Glaser to accuse his Styrian colleagues of doing exactly what his own newspaper did with official correspondence from the Fatherland Front. Moreover, the coverage of news from Yugoslavia in the *Tagespost* was not just a decoy to evade the censors. Throughout the interwar period the *Tagespost* regularly featured lead stories on Yugoslavia, as events over the border in what used to be Greater Styria were still deemed newsworthy to the newspaper's editors and readers.[69] In the month of January 1933, for example, three separate reports from Yugoslavia featured on the second page in one day's edition, while Hitler's appointment as German chancellor on 30 January 1933 was only the second major news item of the day behind the lead story from Yugoslavia about tensions between the Catholic Church and the Sokol gymnastics association.[70] Putting Yugoslavia on the front page was not a circumvention of the Austrian press laws, but rather a conscious strategy by Styrian German-nationalists to keep alive in readers' imagination their lost borderland.

Initially the *Tagespost* appeared not to be concerned with Slovenian minority rights and schools in Carinthia, but a front-page editorial on 10 April 1936 expressed the newspaper's view on the Carinthian Slovene 'problem'. The issue was not minority schools, but the question of whether Carinthia even had an ethnically mixed population. If it did, then minority rights would be a relevant point of debate, but in fact everywhere one looked one could find evidence that Carinthia's culture and inhabitants had been woven together under a dominant German influence and were no longer 'mixed'. The editorial asserted firstly that German tribes had converted the Slavic inhabitants of Carinthia to Christianity in the eighth century, invalidating any claim to an earlier conversion dating to Saints Cyril and Methodius. Secondly, the editorial alleged that the Germans heavily influenced most of the province's traditions and customs. Although there was some hybridity in music and regional dress, the editorial conceded, 'Germans were always the givers, while Slovenes were always the takers'. Finally, the editors argued that the German influence and the intermixing of both groups had erased the ethnic divide between them and left only a marginal linguistic difference. 'Today when we are dealing with the concept "Slovenian", we do not mean a racial or cultural characteristic, but only a linguistic one.' Indeed the Slovenian dialect spoken in Carinthia was actually a derivative of the German, the editorial argued and gave a few illustrations from the vernacular.[71] With this assertion that there were no Slovenes in Carinthia, only Slovenian-speakers, the editors rendered obsolete talk of assimilation to an Austrian state identity, even if that identity was characterized by German culture and language. The claim that a more superior German language and culture had offset any lingering trace of Slovenian dialect or dress, creating homogeneity where real ethnic diversity had apparently ceased to exist, was a foretelling of what later was to eventuate under the Nazis' policies of Aryanization towards Slovenes in Austria after 1938.

Yet we must also be careful of the kind of teleological explanations that link German-nationalist statements in the 1930s with later Nazi policies, while emphasizing the differences between the voluntarist model of assimilation that the Austrofascist state upheld and the model of ethnic dissimilation that German-nationalists preferred. I have already described the response of the chancellor's office to a request for an official Slovenian translation of the Austrian anthem, a response that undermined any claim Schuschnigg made publicly about the civic voluntarism of the Slovenian population. To be a patriot, one had to be a German-speaker, or singer, which blurs the distinction between ethnic and civic arguments about identity. German-nationalist editors also appropriated ethnic and civic arguments about Slovenes: those who went to foreign schools and learned Slovenian were irredentist Slovenian nationalists who posed a threat to the Austrian state, an argument grounded in civic principles of voluntarism and integration, while those who chose local German language schools lost their Slovenian identity and became Germanized Slovenes, this view underpinning the ethnic arguments of *Windisch*-theorists. Nor were German-nationalists alone in their arguments about ethnic dissimilation: the leader of the Carinthian *Ostmärkische Sturmscharen* declared that Carinthia was 'purely German according to blood and race alone.'[72] As we have seen, statements like this resonated repeatedly in the public organs of the Austrofascist state, be they newspapers or school textbooks. There was virtually little rhetorical difference between German-nationalists and Austrofascists, nor did their actions vary towards the Slovenian-speakers. German-nationalists and Austrofascists mobilized their respective followers to reassert their presence in Carinthia during the anniversary year of the plebiscite. Carinthia attracted the greatest attention as the border under siege, but as other irredentist threats emerged in Lower Austria and in the Burgenland, it seemed to both German-nationalists and Austrofascists that the state was in permanent danger of 'Slavicization' unless 'German Austria' did not arise from its slumbering state and reclaim the borderlands for good.

Czech invaders

Like the Slovene 'problem' in Carinthia, the issue of Czech schools was central to German-nationalist and Austrofascist claims about Slavic irredentism in Austria. However, whereas the Slovenian minority schools in Carinthia were nearly all bilingual and governed by Austrian authorities in line with Allied provisions for schools in linguistically mixed regions, the Czech minority schools in Vienna were a mix of state schools, offering streamlined Czech and German language classes, and private schools. The private schools had been run by the Komenský school association – named after the Moravian Reformation-era teacher and theologian, Jan Komenský (1592–1670) – since its establishment in 1872. The Brno Treaty, signed by Austria and Czechoslovakia on 7 June 1920, governed the respective rights of Czech- and German-speaking minorities to establish and maintain their private schools and to have access to state funding for bilingual public schools. This was a departure from the early years of the First Republic when bilingual schools had been banned altogether and Czech-speaking families had been forced to home-school unless their children were already enrolled in the Komenský schools.[73] By 1933, the Czech community in Vienna had 17 kindergartens, 6 primary schools, 6 technical high schools, 2 high schools, 1 trade school, and 1 vocational school for women, and there were a further 9 Czech language schools in Lower Austrian towns outside Vienna. Czech-speaking children could also attend 10 public schools in Vienna that taught Czech language classes. All told, a total of 5,264 Czech-speakers attended these private, state and language schools in Vienna and Lower Austria.[74] How 'Czech' the children were who attended these schools mirrored similar ambiguities facing school authorities in interwar Czechoslovakia.[75] In Vienna children with only one Czech parent could be admitted to the Komenský schools, and there appears to have been neither scrutiny into the children's background by the Komenský authorities nor any attempt by Austrian school officials to force them to attend mainstream schools. Antonie Bruha (1915–2006), who later joined the Communist Resistance in Austria during the Second World War, was born in Vienna to a Czech-speaking mother from southern Bohemia and a German-speaking Viennese father. Her father insisted his daughter learn the language of her grandparents and sent her to a private Czech school in Vienna.[76] Possibly there were fewer disputes in Austria than in Czechoslovakia because Austrian state officials were happy to keep the Czech-speakers outside the mainstream education system to encourage emigration abroad and Czech community leaders were just as happy to keep them out. At any rate, the choice to send children to the Komenský or Austrian schools was already complicated by the third option of state schools offering Czech language classes. Parents may have opted for such a compromise either due to financial pressures or because they preferred their child to be immersed in the German language system for mobility or other practical reasons, which was the case for seasonal migrant workers from Croatian-speaking families in the Burgenland as we will see.

The Czech schools were allowed to continue under the Austrofascist state and the Komenský school association celebrated its sixtieth anniversary during the school year 1932–33. The number of teachers in these schools also did not appear to be affected by the 1934 ban on the Czech Social Democrats and the socialist teachers' unions to which many Czech teachers also belonged. They were simply required to join the Fatherland Front.[77] However, the issue of Czech membership in the Fatherland Front was contentious on both sides as we learn from a report in the *Wiener Neueste Nachrichten* in January 1935. According to the newspaper, the leaders of the Komenský school association had written to Adam, general secretary of the Fatherland Front, affirming their commitment. The Komenský schools taught their children 'to believe in a free and independent Austria' in which they deserved to be treated not as second-class citizens but as equals 'with the same rights but also with the same duties to the state'. In educating the children in their mother tongue, the Komenský schools were instilling a love of the Czech language that was compatible with the Fatherland Front's mission to create a strong Austrian state. But some parents were confused about what membership in the Fatherland Front entailed: they believed that the Fatherland Front sought to discourage Austrian citizens of Czech and Slovak descent from joining because the state's goal was to build 'German Austria', not to cultivate non-German nationalities. Adam's reply to the Komenský leaders was that the Fatherland Front represented the majority German-speaking population in Austria, but that did not preclude non-German-speakers from joining as long as they identified wholeheartedly with Austria. However, non-Austrian citizens were not eligible for membership.[78] We have no way of knowing if such an exchange took place between the leaders of the Komenský school association and Adam. The article was in the files of the press and propaganda ministry so presumably the editors of the newspaper would not intentionally have fabricated an account that directly implicated the country's highest representative of the Fatherland Front. Nevertheless the newspaper was wont to manipulate and exaggerate certain 'facts' as we have seen regarding the Carinthian Slovenes. It is plausible that the editors cobbled together pieces of the story from articles in the Czech language press, for example, with published statements from the Fatherland Front about non-German minorities to create this 'exchange'. The larger intention of the editors was to portray Czechs and Slovaks as reluctant

Austrians, if indeed they were Austrian citizens at all, who joined the Fatherland Front only to keep their jobs while continuing to indoctrinate their children with a dose of Czech language and culture that was incommensurate with their claim to be educating Austrian patriots.

Following the July Agreement the editors no longer needed to veil their accusations behind such insinuations. An editorial in August 1937 claimed that Austrian schools in non-metropolitan areas were left with insufficient enrolments because the Komenský association was shuttling Czech-speaking children from the industrial districts in Lower Austria to attend classes at the Komenský schools in Vienna and, the editorial added, to get a free meal. One of the Komenský schools in Vienna's twelfth district had a large painting of Prague hanging in the main stairwell to remind the students, according to a Komenský textbook the editorial cited, that although Vienna was their place of residence, Czechoslovakia was their fatherland. As further evidence of the misdirected patriotism of these schools, the editorial quoted the wife of a Czech general who had remarked upon visiting one of the schools that 'in these schools, a child certainly does not have a feeling of inferiority . . . The Komenský schools are the pride not only of the Czech minority in Vienna but also the whole Czecho-slovakian nation.'[79] The newspaper did not report that parents had been taking their children out of the Czech schools in response to vandal attacks, presumably by illegal Nazi gangs: one school had had twenty-one windows broken in October 1935, the fourth attack on a Czech school according to the Czech press.[80] The *Wiener Neueste Nachrichten* kept up its own verbal assault on minorities by accusing Czech schools of making Czechoslovak patriots out of children and families whose national loyalty could be bought for the price of a meal and a decorated classroom. As we will see, this was the same propaganda method used by the Fatherland Front to create Austrian citizens out of German minorities in Czechoslovakia by giving them a free summer holiday. Both on this occasion and in the 'exchange' between Adam and the Komenský leaders, the German-nationalist press was acting as an effective mouthpiece of the Fatherland Front, rather than challenging its authority on minority politics.

Another important strand of anti-Czech sentiment that can be detected in the German-nationalist press is the issue of Czechoslovak citizens living in Austria. Neither of the above articles directly mentions whether the parents of the children attending the Komenský schools were Austrian citizens, but they do express doubt over the citizenship credentials of these supposedly Austrian Czechs. Adam's reply to the leaders of the Komenský school association that non-citizens need not apply for membership in the Fatherland Front is an indication of the newspaper's (and the state's) tendency to doubt the legal status of these Czech patriots. Austrian education authorities and German-nationalist activists were less concerned with the schools in Vienna than with the activities of groups like the Komenský school association in educating the children of Czech and Slovak migrants in Austria. In Carinthia the apparent threat of 'Slavicization' appeared to come both from within Austria and without, but the presence of seasonal workers from Czechoslovakia appeared to be a foreign invasion that had state officials as well as German-nationalists alarmed.

Between 1925 and 1937 the Austrian Migration Office issued over 140,000 seasonal permits for Czechoslovak citizens to come to Austria to work on sugar farms and in textile factories. We do not know whether these migrant workers returned home or if more came who were not granted a permit, but we do know that the numbers from Czechoslovakia continued to rise annually before 1938 despite pressure from both socialist and Christian Social labour groups for the migration authorities to ban foreign workers.[81] In Gänserndorf, near the Lower Austrian border with Czechoslovakia, the district governor protested in 1935 that 70 per cent of the students at one local primary school were permanent residents of Czechoslovakia and that their parents, who hardly spoke any German, wanted to live and work in Austria so they could send their children to Austrian schools. He warned of the threat posed by Slovak workers to the German character of Gänserndorf's farming and town communities and claimed that Austrian farmers were hiring Slovak labourers on sugar farms in preference to German-speakers because the Slovaks allegedly lived off more modest wages, were better educated and were more desirable marriage partners.[82]

Similar fears that the workers were not just taking jobs from Austrians, but were also seeking to remake a 'German' town into a Czech one, appeared in the German-nationalist press, this time not in a Styrian or Viennese organ, but in Salzburg where there was a long association with the Bohemian lands as we have seen. The *Salzburger Volksblatt* ran a front-page editorial in August 1937 decrying the 'Czechification' of the Lower Austrian village of Dürnkrut on the Czechoslovakian border. Migrant workers from Czechoslovakia who came to work on the sugar farms in Dürnkrut were not only swamping the Austrian labour market, but also threatening to take over Austria's public spaces. The newspaper claimed that the Czechs in Dürnkrut wanted to build a memorial to the Bohemian King Otakar II, who had defeated the first Habsburg, Rudolf, in 1278. Calling on Austrians to fight 'with all available means' the 'attempt from the Czech side to give an Austrian border spot the character of a Slavic cultural bulwark', the editorial warned it readers that 'this memorial is directed not just against the German character of little Dürnkrut but, rather, against the entire Austrian German character'.[83] Given Glaser's own

Moravian background, it was not surprising that the *Salzburger Volksblatt* would magnify a local scenario of German–Czech rivalries into a larger question about the national identity of Austrian Germans. The newspaper's portrayal of local antagonisms as a 'Slavic' threat to 'German' Austria also reflected a well-worn strategy of the German-nationalist press under the Austro-Hungarian Empire. In the 1930s, Austrian pan-German identity was again constructed in both ethnic and civic terms of a 'Slavic' invasion of Austria's public spaces, which in turn were identified by the newspaper as bastions of 'German' cultural hegemony. Czech migrants were invading Austria's civic identity and Austrian Germans were urged to stage an ethnic barrier of defence. Just as the governor in Gänserndorf feared that the German pride of his community was under threat unless Austrian farmers desisted from employing and intermarrying with Slovaks, the *Salzburger Volksblatt* also called on Austrian Germans to unite in the face of an invasion of Czech migrants. Austrofascists and German-nationalists were in agreement that Austria's borderlands remain in the possession of Germans if Austria was to retain its identity as a German state.

Model Croats

At the official festivities in the Hofburg palace marking 400 years of 'Burgenlander Croatdom' in March 1934, Dollfuss addressed his 'good Croats' and promised to guard and protect Croatian culture in Austria in the same way that he would uphold German culture in the state. He told them they were not only an example to other minorities in Austria, but also a model for Austria's neighbouring countries in promoting similar rights for their German minorities. 'We will be proud to tell the leaders of other countries . . . look at the Austrian Croats, ask them if they feel at home in Austria, whether they call Austria their fatherland, and then follow Austria's example.'[84] As if inheriting the mantle of another self-styled father of the Croats, Emperor Franz Josef, who would also hold court in the Hofburg with men and women from far flung regions of his domain, neither Dollfuss nor his successor Schuschnigg were so much interested in the 'good Croats' as in the ways that the Austrian state might be able to win the hearts and minds of German-speaking minorities abroad.

Two other sites of the 400th year anniversary celebrations, Zagreb and Mariazell, showed that Dollfuss was not the object of the Burgenland Croats' affections either. Rather, the commemorations were occasions to deepen the new bonds of fraternity with Croats from Yugoslavia, who took part in the pilgrimages to Mariazell in 1933 and hosted Burgenlander Croats during the festivities in Zagreb.[85] Relations had been more ambivalent in the earlier interwar years: shut out from Hungary after the

Inter-Allied Military Commission awarded the territories of western Hungary to Austria in 1922, and dismayed by the treatment of Croats in the new South Slav state, Croatian-speakers in the newly formed province of the Burgenland pragmatically chose Austria.[86] They established new associations and newspapers to realign their loyalty to the Austrian state and provide a united voice for all Croats in Austria, including those workers and their families who had fled Horthý's White Terror in 1919 and started new lives in Vienna and Lower Austria. In December 1922 a group of Croatian students and intellectuals in Vienna, with the financial backing of the Yugoslav embassy in Vienna, founded a weekly newspaper, *Hrvatske Novine*, as the organ of Croatian-speakers in Austria. Its subtitle 'Sloga je moć' (Unity is Power) was intended to convey the newspaper's independence from political parties, but from the start it leaned towards the Christian Social Party and the Croatian-speaking priests who represented the party in the Burgenland parliament. In May 1923 a second newspaper, *Naš Glas*, was founded as the Croatian language counterpart of the Burgenland's Social Democratic newspaper, *Burgenländische Freiheit*.[87]

Yet apart from this initial contact with the embassy and some sporadic contacts with Croatian émigrés living in Vienna, there was virtually no relationship with Croats in Yugoslavia during the 1920s. The first gesture came from the Yugoslavian side when organizers of the 1930 Eucharistic Congress in Zagreb invited Burgenlander Croats to attend. Only three turned up: Ignaz Horvat, priest, and president of the Croatian Cultural Association and member of the Burgenland parliament, and two school-teachers. Nonetheless, this contact spawned many more over the next few years as Horvat was introduced to the founder of the St Jerome press in Zagreb, Josip Andrić, who contracted him to write historical and ethnological studies of the Burgenlander Croats and edit literary and musical anthologies from the region. The *Hrvatske Novine* reviewed books published by the St Jerome press and advertised special subscription rates for its journals. Andrić was also able to establish a fund in the Burgenland through his connections with Horvat and the *Hrvatske Novine* for a shrine in Jerusalem to the fourteenth-century martyr Nikola Tavelić. In 1932 the Association of Friends of Burgenlander Croats was established in Zagreb with chapters in Split, Osijek, Varaždin and Slavonski Brod. Belgrade authorities shut down the 'Friends' in May 1933 and parishes took over the initiative in supporting the associational life of Burgenlander Croats, for example attending the 400th anniversary celebrations.[88]

Dollfuss's exhortations to his 'good Croats' was thus a pointed reminder to his listeners that it was the Austrian state, not Croatian-speakers in Yugoslavia, who had given them the opportunity to cultivate their culture and language. The fact that the pilgrimage to Mariazell took place at the same time as the All-German Catholic Congress in Vienna the previous September may also have played on his mind as he reassured Croatian-speakers that the state represented them as much as German-speaking Catholics. He could still count on their formal support for his government: the editors of the *Hrvatske Novine* had welcomed Dollfuss's decision to prorogue the parliament in March 1933 and they continued to champion the state's efforts to create a 'Christian' Austria.[89] But their support wavered when it came to the issue of the new Austrian state youth organization (*Österreichisches Jungvolk* – ÖJV), which Schuschnigg established in August 1936. Catholic youth groups were exempt from the new organization under Article 14 of the 1934 concordat, but church leaders quickly moved to bring all Catholic youth groups into a single organization, *Katholisches Jungvolk* under the mantle of Catholic Action.[90] While the issue had already caused friction between state and church authorities in Austria, for Croatian-speaking Catholics the issue was not just about religion but also about national identity.

In 1937 a series of 'exchanges' took place between the *Hrvatske Novine* and the Austrian press and propaganda ministry. Unlike the correspondence between the leaders of the Komenský school association and Adam, which was constructed and transmitted by the German-nationalist press, the articles in the *Hrvatske Novine* were translated into German and held on file in the Austrian press and propaganda ministry. We do not know if the Austrian authorities responded to any of the concerns raised in the correspondence, but as we will see in the final section of this chapter the surge in state-sponsored activism promoting German culture and language from 1937 onwards showed that the protests of the Croatian-speakers fell on deaf ears. Moreover, in view of the growing ties to Croats in Yugoslavia, these protests possibly aroused official suspicions of the Burgenlander Croats' counter-loyalties.

Stolaric Vojtek, a young Burgenlander Croat, wrote to the *Hrvatske Novine* in April 1937 defending the rights of Croatian youth to cultivate their own national traditions while remaining loyal to the Austrian state. He claimed that the state curriculum and the compulsory classes run by leaders of the ÖJV that had recently been introduced in Austrian state schools, were planting a foreign spirit in the hearts of young Croats. Croatian children should learn songs in their native dialect instead of Tyrolean yodelling and even if German songs were to be translated into Croatian the result would be 'mush' that belongs 'neither to us nor them'. Vojtek foresaw the day when Croatian parents would talk to their children as if speaking to the wind. 'Weep, Croatian mother, for so will you become alienated from our youth!' Vojtek affirmed that Croatian youth wanted to participate as full members of the ÖJV because they, too, bore responsibility 'for our Austria', but they needed a leader to represent them at the federal level of the ÖJV. A representative would then be able to ensure that Croatian-speaking members received materials in their language and could wear their own national hat with a crane feather, instead of the uniform cap. Thinking himself the ideal candidate for leader, Vojtek wrote: 'We, too, want to work with the ÖJV towards its goals, but in our ways and traditions!'[91]

Ignaz Horvat reiterated 'the young patriot' Vojtek's claims the following month, acknowledging that there was much that bound Austrian youth together – be they German, Croatian or Hungarian – in their common religion and love of their Austrian fatherland. But what set them apart were their cultural traditions and national character, the same way that a Tyrolean would not wear Styrian dress or sing any songs other than Tyrolean ones. Horvat also addressed the tensions between Catholic and state youth groups, explaining that the creation of a state youth organization would put pressure on Burgenlander Croats to join the ÖJV unless they were already members of Catholic youth groups under the umbrella of Catholic Action. Horvat argued that the Catholic groups were better equipped than the state organization to address the needs of Croatian youth. Firstly, the Catholic associations were able to cultivate the traditions and character of Croatian-speakers by caring for their spiritual needs, which the state youth groups could not do. Secondly, whereas state youth groups came and went with each new political group, the Catholic groups provided a constant presence in the life of young people. And thirdly, it was far easier to expand the Catholic groups that already existed and to find leaders for them, than to start from scratch building a new state organization.[92]

Horvat's article evidently sparked more controversy than he intended, for in a speech three weeks later at a flag consecration ceremony of the Catholic Boys' League in Zillingdorf, reprinted in the *Hrvatske Novine* under the headline 'for a free fatherland and Croatdom', Horvat stressed that the creation of local state-run youth groups depended on local circumstances. If it was easier to establish a state-run group where a Catholic one did not exist, then the state should do so. He and his fellow leaders of the Croatian Cultural Association supported both the state and church groups because they wanted to nurture youth in a Catholic and patriotic spirit. But he rejected claims that their emphasis on 'Croatdom' was disrespectful towards Germans, for it was obvious that Croats and Germans got along very well. It was simply his view that one needed both religious faith and national identity to be a full person. 'Our Croatian national character is in danger', Horvat told the boys, 'not because someone wishes to make us extinct, but because we are in the midst of a <u>German ocean</u>'.[93] The translator from the press and propaganda ministry underlined Horvat's description, which apparently belied his earlier statement that Croats and Germans got along swimmingly. Horvat recognized the practical needs of communities like Zillingdorf where working families had to earn a living by migrating to Vienna or Lower Austria, but in doing so they also risked losing their roots. It was up to groups like the Catholic Boys' League 'to arm themselves for a new battle . . . for a true Catholic homeland and for the preservation of the Croatian nation'.[94]

Horvat acknowledged the difficulties facing the small rural and working-class Croatian-speaking community and recognized the advantages of a bilingual education system. Minority schools in the Burgenland had had a less contentious history than in Carinthia. The Burgenland system had catered more generously to the Croatian-speakers by allowing three types of minority schools. Type one offered Croatian as the principal language of instruction with German taught only for the required minimum of 5 hours per week from the fourth year of school; type two increased German language instruction after the third year of schooling so that by the end of the compulsory eight years of school, classes were equally split into German and Croatian; and the third type immersed pupils entirely in the Croatian language for the first two years of school before classes switched to German. Parents who depended on seasonal work in Vienna and Lower Austria favoured the third type because their children had to switch between schools and because it required a more intensive German language education; this interest in German was another difference from the Slovenian-speakers in Carinthia. However, the difficulty with the first two models of minority schools, which had operated under the old Hungarian state system, was the shortage of teachers and textbooks. Most teachers had trained in Hungary, their second language was Hungarian, not German, and the old textbooks that had been published by the Hungarian Education Ministry were not permitted in the new Austrian state. Bibles and catechisms were allowed, but there were no textbooks for history, geography or science.[95] Austrian education authorities would certainly have looked with suspicion on the developing ties with Croatian publishing houses in Zagreb, fearing that some of these books may be used to teach an anti-Austrian history, although the authorization of a new curriculum and textbooks by the Austrofascist Education Ministry in 1935 mitigated some of these concerns, at least in the short term.

A new provincial school law introduced in the Burgenland in 1937 appeared to be a conciliatory gesture on the part of the Austrofascist authorities and a welcome sign for Croatian community leaders like Horvat that their youth would receive a proper education in both their mother tongue and the language of the state. The law applied only to state schools,

not confessional schools, and formalized the system already in place elsewhere, such as Carinthia, of establishing minority schools on the basis of
census data. Type one schools that taught only in Croatian would now
operate in districts and villages with more than a two-thirds majority
Croatian-speaking population (according to the 1934 census). Type two
schools of bilingual instruction would be set up where the Croatian-
speakers made up a third of the population. But where the Croatian-
speakers represented less than a third of the population only German
schools would be permitted with voluntary Croatian language classes
offered outside school hours. Unlike in Carinthia, the law actually increased
the numbers of schools that taught in Croatian: sixteen schools that had
previously taught only German with the exception of the first two years of
schooling were now required to offer Croatian language classes under the
new system. However, the problem was still where to find teachers and
textbooks, and how to bring the children up to speed on their Croatian if
they had previously learnt only German.[96] Horvat welcomed the new
school law and stressed the importance of the bilingual system in a region
whose population was forced to migrate to earn a living. The value of a
bilingual education was to cultivate one's roots but, at the same time,
provide a full education in the language of the state so that 'all doors to
the good [and] the best positions are open for our children'. Horvat urged
teachers and educators to bring the new law into full effect so that 'our
Croat' can receive a proper education and preparation for life in equality
with other citizens of Austria.[97] He saw the law as an opportunity for
greater engagement in the state, in which new generations of teachers
would be trained, and where upright citizens like himself and the young
Vojtek would work with the authorities to produce educational materials
that invoked a sense of both Croatian nationhood and Austrian patriotism.
He believed that full integration was possible under the Austrofascist state
in spite of the 'German ocean' in which he saw his fellow Croats swimming
against the current.

   Horvat was an optimist, and Croatian-speakers certainly fared better
under the Austrofascist state than their Slovenian-speaking counterparts
in Carinthia. But it was Carinthia, not the Burgenland, which came to
represent the borderland under siege in the new Austria and carried with
it memories of past national battles. The new borderland of Burgenland
did not yet have a long memory in the minds of Austrian authorities and
German-nationalists were too preoccupied with the new era of Austro-
German détente to pass comment on the Burgenland's minority schools.
By 1937 German-nationalists and Austrofascists were also preoccupied
with the work of the 'Germandom' section of the Fatherland Front, whose
mission was to engage Austrians with their fellow German-speakers
outside Austria. Horvat's dream of integration for 'his Croats' was

ultimately a delusion in the face of those who saw them only as fodder for their grander dreams of a greater-German community in which non-German-speakers would indeed have only the wind to hear them.

Auslandsdeutsche in Austria

Emmerich Czermak, the former Christian Social Education Minister, chaired a working party that met in February 1934 to form what was to become two months later the Austrian Association of Germandom Work Abroad (ÖVVA). Heinrich Mataja, co-editor of the *Reichspost*, was part of the working party along with the Benedictine historian and professor at the University of Graz, Hugo Hantsch, who took over the leadership of the ÖVVA in January 1936 and was also appointed adviser to the federal leadership of the Fatherland Front on all *Volkstum* matters. These men believed that by establishing an organization to serve the interests of German-speaking minorities abroad and continue the work of Germanizing Austria's own minorities, and by bringing this organization under the direct authority of the Fatherland Front, they could foil the attempt of National Socialists to gain a stronghold in German-nationalist groups like the *Südmark* association and redirect the activism of these groups towards the Austrian state rather than Nazi Germany. Accordingly, the ÖVVA invited *Südmark* leaders to sit on its leadership in exchange for ÖVVA leaders to be represented on the leadership of the *Südmark* association. The battle for German Austria was a turf war over the fruits of Germanization and the ÖVVA wanted to ensure that the Germanized inhabitants of Carinthia would be claimed for Austria not Germany.[98]

In addition to rivalry with local nationalist groups, the ÖVVA had to contend with other *Auslandsdeutsche* organizations, especially those with links to German-speaking Catholics in Czechoslovakia. The leader of the Reich Union for Catholic Germans Abroad wrote to Czermak in June 1934 demanding the ÖVVA's dissolution; the two men came to a mutual understanding but the hostility from the German side did not deter Austrian authorities from inviting children from Czechoslovakia for the Fatherland Front's children's summer holiday programme (*Kinderferienwerk*) that year. Although Dollfuss's original idea was to provide malnourished children from poor rural and working-class families in Austria with a time of rest, outdoor activities and a nutritious diet, the invitation was extended to children abroad after 1933. Only 7 came in 1934, but the following year 102 spent the summer in Austria, the majority from Czechoslovakia, but some from Yugoslavia as well.[99] In its efforts to make children from bilingual areas in neighbouring countries into German-speaking Austrians, and so prevent them becoming Czechs, Slovenes or Reich Germans, the

Kinderferienwerk was a variation on the earlier private exchanges of children (*Kindertausche*) in Bohemia and Moravia. Czech activists in the empire had originally sought to discourage these *Kindertausche* in rural areas, but after 1918 they invented their own state-sponsored programmes with invitations extended abroad to children of Czech-speaking families in Vienna to spend a summer in Czechoslovakia.[100] Whereas prior to 1918 it had been nationalist groups like the German and Komenský school associations that laid claim on bilingual communities, in interwar Czechoslovakia, as in the Austrofascist state, it was the state acting as guardian, educating children in the right language and training them for citizenship in the right state when the time came for them to join. The state might have conscripted activists to carry out these tasks, but it was the state nonetheless seeking to nationalize its citizens.

Recruiting the young was the focus of the ÖVVA especially after the formation of the ÖJV in August 1936. ÖVVA leaders worked closely with the ÖJV supplying their leaders with teaching manuals so they could instruct their followers and recruit volunteers to collect money and books to donate to German-speakers abroad. The first major fundraising initiative of the ÖJV in June 1937 raised 20,000 schillings to build German schools along the Upper Austrian border with Czechoslovakia, evidence that 'Germandom work' was as much directed at Austria's own bilingual areas as at those across the border.[101] The ÖVVA also joined forces with the Lower Austrian farmers' league to invite a group of farmers from Hungary for a visit in January 1937 and in October that year a whole class of young farming apprentices to take part in a course on national education in Graz. Even the Vienna Boys' Choir were recruited as youth ambassadors of Austrian Germandom, touring abroad along with the 'Waltharia' university choral society, which held concerts as well as lectures in German-speaking areas of Hungary and Czechoslovakia.[102] To be sure, these activities under the leadership of the ÖVVA and ÖJV were not on the scale of the borderland 'pilgrimages' in interwar Germany, where youth groups, women's leagues and academics were also recruited by state-sponsored agencies seeking to keep alive memories of Germany's lost borderland in the East, and were later incorporated wholesale into Nazi agencies in 1933 to continue the work abroad.[103] But despite the relatively late mobilization of Austria's youth and women's groups on behalf of 'Germandom', the ÖVVA leadership wasted no time getting the ÖJV on board straight away, as well as recruiting a women's auxiliary committee in Vienna and appointing a woman as deputy adviser under Hantsch to the federal leadership of the Fatherland Front.[104] That women were excluded from all public offices other than in the women's section of the Fatherland Front makes this achievement all the more remarkable. It indicates that there were many women in the Austrofascist state who saw their service to the state not just in terms of motherhood and in the broader cultural and social function of motherhood in state- and church-sponsored maternal and child welfare initiatives, but also in the realm of 'Germandom' work, as the letter to the editors of the *Wiener Neueste Nachrichten* from the leader of a German-nationalist women's league also attests. The success of this initiative shows that the Austrofascist state had little trouble mobilizing followers behind its goal of Germanizing the borderlands, thanks to its ingenious idea to co-opt activists who had already cut their teeth on the borderlands of the empire.

Activism required publicity and the ÖVVA founded its own press agency, the Austrian Correspondence for Germandom Work (*Österreich-ische Korrespondenz für volksdeutsche Arbeit* – ÖKVDA), to file stories from the front lines of the organization's work abroad.[105] Articles in the ÖKVDA resembled reports in the German-nationalist press on the lack of schools for German-speakers in Slovenia and the 'Czechification' of towns with a German-speaking population.[106] The work was often described as a mission field to which the faithful should give donations, if not their labour. An article in May 1937 reported that German Catholics outside the borders of Austria and Germany were forced to attend Protestant churches because they could not attend mass in their mother tongue and called on readers to donate German prayer books, catechisms, Catholic newspapers and Bibles to these stranded believers. 'Work in this mission field is Catholic work and German work, a service to the faith and the Church and a service to the German people at the same time.' One only had to look to the 'shining' example of the Holy Father himself, who had ministered to German Catholics in their mother tongue in Milan during the Great War.[107] Here the analogy to the mission field was embodied in the man who became Pius XI in 1922, whose papacy was marked by a call to lay mis-sionary activism. The work of 'Germandom' abroad required missionaries who, like soldiers, would be sent by their families and fellow believers in the cause to achieve victories for the nation. In its descriptions of a frontier world, the ÖKVDA resembled the German newspapers from the Eastern Front that had brought the 'lands and peoples' of the East into the kitchens and on to the trains of Germans at home.[108] But unlike German colonizers in the East, Austrian 'Germandom' workers made both a religious and a national claim on the *Auslandsdeutsche*, whose German-speaking creden-tials were as important as their Catholicism. Only by making such a dual claim could Austrofascists fulfil their mission to be the true bearers of Germandom.

The previous chapter showed how 'Christian' and 'German' were twinned together in Salzburg to produce very different versions of pan-Germanism,

from Steinwender's 'Christ the King of the Germans' to Reitter's positive
Christianity, which sought to reform religion from a community bound by
confession and belief to one of common destiny and action. If we return
to the Boniface Day celebrations in June 1937 we can observe at close hand
the process of accommodating different versions of pan-Germanism within
the institutional structures of the ÖVVA and the Fatherland Front.

Among the dignitaries who attended the Boniface Day festivities, as we
have seen, were Cardinal Innitzer; the Education Minister, Perntner; and
leaders of the Fatherland Front. Hugo Hantsch opened and chaired the
proceedings. In his opening remarks, he stated that this was the second
Boniface Day he had organized under the umbrella of the ÖVVA and
explained why he had chosen to appropriate the legacy of Boniface for the
work of 'Germandom' abroad. Firstly because the very existence of the
Auslandsdeutsche was due to the missionary work of St Boniface who had
woken the German lands from 'a slumbering Christendom'; and secondly,
because if the ÖVVA and its supporters did not continue Boniface's mission
to the German-speakers abroad, if they did not see to it that their co-
religionists continued to say German prayers, sing German hymns, and
hear German sermons, then these people would be lost to the German
nation.[109] Perntner then spoke on behalf of Schuschnigg, praising the work
of the ÖVVA for continuing the 'old and established tradition of the pioneering cultural work of the *Ostmarkdeutschtum*' and called on St Boniface to bless 'this German cultural work . . . for our fatherland Austria'.[110]
Finally, it was Innitzer's turn to address the gathering. The cardinal began
by acknowledging the importance of the ÖVVA in providing succour to
the German people abroad especially at a time when the German Church
was under attack in Germany. 'It is a bishop's duty of conscience, above
all, that he also speak up regarding these regrettable events.' He went on
to express on behalf of Austria and 'in the interests of the German people'
his deep remorse over the treatment of the German clergy and the battle
against Christianity that was without precedent in history.[111] Innitzer's
personal grief over the events in Germany was obvious on this occasion
and his speech prompted the Austrian bishops' conference to issue a statement later that year expressing solidarity with the German clergy in sharing
their suffering.[112]

Just as Steinwender had strayed somewhat from the official message of
Germandom work abroad in his keynote address, Innitzer's speech also
failed to link the work of the ÖVVA with its goal of reaching out to the
German minority in Czechoslovakia. Innitzer himself was of Sudeten
German background but he chose not to mention his heritage or the
Sudeten Germans other than to recognize their part of a larger 'splintered'
German whole.[113] The previous year the cardinal had been the guest of

honour of Vienna's Czech community when he attended the opening of the new Komenský middle school in Vienna's 3rd district, evidence at least that in his public office he made no distinction between assisting German-speakers in Czechoslovakia and Czech-speakers in Austria.[114] Celebrating the achievements of Austria's Czech-speakers at a time when Perntner's Education Ministry was writing them out of school textbooks was not exactly what the ÖVVA understood by 'German cultural work'.

This is not to say that the Austrian Church and its leading representatives did not see their mission also in terms of 'Germandom' work. I have already shown in Chapter 3 how a very strong Catholic attachment to the German nation persisted until the end of the Second World War and even in the aftermath of the war's bitter experiences for some of Austria's clergy. After 1938 Innitzer was shunned by Western Catholic leaders for his 'yes' vote in the 10 April plebiscite following the *Anschluss* and for signing letters to Nazi authorities with 'Heil Hitler'. But there was little difference between the Innitzer before and after 1938: both under the Austrofascist and Nazi regimes the cardinal intervened in politics only where the interests of lay Catholics were concerned, even if he misjudged the political implications of his actions.[115] More will be said on Innitzer and other church leaders in the following chapter on anti-Semitism. But my point here is that within the Church as outside it, multiple versions of pan-Germanism could be accommodated so long as the Austrofascist state continued to promote a 'German Christian' identity. The ÖVVA was one of the most successful programmes of the Fatherland Front precisely because it drew on the breadth and depth of pan-Germanism in the new Austria. Having made its pact with *Südmark* leaders and other German-nationalist activists the organization was able to assemble a wealth of experience on Austria's linguistic frontiers that contributed to its astonishing success and diversity of activities across state borders.

In the end, however, the ÖVVA mirrored the larger fate of the Austrian state. The organization, whose determined push into Czechoslovakia was initially motivated by rivalry with Reich organizations, gave way to cooperation with Nazi Germans just as it had already done with their sympathizers in Austria. In December 1937 the German ambassador in Prague wrote to the German Foreign Office reporting on the ÖVVA and the reactions of Sudeten German groups and Sudeten German Party (SdP) leaders to the Austrian manoeuvres. According to the ambassador, leaders of the Sudeten German *Turnverein* and SdP leaders had been invited by leaders of the Fatherland Front's ÖJV to a retreat in the Tyrolean mountains in early 1938 to discuss cooperation between the Sudeten German and Austrian organizations. The discussions included a proposal to establish a central agency for *Auslandsdeutsche* that would work alongside similar agencies in Berlin and Stuttgart, and a number of cultural initiatives, such as a press agreement between the ÖKVDA and Sudeten German press agencies.[116] Plans were also discussed for a combined programme of concerts and exhibitions, and the joint participation of Austrian and Sudeten German *Turnverein* at the German *Turnfest* in Breslau. The German ambassador assured the Foreign Office that the SdP representatives had declined these offers because the party's leader, Konrad Henlein, had turned to Nazi Germany for assistance.[117] However, this appears to have been wishful thinking on the ambassador's part. It is not clear at all what Henlein's intentions were during 1937 and he may well have seen the ÖVVA's push into Czechoslovakia as an opportunity to build alliances with Austrian 'Germandom' groups against a Czech nationalist onslaught against his party and Sudeten German associational life.[118] What is clear from the Austrian side is that the cooperation between state youth groups, German-nationalist groups like the *Turnverein*, the Fatherland Front's highest dignitaries in the ÖVVA, and a broad spectrum of its supporters in the Catholic Church, the German-nationalist press, women's auxiliary groups and cultural associations, were all working towards the Germanization of Austria and the German nation across political borders.

When the *Wiener Neueste Nachrichten* greeted the *Anschluss* on 12 March 1938 as the fulfilment of the 'Greater German Empire', the editors openly expressed what they long had envisaged was the true national community to which Austria belonged. Their vision of a universal pan-German nation included German minorities living outside Germany and Austria and resembled the National Socialist vision of a *Volksgemeinschaft*. But as we have seen in this chapter the German-nationalist idea of a pan-German community was also compatible with the views of German-speaking Catholics who saw themselves as the heirs of St Boniface and the Holy Roman Empire. The Austrofascist state accommodated all of these visions and had much in common with German-nationalist editors' views of National Socialists and the place of non-German minorities in Austria. Not all German-nationalists saw National Socialists as the leaders of a nationalist front in Austria, and not every Austrofascist functionary dismissed National Socialism's place in the new Austria. They might have disagreed on the role of Christianity in the state, even if they both drew on religious themes to construct the boundaries of the national community. However, when it came to defending 'German' Austria against 'Slavic' irredentism, or promoting German culture abroad in the name of the universal pan-German nation, Austrofascists and German-nationalists found – perhaps to their own surprise – they were fighting on the same front.

Notes

1 *Wiener Neueste Nachrichten*, 12 March 1938, p. 1; 13 March 1938, p. 1.
2 Anton Staudinger, 'Katholischer Antisemitismus in der Ersten Republik', in Gerhard Botz, et al. (eds), *Eine zerstörte Kultur: Jüdisches Leben und Antisemitismus in Wien seit dem 19. Jahrhundert* (Vienna: Czernin, 2002), pp. 275–77.
3 *Wiener Neueste Nachrichten*, 24 January 1933, p. 4.
4 *Wiener Neueste Nachrichten*, 7 March 1933, pp. 1–2. Figures for Lower Bavaria, according to the newspaper, were 281,072 and 632,705 for Upper Bavaria and Swabia, totalling 913,777 for the province.
5 See Geoffrey Pridham, *Hitler's Rise to Power: The Nazi Movement in Bavaria, 1923–1933* (London: Hart-Davis, MacGibbon, 1973), pp. 303–6. Table 7 on p. 306 lists the figures for rural districts of Lower Bavaria, showing that the NSDAP gained 97,900 votes from new voters while the Bavarian Peasants' and Middle-Class League, and the Bavarian People's Party had combined losses of 18,900.
6 Ebneth, *Die österreichische Wochenschrift*, p. 33.
7 Ibid. This occurred in Germany during the height of the Nazi movement in the early 1930s, when Nazi leaders attacked the Centre Party not because it represented Catholics, but because it had collaborated with the Social Democrats during the Weimar period. See Steigmann-Gall, *The Holy Reich*, p. 56.
8 *Wiener Neueste Nachrichten*, 14 April 1933, p. 3.
9 *Wiener Neueste Nachrichten*, 31 May 1933, p. 1. Frank was expelled three days after his arrival in Austria on a visit that had turned into a propaganda tour, during which his speeches had urged opposition to Chancellor Dollfuss. See Edmondson, *The Heimwehr and Austrian Politics*, p. 190; Brook-Shepherd, *The Austrians*, p. 273.
10 *Wiener Neueste Nachrichten*, 12 June 1933, p. 1; 13 June 1933, p. 5.
11 *Wiener Neueste Nachrichten*, 13 June 1933, p. 1.
12 *Wiener Neueste Nachrichten*, 14 June 1933, p. 1.
13 *Wiener Neueste Nachrichten*, 26 July 1934, p. 1.
14 Mauthe's greater-German leanings were evidently stronger than his opposition to National Socialism for after the *Anschluss*, he was simply replaced as chief editor of the *Wiener Neueste Nachrichten* and spared the fate of denunciation or incarceration. See Dubrovic, *Veruntreute Geschichte*, pp. 213, 229–31. See also Fritz Hausjell, *Journalisten für das Reich: Der Reichsverband der deutschen Presse in Österreich 1938–45* (Vienna: Verlag für Gesellschaftskritik, 1993), p. 153; Gabriele Melischek and Josef Seethaler (eds), *Die Wiener Tageszeitungen: Eine Dokumentation 1918–1938*, vol. 3 (Frankfurt am Main: Peter Lang, 1992), p. 207; Paupié, *Handbuch der Österreichischen Presseges-chichte*, vol. 1, pp. 111–12; Jagschitz, 'Die Presse in Österreich von 1918 bis 1945', p. 50.
15 Gerhard Jagschitz, 'Zwischen Befriedung und Konfrontation: Zur Lage der NSDAP in Österreich 1934 bis 1936', in Jedlicka and Neck (eds), *Das*

Juliabkommen von 1936, pp. 163–67; Pauley, *Hitler and the Forgotten Nazis*, pp. 148–50; Bukey, *Hitler's Hometown*, p. 157.

16 On German Catholic refugees and *Der Christliche Ständestaat*, especially the rivalry with the *Reichpost* editors, see Ebneth, *Die österreichische Wochenschrift*. See also Anton Staudinger, 'Zur "Österreich"-Ideologie des Ständestaates', in Jedlicka and Neck (eds), *Das Juliabkommen von 1936*, pp. 209–12. I address this further in Chapter 6.

17 Peter Malina, 'Berichte aus einem fernen Land? Die Berichterstattung der *Reichspost* über die Lage der Kirchen in Deutchland 1933', *Medien & Zeit* 5, 4 (1990): 11–17.

18 Staudinger, 'Zur "Österreich"-Ideologie des Ständestaates', pp. 238–39.

19 On Funder, see Hedwig Pfarrhofer, *Friedrich Funder: Ein Mann zwischen Gestern und Morgen* (Graz: Styria, 1978), as well as Malina, 'Berichte aus einem fernen Land?' and Michael Schmolke, 'Katholische Journalistik in Österreich 1933–1938', *Medien & Zeit* 3, 4 (1988): 17–24. See also his two autobiographical works, Friedrich Funder, *Als Österreich den Sturm bestand: Aus der Ersten in die Zweite Republik* (Vienna: Herold, 1957) and *Vom Gestern ins Heute: Aus dem Kaiserreich in die Republik* (Vienna: Herold, 1971).

20 Stanley Suval, *The Anschluss Question in the Weimar Era: A Study of Nationalism in Germany and Austria 1918–32* (Baltimore: Johns Hopkins University Press, 1974), pp. 198–202; Bluhm, *Building an Austrian Nation*, pp. 42–43. For a detailed discussion of the Austrian Action programme, and Winter's ideas on Catholic socialism, see Alfred Diament, *Austrian Catholics and the First Republic: Democracy, Capitalism and the Social Order, 1918–1934* (Princeton: Princeton University Press, 1960), pp. 125–30, 220–29.

21 Winter fled Austria in 1938 and only returned in 1955, when his formerly radical ideas about Austrian nationhood and Catholic-socialist cooperation became mainstream thought in the post-war successor party to the Christian Socials, the ÖVP (Austrian People's Party). See Bluhm, *Building an Austrian Nation*, p. 43; Friedrich Scheu, *Der Weg ins Ungewisse: Österreichs Schicksalskurve 1929–1938* (Vienna: Molden, 1972), pp. 200–1; Fritz Fellner, 'The Problem of the Austrian Nation after 1945', *Journal of Modern History* 60, 2 (1988), pp. 271–73.

22 Pfarrhofer, *Friedrich Funder*, pp. 183–84.

23 Ibid., p. 184.

24 *Tagespost*, 4 January 1933, p. 1.

25 Ibid.

26 *Tagespost*, 4 July 1933 (Abendblatt), p. 1.

27 *Tagespost*, 23 April 1933, pp. 1–2. On the NSDAP-*Heimatschutz* agreement, see Edmondson, *The Heimwehr and Austrian Politics*, pp. 185–86.

28 *Tagespost*, 29 April 1933 (Abendblatt), p. 1.

29 Schmied, 'Presse und Diktatur', pp. 49, 52, 64. Prior to the drop in subscriptions, the *Tagespost* had sold around 30,000 copies on weekdays and 40,000 on Sundays. Schmied notes that the loss of readership was also attributed to a general readership fatigue in Austria that saw many readers drift away from

established Austrian newspapers towards the international German language press in Switzerland especially. See also Csoklich, 'Presse und Rundfunk', p. 725.

30 Schmied, 'Presse und Diktatur', pp. 65–66, 77–78.

31 Ibid., pp. 77–78.

32 See Chapter 2.

33 See both morning and evening editions of *Tagespost*, 24 February 1937, p. 1.

34 Low, *The Anschluss Movement*, pp. 180, 202–3.

35 *Tagespost*, 26 November 1937, p. 1.

36 El Refaie, 'Keeping the Truce?', p. 63.

37 Low, *The Anschluss Movement*, pp. 365–66.

38 *Tagespost*, 13 February 1938, p. 1. Hitler had originally sent von Papen to Vienna after the assassination of Dollfuss to replace Theo Habicht, who had masterminded the July putsch. See Hanisch, *Der Lange Schatten des Staates*, p. 321.

39 *Tagespost*, 16 February 1938 (Abendblatt), p. 1.

40 *Tagespost*, 5 March 1938 (Abendblatt), p. 1.

41 Stefan Karner, *Die Steiermark im Dritten Reich 1938–1945: Aspekte ihrer politischen, wirtschaftlichen-sozialen und kulturellen Entwicklung* (Graz: Leykam, 1986), p. 71; Dubrovic, *Veruntreute Geschichte*, p. 257.

42 These messages appeared in the *Heimatdienst* files, too, presumably to monitor the newspaper's readership. ÖStA/AdR, BKA/HD, Carton 8, *Wiener Neueste Nachrichten*, 29 and 31 October 1935.

43 ÖStA/AdR, BKA/HD, Carton 8, *Wiener Neueste Nachrichten*, 31 October 1935.

44 *Wiener Neueste Nachrichten*, 27 October 1935, p. 2.

45 Pieter Judson, *Guardians of the Nation: Activists on the Language Frontiers of Imperial Austria* (Cambridge, MA: Harvard University Press, 2006), pp. 253–54.

46 Thomas M. Barker, *The Slovene Minority of Carinthia* (Boulder: Columbia University Press, 1984), pp. 172–73.

47 Felder, *Die historische Identität der österreichischen Bundesländer*, p. 55; Barker, *The Slovene Minority of Carinthia*, pp. 165, 179; Brigitta Busch, 'Shifting Political and Cultural Borders: Language and Identity in the Border Region of Austria and Slovenia', *European Studies* 19 (2003), pp. 130–31; Judson, *Guardians of the Nation*, pp. 237–38. On the *Windischentheorie*, see especially Tom Priestly, 'Denial of Ethnic Identity: The Political Manipulation of Beliefs about Language in Slovene Minority Areas of Austria and Hungary', *Slavic Review* 55, 2 (1996): 364–98. On *Südostforschung* and the anti-Slavic discourse of Austrian 'experts' from the eighteenth to the early twentieth centuries, see Promitzer, 'The South Slavs in the Austrian Imagination', pp. 183–215.

48 ÖStA/AdR, BKA/HD, Carton 6, *Wiener Neueste Nachrichten*, 9 March 1935.

49 ÖStA/AdR, BKA/HD, Carton 6, *Wiener Neueste Nachrichten*, 8 May 1935.

50 Barker, *The Slovene Minority in Carinthia*, pp. 73–74. See also Priestly, 'Denial of Ethnic Identity', p. 377; Felder, *Die historische Identität der österreichischen Bundesländer*, p. 53.

51 Hanns Haas and Karl Stuhlpfarrer, *Österreich und seine Slowenen* (Vienna: Löcker & Wögenstein, 1977), p. 42; Erwin Steinböck, 'Kärnten', in Weinzierl and Skalnik (eds), *Österreich 1918–1938*, vol. 2, pp. 810–13; Barker, *The Slovene Minority of Carinthia*, pp. 181–89.

52 Steinböck, 'Kärnten', pp. 817–19, 827.

53 After the *Anschluss*, the *Heimatbund* became the instrument of National Socialism's policy of Germanization: of the 78 Slovene and utraquistic schools in operation prior to *Anschluss*, 50 were closed down by the end of 1938. The resettlement and deportations of Carinthian Slovenes did not begin until after Germany's occupation of Yugoslavia in 1941, as Nazi authorities in Berlin did not want to incite premature anti-German hostilities in Yugoslavia. By war's end, the Nazis had forcibly resettled around 1,300 Carinthian Slovenes and incarcerated another 1,000 in prisons and camps, including 200 who died in concentration camps. See Haas and Stuhlpfarrer, *Österreich und seine Slowenen*, pp. 67–70; Barker, *The Slovene Minority of Carinthia*, pp. 189–90. On the National Socialist period, see Michael John, 'Angst, Kooperation und Widerstand: Die autochthonen Minderheiten Österreichs 1938–1945', *Zeitgeschichte* 17, 2 (1989), pp. 74–77.

54 ÖStA/AdR, BKA/HD, Carton 7, *Wiener Neueste Nachrichten*, 8 June 1935. Dozens of articles from the *Freie Stimme* were also included in the press files of the *Heimatdienst*.

55 ÖStA/AdR, BKA/HD, Carton 7, *Wiener Neueste Nachrichten*, 9 June 1935.

56 *Wiener Neueste Nachrichten*, 22 July 1936, p. 4.

57 ÖStA/AdR, BKA/HD, Carton 7, *Wiener Neueste Nachrichten*, 11 June 1935.

58 Staudinger, 'Austrofaschistische "Österreich"-Ideologie', p. 44.

59 On a separate occasion from Schuschnigg's visit, the leader of the Carinthian *Ostmärkische Sturmscharen* described Carinthia as the 'cradle of Germany' indicating he saw no distinction between the new Austria and Nazi Germany. See ibid., p. 43.

60 Claudia Fräss-Ehrfeld, *Geschichte Kärntens* vol. 2, *Kärnten 1918–1920* (Klagenfurt: Heyn, 2000), pp. 35–38.

61 ÖStA/AdR, BKA/HD, Carton 8, *Wiener Neueste Nachrichten*, 21 September 1935.

62 Ibid.

63 Ibid.

64 On the relationship between British diplomats and intellectuals and the Yugoslav King Alexander during and after the First World War, see Vesna Drapac, *Constructing Yugoslavia: A Transnational History* (Basingstoke: Palgrave Macmillan, 2010).

65 According to census figures of 1846 and 1850, Styria had 363,000 Slovenes, which represented 36 per cent of Styria's population. See Fran Zwitter, 'The Slovenes and the Habsburg Monarchy', *Austrian History Yearbook* 3, 2 (1967),

p. 159. The number of Slovenes in Styria in the interwar period is based on the 1939 Nazis census, in which 3,607 declared themselves to be Slovene. Felder, *Die historische Identität der österreichischen Bundesländer*, p. 43. However, there were two censuses in 1939 following the National Socialist takeover in Austria: one on the basis of 'mother tongue' (*Muttersprache*), and the second to determine those who identified ethnically with the *Volkstum*. We can be sure that the number of Slovene-speakers who identified themselves publicly with the Slovene *Volk* was dramatically lower than those who declared only that their mother tongue was Slovenian. Even the latter figure would have represented only a proportion of the population who could and did speak Slovenian, but had long been acculturated into German-speaking society. See John, 'Angst, Kooperation und Widerstand'.

66 Aschacher, 'Die Presse der Steiermark', p. 59.
67 Ibid., pp. 61–62.
68 Glaser, *Tagebuch*, 22 June 1934.
69 Aschacher, 'Die Presse der Steiermark', pp. 59–60.
70 *Tagespost*, 4 January 1933, p. 2; 30 January 1933, p. 1.
71 *Tagespost*, 10 April 1936, p. 1.
72 Staudinger, 'Austrofaschistische "Österreich"-Ideologie', p. 44.
73 Karl M. Brousek, *Wien und seine Tschechen: Integration und Assimilation einer Minderheit im 20. Jahrhundert* (Munich: Oldenbourg, 1980), pp. 39–41.
74 Ibid., pp. 45–47.
75 See Tara Zahra, *Kidnapped Souls: National Indifference and the Battle for Children in the Bohemian Lands, 1900–1948* (Ithaca: Cornell University Press, 2008).
76 Interview with Antonie Bruha in Marie Brandeis, *Wir kamen von anderswo: Interviewbuch mit Tschechen und Slowaken in Österreich* (Prague: KLP, 2003), pp. 17–23, held in Forschungszentrum für historische Minderheiten (FZHM), Vienna.
77 Brousek, *Wien und seine Tschechen*, pp. 47–48.
78 ÖStA/AdR, BKA/HD, Carton 5, *Wiener Neueste Nachrichten*, 30 January 1935.
79 *Wiener Neueste Nachrichten*, 6 August 1937, pp. 1–2.
80 Brousek, *Wien und seine Tschechen*, pp. 48–49.
81 Jürgen Illigasch, 'Migration aus und nach Österreich in der Zwischenkriegszeit', *Zeitgeschichte* 26, 1 (1999), pp. 19–20. There are no statistics for the early 1920s as the Migration Office only kept records for emigration before 1925. See also Chapter 6.
82 Staudinger, 'Austrofaschistische "Österreich"-Ideologie', p. 43.
83 *Salzburger Volskblatt*, 25 August 1937, p. 1.
84 Cited in Brousek, *Wien und seine Tschechen*, p. 43; see also Gerald Schlag, 'Die Kroaten im Burgenland 1918 bis 1945', in Stefan Geosits (ed.), *Die burgenländischen Kroaten im Wandel der Zeiten* (Vienna: Edition Tusch, 1986), p. 202.
85 In the same year as the 400th anniversary celebrations, for example, the theological seminary in Zagreb invited seminarians from the Burgenland to attend

their summer retreat and gave them books and musical instruments to take back with them. Franz Szucsich, 'Das Vereinswesen der burgenländischen Kroaten', in Geosits (ed.), *Die burgenländischen Kroaten*, p. 245.

86 Schlag, 'Die Kroaten im Burgenland 1918 bis 1945', p. 199. For example, when Yugoslavia's Education Minister, Svetozar Pribičević, shut German schools in 1925 as revenge for the treatment of Slovenian schools in Austria, Croatian-speaking deputies in the Burgenland parliament protested by declaring their loyalty and belonging to Austria: 'We were and we remain Austrians!'

87 Ibid., pp. 178–81, 188.

88 Ibid., pp. 199–200. See also Szucsich, 'Das Vereinswesen der burgenländischen Kroaten', pp. 244–45.

89 Schlag, 'Die Kroaten im Burgenland 1918 bis 1945', p. 201.

90 Catholic Action groups in Austria were granted full autonomy under the terms of the May 1934 concordat, which the Austrian bishops successfully negotiated to ensure that no loophole existed for state organizations to exploit the freedom of Catholic youth groups and welfare auxiliaries, as had already happened in Germany. Catholic Action groups in Germany were to have been protected under Article 31 of the 1933 Concordat, but negotiations concluded before these groups could be specified in the wording of the document. See Gellot, 'Defending Catholic Interests in the Christian State', pp. 574, 580.

91 ÖStA/AdR, BKA/HD, Carton 11, *Hrvatske Novine*, 24 April 1937.

92 ÖStA/AdR, BKA/HD, Carton 11, *Hrvatske Novine*, 8 May 1937.

93 ÖStA/AdR, BKA/HD, Carton 11, *Hrvatske Novine*, 29 May 1937. Underline in original translation.

94 Ibid.

95 Schlag, 'Die Kroaten im Burgenland 1918 bis 1945', pp. 192–93.

96 Ibid., pp. 202–3.

97 ÖStA/AdR, BKA/HD, Carton 11, *Hrvatske Novine*, 5 June 1937.

98 Bärnthaler, 'Geschichte und Organisation der Vaterländischen Front', pp. 265–68.

99 Ibid., p. 261.

100 See Zahra, *Kidnapped Souls*.

101 ÖStA/AdR, BKA/HD, Carton 10, ÖKVDA, 24 April 1937 and 19 June 1937; Bärnthaler, 'Geschichte und Organisation der Vaterländischen Front', p. 269.

102 Bärnthaler, 'Geschichte und Organisation der Vaterländischen Front', pp. 268–69.

103 See Elizabeth Harvey, 'Pilgrimages to the "Bleeding Border": Gender and Rituals of Nationalist Protest in Germany, 1919–39', *Women's History Review* 9, 2 (2000): 201–29; Harvey, *Women and the Nazi East: Agents and Witnesses of Germanization* (New Haven: Yale University Press, 2003). There are many studies of the German '*Ostforscher*', notably Michael Burleigh, *Germany Turns Eastward: A Study of* Ostforschung *in the Third Reich* (Cambridge: Cambridge University Press, 1988).

104 Bärnthaler, 'Geschichte und Organisation der Vaterländischen Front', p. 268.

105 Ibid., pp. 267–68. The ÖKVDA began publication in November 1935 and was edited by Josef Tzöbl.
106 ÖStA/AdR, BKA/HD, Carton 10, ÖKVDA, 20 March 1937 on Germans in Slovenia, for example, and 24 April 1937 on plans to build a Czech commerce academy and teachers' college in Iglau.
107 ÖStA/AdR, BKA/HD, Carton 10, ÖKVDA, 8 May 1937.
108 See Vejas Gabriel Liulevicius, *War Land on the Eastern Front: Culture, National Identity, and German Occupation in World War I* (Cambridge: Cambridge University Press, 2000) on these encounters with the regions and people under German military occupation after 1915. The agricultural bounty from the new territories, farmed by locals under German 'tutelage', quite literally did enter the kitchens of German homes during an exhibition in Berlin in 1916.
109 ÖStA/AdR, BKA/HD, Carton 10, ÖKVDA, 19 June 1937.
110 Ibid.
111 Ibid.
112 Viktor Reimann, *Innitzer: Kardinal zwischen Hitler und Rom*, rev. and expanded edn (Vienna: Amalthea, 1988), p. 90.
113 Ibid.
114 On the opening of the new school see Brousek, *Wien und seine Tschechen*, p. 48.
115 See Reimann, *Innitzer*. Innitzer intervened on behalf of Austrian Nazis imprisoned in Wollersdorf in 1934 and again in 1935 when a request came from families of the prisoners to send Christmas parcels to their loved ones. He also vigorously defended the young priests and members of the Catholic '*Neubund*' when Rome sought an official explanation for the numbers of Nazis in the organization.
116 Bärnthaler, 'Geschichte und Organisation der Vaterländischen Front', pp. 269–70. The Austrian press and propaganda ministry already had on file all the publications of the *Volksdeutsche Presse- und Informationsdienst* and the *Sudetendeutsche Presse-Briefe*, the press agency of the SdP. See ÖStA/AdR, BKA/HD, Carton 11.
117 Bärnthaler, 'Geschichte und Organisation der Vaterländischen Front', pp. 269–90.
118 Henlein had already sought out Hungary, Italy, Sweden, Britain and even the League of Nations as allies to the cause of the Sudeten minority, and his political alliances remained flexible right up until the end of 1937, as Mark Cornwall has recently shown. Even Henlein's famous letter to Hitler in November 1937 asking him to invade Czechoslovakia (before Hitler had even annexed Austria) does not indicate that Henlein saw Nazi Germany as the only chance for the Sudeten Germans, but simply that this was another one of Henlein's 'manoeuvres'. See Cornwall, ' "A Leap into Ice-Cold Water": The Manoeuvres of the Henlein Movement in Czechoslovakia, 1933–1938', in Cornwall and Evans (eds), *Czechoslovakia in a Nationalist and Fascist Europe*, pp. 123–42.

5

'Ostjude' as anti-Semitic stereotype

Just as minority politics drew activists and politicians into a common league on behalf of Austrian 'Germandom', anti-Semitism united German-nationalists and Austrofascists into a common pan-German front. We saw in the previous two chapters that while German-nationalists and Austro-fascists sometimes differed in where they drew the boundaries of a universal pan-German community – notably over the question of religion – they found a common footing when it came to constructing a pan-German identity within the Austrian state. Austria was a German state with German-language institutions and a German cultural heritage and minorities had to dissimilate from their non-German identities and become Germanized citizens of Austria. Similarly the question of Jewish assimilation and citizenship in the Austrian state bound Austrofascists and German-nationalists even as religion again proved a sticking point. State functionaries preferred comparisons between Jews and Ottoman Turks as twin threats from 'the East', while German-nationalist editors focused their attacks on vagrant Jewish criminals from Eastern Europe. All of these images of Jews were conflated into a single anti-Semitic stereotype of the foreign Eastern Jew, the '*Ostjude*'.

In the remaining two chapters I argue that anti-Semitism and the debate on immigration and citizenship were as integral to the construction of an Austrian pan-German identity as were the questions of Austro-German unity and minorities. This chapter shows the construction of cultural, political and racial barriers to Jews and demonstrates that German-nationalists and Austrofascists were equally defamatory in their anti-Semitism: an editor of a German-nationalist newspaper was no more or less predisposed to anti-Semitism than a functionary of the state. Furthermore, I argue that a typology of anti-Semitism does not help us draw useful distinctions between the violent and genocidal actions of some anti-Semites and the 'merely' exclusionary and xenophobic attitudes and politics of others. Rather, I suggest that it is more fruitful to see anti-Semitism, like national identity, as a construction of civic and ethnic boundaries.

Chapter 6 will then demonstrate how these boundaries turned into legal barriers to bar Jews from residency and citizenship in the Austrofascist state.

'Constructing the Jew' in Austria[1]

We cannot begin to understand anti-Semitism in all of its dimensions or even at its core by approaching it as a typology. Historians often make distinctions between types of anti-Semitism, ranging from personal prejudice, to anti-modernist critiques, to racial anti-Semitism and to genocide at the far end of the scale.[2] Yet they also recognize the relative ease with which one type can mobilize into another. Sigurd Paul Scheichl has shown how personal dislike of Jewish students in the Austrian German-nationalist student fraternities rapidly developed into a political and racial programme under the patronage of Georg von Schönerer.[3] Similarly, Günter Fellner has argued that a 'verbal' anti-Semite cannot be compared to a pogromist, but neither is it implausible that verbal attacks might later turn into genocide.[4] In his analysis of different categories of anti-Semitism in Austria, Bruce Pauley comes to the same conclusion as Fellner and Scheichl that 'from an anti-Semitism of words it was only one small step to an anti-Semitism of deeds.'[5] But like nationalism, anti-Semitism cannot be understood in terms of static categories that tell us little about how it functioned in society, even allowing for the fluidity of those categories. Rather, anti-Semitism can be seen as a constructed image of Jews, just as nationalism is also understood in constructivist terms. Such a mode of analysis also avoids teleological readings of modern anti-Semitism that place its origins in the late nineteenth century (Schönerer in Austria, the Dreyfus affair in France), the mid-point after the First World War (the 'stab in the back' myth), and the final stage in the Holocaust, or the more subtle teleology that explains the origins of disinfection regimes in Nazi concentration camps in the disinfection stations on the Eastern Front in the First World War.[6]

The image of the foreign Jew – Hannah Arendt, falling into the contemporary trap of typologies, referred to this image as 'nationalistic anti-Semitism'[7] – was a product of the First World War and the post-war peace settlements. In France, for example, the construction of the foreign Jew surfaced in the immediate aftermath of the re-annexation of Alsace-Lorraine and again in the 1930s, following the arrival of Jewish refugees from Germany. Although anti-Dreyfusards had already depicted Jews as France's national enemy in the late nineteenth century, Jews then were not seen as a threat to France's borders but to the idea of France as a nation of Christian piety untainted by republican mores. After 1918, however, Jews were seen as invaders of the French state, living off the generosity of the French and capable of switching sides at the moment of necessity and opportunity.[8]

Similarly in Austria, anti-Semitism in the interwar period inherited some of the nineteenth-century stereotypes of Jews as a threat to good and industrious Christian men and women most famously propounded by Vienna's mayor of the 'little people' and founder of the Christian Social Party, Lueger. But the war transformed these earlier images of Jews as stains on the moral and material fabric of the empire to being, almost overnight, illegal aliens in Austria. Peter Pulzer has argued that anti-Semitism in Germany and Austria was 'exceptional' in the nineteenth century because of its genesis in the revolutionary civil and constitutional codes (1848 in Germany and 1867 in Austria) and there are many who would see anti-Semitism in Austria and Germany – or indeed all of Eastern Europe – as 'exceptional' for the entire interwar period and Second World War.[9] But as in France, it was not the nineteenth-century debates that determined anti-Semitism's development in the twentieth century. More than any innate or exceptional political culture, it was imperial collapse, international treaties and the regulation of citizenship in the new republics in Germany and Austria that provided the legal and political framework in which anti-Semitism radicalized during the interwar period.[10] While the antecedents for modern anti-Semitism certainly lay in the experiences of national politics in the empire before the war, I argue that the creation of an anti-Semitic stereotype in the interwar period was a specific product of the wartime experience of Jewish refugees and drew on images of Jews as illegal, stateless criminals invading Austria's borders and marauding its public resources.

Most of the agitation against Jews in post-war Austria was directed against wartime refugees from Galicia who remained in Vienna and initially were excluded from citizenship in the new Austrian state.[11] Food and housing shortages, coupled with the popular perception that Jewish refugees were using up meagre resources, fuelled hostilities towards them in all sectors of public life in politics, universities, the professions and the press. Nor was the hostility towards the refugees limited to any one 'camp': the Social Democrats had their own anti-Semitic spokesperson in the governor of Lower Austria and Vienna, Albert Sever.[12] In September 1919, Sever issued a decree for the expulsion of all foreigners who did not have residency prior to 1914 in the territories that made up the post-war Austrian state. The federal Social Democratic party leadership tried to distance itself from the provincial party's actions, but in the end Sever only succeeded in deporting around 12,000 of the refugees due to insufficient coal and transportation and the unwillingness of Poland and Czechoslovakia to approve the transports through their territory.[13]

In Vienna, anti-Semites took to the streets and their printing presses to protest against the refugees, wildly inflating the numbers of the refugees to represent the entire Jewish population of the city. The leader of the Nazi Party, Walter Riehl, initially played an active role in organizing public demonstrations. At a rally held in the Prater fairground in September 1920, he called for the deportation of the city's 200,000 Jews to vacate housing for the 150,000 homeless in Vienna. The scars of defeat and the post-war economic crisis exacerbated this suspicion and resentment towards Jewish refugees so that the collective label of '*Ostjuden*' functioned as a means of alienating Jews from society and vindicating attempts to have them removed. One Zionist daily newspaper in Vienna remarked bitterly in September 1921 that 'since the collapse [of Austria-Hungary] the good people of Austria have condensed everything into the little word *Ostjude* . . . It is a wondrous expression which alleviates every pain and takes away every shame. Complaints over the rising costs of bread, and the falling morals of women, over bad railroad transportation, the lack of coal, the unruliness of school children, and the watering down of milk find their solution: Out with the *Ostjuden!*'[14]

Riehl's efforts were soon overtaken by the Christian Social politician, Anton Jerzabek, leader of the League of Anti-Semites (*Antisemitenbund*), whose members included many prominent Christian Social figures including the future Chancellor Dollfuss, who spoke at several League meetings in 1920 while he was president of the Catholic student body in Vienna. The League's first activity was to organize an international congress in Vienna in March 1921 for 40,000 Austrian and other European delegates to discuss a proposal for Europe-wide restrictions on Jewish minorities. The delegates defined Jews as any persons with a Jewish great-grandparent, surpassing Hitler's classification of third-generation Jews under the later Nuremberg Laws. The *Antisemitenbund* also went further than any other group in Austria by demanding the legal separation of Jews and non-Jews in government services, such as education and welfare support, and the total exclusion of Jews from law, medicine and teaching. In addition to these demands, its leaders called for a moratorium on Jewish immigration to Austria, the deportation of all Jewish arrivals since 1914, the official label of 'Jewish' for any business or newspaper that employed Jews, a pro rata restriction on Jews in the arts, disenfranchisement of the Jews and, finally, a prohibition on ownership of land or holding public office. After 1924, Riehl forced Nazi party members to relinquish their membership in the *Antisemitenbund* so that, until 1933, the Nazi Party held a monopoly on all anti-Semitic activities in Austria. The League reformed in 1933 following the ban on the NSDAP and came under scrutiny by the Austrofascist state not because of its anti-Semitism, but due to the government's suspicions that it was a cover for illegal Nazis. Its leaders attempted to demonstrate their Austrian credentials by drawing up new organizational rules in 1936, but the government continued to hold them at arm's length.[15]

Thus the *Antisemitenbund* never had the institutional status of the ÖVVA, which also recruited Nazi sympathizers as we saw in Chapter 4. Part of the reason for this distance lay in the government's own anti-Semitic programme, which we will see below did not require an army of activists to carry it out but only a handful of politicians and administrators. A further reason why the Austrofascist state distanced itself from the League is that Dollfuss and other Christian Social politicians no longer needed it as a platform for their own careers as they had done in 1920. As noted above Dollfuss himself addressed the early League gatherings and several other Christian Social politicians also campaigned after the war for Jews to be given a minority status in Austria. In 1919, even before the *Antisemitenbund* was founded, the leader of the Christian Social Party, Leopold Kunschak, proposed a *numerus clausus* bill that – had it been accepted – would have given Austrian Jews separate political rights and restricted their representation in the public service and academia. In 1920, Kunschak went further by suggesting that Jewish refugees be given the choice either to emigrate or be interned in a concentration camp. Kunschak's views alarmed his more conservative colleagues, Ignaz Seipel counselling him not to promulgate the bill in 1919, although he conceded it might well be a political possibility in the future. Nonetheless, the tolerance shown for such inflammatory debate reveals the high profile of anti-Semitism in Christian Social circles. Although anti-Semitism had been one of the political pillars on which Lueger had founded the party, he had only used anti-Semitism as a weapon against his political rivals and never enacted any anti-Semitic legislation. Not until the Austrofascist period did state functionaries have both the power and the legislative resources to create anti-Semitic laws, while German-nationalist polemicists looked on from the sidelines either in approval or resigning themselves to a day when more extensive legal measures would be possible in Austria.

Kunschak's proposal in 1919 for a *numerus clausus* also pre-dated the 1920 Hungarian *numerus clausus* on Jewish enrolments in universities, as part of a larger counter-revolutionary campaign against Jews who had participated in Béla Kún's revolution. While the legislation did not explicitly mention Jews as the target minority, its references to Christian representation at the universities, along with the anti-Semitic nature of Hungarian debate surrounding the law, showed that its intended result was to reduce the numbers of Jews in Hungary's universities.[16] The international community did not condone the law but, having assisted Miklós Horthy to form a counter-revolutionary government in 1920 in return for his cooperation in signing the Treaty of Trianon, the Allies could turn a blind eye to Hungary's anti-Semitic legislation, especially at a time when America's Ivy League universities were unofficially imposing quotas of their own on Jewish immigrants.[17] As we will see with Austria's citizenship laws, legislators in the new states were simply following ethnic principles already enshrined in the Allied policy of self-determination and in minority treaties created by the League of Nations. Such a conclusion does not, of course, underplay the political agency and will of the respective governments that enacted the legislation, but it does highlight the international conditions under which moves towards exclusionary politics were possible in the interwar years.

Hungary's *numerus clausus* became a cause célèbre for student activists and their patrons at the highest level of university governance in Austrian universities. The German Students for the East March (*Deutsche Studenschaft für Ostmark*) led a campaign to have the number of Jewish students at Austrian universities restricted to 10 per cent of all student enrolments in accord with the demographic ratio of Jews to non-Jews in Austria. The numbers of Jewish enrolments were disproportionately high, constituting over a third of all tertiary enrolments at Austrian universities, due partly to the number of Jewish immigrants before and after 1918, and partly to the tendency of Jewish families to place greater value on higher education for both males and females. Jewish enrolments at the University of Vienna, for example, rose from 27 per cent before 1914 to 42 per cent in 1920–21. The rector of the University of Vienna, Karl Diener, publicly supported the efforts of the *Deutsche Studentenschaft* in 1922 to halt what he described as the 'shocking invasion of racially and organically alien elements, whose culture, upbringing, and morals are far below every native German student ... The reduction of the Eastern Jews must today take a leading place in the program of every rector and senate of a German university (*Hochschule*). The progressive orientalization of Vienna must at least be stopped at the *Hochschulen*.'[18] At the Technical College in Vienna, where more than 41 per cent of students were Jewish, the academic senate approved a *numerus clausus* on Jewish students in March 1923 by prohibiting Jewish immigrants from enrolling in those courses that already filled a 10 per cent Jewish quota. When efforts to impose similar conditions on Jewish enrolments at the University of Vienna failed, student groups staged violent riots and disrupted lectures, forcing the university to close its doors temporarily in November 1923 for the first time since 1897, when students had rioted against the Badeni Decrees. The general climate of academic anti-Semitism deterred Jews from seeking a university place so that, between 1921 and 1927, Jewish enrolments at the University of Vienna dropped from 42 per cent to 17.5 per cent.[19]

Opinion makers outside the academy looked disparagingly upon what they saw as rabble-rousing student antics, but their own views were no less hostile. When the University of Vienna was forced to close in November 1923, the Christian Social press and university professors condemned the violence because it disrupted teaching and research, not because it was racially motivated. The *Reichspost* warned that Jewish dominance would be contained not by violence, but by the intellectual dissemination of pan-German ideas.[20] One of the few academics who spoke out against the anti-Semitism was Theodor Innitzer, who had been on the university's theological faculty since 1913 and was appointed rector of the University of Vienna between 1928 and 1929.[21] He had assisted poor Jewish students and, as rector, threatened to close the university for an academic year when violence broke out against Jewish students.[22] Later, however, as the Austrian cardinal, Innitzer endorsed the views of the head of the Anima German seminary and church in Rome, Alois Hudal (1885–1963), whose book, *Die Grundlagen des Nationalsozialismus* (The Foundations of National Socialism), published in 1936, argued in favour of racial laws on the basis that all races and people were equal before God, but not all races and people were equal in their intellectual, moral and physiological capacities.[23]

Hudal's ideas and their reception in Austria will be explored in more detail below, but the example of Innitzer here highlights the problem of boxing anti-Semitism into categories or types in order to be able to classify a phenomenon that appeared to be more widespread and deep-seated in Austria than anywhere else in Europe. Just as a university professor, a politician and a cardinal could find themselves on the same platform promoting 'Germandom work', so at different times could the place of Jews in Austria's public institutions draw a common response as well as differences on other occasions. If we are to avoid the problematic and blurred categories of anti-Semitism as religious prejudice or racism, and instead see how anti-Semitism functioned in politics and in the wider public sphere as a social and cultural stereotype, then we must ask how and in what context such stereotypes were constructed by an individual, a group or a government. The views of a politician, a university professor, a cardinal or a newspaper editor then become significant because they are connected directly with the particular social and political context in which they are expressed. There is little sense in arguing that the anti-Semitism of state functionaries was less obstreperous than that of groups such as the *Antisemitenbund* or the *Deutsche Studentenschaft*, which we have seen was not true anyway for the immediate post-1918 period. Nor does the much cited qualification that Jews fared better under Austrofascism than under Nazism help us to understand the nature of anti-Semitism before 1938. On the other hand, it is equally banal to argue that all anti-Semitism, regardless of where it occurred or how it was formulated or by whom it was expressed, had similar intentions and equal consequences. It is much more significant to investigate how and why certain stereotypes of Jews emerged and became pervasive at a particular time. The image of Jews as morally and materially corruptive in 'Christian Austria', for example, had evolved over a longer period than the stereotype of Jews as foreigners. When Gföllner's pastoral letter in January 1933 condemned Jews for their 'mammonism' and blamed them for the 'spiritual trash' in society, and at the same time attacked National Socialism as 'un-Christian', we have to consider which anti-Semitic stereotype was behind the bishop's denunciations.[24] Was the push to remove Jews from public life in Austria after 1933 prompted by stereotypes of the Jews as religious or ideological enemies, or by another more recent perception of the Jews as aliens in a state framed by ethnic and civic boundaries of belonging? The following section will address these images of Jews from the perspective of the state, church leaders and the Jewish community itself. The final two sections of the chapter will then analyse the stereotypes of Jews in the German-nationalist press.

Jews in the 'Christian' state

The history of religion in the Austrofascist state, a field rich in potential for future research, would benefit considerably from more comparative approaches that locate the Austrian experiences within broader social and cultural histories of the Church during the first half of the twentieth century. I state this here because notwithstanding the headway already made by Laura Gellott, Irene Bandhauer-Schöffmann and others, the lack of attention in this important area of twentieth-century Austrian history means that any understanding of religious belief and practices during the 1930s is obscured by arguments about the Church's role in politics.[25] For the same reason I suggest that the question of anti-Semitism in the Austrofascist state has been obscured by arguments that narrowly link the politics of the Church with that of the 'Christian' Austrian state. These arguments are predicated on an assumption that the statements of church leaders can be placed alongside the speeches of state leaders as evidence for a church-state alliance on the issue of Jews in Austria, but as Gellott and others have pointed out, the question of anti-Semitism and the Catholic Church in Austria – both before and after 1938 – is much more ambiguous than some have claimed.[26]

Instead of starting with the premise that crucifixes in classrooms and on country roads were a constant reminder to school children and uneducated peasants that Jews killed Christ, Austrian historians have still many more sources to mine to reach the complexity and sophistication of arguments about anti-Semitism and popular religion elsewhere, in France notably.[27] This book is not intended to make that contribution, but my argument here is simply that the evidence of a cardinal or priest attending a speech or festivity does not demonstrate the individual's – or entire Church's – support for the state ideology. To take Vichy France as an example, Vesna Drapac has argued that the evidence of a French cardinal attending an official celebration flanked by German officials in Nazi-occupied Paris, then a few hours later directing parishioners in a local gathering on their double obligation as Christians and patriots to relieve suffering and endure hardship, is reason to dispense with conventional wisdom about the Church's support for the Vichy regime.[28] So also Austrian historians might begin to examine the many nuances of Catholic life under the Austrofascist state. We have already seen the multiple meanings that 'Germandom' work held for the organizers and supporters of the Boniface Day celebrations. Similarly, we will see here that the anti-Semitism of Bishop Hudal received mixed responses from Austrian Catholics, and not everyone who attended the All-German Catholic Congress in Vienna in September 1933 equated Ottoman Turks with Jews. Church and state leaders did sit alongside one another both during the 1933 Congress and at Hudal's public lectures in Vienna in 1936, but that does not mean they were equally receptive to the various ideas expressed on those occasions.

Indeed, uppermost in the minds of the organizers of the Catholic Congress was not the 'Jewish question' but the absence of German Catholics at what was supposed to be an 'All-German' celebration. Over 30,000 German Catholics had already registered to attend when the Reich Chancellery informed the Central Committee of the Catholic Congress that the 1,000-mark tariff would also apply to pilgrims travelling to Vienna.[29] The absence of Germany's Cardinal Faulhaber, who was to have been the papal representative, was a further blow to the organizers. Funder, chief editor of the *Reichspost* and a member of the Central Committee, travelled to Rome in July 1933 to ask the pope to send a papal legate in place of Cardinal Faulhaber. In the end, Cardinal La Fountaine, the archbishop of Venice, came to Vienna as the pope's representative along with the cardinals of Hungary, France and Poland.[30] Around 33,000 pilgrims travelled to Vienna from all over Europe: a delegation of Belgian women pilgrims came, Hungarians, Poles and Italians celebrated their own masses during the week's programme, Croats from Yugoslavia came in support of Croatian-speakers in the Burgenland, who were preparing to celebrate a different anniversary as we saw in Chapter 4, and Czech-speaking Viennese Catholics attended along with pilgrims from Czechoslovakia. Even a priest from China showed as one of the invited speakers.[31] The German pilgrims were not forgotten by the organizers, nor by Cardinal Innitzer who was personally saddened by their absence, but for the rest of the pilgrims the 'All-German' Catholic Congress was an international affair, a celebration of the universal Church where laity, clergy and bishops gathered as one.[32]

Others who attended the various events throughout the week of the Catholic Congress might have been more interested in the special events for women than the missing Germans. A women's public meeting was held in Vienna's Concert Hall on the Saturday evening on the third day of the Congress. Alma Motzko (1887–1968), academic, member of the Vienna city council and leader of the Catholic Women's Organization for the archdiocese of Vienna, gave the keynote address. The following Monday members of the Catholic women's movement were invited to hear a lecture by another female politician, Emma Kapral (1877–1969), a former Christian Social member of parliament and leader of the Catholic Union of Women School Teachers. Both women affirmed church teaching about 'God-given differences' between men and women and the role of motherhood as the social and spiritual basis on which a society and a state could be renewed, or re-Catholicized. But each speaker carefully addressed the definition of women's work that the state wanted to restrict to the private sphere of the home. At the time of the Catholic Congress, the government was debating the proposed Double Wage Act that would exclude married women from paid employment. With Chancellor Dollfuss in the audience, Motzko argued that Catholic women wanted to perform their full duties as citizens in the state not just in their private lives, but also in the public spheres of education, politics and professional life. She also rejected both the state's and the Church's attempts to redirect women's activism towards the charitable work of Catholic Action, maintaining that charity was not the only type of work women could perform outside the home. In her talk two days later Kapral reasoned on both theological and political grounds that all women had a vocation in the state, although she differed from Motzko in her view that married women's vocations were either in the home or in the family business where they contributed to the family income. Kapral addressed only the rights of unmarried women to be paid equal wages to men and to have political representation in the state. She also praised the state's effort to ban 'false' images of women's bodies in the media. A further clue as to what the two women and their audiences saw as the prevailing *Zeitgeist* was a play performed by a lay drama group following Motzko's address. Neither Jews nor Communists were among the various characters in the play; instead, an unbeliever, a beggar, the unemployed, a neglected boy, a prostitute, the sick, the homeless and the poor represented the full spectrum of social and spiritual poverty to mobilize Catholic women activists in the audience.[33]

So when Dollfuss addressed delegates at the Vienna Stadium in his famous speech on 11 September, in which he spoke of Austria's defeat of the 'hordes from the East' in 1683 and called for a German Christian spirit of renewal that would again repel the newest threat from 'the East', not all of his listeners would have interpreted this denunciation of communism in anti-Semitic terms.[34] The women who had heard Motzko's and Kapral's talks may have been asking themselves whether he was also speaking to their place within the 'German Christian' state. Both Kapral and Motzko had rejected the Nazi German view of women as biological agents of national renewal, and one wonders what their listeners made of the chancellor's words on this occasion. Moreover, the theme of liberation from 'the East' was celebrated throughout 1933, not only by the organizers of the Catholic Congress. Forty thousand *Heimwehr* troops had marched in Vienna earlier in May to commemorate the 250th anniversary of the city's liberation even though the actual anniversary was 12 September, the day after Dollfuss's speech.[35] We have seen that Archbishop Rieder in Salzburg described 1933 as a holy year for Germans, while the Vatican's own illustrated coverage of the celebrations in Vienna proclaimed a 'holy year' not just for Germans but for the united forces of Christendom – symbolized in the cross presented by Pope Innocent XI to Marco d'Aviano – who had triumphed over a common enemy, the Ottoman Turks under the Grand Vizier Kara Mustafa.[36] Pius XI sent a personal message to Dollfuss to congratulate him on his speech at the Catholic Congress, not for his defiance of the 'hordes from the East' but for his public declaration that he would build Austria according to papal teaching in the encyclical, *Quadragesimo Anno*.[37] The Catholic Congress was not only an occasion for commemorating the past and present triumphs of Christendom over its enemies, but it was also a platform for upholding conservative values and role models and challenging the views of those within and outside Austria who would seek to restrict the full expression of those values in both public and private life.

The debate over women's work at the 1933 Catholic Congress also provides a context in which to examine the Austrofascist state's coordination of Zionist groups, including women's associations, within the Fatherland Front. Zionist groups were the most prominent Jewish organizations in the Austrofascist state following the ban on the Social Democratic and Communist parties. Even Zionist workers' groups, like Poale-Zion, remained legal while all other Jewish workers' organizations were banned. Zionist women activists were engaged in a number of state-sponsored charitable initiatives alongside Catholic, liberal and nationalist women's groups. Although Jewish women also belonged to the inter-confessional League of Austrian Women's Associations (BÖFV), many withdrew from its activities due to the anti-Semitic views of some of its members. Sofie

Löwenherz, whose husband was the director of Vienna's Jewish religious and political organization, the *Israelitische Kultusgemeinde* (IKG), led the largest Zionist women's association, the World Organization of Zionist Women (WIZO). WIZO played a leading role in the formation of the Women's Emergency Service, a national welfare organization founded in 1934 by Leopoldine Miklas – wife of the Austrian federal president, Wilhelm Miklas – to replace the former socialist welfare groups. Löwenherz was on the organizing committee of the Women's Emergency Service along with Motzko and other representatives of Austrian women's associations. Löwenherz again took a prominent role in organizing the Fatherland Front's Mother's Day celebrations and exhibition in Vienna's Natural History Museum in 1936. Her organization published a commemorative booklet honouring the memory of Jeanette Herzl (1836–1911), mother of the founder of Zionism, Theodor Herzl, whose 100th birthday coincided with the 1936 Mother's Day celebrations.[38]

Official tolerance of Zionist groups and coordination of their activities within the Fatherland Front allowed the state to delineate clear boundaries between 'German Christian' Austrians and the Jewish minority living alongside them. Zionist Jews were neither Christian nor German, and even if they spoke German their national loyalties lay elsewhere. Thus the state could be absolved of its responsibilities towards all Jews by ensuring their needs were met by the Jewish community. By creating these social, political and eventually legal boundaries between Austrian citizens, the state could expedite the process of Jewish emigration from Austria.[39] The Austrofascist state's support for Zionism was the inverse of its own policies of Germanization: Austrofascists promoted the dissimilation of German-speaking Jews from an Austrian German identity while encouraging Slovene, Czech and Croatian minorities to dissimilate from their non-German identities to become Germanized Austrians.

One of the most prominent supporters of Zionism within the Austrofascist state was Emmerich Czermak, who we have already seen was instrumental in the founding of the Fatherland Front's 'Germandom Work' organization. In 1933 Czermak co-authored a book with a well-known Zionist, Oskar Karbach, entitled *Ordnung in der Judenfrage* (Order in the Jewish Question), in which he argued for a reversal of Jewish assimilation in the Austrian state and a religious awakening among the Jewish people. The Jews themselves, Czermak claimed, recognized that assimilation had failed. In keeping with the earlier Christian Social proposals for a *numerus clausus*, Czermak outlined his proposal for the segregation of Jews as a minority group to regulate their participation in the 'host' nation. This was necessary, he believed, because Palestine would not be able to accommodate all the Jews in Germany let alone in Europe. Karbach's shorter contribution to the book welcomed the authoritarian measures of states that could enforce dissimilation as a state policy and thereby convince Jews that in the long term such a reform would lead to their becoming active and valuable citizens in the state. Moderate Zionists, although they also sought minority representation and greater control over Jewish affairs in the state, opposed Czermak's proposal because it did not address the under-representation of Jews in the civil service, among other areas of public life.[40]

Thus although the 1934 constitution guaranteed the equality of all citizens and the freedom of all religions, and in spite of both Dollfuss's and Schuschnigg's assurances to Austrian Jews that they were not second-class citizens, from the outset Austrofascist functionaries were drawing up plans to count and regulate the numbers of Jews in the state. Even before the new constitution was promulgated, the government used the ban on the Social Democratic Party as a pretext for firing Jewish doctors from public hospitals. The Association of Jewish Physicians in Vienna reported that 56 of the 58 physicians dismissed after February 1934 were Jewish, although the majority of them were not members of the Social Democratic Party and many non-Jewish doctors who were kept their jobs. The government also put a freeze on all new Jewish appointments in hospitals with the intent of reducing the quota of Jewish physicians to 20 per cent in line with Czermak's proposal. Further, no Jewish physician was appointed to the Fatherland Front's committee of physicians despite the fact that the Association of Jewish Physicians had joined the Fatherland Front in February 1934.[41] Similarly, in the legal profession the government sought to reduce the quota of Jewish lawyers by appointing only two of twelve Jewish members of the former executive committee of the Bar association to the new Ministry of Justice legal association. In commerce, no Jew was appointed to sit on the state Economic Council's sub-council for trade and banking and the Fatherland Front's Trade Association and Trade Union excluded Jewish members, leading a campaign in 1937 to boycott Jewish businesses. Short of barring Jewish doctors and lawyers from practising in private clinics and law firms, the Austrofascist state mobilized its full political powers to reduce Jewish representation in public life and ensure the professional existence of Jews was dependent upon the Jewish community alone. And just as Zionists had feared, none of these reforms addressed the representation of Jews in public administration. In the arts, too, Jews were not allowed to publish in Austrian presses or appear in Austrian films and state theatres would not employ Jewish directors or actors, unless they were world-renowned.[42] We will see the exceptional status that Max Reinhardt had in Austria, and in Salzburg especially, not least because he had brought international fame to Austria through the Festival he founded in 1920.

Education in public schools was one of the most visible spheres of discrimination against Jews under the Austrofascist state. Just as non-socialist Jewish doctors had been fired in February 1934 and replaced with non-Jewish doctors, so too the majority of Jewish schoolteachers dismissed in 1934 had not been members of the Social Democratic Party.[43] Shortly after the dismissal of Jewish schoolteachers, in September 1934, the Ministry of Education decreed that non-Catholic students were to be streamlined into parallel classes, ostensibly on the grounds that some middle and elementary schools were overcrowded and that it would release Jews and Protestants from the compulsory Catholic religion classes that Dollfuss had introduced the previous year.[44] In his memoir, *Last Waltz in Vienna*, George Clare describes how the discrimination against him and his fellow Jewish students did not end at the point of segregation. Clare attended Vienna's prestigious grammar school, *Schopenhauergymnasium*, and, since the 1934–35 school year, had been placed in Form A, a mixed class for Jewish and non-Jewish students, while Form B was for non-Jews only. Clare recounts how on one occasion, when the two classes in his year took part together in a march in the Viennese Woods, the Form B boys started singing the *Horst-Wessel Lied*, the unofficial Nazi anthem that had been banned in 1933. Clare informed the school headmaster and was promptly expelled from the school, not on the grounds of his opposition to the song, but because Clare had flippantly remarked to another Form A pupil that the teacher who had been supervising the students was 'a Nazi anyway' and the student had in turn blown the whistle on Clare. The teacher in question, unknown to Clare at the time, was in fact a leader in the Austrian state youth organization and may well have been a Nazi sympathizer – we have seen the close relationship of ÖJV to former Nazis in the ÖVVA.[45] From Clare's account, we see that the segregation in schools was not intended to separate Jewish students from non-Jews entirely, since there were still mixed classes, but rather to reinforce the idea that Jews could not assimilate fully into the social and academic sphere of other Austrians. The effect of this discrimination was to foster a minority identity in Jewish students and leave them vulnerable to attacks or taunts from the majority population, often under the wilful supervision and encouragement of state functionaries.

Jewish leaders unequivocally condemned the segregation of Jewish and non-Jewish students, but disagreed among themselves over what provisions the state should make for education for Jews. Liberals advocated integration in public schools, while Zionists wanted secular Jewish schools, but reiterated that these should not be made compulsory and that Jewish children should have the same educational opportunities as non-Jews. Orthodox Jews opposed the Zionists' proposal for secular Jewish schools in favour of religious-based education.[46] A similar disagreement within the Jewish community arose when the Fatherland Front segregated Jews into their own youth group separate from the ÖJV but still under the umbrella of the Fatherland Front. Liberals again protested the segregation, but Orthodox and Zionist Jews welcomed what they regarded as greater autonomy for Austrian Jews.[47]

Factions in the Jewish community over the issues of education and youth groups reflected a larger tension between assimilated Viennese Jews and the newer arrivals from Galicia and Bukowina who had been in Vienna for barely a generation. Clare saw himself as 'already second-generation Viennese, and Viennese-born Jews felt resentment towards the less assimilated Jews from the East. 'We were, or rather thought we were, quite different from that bearded, caftaned lot. We were not just Austrian, but German-Austrian.' After the *Anschluss* Clare emigrated to Ireland and, along with other Jewish refugees, changed his name from Klaar when he joined the British army to avoid capture by the Nazis. But this decision for Clare also severed a link to his forebears, who had risen to imperial rank in the military and medical fields of the Habsburg Monarchy. His Bukowinan-born great-grandfather, Herrmann Klaar, studied medicine in Vienna and went on to become a surgeon in the army, eventually earning the imperial title of Surgeon-Major. Clare held a warmer affection for his paternal grandmother, Julie, whom he described as 'totally Viennese', than for his mother's mother, Adele, who 'was very much the East European ghetto Jewess.'[48] Both women had been born in the empire's periphery, in Bukowina and Galicia respectively, but Clare's memory distinguished between them on the basis of their assimilation to the language, education and culture of Viennese society with which he also personally identified.

Other Jewish memoirs recount anecdotal illustrations of antipathy between assimilated and unassimilated Jews. The assimilated Viennese Jews used disparaging labels such as '*Polak*' for the Galician Jews and Jewish spectators jeered the '*Ostjuden*' on the field at soccer matches between Austria Wien and Hakoah Wien. There was just as much retaliation from the Jewish immigrants, who made fun of assimilated Jewish intellectuals through poetry and song lyrics and schoolyard taunts of '*Assimilant*' against fellow pupils.[49] Taxes paid to the IKG indicate the economic gap between assimilated and newly arrived Jews: while Jews from Bohemia were the largest taxpaying group, the Galicians, who constituted one-fifth of the Jewish population in Vienna between 1870 and 1910, represented only 8 per cent of all IKG taxpayers. Religious differences also provoked some embarrassment on the part of assimilated Jews who complained that the Orthodox Galicians were disruptive in the synagogue with their noisy prayers.[50]

However, relations between assimilated and unassimilated Jews in Austria need to be seen in a separate context from anti-Semitism in the Austrofascist state. The resentment of the Galician Jewish arrivals towards second- and third-generation Viennese Jews, and the social awkwardness on the part of the latter towards the new arrivals, stemmed from a pro-tracted process of Jewish self-identification with the Austrian state that had stagnated and then regressed during the interwar period as Austrian Jews began to cultivate an ethnic Jewish identity in response to the loss of identification with the Austro-Hungarian Empire. This nascent Jewish eth-nicity was based not on language, but on religious and familial notions of Jewish identity. Instead of identifying with the nation or the state, as they had done before 1918, and because they were denied full integration in the new state after 1918, Jews turned inward to the Jewish community and especially to their family.[51] Jewish women activists left the liberal women's organizations to which they had belonged and withdrew into their family or, in a few cases, joined Zionist ones as a way to continue their activism.[52] Similarly Clare's memoir can be seen as his primary identification with his family rather than the country he grew up in. While the formation and expression of Jewish self-identity in the interwar period led to friction and social barriers between the two groups, this disharmony differed from the state's anti-Semitism both in its intent and function in society. As we have seen, Austrofascists sought to exclude all Jews, not just unassimilated Jews, and they supported Zionist groups because they believed this would aid the segregation of Jews and their eventual emigration from Austria.

I have argued that it is a false premise to compare the discrimination of Jews in the Austrofascist state with that in Nazi Germany in the same period, or with the persecution of Austrian Jews after 1938.[53] The absence of physical violence and deportations should not lead us to conclude that anti-Semitism in the Austrofascist state was 'moderate', for even scholars of Nazi Germany argue that the early anti-Semitism of Hitler's regime was moderate compared to the period after 1941. The evidence above demon-strates the government's execution of a systematic plan to remove Jews from public life, to reduce their status to a legal minority and to shift responsibility for this minority from the state to the Jewish community. All of this followed to the letter Czermak's 1933 programme and the fears that Zionists expressed at the time of the book's publication did indeed come to fruition. Church leaders and others in the wider community could say all they liked for or against the measures: the state was on a mission of its own and this time did not need to recruit activists for the cause.

When anti-Semites did speak up either within the Catholic Church or in the German-nationalist press, the state and its functionaries did not always take notice. However, state functionaries chose to notice when those outside views were relevant to Austria's domestic and foreign affairs. The views of Bishop Hudal in the book he dedicated to Hitler and in the lectures he gave in Austria in March 1936 can be understood within this context of state functionaries choosing to listen to a church leader, rather than as the statements by a bishop standing to represent the views of the state. And it is in the context of Hudal's lecture tour in Austria that we can interpret the comments made by the Jesuit leader of St Paul's Mission, Georg Bichlmair (1890–1953), who believed that first- and second-generation baptized Jews should not hold public office because their national character and 'spiritual homelessness' would have a dangerous effect on Austria's German Christian culture.[54] Bichlmair had been one of the few priests to support Motzko after her public speech at the Catholic Congress, so his views did not always represent mainstream clerical teaching.[55] What is important here, however, is not whether his views were exceptional, but the context in which they were made and the responses they received from state and church leaders as well as lay Catholics and non-Catholics.

During Hudal's visit to Austria in March 1936 the *Reichspost* and other government organs gave coverage of his ideas about race and his views on Austria's relationship with Fascist Italy and Nazi Germany. In a press conference he gave in Vienna to members of the official press corps, Hudal spoke of his personal admiration for Mussolini, who in Hudal's eyes had been sent by God to the Italian people at exactly the right time in their history. He also assured journalists that Mussolini was a friend of Austria and an example to Austria of what a self-assured leader with the strong will of the people behind him could do for the future of a country battling against international pressures, Hudal referring to the League of Nations' sanctions on Italy after its invasion of Ethiopia. At the press conference Hudal also noted that his forthcoming book, *The Foundations of National Socialism*, had already been listed on the German *Reichsschriftkammer* (Reich Chamber of Literature) for its 'negative tendencies', but he shrugged off this label by identifying with the 'positive direction' of fascism, which he claimed had successfully synthesized state, nation, religion, church and politics. According to Hudal, the likes of the neo-pagan Nazi ideologue, Alfred Rosenberg, could not possibly understand this synthesis because he held to a 'Slavic' worldview: Rosenberg was a Baltic German and had lived 'entirely in the Russian world' before he came to prominence in Nazi Germany. Hudal claimed it was now up to Austrians to demonstrate this synthesis between Christendom and Germandom, not as the '*Grenzmark*', or borderland, of the German nation or as a bridge between Germans and the other nationalities of Central Europe, but as a 'continuous protest against the Herostratic deed' that was the dissolution of the old monarchy.[56] Rejecting both the German-nationalist conception of an *Ostmark* and the traditional Catholic version of pan-Germanism that saw Austria as the bearer of true German Christendom, Hudal instead believed that Austrian Germans should preserve Austria's more recent memories of statehood, a strong attachment to Rome and Italy, and the achievements of Germandom in a state that had been separated from Germany for seven decades.

Hudal took up the theme of 'Germandom and Rome' later on during his lecture tour, arguing that Nazi Germany's efforts to remove the influence of the Catholic Church from the German nation – like those of the nineteenth-century '*Los von Rom*' movement before it – were premised on a false belief that the Roman Church was in opposition to the development of the German nation. In fact, Hudal explained, the Roman Church was not bound to 'Roman culture', but had throughout the medieval period been part of a 'holy triad' of Roman-Hellenistic antiquity, Germandom, and Christendom. German culture had shaped the Church in the Middle Ages and together both had shaped Western Christendom until the 'linguistic genius' of Martin Luther split the Church in two, and 'German genius' triumphed over Rome. But the Catholic part of Germany and Austria remained most of all a protector and guardian of that synthesis between Christendom and Germandom, the true Occident, which now had to withstand the 'floods of neo-pagan radicalism and bolshevism'.[57]

If this sounds like the views of an ultramontane Catholic and not the Nazi sympathizer who openly confessed to hiding known Nazis – including Adolf Eichmann – in the Anima seminary in the last days of the Second World War, then we have to examine what else Hudal said on his visit that revealed his support for National Socialists, neo-pagan radicals notwithstanding.[58] His lecture on 18 March 1936 in the Lower Austrian parliament, entitled 'The Problem of Racial Influence on Western Christendom', printed the following day in the *Reichspost*, was delivered in front of an audience that included Cardinal Innitzer; Secretary of State Perntner (the later Education Minister); head of the federal press agency, Ludwig; and other senior functionaries, church representatives and members of the German, Italian and Polish consular staffs. On this occasion Hudal explained that race was more than a 'purely intellectual abstraction' or a 'purely biological' matter, but rather something that had to be understood in connection with culture and religion to which races had constantly adapted and changed. Only in the context of the Church's teachings about salvation and grace could theories of race make sense, Hudal claimed, for every person had an eternal soul and if racial theory ignored this principle then it was in danger of becoming another form of materialism that would do more harm than good to 'our German spiritual culture'.[59] In short, Hudal was in favour of racial theories so long as the Church, not scientists and statesmen, had the final say.

On the same day as Hudal's lecture, Bichlmair gave his talk on 'the Christian and the Jew', which was reprinted in the same day's edition of the *Reichspost*. Bichlmair's lecture was part of a series organized by Catholic Action on 'The Church in Struggle', though on this occasion neither state nor church leaders were present except the Justice Minister, Hans Hammerstein-Equord. Bichlmair set out to inform the 'thousands of Austrian Catholics' who expected from Catholic Action a clear explanation for their response to the 'Jewish question'. The problem, as Bichlmair saw it, was that the Church had no single position: between the radical anti-Semites and those who took a political or religious stance against Jews lay the 'great mass' of ordinary Catholics who did not know what their response should be. The editors of the *Reichspost* obviously saw themselves as bearers of that same enlightening mission since they devoted two entire pages to his talk where they had only allowed a cursory half-page summary of Hudal's lecture. Bichlmair and the *Reichspost* were talking to the 'little people', like Lueger before them, those who might have gone along to the Catholic Congress and wondered what the chancellor meant by the 'hordes from the East': Turks, Russians or Jews? Bichlmair reduced all the historical, theological, political and cultural arguments down to a single issue: the Jewish question was above all a question of the law. Christians were obliged to obey God's law of love for their neighbours, and for that reason every Christian should reject those who preached hatred of the Jews, but God's law was not incompatible with human laws based on Christian ethics. That meant Christians had a religious duty to refrain from anti-Jewish attacks, but they also had an ethical obligation to reduce numerically the Jewish presence in every sphere of society from the arts, to medicine and education, and the media. Quoting the title of Czermak's book, Bichlmair said that it did not matter whether 'order in the Jewish question' was achieved in Austria by a minority law or by constitutional means, the main task was that Christians took the lead in determining the proper place of Jews in society. Even better would be that the Jews remove themselves, Bichlmair again chiming with Czermak's view that the Jews also wished to dissimilate and emigrate, and the state should give full assistance to fulfil their wish. Finally, on the question of converted Jews, Bichlmair distinguished between baptized Jewish children, who were schooled in 'German Christian' principles from a young age, and adult converts whose main motivation for baptism was often political expedience. For this reason it was acceptable for certain professions to have an

Aryan paragraph, but Bichlmair rejected a universal Aryan law on ethical grounds.[60]

Thus the views of both Hudal and Bichlmair can be placed within the political context of the Austrofascist state and its external and internal affairs. Hudal was not yet a Nazi-harbourer, though he did not distance himself in his public remarks in Austria from Nazis other than those whom he regarded as neo-pagan radicals. He was also sensitive to Austria's political relations with Italy. At the time he was in Austria a delegation of Austrian journalists were visiting Rome to cover the upcoming talks between the Hungarian, Italian and Austrian foreign ministers.[61] His comments on Mussolini and the Rome-Austrian axis can be understood within this support for Italy, and, as the Austrian bishop in Rome, both state and church leaders in Austria were eager to hear his views. (Later that year Hudal would host Fatherland Front functionaries on their visit to Rome.) Hudal's book had not yet appeared and his ideas on race, and his position on Nazi Germany, at this point during his visit to Austria did not raise as much attention as they would later in the year following the July Agreement. Hudal caused controversy when he wrote an anonymous article in the *Reichspost* on 16 July 1936 calling for Austrian Catholics to engage wholeheartedly with Nazi Germany to prevent the anti-Christian 'radical left-wing' of National Socialism gaining an upper hand over the conservative Christian wing of the party. He also saw in this renewed engagement the chance to stem another '*Los von Rom*' movement in Austria from Catholicism to Protestantism. When the *Reichspost* editors finally revealed the author's identity, the reaction from Catholics who opposed National Socialism, above all the editors of the rival Catholic organ, *Der Christliche Ständestaat*, forced Hudal to defend his comments again in the *Reichspost* in August. The editors of the *Christliche Ständestaat*, including the German Catholic émigré Dietrich von Hildebrand, responded to Hudal's articles accusing him of misrepresenting both Nazis and Catholics under the cover of anonymity, a tactic the editors saw as playing further with truth.[62] We will revisit the Austrofascist state's response to German Catholic émigrés in the following chapter. Important to note here is that Hudal's statements on National Socialism after the July Agreement were no different from what he had expressed publicly during his lecture tour in Austria when he had argued that Christendom and Germandom were the synthetic fibres of the West and wished for National Socialism to embody that synthesis, rather than succumb to bolshevist and neo-pagan elements in the party. It was the political context of Austro-German relations that had changed, not Hudal.[63]

Bichlmair, on the other hand, was addressing domestic concerns about the legal status that Jews should have in Austria. It was significant that he was speaking to an audience of mostly Catholic Action members whose activities, although they came under the umbrella of the Church, also extended into the sphere of state-sponsored charity work. Catholic women's groups operating within Catholic Action cooperated with Zionist groups, as we saw with the Fatherland Front's Mother's Day activities that took place two months after Bichlmair's talk. Preparations would already have been underway for the Mother's Day exhibition and it was these women, and others within Catholic Action, whom Bichlmair sought to enlighten on their religious and civic responsibilities towards their fellow Jewish activists. Of course the Zionists were not the problem, they would leave Austria soon enough; it was the assimilated Jews who needed to be removed by legal means. Bichlmair's efforts to bring about a respectable, civic-minded attitude to Jews that ordinary Catholics could embrace as citizens in the 'Christian' Austrian state, also reveal the way anti-Semitism functioned as a civic argument about rights and citizenship. Ethnic arguments about religion and race were embedded in that civic discourse, but it was the latter that gave shape and legitimacy to the racial view of Jews in the Austrofascist state.

'*Ostjuden*' in Vienna

The Austrofascist state took less notice of German-nationalists than of church dignitaries, but the anti-Semitism of German-nationalists often bore resemblance to the arguments made by state functionaries. Two examples of the German-nationalist press, the *Wiener Neueste Nachrichten* and the *Salzburger Volksblatt*, bear out these parallels and demonstrate the multiplicity of views within the German-nationalist 'camp'. German-nationalists tended not to moralize about the dangerous materialism and spiritual barrenness of the Jews and instead sensationalized stories about the crimes of Jewish immigrants. However, they couched their anti-Semitism in the same civic arguments as Austrofascists: Jews were a threat to public law and order in the Austrian state who were incapable of assimilation. Whether conspicuous as Eastern-types in Vienna's 2nd district or disguised in local costume in the Salzburg lakes and mountains, Jews were foreigners who did not belong in Austria.

A favourite target of anti-Semites in Vienna was the city's second district and unofficial Jewish quarter, Leopoldstadt. The *Wiener Neueste Nachrichten* constructed the image of a Jewish 'ghetto' by mapping the physical boundary of the Danube canal and Danube river, which segregated Leopoldstadt and the adjacent district of Brigittenau from the rest of Vienna, on to a mental boundary between foreign Jews and native Viennese. The editors even proposed that Leopoldstadt and Brigittenau officially be renamed as the Jewish quarter.[64] A photographic essay on the Jews of Leopoldstadt constructed this mental boundary of exclusion. The photographs showed Jewish men with side-locks wearing caftans, standing in streets and exchanging wares, women and children sitting on park benches, girls listening to a gramophone and a woman posing in a bathing costume.[65] The woman in her bathing costume reflected a popular anti-Semitic stereotype that surfaced every summer in Austrian resort towns, where anti-Semites ran 'Jew-free' campaigns to ban Jewish tourists from hotels, cafes and entire towns.[66] The pictures reinforced the popular anti-Semitic stereotype image of foreign Eastern-types with their inability or unwillingness to blend into Austrian society. The photographs ridiculed Jews who were audacious enough to enter Austria's public spaces, by conducting their business on the street or attempting to bathe in an Austrian pool or lake, for example, only to end up becoming a self-parody of their own alienation.

The pictures were not just intended as satire, however, but as a warning that Jews were growing steadily in numbers and gaining entry into society. The editors claimed that the census in March 1934 had only counted Jews who formally identified with Judaism and estimated that the real number with 'Jewish blood' was closer to 400,000, more than double the census figure. The rise in population was not due to the Jewish birth rate, which was lower than the Austrian average, but rather, to the 'continuous immigration and alarming increase in mixed marriages', which resulted in Vienna having more Jews than Palestine. 'Under such circumstances', the editors declared, 'it is difficult not to deny the existence of a Jewish problem in Austria'. Anti-Semitism was not 'a malicious invention of intolerant fanatics', but something that the Jews of Vienna had brought upon themselves through their 'importunity'. 'The characters that are captured in these pictures may yet be the least dangerous ones. But their children could, if permitted, assimilate as doctors, lawyers, journalists and Marxist leaders, and that must not be tolerated now or ever.'[67] The text and the images combined racial images of Jewish blood spreading through Vienna through intermarriage with non-Jews, with a civic argument about the Jewish assimilation from fringe-dwelling immigrants to prominent members of Vienna's professional classes who voted for the Social Democrats.

The ghetto-stereotype of Leopoldstadt and assimilated Jews was not entirely an imagined construct of German-nationalists. Leopoldstadt had been named after Emperor Leopold I, who expelled the Jews living along the Danube in 1670, but after Emperor Franz Josef granted them legal equality and lifted residential restrictions against them in 1867, Jews began to resettle Leopoldstadt.[68] By the 1930s, approximately 65,000 Jews lived

in Leopoldstadt, which represented around 40 per cent of the neighbourhood's residents and a third of Vienna's total Jewish population.[69] Robert
Wistrich argues that the figures do not reflect real segregation of Jews and
non-Jews, which was more visible in other cities of the former Austro-
Hungarian Empire, such as Prague, or in comparison with the Jewish villages and urban ghettos in Galicia and Hungary. He points out that
Viennese Jews had a high level of interaction with non-Jewish residents
through the practice of subletting accommodation to boarders and apprentices to cope with housing shortages. Even in Leopoldstadt, which was the
most densely populated Jewish neighbourhood in Vienna and where destitute immigrants crowded together in single rooms, Jews still lived among
a non-Jewish majority.[70] On the other hand, Marsha Rozenblit has shown
that segregationist tendencies did exist insofar as poorer Jews tended to
live alongside middle-class Jews in the same neighbourhood, albeit in
impoverished, cramped conditions and in a different street from their
wealthier neighbours. She argues that neighbourhood encounters with
Jewish shops shut on Saturdays and women wearing wigs in compliance
with Orthodox Jewish law on modesty, for example, reinforced the popular
image of a Jewish ghetto in Leopoldstadt.[71]

Joseph Roth (1894–1939) – author, feuilletonist, journalist and himself
a Galician Jew – immortalized the Jews of Leopoldstadt in his book, *Juden
auf Wanderschaft* (Wandering Jews), first published in 1937. Roth wrote
with curiosity and personal empathy for the displaced Jews, whom he
encountered first in Vienna and later as a correspondent in Russia.[72] He
famously described Leopoldstadt as a 'voluntary ghetto':

> Many bridges join it to the other districts of the city. Every day traders,
> peddlers, stockbrokers, dealers, all the unproductive elements of immigrant
> Eastern Jewry, cross over these bridges. But in the evenings the offspring of
> these unproductive elements, the sons and daughters of the traders, who
> work in the factories, offices, banks, editorships and art studios, cross over
> the same bridges . . . Leopoldstadt is a poor district. There are many small
> apartments, where families of six live. There are dormitories where fifty, sixty
> people sleep on the floor overnight. The homeless sleep in the Prater. The
> poorest of all the workers live near the railway stations. The *Ostjuden* do not
> live any better than the Christian residents in this part of the city. They have
> many children, they are not accustomed to hygiene and cleanliness and they
> are hated. No one looks after them. Their cousins and co-religionists sitting
> in the editorial offices in the first district are 'already' Viennese and do not
> want to be related to or confused with the *Ostjuden* . . . The *Ostjuden* are
> dependent on the support of middle-class charities. One is inclined to regard
> compassion to Jews as higher than it should be. Jewish charity is equally
> imperfect an institution as any other. Charity gratifies the charity-giver first
> and foremost. Often the co-religionists of the *Ostjude* or even his compatriots

in a Jewish charitable institution do not treat him any better than Christians do. It is terribly hard to be an *Ostjude*; there is no lot worse than that of a foreign *Ostjude* in Vienna.[73]

Roth was not constructing a stereotype, however. He was simply highlighting the social stigma of being both foreign and Jewish in Vienna. He was sensitive to the tensions that existed between assimilated and unassimilated Jews, unlike the Viennese-born Clare, and to the ways in which anti-Semites might perceive all Jews as 'unproductive elements'. But instead of depicting the physical boundary separating Leopoldstadt from the rest of Vienna as a barrier to assimilation, as the *Wiener Neueste Nachrichten* did, Roth described a literal and allegorical bridge, joining the traditions of the past with the possibilities of assimilation for the children and grandchildren of the *Ostjuden*. The editors of the *Wiener Neueste Nachrichten* wanted to prevent assimilation, whereas Roth, who identified spiritually with Orthodox Jews and perhaps saw himself as the social conscience of Vienna's Jewry, chided the 'already' assimilated Jews for their moral failure to help integrate the newer arrivals.[74]

The *Wiener Neueste Nachrichten* exaggerated the disaffection between assimilated and unassimilated Jews in order to reinforce a stereotype of the foreign Jew. An article in March 1935 referred to the *Ostjuden* as 'guests' who had abused Austrian hospitality and vexed the 'native' Jews. The article cited a letter, allegedly written by a Jewish woman who had lived in Vienna since 1905: 'Again and again I bump into Polish Jews who have the best furnished houses, good businesses, who take part in all possible forms of dirty competition, and who make life difficult for the decent Jewish businessman. Nearly all of the businesses in the 2nd district are in the hands of my co-religionists, of whom I am honestly ashamed.' The 'native' Jewish woman continued to berate the 'Poles': 'If you sell an article for 26 Groschen, just as swiftly a Pole comes along and sells it for 25 Groschen ... These immigrant Polish Jews are the ruin of us all.'[75] It is highly implausible that a Jewish woman would write to an anti-Semitic newspaper to complain about other Jews. As in the case of the '*Windische*' who wrote to the editors to complain about Slovene nationalists, it is likely in this case that the editors were exploiting a popular stereotype of *Ostjuden* as criminals. The letter did not attempt to validate the woman's concerns or point out the positive contribution that she or any other 'decent' Jew had made to the community. Rather, it highlighted that 'native' Jews were themselves recent immigrants to Vienna and suggested that, in spite of their purported indignation at 'Polish' Jews, these already domiciled Viennese Jews still identified with their 'co-religionists'.

The most sensational articles in the *Wiener Neueste Nachrichten* featured anti-Semitic stereotypes of vagrancy. On 9 March 1937, the newspaper reported that police at the Vienna Fair had arrested a pick-pocketing band of Jewish immigrants, whose leader, a Jewish merchant, had been arrested two years earlier in a separate pick-pocketing scheme at the Prague Fair. These tenuous claims were significant for their caricature of the nomadic merchant Jew whose criminal activities had begun to seep into Austria.[76] In September 1937, the newspaper published two reports on passport forgery operations run by international rings of Jewish immigrants. The first article said that the suspected leader of one organization, Frau Silberstein, had been arrested in Paris along with six other Jewish immigrants from Czechoslovakia, Poland and Russia. More arrests of Jews from Poland and Russia had reportedly been made in Danzig. The article highlighted the illegal activities of *Ostjuden* in its headline – 'Frau Silberstein distributes passports to *Ostjuden*' – giving the impression that Jews were helping other Jews cross Europe's borders illegally and, more importantly, that they were helping those most unwanted of all Jews, the *Ostjuden*.[77] The second article reported that another 'international band of Jewish passport forgers' had been uncovered in Pressburg (Bratislava), just across the Austrian border in Czechoslovakia. The report told how this smuggling operation, based in Warsaw, falsified documents to bring Polish refugees to France from Czechoslovakia via Austria. The head of the organization, Judas Rubenstein, was himself a refugee from Poland who operated under the name of Max Schöpfel, a remark that might have been construed by readers to mean that Jews were posturing as Germans. The article also mentioned that two arrests had been made in connection with the smuggling operations on the Austrian border and that possible links between Czechoslovakia and the Paris-based organization under Frau Silberstein were being investigated.[78] These allegations of a chain of Jewish gang operations across Europe suggested that the porosity of international borders was playing into the hands of Jewish immigrants.

The stereotype of Jews as criminals first developed in late nineteenth-century academic and popular discourses of Jewish felony. Criminologists in Austria-Hungary and Germany attributed the criminal behaviour of Jews to ethnic and cultural factors, such as language, religion and ancestral heritage, often specifically related to the socio-economic position and family vocations of Jews, rather than the racial idea of a biological predisposition towards crime. Thus prostitution was construed as part of an international slave trade run by Jews, rather than attributed to the sexual perversion of alleged offenders. Criminologists attempted to prove their theories by claiming that non-Jewish accomplices adopted the same behaviour, vocabulary and religious practices of Jews in the criminal underworld, reinforcing the notion that common linguistic and cultural traits were to be found among criminal populations. Austrian newspapers popularized these academic discourses by constructing a narrative of crimes committed, aided and defended by Jewish lawyers, journalists, scientists, and other perpetrators connected to a Jewish economic and social underworld. No specific crime was ever mentioned; instead, the newspapers collapsed multiple anti-Semitic stereotypes into a single stereotype of Jewish criminality.[79] The same popular accounts of Jewish refugees as criminals, profiteers and speculators appeared in wartime newspapers, denunciations by fellow Viennese, and in political debate after parliament reconvened in 1917.[80]

In the 1930s the German-nationalist press streamlined the various anti-Semitic references to Jewish criminal behaviour, which was allegedly conditioned by their ghetto backgrounds, into the stereotype of the foreign and fraudulent Jew. However, this stereotype was specific to the interwar period in its association with illegal immigrants and refugees, as we will see in the next chapter. The stereotype of the Ostjuden infiltrating Austria's public spaces and institutions had its origins in the late Habsburg era and in the immediate post-war period. But it gained new legitimacy in the Austrofascist period through the state's efforts to legalize the boundaries between Jews and non-Jews in Austria. As the following section demonstrates, the stereotype of the Ostjuden extended beyond Vienna to Salzburg, where anti-Semitism drew on provincial sites of exclusion and assimilation.

'Anti-Semitism without Jews'

According to the 1934 census, Salzburg had 239 Jews out of a total population of 245,801 (less than 0.1 per cent), a figure that has prompted historians to describe anti-Semitism in Salzburg as 'Antisemitismus ohne Juden' (Anti-Semitism without Jews). Although this phrase mostly refers to the period after 1945, Günter Fellner has suggested that it is also an apt description of anti-Semitism in Salzburg during the interwar years.[81] Yet the nature of Salzburg's hostility towards Jews was neither grounded in a perception that the local population was under threat from a minority group, nor associated with any of the traditional factors, such as an established Jewish presence in the economy, politics, society or culture.[82] Interwar anti-Semitism in Salzburg was directed instead at visitors: Jewish artists at the annual Salzburg Festival and middle-class Jewish families who holidayed each summer in the province's popular lakeside resorts. By the 1930s, the stereotype of Ostjuden as criminals was grafted on to these provincial stereotypes to create a single image of Jews invading and corrupting Austria's public spaces.

The anti-Semitic protest against Jewish visitors in Salzburg reflected a general xenophobic reaction in Salzburg directed, firstly, at wartime refugees and, secondly, at tourists after the war who were seen to be consuming the meagre resources of the local population. During the First World War, anti-Semites in Salzburg referred to the refugees from Russian-occupied Galicia and Bukowina as 'foreign bodies' (*Fremdkörper*) and 'intruders' (*Eindringlingen*), even though not more than a fifth of all wartime refugees in Salzburg (about 2,000 out of a total 10,000–13,000) were Jews. Jewish relief organizations in Vienna were 'robbing the state for Israel', while the 'material extravagance' (*Toilettenluxus*) of Jewish 'war profiteers' amid wartime food shortages reinforced the popular anti-Semitic stereotype of greed and self-preservation.[83] Hans Glaser summed up the views of many in Salzburg who resented the intrusion of the Jewish refugees and resented even more the Jewish agencies in Vienna. He wrote in his diary in January 1918: 'It is truly impossible, after the experiences we have had with the Jews in the war, to think as a Judaophile.'[84] After the war, anti-Jewish sentiments were symptomatic of a general reaction to food shortages after the main supply regions in the newly independent states of Czechoslovakia, Hungary and Yugoslavia had been cut off from Austria. The resentment against foreigners in Salzburg extended to all visitors, not just Jewish, in the form of a strictly limited tourist season. Yet the desperate food situation in Salzburg also heightened animosity towards Vienna as the centre of a 'Jewish-Socialist republic' that profited from the post-war conditions while the rest of 'Christian-German Austria' starved.[85]

If there was a strong xenophobic undercurrent in Salzburg's response to Jews during and after the First World War, provincial anti-Semitic stereotypes lingered beyond the immediate post-war period of economic crisis. Anti-Semitism became a permanent fixture on the landscape of regional tourism in Salzburg during the interwar years, especially in the lakeside resort towns of St Gilgen, Bad Gastein and Wallersee.[86] This form of anti-Semitism during the tourist season – '*Sommerfrischen-Antisemitismus*' – was also prevalent in Weimar Germany, especially in the seaside resort areas of the North and Baltic seas, and belonged to a broader phenomenon of 'everyday anti-Semitism' in the Weimar era.[87] As in Germany, anti-Semitism in Austria's tourist industry facilitated the widespread acceptance of a popular stereotype that allowed it to enter mainstream politics and society. Jacob Borut's observation of anti-Semitism in Weimar Germany is equally applicable to interwar Austria, that it 'was not the view of Judaism as an alien race, but the strong hold of stereotypes – old and new – regarding the Jews, which ensured that anti-Semitic actions initiated or supported by an anti-Semitic government would not encounter wide disagreement (let alone opposition).'[88] As the photographs in the *Wiener*

Neueste Nachrichten showed, the popular stereotype of foreign Jews con-verged with another stereotype of Jews as '*Assimilanten*'. The provincial press and the tourist industry constructed and popularized these stereo-types, fuelling an 'everyday' anti-Semitism that vindicated the actions of local anti-Semites.

The *Trachtvereine* – local associations that promoted the wearing of folk costume – were another site of popular anti-Semitism in the province. Many of these associations in Salzburg sprang up before the First World War, partly through a revival of the rural idyll, and partly also as a defence against the cosmopolitan modernism of Vienna. *Tracht* symbolized 'care-free summer living, vivacity, sensuality and intimacy far away from the everyday world'.[89] After 1918, it also represented nostalgia for the multina-tional empire, in which regional clothing and dialect had defined local identity. *Tracht* also held symbolic meaning for Austrian Jews: it symbol-ized their assimilation under the Habsburg Monarchy and became an important source of identification with the summer lifestyle of Austria's middle classes.[90] Viennese Jewish women only ever wore the traditional dress (*Dirndl*) during the summer in Salzburg, never in Vienna.[91] George Clare and his parents spent each summer at Bad Ischl, trying to blend in by wearing their *Tracht*, along with other Jewish tourists and famous artists at the Festival, with nostalgia for the empire and the slightest of smirks at their non-Jewish country cousins:

> On the other side of the river Franz Lehar was in his residence, you rubbed shoulders with Emmerich Kalman, you giggled when you saw the twin brothers Goltz, the operetta librettists, looking as alike as one egg from a Jewish mother hen looks to another, both rather incongruously disguised in the local dress, as we were, as genuine Austrian hillbillies . . . Mixing with the crowd at Zauner's tea-room as if they were just perfectly ordinary human beings, you saw princes and even Habsburg archdukes, and you felt sure that from somewhere up above the rain clouds, always plentiful over Ischl, the man who had made the spa so famous, had so loved its mountains, where he had stalked stag and chamois, Franz Josef himself, no less, looked down benevolently on his people, Jews and non-Jews alike.[92]

As self-proclaimed defenders of this national tradition, *Tracht* associations took their role seriously, aiming to refine the social art of wearing national costume to reflect the probity and purity of alpine Aus-trians. Salzburg had the dubious honour of founding in 1909 the First Austrian Imperial Organization for Alpine National- and Mountain-Costumes Associations, which protested against Jews wearing *Tracht*. After Dollfuss banned the wearing of uniforms in 1933, the organization attached political meaning to the wearing of *Tracht* by instructing their members to wear shorter leather trousers with white buttons sewn with black and red thread to represent the Nazi tricolour. In 1935, the Austro-fascist authorities in Salzburg introduced a civil uniform for teachers and civil servants, the so-called *Landestracht*, which the *Tracht* associations refused to wear. After 1938, *Tracht* became a symbol of racial belonging to the national community as the associations first banned Jews from wearing *Tracht*, then non-German minorities in 1939 and, in 1943, foreign workers, mainly Poles and other workers from Nazi-occupied Eastern Europe.[93]

The Salzburg Festival also became a focal point of local anti-Semitism. As we saw in Chapter 3, Nazi newspapers in Salzburg ran a smear campaign against the Jewish director, Max Reinhardt, and tried to prevent him from staging his plays in churches. An article from *Der Eiserne Besen*, which led the campaign against Reinhardt in 1924, declared that 'Smoking Jewesses inside our Christian houses of God, collected by the Semites Max Reinhardt, [Alexander] Moissi and [Hugo von] Hoffmansthal [sic]' would no longer be tolerated.[94] The reference to Hofmannsthal was characteristic of a particularly virulent expression of anti-Semitism posing as religious distaste. Hofmannsthal's great-grandfather had been a Jewish rabbi, his grandfather had converted to Catholicism and the young Hugo had been raised a Catholic, only discovering his Jewish heritage during his childhood.[95] Hofmannsthal's plays reflected his deep religious faith and he consulted Archbishop Rieder on his work. For the editors and readers of the *Eiserne Besen*, however, he remained a Jew in the company of Reinhardt and other Jewish performers in the Festival.

In contrast to these Nazi organs, the *Salzburger Volksblatt* saw the Festival solely in terms of economic gain and distanced itself from any view that might be harmful in the short term. The newspaper wrote in 1921 that it would be 'foolish' to show inhospitality as the Festival visitors brought money into the province.[96] Yet on another occasion in 1921, when the newspaper called for 'assiduous propaganda to attract Aryan travellers so that there will be no room left for the Jews', its anti-Semitism chimed with the *judenrein* platitudes elsewhere in the province.[97] In 1929, the newspaper published a letter from an international Jewish visitor to the Salzburg Festival, who wrote to the newspaper in disgust at an article he had read in the *Eiserne Besen*. 'I am a German American, a Jew ... just arrived in Salzburg. I happened to read a copy of *Der Eiserne Besen*. I was struck speechless. How is it possible, in a city that publicizes international tourism, that such a paper, with such shameful language, which is really a cultural disgrace for Salzburg, can be tolerated? I immediately left this otherwise beautiful city, and I plan to propagandize against the Festival.' The editors published the letter without comment, giving silent assent to the views of the *Eiserne Besen*.[98]

The dilemma for the *Salzburger Volksblatt* was that it relied on advertising fees from local Jewish businesses. In 1923, local business leaders had pressured Glaser to ban Jews from advertising in the *Salzburger Volksblatt*, which would have lost the newspaper over 500 million crowns. Glaser refused and non-Jewish businesses in Salzburg boycotted the newspaper for several months.[99] However, in 1934, two Jewish firms, Ornstein and Pasch, boycotted the *Salzburger Volksblatt* by placing their notices in the rival *Salzburger Chronik*. Glaser wrote to the director of a third Jewish firm in Salzburg, Löwry, to inform him that their business relationship could no longer continue, presumably in view of the increased pressure from National Socialists from within the editorship and from outside businesses. After Glaser had informed the director of the Löwry firm that future notices in the *Salzburger Volksblatt* from the rabbinate would have to be paid for, the rabbi sought to mediate with the newspaper. Glaser himself was not an anti-Semite and he maintained purely professional relationships with Jewish business-owners, with Löwry in particular, who assured Glaser personally that his firm was not involved in the boycott.[100] Glaser's private notes in his diary carry no acrimony towards Jews. Although he had regular professional and personal contact with National Socialists, Glaser referred to the radical anti-Semites among them as 'fanatic' and 'peculiar birds'.[101] We will see a pattern emerging between 1933 and 1938 that was consistent with the anti-Semitic position of the newspaper prior to 1933: acquiescence in anti-Jewish denigration yet diligence in promoting the popular stereotype of the foreign Jew.

The newspaper's tolerance of Jews who brought economic benefits to Salzburg was evident in its defence of Max Reinhardt as an exceptional Jew, as opposed to other 'runaway *Ostjuden*'. An article in the *Salzburger Volksblatt* on 23 March 1933 published an extract from the Nazi German newspaper, the *Völkische Beobachter*, denouncing Jewish refugees who had fled Germany to find work in Austria as 'nothing other than a pile of rabble-rousing *ostjüdischen* journalists and shallow literati'. Among the list of names cited by the Nazi newspaper, the *Salzburger Volksblatt* singled out Reinhardt because of his contribution to Salzburg's economy and international reputation. 'The city of Salzburg . . . has every reason to judge objectively . . . that we have a great deal for which to thank Reinhardt, as much for economic as for artistic reasons'. The editors also dismissed claims that Reinhardt was a hatemonger like other *Ostjuden*; nor was he a refugee since he owned a house in Salzburg and the Josefstädter theatre in Vienna.[102] By virtue of Reinhardt's positive contribution to Salzburg's international cultural reputation and tourism, the newspaper regarded him as a 'decent Jew' who knew his place, and did not assert his political opinions but quietly went about his business in the theatrical world. However, this view was given short shrift in the *Salzburger Volksblatt*: the article on Reinhardt appeared on page ten and there were no laudatory tributes to his successes outside Salzburg, in America for example.

The article in defence of Reinhardt was a rare acclamation, either by German-nationalists or Austrofascists, for Jewish assimilation in Austria. The stereotype of Jews as foreign and deviant was more typical in the *Salzburger Volksblatt*. As with the *Wiener Neueste Nachrichten*, this stereotype was seen in reports of Jewish immigrants involved in illegal activities. One article on 9 November 1936, for example, reported that two currency smugglers had been arrested near Salzburg while attempting to cross the border into Germany. The article said that both men had claimed to live in Vienna but were, presumably in view of their names, Leib Schlosser and Raphael Lewinter, 'of Eastern origin'; they were thought to 'in high probability belong to an international smuggling ring'.[103] Although reports often alluded to differences of ethnicity and religion, the anti-Semitic stereotype of *Ostjuden* in the *Salzburger Volksblatt* excluded Jews from Austria not on the grounds of their Jewishness, but because they were illegal immigrants, criminals or both. For example, the newspaper ran regular court stories of Jews appealing against deportation orders and naturalization laws. On 12 February 1937, the newspaper reported that Vienna's municipal court had denied citizenship to a Jewish grocery storekeeper, Moses Leider, on the basis of a federal decree in November 1933 that suspended indefinitely all naturalizations.[104] The jeering headline, 'Moses Leider Wants to Become Austrian', and the pointed reference to the man's Jewish background, ridiculed the foreign Jew whose chances of acquiring citizenship were slim to preposterous. The article appeared among other stories of sensation, crime and tragedy, which made the Leider case simply another tale of popular intrigue.

Other reports in 1937 depicted Jews as illegal immigrants who posed a threat to public order. In March 1937, the *Salzburger Volksblatt* reported that a shop owner, Moses Schattner, had been brought before the trade practice authorities in Vienna for selling spoiled food products out of greed for profits.[105] The following month, the newspaper reported that a German Jewish immigrant, Albert Salomon, had been given a five-year expulsion order for entering and residing in Austria without legal documents. According to this report, Salomon had left Germany for Czechoslovakia in January 1935 and, in March of that year, had illegally entered Austria, where he remained. The Public Security officer in Vienna ruled that he be deported, but Salomon appealed to the federal court on the grounds that he was a refugee from Germany and was therefore under the protection of the League of Nations.[106] The court dismissed the appeal, the newspaper stated, because Salomon did not have the right to enter and remain in

Austria without documents and because Austria's domestic laws were not bound by the League of Nations' conventions.[107]

A different case, reported in the *Salzburger Volksblatt* in October 1937, involved a Polish citizen in Vienna, Jakob Frisch, who had received a court deportation order for illegal hawking. The article challenged the legitimacy of the man's Polish citizenship by placing the adjective 'Polish' in quotation marks, whereas other foreign nationals were left out of such speculation.[108] This use of 'ironic inverted commas', as Viktor Klemperer noted in his study of Nazi terminology, was also a common ploy of Nazi newspapers in Germany to 'declare that the reported remark [was] not true'.[109] Moreover, the title of the article in the *Salzburger Volksblatt* – 'The Deportation of "Polish" Citizens' – suggested that Jakob Frisch's case represented a wider group of foreigners, namely Jewish Poles, whose status in Austria the *Salzburger Volksblatt* had declared illegal. Similarly, the article in April challenged the refugee status of the German Jew, Salomon, by referring to him in the headline as 'The Emigrant without a Passport'.

The headline of another article on 24 January 1938, 'Against Stealthy Refugees', implied a general trend of fraud and illegality among Jewish immigrants in Austria. This report involved the case of a Pole, Juda Buchsbaum, who had received a ten-year expulsion order from Austria for illegally entering Austrian territory. The alleged reason why he had fled his native Poland, the article added, was to evade a six-month parole sentence. The federal court had rejected Buchsbaum's appeal because he had 'endangered the public interests' by entering Austria without a valid passport. That his family was already living in Vienna was not a justifiable claim against deportation, the article explained, even though his deportation would mean separation from his family, 'because according to the law the public interests must be considered ahead of the interest of the individual'.[110] The newspaper omitted to elaborate on what the public interests in Austria were, emphasizing only that the protection of law and order was at stake. The *Salzburger Volksblatt* staged each of these court cases as a dichotomous role-play between the Jewish immigrant and the Austrian legal system, which drew attention to a legal boundary of exclusion that resulted in Jews being expelled literally over Austria's border.

Reports of court cases, like the images of Jews in Leopoldstadt, drew attention to the foreign appearances, names and customs of Jews, but embedded these ethnic discourses within a larger civic framework of the Jews as foreigners, illegal immigrants, smugglers and passport forgers violating the physical and legal boundaries of the Austrian state. Austrofascists and German-nationalists used a common civic discourse to typecast Jews as unassimilated and deviant. That the stereotype of the Jew as foreigner was tied to civic arguments about participation and residency in the

Austrian state shows how anti-Semitism functioned in the interwar years as a tool for excluding Jews from public life. It also demonstrates that Austrofascists and German-nationalists were equally committed to defending the boundaries of the Austrian state. As the final chapter will show, Austrofascists and German-nationalists were more preoccupied with debates about citizenship and immigration than with the question of Austro-German unity before 1938. Anti-Semitism also makes another absurdity out of the *Lager* theory when we consider that Bishop Hudal was a more radical nationalist than Salzburg's Hans Glaser, who thought anti-Semites were 'peculiar birds'.

Notes

1 I have taken this phrase from T.J. Cole, 'Constructing the "Jew", Writing the Holocaust: Hungary 1925–40', *Patterns of Prejudice* 33, 3 (1999): 19–27.

2 Sigurd Paul Scheichl, 'The Contexts and Nuances of Anti-Jewish Language: Were all the "Antisemites" Antisemites?', in Ivar Oxaal (ed.), *Jews, Antisemitism and Culture in Vienna* (London: Routledge and Kegan Paul, 1987), pp. 95–97. On anti-Semitism in the student fraternities, see Chapter 1.

3 Ibid.

4 Günter Fellner, 'Antisemitismus in Salzburg 1918–1938' (PhD dissertation, University of Salzburg, 1979), pp. 8, 47, 55.

5 Bruce Pauley, *From Prejudice to Persecution: A History of Austrian Anti-Semitism* (Chapel Hill: University of North Carolina Press, 1992), especially Part 3, pp. 131–202. The quote from the conclusion on p. 324 is also cited by Gellott, 'Recent Writings on the Ständestaat', as evidence of the ambiguity of much writing about anti-Semitism in pre-*Anschluss* Austria.

6 Paul Weindling, for example, borders on this unhelpful teleological reading of anti-Semitism in his book, *Epidemics and Genocide in Eastern Europe, 1890–1945* (Oxford: Oxford University Press, 2000).

7 See Hannah Arendt, *The Origins of Totalitarianism* 2nd edn (London: Allen & Unwin, 1958), p. 48.

8 France had already expelled Galician Jewish immigrants as 'enemy aliens' at the outset of the First World War, many of whom ended up in Vienna. See Pauley, *From Prejudice to Persecution*, p. 67. On French immigration restrictions in the 1930s, see Vicki Caron, *Uneasy Asylum: France and the Jewish Refugee Crisis, 1933–1942* (Stanford: Stanford University Press, 1999). See also Fay Brauer, 'Commercial Spies and Cultural Invaders: The French Press, *Pénétration Pacifique* and Xenophobic Nationalism in the Shadow of War', in Gee and Kirk (eds), *Printed Matters*, pp. 105–31.

9 Andrei S. Markovits, 'Peter Pulzer's Writing on Political Anti-Semitism and the Jewish Question in Germany and Austria: An Assessment', in Henning Tewes and Jonathan Wright (eds), *Liberalism, Anti-Semitism and Democracy: Essays in Honour of Peter Pulzer* (Oxford: Oxford University Press, 2001),

pp. 49–51. Michael Phayer's otherwise insightful and balanced study of Pius XII and the Holocaust makes a number of sweeping claims about the anti-Semitism of Eastern Europeans vis-à-vis that of their French and British counterparts. Michael Phayer, *The Catholic Church and the Holocaust, 1930–1965* (Bloomington: Indiana University Press, 2000).

10 The legal context will be explored more fully in Chapter 6, but it is important to refute the 'exceptional' label here because of the way it has coloured the entire debate about anti-Semitism in Austria not just in the interwar period. As I will show, anti-Semitism was linked to state building in the interwar Austrian state, and must be seen within a larger context of post-Habsburg Central Europe as well as Western Europe, as the case of France demonstrates.

11 See Chapter 6 on citizenship legislation in the new Austrian state.

12 Vienna was part of Lower Austria until it became a separate province in 1920.

13 Pauley, *From Prejudice to Persecution*, pp. 82–85; Beatrix Hoffmann-Holter, *'Abreisendmachung': Jüdische Kriegsflüchtlinge in Wien 1914–1923* (Vienna: Böhlau, 1995), pp. 162–63, 197–210; Gernot Heiss, 'Ausländer, Flüchtlinge, Bolschewiken: Aufenthalt und Asyl 1918–1933', in Gernot Heiss and Oliver Rathkolb (eds), *Asylland Wider Willen: Flüchtlinge im Europäischen Kontext seit 1914* (Vienna: Jugend & Volk, 1995), p. 90; Edward Timms, 'Citizenship and "Heimatrecht" after the Treaty of Saint-Germain', in Edward Timms and Ritchie Robertson (eds), *The Habsburg Legacy: National Identity in Historical Perspective* (Edinburgh: Edinburgh University Press, 1994), p. 160. See also George E. Berkley, *Vienna and its Jews: The Tragedy of Success 1880s–1980s* (Cambridge, MA: Abt Books, 1988), pp. 156–58.

14 Pauley, *From Prejudice to Persecution*, pp. 80–82.

15 Ibid., pp. 82, 183–87; Bruce F. Pauley, 'Politischer Antisemitismus im Wien der Zwischenkriegszeit', in Botz, et al. (eds), *Eine zerstörte Kultur*, p. 256.

16 Nathaniel Katzburg, *Hungary and the Jews: Policy and Legislation, 1920–1943* (Ramat-Gan: Bar-Ilan University Press, 1981). See also Cole, 'Constructing the "Jew"'.

17 Pauley draws attention to the American academic anti-Semitism in his book. See here, Pauley, *From Prejudice to Persecution*, p. 94. Later some of these Jewish students who had been denied a place in America came to Vienna and found themselves the target of student anti-Semitism, prompting the American ambassador to put pressure on the Austrian authorities to act. Ibid., pp. 127–30.

18 Ibid., pp. 89–100, quote on p. 95.

19 Ibid., pp. 89–100, 121. See also Peter Pulzer, 'Spezifische Momente und Spielarten des österreichischen und des Wiener Antisemitismus', in Botz, et al. (eds), *Eine zerstörte Kutur*, p. 140.

20 Pauley, *From Prejudice to Persecution*, pp. 97–98.

21 Harriet Pass Freidenreich, *Jewish Politics in Vienna 1918–1938* (Bloomington: Indiana University Press, 1991), p. 187.

22 Pauley, *From Prejudice to Persecution*, p. 298.

23 Staudinger, 'Katholischer Antisemitismus in der Ersten Republik', pp. 278, 422n.41. Innitzer's response to the book in a letter he wrote to Hudal in December 1936 was to counsel patience and caution until the time came when a more open and positive discussion about his ideas became possible in Austria. See Maximilian Liebmann, *Theodor Innitzer und der Anschluss: Österreichs Kirche 1938* (Graz: Styria, 1988), p. 50.

24 Gföllner's letter is referred to frequently in accounts of Austrian anti-Semitism. See, for example, the contributions by Angelika Königseder and Ernst Hanisch in Tálos and Neugebauer (eds), *Austrofaschismus* and by Anton Staudinger and Peter Pulzer in Botz, et al. (eds), *Eine zerstörte Kutur*. See also the 24 January 1933 editorial in the *Wiener Neueste Nachrichten* in Chapter 4.

25 See Gellott, *The Catholic Church and the Authoritarian Regime in Austria* and 'Defending Catholic Interests in the Christian State'. See also Gellott and Phayer, 'Dissenting Voices'. Irene Bandhauer-Schöffmann has also written extensively on Catholic women and women's politics more broadly in the Austrofascist state. See Bandhauer-Schöffmann, 'Der "Christliche Ständestaat" als Männerstaat? Frauen- und Geschlechterpolitik im Austrofaschismus', in Tálos and Neugebauer (eds), *Austrofaschismus*, and 'Gottgewollte Geschlechterdifferenzen', in Brigitte Lehmann (ed.), *Dass die Frau zur Frau erzogen wird: Frauenpolitik und Ständestaat* (Vienna: Löcker, 2008). On Catholicism and eugenics in the 1930s, see Monika Löscher, 'Eugenics and Catholicism in Interwar Austria', in Marius Turda and Paul J. Weindling (eds), *'Blood and Homeland': Eugenics and Racial Nationalism in Central and Southeast Europe, 1900–1940* (Budapest: Central European University Press, 2007).

26 Gellott, 'Recent Writings on the Ständestaat', pp. 218–25. For an example of the kind of sweeping statements about Catholicism and anti-Semitism, see Pauley, *From Prejudice to Persecution*, p. 151: 'So widespread was anti-Semitism among Austrian Catholics that organizations that carried the name "Christian" in their title could almost be assumed to be hostile towards Jews.'

27 For an example of the sophistication of this scholarship on popular religion, such as pilgrimage, in the wider context of anti-Semitism and re-Christianization in France, see Ruth Harris, *Lourdes: Body and Spirit in the Secular Age* (New York: Allen Lane, 1999).

28 Vesna Drapac, *War and Religion: Catholics in the Churches of Occupied Paris* (Washington, DC: Catholic University of America, 1998), pp. 33–35. In his address to the parish in Paris's 5th *arrondissement* in December 1940, Cardinal Suhard did not mention Pétain nor did he refer to the military ceremony at Les Invalides from which he had just come.

29 Reimann, *Innitzer*, p. 63.

30 Ibid., p. 55. Pfarrhofer, *Friedrich Funder*, p. 153.

31 Czech-speaking Catholics of the St Methodius Association of Vienna took part in the Congress; see FZHM, 11/476, Wiener St Method-Verein Zentralausschuss. The Vatican's jubilee publication to mark the anniversary celebrations, *Anno Santo: Rassegna illustrata del Givbileo della Redenzione*, on 17 September 1933 included photographs of the delegates in Rome and their

arrival in Vienna, and a double-spread photograph of the Belgian Catholic Women's League in Vienna. ÖStA/AdR, BKA/BPD, Carton 8. For the official guidebook and programme of events, see *Festführer zum Allgemeinen Deutschen Katholikentag in Wien* (Vienna: Pressekomitees des Katholikentages, 1933) and the official report *Allgemeiner Deutscher Katholikentag Wien 1933*, 7. bis 12. September 1933 (Vienna: Verlag des Katholikentagcomitees, 1934).

32 On Innitzer's response to the missing German pilgrims, see Reimann, *Innitzer*, pp. 63–64.

33 Bandhauer-Schöffmann, 'Gottgewollte Geschlechterdifferenzen', pp. 25–42. The Double Wage Act was passed in December that year, and two years later Motzko was pushed aside as leader of the Catholic Women's Organization when it was brought under the umbrella organization of Catholic Action. See Bandhauer-Schöffmann, 'Der "Christliche Ständestaat" als Männerstaat?'

34 Ernst Hanisch, 'Der Politische Katholizismus als ideologischer Träger des "Austrofaschismus"', pp. 76–77; Reimann, *Innitzer*, p. 56.

35 Scheu, *Der Weg ins Ungewisse*, p. 122.

36 ÖStA/AdR, BKA/BPD, Carton 8, *Anno Santo: Rassegna illustrata del Givbileo della Redenzione*, 17 September 1933. In addition to the coverage of events in Rome and Vienna, the publication included a history of the battle and liberation with pictures of Kara Mustafà on horseback, Marco d'Aviano carrying the cross in battle and a photograph of the pulpit in St Stephen's from where Marco d'Aviano spoke.

37 Reimann, *Innitzer*, p. 56.

38 Dieter J. Hecht, 'Jüdische Frauen im Austrofaschismus', in Lehmann (ed.), *Dass die Frau zur Frau erzogen wird*, pp. 157–63.

39 Ibid., p. 166.

40 Pauley, *From Prejudice to Persecution*, pp. 166–67.

41 Ibid., p. 270; Freidenreich, *Jewish Politics in Vienna 1918–1938*, p. 189.

42 Pauley, *From Prejudice to Persecution*, pp. 270–72.

43 Ibid., p. 272.

44 In April 1933, Dollfuss had annulled a law banning compulsory religious observance in schools introduced in April 1919 by the then Undersecretary for Education, Otto Glöckel. The so-called Glöckel Decree had released teachers and students from obligatory classroom prayers and attendance at confession and religious processions, but the new law in 1933 was based on Pope Pius XI's 1929 encyclical, *Divini illius Magistri*, which called for confessional education for all baptized Catholics. See Dachs, ' "Austrofaschismus" und Schule', p. 283; Richard Olechowski, 'Schulpolitik', in Weinzierl and Skalnik (eds), *Österreich 1918–1938*, vol. 2, pp. 592, 603; Michael J. Zeps, *Education and the Crisis of the First Republic* (Boulder: Eastern Europe Monographs, 1987), pp. 33, 168.

45 Clare, *Last Waltz in Vienna*, pp. 50–53.

46 Freidenreich, *Jewish Politics in Vienna 1918–1938*, pp. 198–200.

47 Pauley, *From Prejudice to Persecution*, pp. 271–72. See also Staudinger, 'Zur "Österreich"-Ideologie des Ständestaates', pp. 233–34.

48 Clare, *Last Waltz in Vienna*, p. 31.
49 Michael John, ' "We Do Not Even Possess Ourselves": On Identity and Ethnicity in Austria, 1880–1937', *Austrian History Yearbook* 30 (1999), pp. 57–58.
50 Robert S. Wistrich, *The Jews of Vienna in the Age of Franz Joseph* (Oxford: Oxford University Press, 1989), pp. 45–51.
51 Marsha L. Rozenblit, 'Jewish Ethnicity in a New Nation-State: The Crisis of Identity in the Austrian Republic', in Michael Brenner and Derek J. Penslar (eds), *In Search of Jewish Communities: Jewish Identities in Germany and Austria 1918–1933* (Bloomington: Indiana University Press, 1998), pp. 134–53.
52 Jews in Germany experienced similar 'conversions' to Zionism in the interwar period, often as a result of encounters with Eastern Judaism during the First World War. See Steven E. Aschheim, *Brothers and Strangers: The East European Jews in German and German Jewish Consciousness, 1800–1923* (Madison: University of Wisconsin Press, 1982) and Peter Pulzer, 'Der Erste Weltkrieg', in Steven M. Lowenstein, et al. (eds), *Deutsch-jüdische Geschichte in der Neuzeit*, vol. 3 (Munich: C.H. Beck, 1997), pp. 356–80.
53 As Pauley does on p. 273 in his conclusion to the chapter on the Austrofascist state, 'Friend or Foe?' in *From Prejudice to Persecution*.
54 Pauley, *From Prejudice to Persecution*, pp. 161–62. Bichlmair's words are included in many accounts of anti-Semitism in this period along with Gföllner's pastoral letter and Hudal's book. See, for example, Angelika Königseder, 'Antisemitismus 1935–1938', in Tálos and Neugebauer (eds), *Austrofaschismus*, pp. 58–59.
55 See Bandhauer-Schöffmann, 'Gottgewollte Geschlechterdifferenzen', pp. 22, 57n.15.
56 ÖSta/AdR, BKA/BPD, Carton 8, *Reichspost*, 18 March 1936.
57 ÖSta/AdR, BKA/BPD, Carton 8, *Wiener Zeitung*, 27 March 1936.
58 On Hudal's wartime record, see Phayer, *The Catholic Church and the Holocaust*, pp. 11–12.
59 *Reichspost*, 19 March 1936, p. 6.
60 Ibid., pp. 7–8.
61 The talks and the visit of the Austrian press delegation was the front-page story on the day Hudal's and Bichlmair's lectures were published.
62 Reimann, *Innitzer*, pp. 84–85; Liebmann, *Theodor Innitzer und der Anschluss*, pp. 45–52.
63 It was the changed political context that also prompted Schuschnigg to write to Hudal personally after the publication of his book later asking him to stay within the boundaries of the Austrian press laws for although both Schuschnigg and many educated people in Austria would agree with Hudal, the 'great masses' would interpret Hudal's words as unconditional support for National Socialism and anti-Semitism, something Bichlmair and the organizers of Catholic Action had also been concerned for. See Liebmann, *Theodor Innitzer und der Anschluss*, p. 49.
64 *Wiener Neueste Nachrichten*, 17 November 1934, p. 5.

65 *Wiener Neueste Nachrichten-Bilder*, 6 May 1934, pp. 2–4.

66 On the so-called *Sommerfrische-Antisemitismus*, see Kriechbaumer (ed.), *Der Geschmack der Vergänglichkeit*.

67 *Wiener Neueste Nachrichten-Bilder*, 6 May 1934, pp. 2–4.

68 Klaus Lohrmann, 'Vorgeschichte: Juden in Österreich vor 1867', in Botz, et al. (eds), *Eine zerstörte Kultur*, pp. 38. According to the 1934 census, there were 176,034 Jews in Vienna, which represented less than a tenth of Vienna's population. See 'Einleitung der Herausgeber', in Botz, et al. (eds), *Eine zerstörte Kultur*, p. 19.

69 Christine Klusacek and Kurt Stimmer, *Leopoldstadt* (Vienna: Kurt Mohl, 1978), pp. 58–59.

70 Wistrich, *The Jews of Vienna*, p. 48.

71 Marsha L. Rozenblit, *The Jews of Vienna, 1867–1914: Assimilation and Identity* (Albany: State University of New York Press, 1983), pp. 77–79.

72 On Roth's journalistic career, see Klaus Westermann, *Joseph Roth, Journalist: Eine Karriere 1915–1939* (Bonn: Bouvier, 1987).

73 Joseph Roth, *Juden auf Wanderschaft*, 7th edn (Cologne: Kiepenhauer and Witsch, 2000), p. 40.

74 On Roth's spiritual affinity with Galician Jewry, see Wistrich, *The Jews of Vienna*, pp. 656–58.

75 *Wiener Neueste Nachrichten*, 21 March 1935, p. 2.

76 *Wiener Neueste Nachrichten*, 9 March 1937, p. 3.

77 *Wiener Neueste Nachrichten*, 28 September 1937, p. 6.

78 *Wiener Neueste Nachrichten*, 30 September 1937, p. 5.

79 Daniel Vyleta, 'Jewish Crimes and Misdemeanours: In Search of Jewish Criminality (Germany and Austria, 1890–1914)', *European History Quarterly* 35, 2 (2005): 299–325.

80 See Pauley, *From Prejudice to Persecution*, pp. 69–72. For the wartime denunciations of refugees and other foreigners in Vienna, see Healy, *Vienna and the Fall of the Habsburg Empire*.

81 Fellner, 'Antisemitismus in Salzburg', p. ii.

82 Günter Fellner, 'Judenfreundlichkeit, Judenfeindlichkeit: Spielarten in einem Fremdenverkehrsland', in Kriechbaumer (ed.), *Der Geschmack der Vergänglichkeit*, pp. 119–20.

83 Fellner, 'Antisemitismus in Salzburg', pp. 82–88. By the end of 1918, there were no remaining Jewish refugees in Salzburg. See Hoffmann-Holter, 'Abreisendmachung', p. 143.

84 Hanisch, 'Die Salzburger Presse in der Ersten Republik', p. 347.

85 Fellner, 'Antisemitismus in Salzburg', pp. 90–97.

86 Kriechbaumer (ed.), *Der Geschmack der Vergänglichkeit*.

87 Jacob Borut, 'Antisemitism in Tourist Facilities in Weimar Germany', *Yad Vashem Studies* 28 (2000), pp. 8, 26.

88 Ibid., p. 50.

89 Ulrike Kammerhofer-Aggermann, 'Dirndl, Lederhose und Sommerfrischenidylle', in Kriechbaumer (ed.), *Der Geschmack der Vergänglichkeit*, pp. 317–18.

90 Ibid.

91 Albert Lichtblau, ' "Ein Stück Paradies . . . ": Jüdische Sommerfrischler in St Gilgen', in Kriechbaumer (ed.), *Der Geschmack der Vergänglichkeit*, p. 309.

92 Clare, *Last Waltz in Vienna*, pp. 144–45.

93 Kammerhofer-Aggermann, 'Dirndl, Lederhose und Sommerfrischenidylle', pp. 326–31.

94 Steinberg, *The Meaning of the Salzburg Festival*, p. 167.

95 Robert Kriechbaumer, 'Statt eines Vorwortes: "Der Geschmack der Vergänglichkeit" ', in Kriechbaumer (ed.), *Der Geschmack der Vergänglichkeit*, p. 22.

96 Ibid., p. 12.

97 Steinberg, *The Meaning of the Salzburg Festival*, p. 166.

98 Stephen Gallup, *A History of the Salzburg Festival* (London: Weidenfeld & Nicolson, 1987), p. 59.

99 Hanisch, 'Die Salzburger Presse', p. 353.

100 Glaser, *Tagebuch*, 3 August 1934.

101 Glaser, *Tagebuch*, 2 January 1937; 9 January 1933.

102 *Salzburger Volksblatt*, 23 March 1933, p. 10.

103 *Salzburger Volksblatt*, 9 November 1936, p. 11.

104 *Salzburger Volksblatt*, 12 February 1937, p. 6. The 1933 law followed an earlier restriction on citizenship in 1925, which required applicants to have resided continuously in the same place for four years. See Illigasch, 'Migration aus und nach Österreich in der Zwischenkriegszeit', p. 14.

105 *Salzburger Volksblatt*, 12 March 1937, p. 3.

106 Presumably, that he came under the protection of the High Commission on Refugees (Jewish and Other) Coming from Germany, which was established in October 1933. See Michael R. Marrus, *The Unwanted: European Refugees in the Twentieth Century* (Oxford: Oxford University Press, 1985), p. 161.

107 *Salzburger Volksblatt*, 30 April 1937, p. 7.

108 *Salzburger Volksblatt*, 2 October 1937, p. 6.

109 Klemperer, cited in Pegelow, ' "German Jews", "National Jews", "Jewish Volk" or "Racial Jews"?, p. 215.

110 *Salzburger Volksblatt*, 24 January 1938, pp. 2–3.

6

Citizens, immigrants and refugees

Debates on citizenship, immigration and refugees in the Austrofascist state showed the boundaries of pan-German identity more clearly than any other identity discourse between the world wars. Austrofascists and German-nationalists had different views about who the true refugees were, but both sought to curb immigration of Jews and reduce Jews already living in Austria (both citizens and non-citizens) to the status of a legal minority with few political and social rights, as we saw in Chapter 5. This chapter shows how the German-nationalist press and government organs responded to different groups of refugees and immigrants, terms that were ideologically construed to bolster the case for asylum. Both the German-nationalist and government press attached increasing importance to the right of the state to decide who could live in Austria and endorsed the state's attempts to introduce a new Alien Act and population index after 1935. While the Alien Act built on earlier citizenship legislation in the First Republic, the proposal for a population index was modelled on Italian Fascist legislation and signalled a shift towards totalitarian models of population management. Neither the population index nor the Alien Act was fully implemented prior to Austria's annexation to Nazi Germany in 1938. Nonetheless, the legislation corresponded to a broader pattern of fascist population policy across Europe in the interwar era. Whereas the questions of non-German minorities and Jews had their roots in the multinational empire, the issues of immigration and citizenship presented Austrian politicians with a novel strategy for defining the state's ethnic and civic borders.

Immigration and citizenship in the First Republic

In order to understand the context in which a new immigration bill was proposed by the Austrofascist state, we must briefly study its origins in the legislation under the First Republic. The provisional National Assembly of the Republic of German-Austria had created the first legislation on

Austrian citizenship within a month of the declaration of the republic on 12 November 1918.[1] The law of 5 December 1918 granted automatic citizenship in the Republic of German-Austria to anyone whose legal residence (*Heimatrecht*) had been in the territory of German-Austria prior to August 1914. As in the Austro-Hungarian Empire, the new law conferred citizenship rights through permanent residency in a municipality or region. The law of domicile (*Heimatrecht*) referred primarily to citizenship and welfare eligibility and was implied in the Austrian definition of citizenship.[2] Individuals had to prove their citizenship by possession of a certificate (*Heimatschein*) that recorded their pre-1914 place of residence as German-Austria. Everyone else who lived in the territory of the republic, but had their legal place of residence in one of the former dominions of the empire, had one year after the law was passed to obtain residency in German-Austria and to state their allegiance to the German-Austrian state. This meant that imperial civil servants, railway workers, soldiers and officers, who had been domiciled outside the territory of German-Austria during the war, were able to gain Austrian citizenship after the war.[3]

However, the 1918 law explicitly excluded those whose legal residence was in Galicia, Dalmatia or Istria. This was a deliberate attempt to prevent Galician Jewish refugees in Vienna from applying for citizenship. Given the negligible migration from Dalmatia and Istria, the exclusion of the coastal crown lands was a legal ploy to deflect international accusations of discriminatory action against Jews. Jewish refugees from Bukowina were more fortunate than those from Galicia because a large number of German-speaking administrative personnel had been domiciled in Bukowina. Any attempt to exclude that province would therefore have made both Jews and non-Jewish imperial servants also ineligible for Austrian citizenship.[4] Thus from the outset, citizenship laws in Austria were intended to prevent Jews from becoming citizens in the republic.

International peace treaties after the war sought to govern the rules for citizenship in the new nation-states precisely in order to counteract such cases of discrimination. Article 80 of the Treaty of Saint-Germain, which Austria was forced to sign in 1919, included a provision that allowed citizens of the former Austro-Hungarian Empire to opt for citizenship in any successor state in which they identified 'according to race and language' with the majority of the state's population. However, considerable ambiguity surrounded the wording of Article 80. It was often misquoted as race *or* language, which anti-Semites rejected on the grounds that German-speaking Jews could not be regarded as racially German.[5] The original terms of Article 80 were partially amended after Austria and Czechoslovakia signed the Brno Treaty on 7 June 1920, which recognized language, rather than race, as the condition upon which citizenship could be claimed in either state. Nonetheless, Article 80 was finally adopted into Austrian legal practice on 20 August 1920 with the proviso that proof of one's identification with the German language had to be shown in graduation certificates from German primary, secondary or tertiary schools. This was an exercise in vain for Jewish refugees who usually had no such proof available and for whom retrieval of the necessary documents was next to impossible. Furthermore, Jews from Bohemia and Moravia spoke German ahead of Czech and were more easily able to prove their affinity with the German language than Galician Jews, who spoke mainly Yiddish and had recorded their nationality as Polish in the 1910 census.[6] One prominent exception was Galician-born Joseph Roth, who became an Austrian citizen on 8 June 1921 under the terms of Article 80, although his domicile in Brody would otherwise have made him a Polish citizen.[7]

Anti-Semites were eager to curb what they regarded as the liberal application of Article 80 in Austrian legal practice. They emphasized race, rather than language, as the basis for acquiring citizenship. The legal precedent for this reinterpretation of Article 80 occurred on 9 June 1921 when the federal administrative court, which was responsible for final appeals in citizenship claims, handed down a ruling on the grounds of racial attribution (*Rassenzugehörigkeit*). On this occasion, the court ruled that Galician-born Moses Dym had failed to produce 'tangible evidence for his attribution to the German race', even though he had submitted evidence of his attribution to the German language. The Dym ruling opened the way for the incoming Greater German Interior Minister, Leopold Waber, to interpret Article 80 in specifically anti-Semitic terms.[8] Whereas the Interior Ministry had previously granted citizenship on the grounds of language and ignored the reference to race, Waber disqualified thousands of cases for citizenship solely on the premise that Jews did not identify racially with the majority of the Austrian population. Waber never had the support of the chancellor's office, however, and he was eventually replaced in December 1921. Nonetheless, during his six months in office, the Interior Ministry dismissed almost 180,000 cases for citizenship under the terms of Article 80. Furthermore, the administrative court rejected approximately 200 appeals in cases where the Interior Ministry had already denied grounds for naturalization.[9] The relatively small number of appeals in the administrative court shows that legal practice at the highest federal level was well understood by potential appellants to be racially discriminatory against Jews.

Legal definitions of racial or ethnic attribution (*Volkszugehörigkeit*) had their origins in the Austro-Hungarian Empire. For example, Czech and German school board committees in ethnically mixed regions had appointed members on the basis of ethnic attribution. They determined this legally not only by language, but also by proof of the individual's activities and spheres of involvement in private, public and social life. Authorities also applied the principle of ethnic attribution to German and Czech voting registers in order to avoid 'Trojan Horse' tactics by which individuals with sympathies for one nationality might deliberately have identified themselves as another nationality to agitate for their own national cause. In some cases, these decisions were based on the individual's own willingness to signify his or her ethnic belonging according to the legal criteria. However, in most cases, the decisions rested on the authorities' definition of 'objective' or 'tangible' proof of ethnic attribution, which almost always resulted in discrimination. This aspect of Austrian imperial law is important because of its continuity in the post-1918 legislation on citizenship, notably in the federal administrative court and in Waberian legal practice. There was also continuity in personnel where lawyers involved in cases for the imperial court prior to 1918 later applied the principle of ethnic attribution to citizenship cases during the early 1920s.[10]

In spite of the legal obstacles to acquiring citizenship in the Austrian republic, the number of naturalizations in Austria, including those of Jews, did not decline significantly until 1934. Approximately 120,000 individuals were naturalized between 1919 and 1936, although this figure, based on data from the *Statistischen Handbuch fur die Republik Österreichs* (Statistical Handbook for the Republic of Austria), excluded those who opted for Austrian citizenship under the terms of Article 80. More than 82,000 naturalizations – 70 per cent of the total between 1919 and 1936 – occurred in Vienna under the city's Social Democratic administration, and a further 20,360 citizenships were approved under the terms of Article 80 for Jewish refugees in Vienna between 1920 and 1925.[11] The statistics also show that the overwhelming majority of citizenships in Austria were approved between 1923 and 1933 with only a slight drop after 1925. This refutes two historical misconceptions about citizenship in the First Republic. Firstly, the evidence that there were only 5,102 naturalizations between 1919 and 1921, while the record annual figure occurred in 1923 with 17,650 naturalizations, counters the claim that most naturalizations occurred immediately after the First World War. Secondly, there was no significant drop in naturalizations after 1925, in spite of a law on 30 July 1925 that restricted citizenship to individuals who had resided permanently in the same town or municipality for at least four years. Only after a federal decree of 24 November 1933 placed a moratorium on naturalizations did the annual figures drop dramatically – from 5,135 in 1933 to 2,178 in 1934, and then to 928 in 1935.[12] Therefore, the statistics for naturalization should be seen in the context of the Christian Social government's gradual repression of the Social Democrats after 1932, and the eventual ban of that party in

February 1934, rather than as evidence of an increasingly restrictive policy on citizenship in the First Republic.

Naturalization policies in the First Republic bore some similarities to citizenship laws in the Weimar Republic. Like Austria, Weimar Germany inherited an old imperial legal practice (and many of its practitioners) that conferred citizenship on the basis of residency in a state or municipality. However, unlike in Austria, the terminology of race had already entered German legal practice before 1918. The German Reich Citizenship Act of 1913, which established the law of blood (*jus sanguinis*) as the determining factor in citizenship cases, marked a departure from previous laws when individual German states, i.e. not the Confederation or, after 1871, empire, had granted citizenship. Although the powers of naturalization still rested with the individual states after 1913, the new law ensured that each state could veto naturalizations approved in other states, thereby preventing foreign-born Jews and Poles from acquiring citizenship in 'generous' states. The law also allowed emigrants from Germany to retain their citizenship rights, unless they became citizens of a foreign country.[13] The outbreak of war in 1914 delayed the strict application of this law in order to conscript Jewish soldiers into the army. In the first two years of the war, the imperial government naturalized more than eight times as many Jews than in the entire pre-war period. After the war, however, the strengthened federalist basis of the Weimar Republic meant that the question of citizenship re-emerged amid sharp regional differences along Social Democratic and Centre party political lines. In 1919, the Social Democratic Prussian Interior Minister, Wolfgang Heine, proposed that 'foreigners' (meaning Poles and Jewish immigrants from Eastern Europe) be naturalized if they or their sons had served in the German army in the war. The Bavarian Centrist government, established after the defeat of the revolutionary socialists in May 1919, resisted Prussian attempts to relax the 1913 law. Repeated efforts to federalize the law floundered as the major parties and regional factions disagreed over whether Jews could be defined as immigrants of 'German descent' (*deutschstämmig*), or of 'foreign descent' (*fremdstämmig*). Authorities in Bavaria and Württemberg, on the one hand, interpreted the term '*deutschstämmig*' to mean that religion, rather than language proficiency or assimilation to German culture, precluded Jews from identifying with the German nation. On the other hand, the Prussian Interior Ministry regarded 'Jew' and 'German descent' as mutually inclusive terms if the immigrant had upheld 'German language and customs' abroad. Yet even the Prussian administration restricted naturalization during the early years of the republic by increasing the requirement for prior residency from ten to twenty years. The Prussian Interior Ministry adopted a more liberal practice during the period of economic and political stabilization between 1925 and 1929 by defining Jews from German-speaking areas in Poland as culturally of 'German descent'. The result was that more Jews from Eastern Europe were naturalized in the Weimar Republic than in the German Empire. Nevertheless, the failure of the Weimar era was that the period of stabilization did not lead to a change of policy, merely a looser application of the existing law. This failure had disastrous consequences later in July 1933 when the Nazi government stripped approximately 7,000 of these new German citizens of their citizenship rights.[14]

While the Prussian Interior Ministry's actions after 1925 can be compared to the liberal application of Article 80 under Vienna's municipal government, the similarities should not be overstated. In Austria, the Social Democrats remained outside federal government after 1920 and were a party already under siege by 1927. In 1929, therefore, the Christian Socials could embark single-handedly on a programme of systematic repression of the rights of foreigners, which culminated in the November moratorium on naturalizations in 1933 and set the scene for further restrictions under the Austrofascist state. The border regime to regulate the entry and residency of foreigners in Austria was in place at a federal level by the end of the 1920s and, therefore, must be interpreted in a different light from the restrictive practices of regional authorities in Weimar Germany. Moreover, the fact that the Austrofascist authorities did not consider it necessary to introduce an Alien Act until 1936 shows the extent to which previous practices had already established sufficient barriers of entry and residency.

Few studies of immigration and citizenship in Austria deal with the interwar period specifically. Most research on immigration to Austria focuses on the Second Republic and characterizes interwar Austria as a country of emigration, rather than immigration.[15] However, a study by Jürgen Illigasch has shown that immigration was actually higher than emigration in the interwar period, especially when seasonal labour immigration is taken into account. There are further discrepancies because the Austrian Migration Office did not begin to collect data on immigration to Austria until 1925. The Migration Office had originally been established in 1919 to facilitate emigration from Austria as a means of alleviating the war-shattered economy, but immigration statistics were not recorded until a law was introduced in 1925 to curb economic immigration. Thus the statistics for immigration between 1925 and 1937 present an incomplete picture of the interwar period as a whole.[16] Moreover, as Michael Marrus reminds us in his authoritative study of Europe's refugees in the twentieth century, statistical data on illegal immigration are notoriously difficult to obtain since refugees were excluded from census counts and the definition of who was a refugee varied in every country.[17] At best, we can only rely on official immigration data and surmise that the actual number of foreigners entering a country was significantly higher, particularly after German Jews began emigrating in 1933.

Austria was a destination for both political and labour immigration during the 1920s. Immigrants from Hungary, Italy, Germany, Russia and the Balkan states came to Austria seeking political refuge from authoritarian, communist and Fascist governments. Hungarian communists fled to Austria in 1919 after the fall of Béla Kun's revolutionary government, including, briefly, Béla Kun himself. German communists fled after the collapse of the short-lived soviet regime in Bavaria and anti-Fascist émigrés from Italy began arriving after Mussolini's March on Rome in 1922. German Nazis made up another group of political émigrés after the failed Beer Hall putsch in Munich in 1923. From the Balkan states, Greek legitimists, Croatian and Macedonian autonomists, and numerous Albanian and Montenegrin refugees, sought either transitory or permanent asylum in Austria. In addition, Russian tsarist supporters and Ukrainian military officials came to Austria in the 1920s as political refugees from the Soviet Union.[18]

One of Austria's literary discoveries of the twentieth century, Alexandra von Hoyer (1898–1991), represented the latter group of refugees from Soviet Russia. Her Austrian husband had been in a Russian prison camp in the First World War and, together with their young son, the couple fled their home in Siberia in 1925 to escape political persecution from communists. Writing in Austria under her pseudonym, Alja Rachmanova became famous through her diary, *Milchfrau in Ottakring* (The Milkwoman in Ottakring), which chronicles her experiences of social and intellectual isolation and daily survival in a foreign land after being forced to abandon her academic career in Russia for a meagre existence selling milk in a suburban Viennese shop.[19] Rachmanova's diary was eventually published in 1931 in three volumes and translated into 21 languages, selling 600,000 copies before the Nazis banned it in 1938 for its religious undertones.[20] *Milchfrau in Ottakring* is a poignant testament to the millions of refugees and immigrants forced to rebuild their lives during the massive population upheavals after the First World War, a phenomenon often overshadowed in historical scholarship by the wave of emigration from Germany during the 1930s.[21]

Along with Belgium, Holland and France, Austria took steps to regulate its domestic labour market against foreign workers in the mid-1920s.[22] On 19 December 1925, the Austrian parliament passed a Domestic Workforce Protection Act (*Inlandarbeiterschutzgesetz*), which banned foreigners from working without permanent residency.[23] This measure was a result of pressure from both Social Democratic unions and Christian Social labour representatives on the government to reduce the numbers of Czech and Slovak textile workers and sugar plantation labourers.[24] However, statistics for the period 1925–1937 show that the Migration Office still approved an average annual quota of 6,419 immigration and work permits. Furthermore, the numbers emigrating from Austria outside Europe between 1925 and 1937 represented half of all immigration and work visas issued in the same period, that is 41,253 emigrants and 83,441 visas. This suggests that most immigrants tended not to stay long in Austria, but emigrated overseas instead. Furthermore, these figures exclude the seasonal migrants from Czechoslovakia, whose numbers exceeded 140,000 in the period from 1925 to 1937. Therefore, we can see that the 1925 law did not have the desired effect of reducing the number of foreign workers in Austria, either through seasonal immigration or through work visas.[25] We might conclude, speculatively, that contemporary attitudes towards foreign workers varied to such a degree that it was possible to have a law in place to satisfy workers' protests, while in practice the government continued to approve visas and employers turned a blind eye to illegal workers in order to avoid paying union wages.

In contrast with these ineffectual protectionist policies against foreign workers, Austria's response to political immigration was one of hard-line intimidation and frequent deportations. The legal basis for deportation came from an obscure imperial law of 1871, the so-called 'Schubgesetz', which justified deportation by a provincial or municipal authority of any individual who had become a public burden on charities and welfare, had a criminal record or had an infectious disease. This practice continued unofficially under the First Republic and was formalized in a law of 7 December 1929, which was Austria's first de facto Alien Act. It was used in many cases to justify the expulsion of Roma and Sinti from towns or outlying regions. The governor of Vorarlberg, Otto Ender, invoked the 1929 law to deport any jobless person who was not eligible for unemployment benefits in Vorarlberg if his or her legal residence was in another province. It also enabled local authorities to expel foreigners who had committed a criminal offence or disturbed the 'public order, safety and peace' of citizens. Consequently, Nazi putschists in 1923, and communists in general, were targeted and often deported for minor transgressions, such as giving false information to authorities or possessing foreign currencies. Although the authorities' actions were directed against political immigrants, they could only legally justify expulsion if foreigners were seen to be disrupting the peace. In 1932, for example, the Austrian State Secretary, Emil Fey, denied entry to the Czechoslovakian-born German communist, Egon Erwin Kisch, on the grounds that Kisch's proposed lecture on Russia and China contained 'communist propaganda' that would undermine public order. Given that Kisch had still been allowed into Austria in 1930, Fey's statement indicated the government's growing inclination to ban left-wing political immigration to Austria.[26]

The practice of deporting foreigners for political reasons was not actually legislated until 1932, amid government opposition to the German leader of the Austrian NSDAP, Theo Habicht. Hitler had sent Habicht as his envoy to the Austrian party headquarters in Linz in July 1931 to unite the provincial Nazi groups and bring them under the control of the leadership in Germany. Habicht's appointment had met with objection from the Christian Social government and divided the Greater German camp, whose moderate wing in coalition with the Christian Socials was opposed to National Socialist dominance. In mid-1932, the Austrian government finally declared that foreigners who engaged in political activity would be deported according to Paragraph 8 of the Law of Assembly.[27] Habicht did not leave Austria until the ban on the NSDAP in June 1933, after which he continued to oversee the party's underground activities in Austria from his base in Munich. Nonetheless, his presence in Austria had been a catalyst for the government's policy shift. Whereas deportations of Nazis and communists had previously been justified for the sake of public order, the government's response to political immigration was couched in explicitly political terms after 1932, and even more so after 1933. However, concrete attempts to develop an immigration law did not begin until 1936 and, as we will see, remained unrealized at the time of *Anschluss*.

To summarize, successive Austrian governments had already exercised vigilance against foreigners prior to the Austrofascist state coming to power. Restrictions on citizenship, residency and work opportunities, as well as efforts to clamp down on political freedoms, were directed against groups who threatened the political and social power of the Christian Socials, namely, Jews, communists and Nazis. The federal government's increasingly hard-line approach after 1929, and especially after 1932, reflected the radicalizing tendencies within the Christian Social Party that escalated under the Austrofascist state. Under these conditions, it was relatively easy for the German-nationalist press to sensationalize reports on Jewish refugees from Germany and argue for a stricter border protection regime without violating the state censorship laws.

Who is the true refugee?

Making a case for greater border protection also entailed stricter definitions of Europe's true refugees. German-nationalist editors and their readers sympathized with the plight of Austrian Nazis languishing in camps in Yugoslavia after the failed putsch of 1934, while church leaders and a few Austrofascist functionaries welcomed German Catholics fleeing Hitler's regime. (Not every organ of the state welcomed the Catholic émigré intellectuals, as we will see). Expatriate Austrians forced to flee republican Spain were given a hero's welcome in train stations all over Austria, but rumours and reports of Jews crossing borders triggered hysterical responses in both government circles and the press.

Jews from Germany

The 'unwanted' refugees of Europe's twentieth century, as Michael Marrus has shown, were the Jews from Hitler's Germany. Whereas anti-Semitism was often expressed in localized terms of Jewish invasions of Vienna's 2nd district or Salzburg's tourist towns, the refugee issue was an Austrian-wide concern. The Viennese and, most surprisingly, the Styrian organs had the most to say about Jewish refugees. It was characteristic that the *Wiener Neueste Nachrichten* would seek to exploit the *Ostjude* stereotype to generate hysteria over Jewish immigration to Austria, but the *Grazer Tagespost* had less inclination towards anti-Semitism given its preoccupation with its lost borderland in Yugoslavia and, as we will see, the plight of Austrian Nazi refugees in Yugoslavia. However, the *Tagespost* was less concerned with the threat of Jewish immigrants in Austria, than with the problem that Austria's identity as a German state could potentially be tainted by an influx of 'non-Germans' into the country. In this respect, the editors' reaction was less sensationalism than xenophobia. Refugees had come to Styria during the war but that had been temporary and they had been repatriated by war's end, unlike the Jewish refugees who stayed on in Vienna. Jewish refugees from Germany, however, had no option to return and their stay in Austria might turn out to be indefinite unless Austria closed its borders.

It was this fear that prompted editors of the *Tagespost* to defend the Austrian government's border block against political refugees from Germany following Hitler's appointment as chancellor. On 10 February 1933, the newspaper reported that State Secretary Fey had ordered police on the Austro-German border to refuse entry to all German political refugees and to deport any found already to be in Austrian territory.[28] The next day, the newspaper explained that these measures were a matter of course 'for the protection of the native population' against 'non-Germans' (*Nichtdeutscher*) who were entering Austria from Germany 'in great hordes'. The article on 11 February explained that the concern of the government was not to restrict political asylum, but to keep political agitators out of Austria.[29] This sentiment was echoed in the government press with the *Reichspost* also headlining the state's intent to ban entry of any individuals claiming to be political refugees, whom the newspaper deemed to be criminals.[30]

The burning of the German parliament in Berlin on 27 February sparked fears from both the government and the *Tagespost* of a potential 'invasion' of German communists, whom the German government held responsible for the arson. On 1 March, the *Tagespost* claimed that Austrian border police units would have to check more thoroughly the documentation of Germans crossing the border and deport 'suspicious persons' immediately.[31] On the front page of the same day's evening edition, an editorial decried a 'bolshevist invasion' and called for the Austrian government to refuse asylum to communists.[32] These reactions in the *Tagespost* mirrored the paranoia of the government, which had announced plans to expel any German citizen without a passport or immigration permit. According to reports in the Social Democratic *Arbeiter-Zeitung*, the police had also begun raids in Vienna's working districts, arresting anyone with a German passport and deporting individuals suspected of left-wing political activities.[33]

The *Tagespost* continued to report on the government response to the refugees for the remainder of 1933. On 3 June, for example, the *Tagespost* reported the Lower Austrian government's proposal to denaturalize foreign-born individuals living in the province.[34] Another lead article on 1 September 1933 said that police in Vienna had ordered a group of German Jews to leave Austria because they had been unable to find work and had become dependent on state funds and private charities.[35] This report in September is corroborated by evidence that the Austrian authorities had begun to restrict the entry of anyone who could not produce evidence of adequate financial means. The fears of the Austrian government were such that border guards simply regarded all arrivals on the border as destitute immigrants. When a Jewish film writer in exile in Czechoslovakia was denied entry into Austria to attend a business meeting, the official statement from the chancellor's office was that 'we cannot allow persons without identity papers and without sufficient funds to be let into Austria. Only when there is evidence to us of a secure existence, do we permit entry.'[36]

The government's alarm and the *Tagespost*'s support for a zero tolerance policy towards refugees who allegedly posed a political and material threat to Austria were disproportionate reactions to what was a comparatively low level of immigration by international standards. According to a 1935 report from the League of Nations' High Commission for Refugees (Jewish and Other) Coming from Germany, which had been established in October 1933 under the helm of James G. McDonald, Austria was ranked eighth as a receiving country for refugees from Germany.[37] Austrian migration statistics indicate that 7,249 Germans acquired immigration and work permits between 1933 and 1937, a figure that accounted only for legal entries into Austria.[38] The number of illegal entries was at least half as high again: between January 1933 and April 1936, the IKG in Vienna sponsored 4,600 refugees, which excluded the additional numbers of refugees who found other means of subsistence through black market employment or through family support.[39] Some of these refugees were Austrians who had been living and working permanently in Germany, including many who had acquired German citizenship and were not classified as returnees upon their arrival in Austria.[40]

By drawing attention to German Jews in other European countries than Austria, the *Tagespost* could create a sensational story of mass migration at the threshold of Austria's borders. Reports in April 1933 estimated that up to 300 Jews, communists and socialists had arrived in Switzerland from Germany in the three days after the burning of parliament, and that a further 3,000 Jews had fled to Switzerland following the anti-Jewish boycott on 1 April.[41] In the same month, another report from Poland said that 900 Polish Jews and 400 German Jews had crossed over the Polish-German border.[42] On 25 August, the newspaper reported that the numbers of German refugees in France had risen to 18,000. The next day, a report from Czechoslovakia warned that the growing number of Jewish refugees from Germany would become a burden to countries of asylum, such as Czechoslovakia and France.[43] Two articles in December reported that there were still 600 German Jews in Yugoslavia who had not yet emigrated to Palestine.[44]

None of these reports in the *Tagespost* were misleading in the light of refugee statistics compiled by the League of Nations. In Switzerland, for example, some 10,000 German refugees entered the country through one border station alone between May and September 1933.[45] France had the highest intake of German refugees in Europe with 25,000 by the end of 1933, which substantiates the *Tagespost*'s reports of up to 18,000 at the end of August.[46] The mass deportation of up to 20,000 Polish Jews from Germany in 1933 was also consistent with the *Tagespost*'s reports of Jewish refugees crossing the Polish-German border.[47] If there was any hint that the newspaper might have inflated the statistics to exaggerate the threat of Jewish refugees, it was in the headline reports of Jewish refugees in Yugoslavia. Like the reports on Carinthian Slovenes, these reports on Jewish refugees south of the Austrian border reflected the newspaper's tendency to localize topics of concern to a German-nationalist readership. In this respect, the newspaper was simply continuing an established editorial practice from imperial times when a threat to local identity could be magnified as a threat to the wider Austrian pan-German identity, just as

Slovene nationalists in Styria had been conflated with Czech nationalists in Bohemia into a single threat to the Germans of Austria-Hungary.

As Yugoslavia was to Styrian readers, Jewish refugees were historically and geographically proximate to readers of the *Wiener Neueste Nachrichten*. Throughout 1933 and 1934, the Viennese newspaper closely observed the various restrictions imposed on Jewish refugees in other European countries. An article on 12 July 1933 defended Switzerland's right to pursue restrictive asylum policies against 'the stream of political refugees who have flooded into Switzerland to claim freedom of asylum'. The newspaper described the refugees as 'asylum politicians' (*Asylpolitiker*) whose intent it was to agitate against Germany and 'spin their communist webs of intrigue further'. The newspaper defended the Swiss, who it claimed 'began seeing it as rather strange to take a growing invasion of Jews into their country, which threatened to turn the concept of asylum into its opposite. So the Swiss, who always show consideration for the individual, have decided not to remove the clause on asylum, for instance, but rather, to banish the unwanted intruders from the country by various emergency measures.'[48] The sentiment behind this veiled remark was that Jews, not refugees, posed a threat to European traditions of asylum because they abused the terms of asylum in order to spread their political influence. A separate editorial in the newspaper claimed that Jewish immigration to Switzerland had unleashed a heightened sense of national consciousness among Swiss Germans and pointed to the daily protest rallies and marches as evidence that 'feelings have been brought to life that until now have slumbered'.[49]

The *Wiener Neueste Nachrichten* also backed the efforts of European governments to restrict or ban refugees and immigrants from participating in the public life of the host country. An article on 29 November 1933 cited a report in the French right-wing newspaper, *Midi*, which claimed that 'certain Israelite circles' were attempting to influence France's relations with Germany.[50] Just over a month later, the *Wiener Neueste Nachrichten* reported that the French government had withdrawn the residence permits of approximately 2,500 German 'emigrants' in Alsace.[51] An article followed three weeks later with allegations that German refugees in England had been prohibited from practising or training in medicine at English hospitals or universities.[52] These articles gave silent approval of discriminatory policies against refugees from Germany, justifying and promoting international measures against what the newspaper regarded as the universal threat of Jewish immigration in Europe.

The newspaper's reports on refugees housed in military barracks in Paris were an example of this anti-Semitic bias. A front-page editorial on 22 February 1934 described the 'floods' of Jews who 'swarm' around the

Boulevard Saint-Michel with nothing to occupy their time. The newspaper referred to the barracks as a 'ghetto', whose occupants derived a meagre income from petty trading because they 'are not used to physical work and manual labour [and because] the police ban peddling on the streets of Paris'.[53] This statement resembled an anti-Semitic stereotype that the newspaper depicted elsewhere in its reports about the Jews of Leopoldstadt, who conducted an allegedly unscrupulous trade in selling and exchanging small goods.[54] The American journalist, Emil Lengyel, visited the military barracks in Paris at the end of 1933 and, observing the impoverishment and suicidal tendencies of the refugees, described their story as 'one of the darkest chapters of Europe's post-war history'.[55] However, the *Wiener Neueste Nachrichten* guarded against such compassion by omitting any reference to their physical or emotional duress, dehumanizing them instead by likening them to insects, whose inability to do manual work precluded them from any productive or meaningful existence.

National Socialist refugees

Unlike the articles on Jewish refugees, stories of Austrian Nazis crossing into Germany and Yugoslavia presented a human face to refugees. These reports allowed German-nationalist newspapers to distinguish between Nazi 'refugees' and Jewish 'emigrants' to suit their ideological vantage point. The *Tagespost* published numerous front-page articles about Austrian Nazis crossing into Germany during the months following the party's ban in June 1933. These stories served two purposes: firstly, to delegitimize the Austrian government's struggle against a stronger foe across the German border and, secondly, to portray the heroism of Austrian Nazis as they risked life and possessions to escape the Austrian authorities. There were frequent reports of arrests on the Bavarian border as well as detailed reports on Austrian Nazis, and the smugglers assisting them, who successfully evaded the border guard as they fled into Bavaria.[56] Other articles gave extensive coverage to the government's border security measures intended to prevent Nazi incursions from the German side as well as Austrians escaping into Germany. Two articles in July reported that a Nazi Party rally in the Bavarian town of Kiefersfeld across the border from Kufstein in Tyrol, attended by up to four thousand German SA and SS soldiers, had prompted a full border alert by the Austrian authorities.[57] On 26 July, the *Tagespost* reported a border violation by a German aeroplane that had flown over the Austrian province of Vorarlberg and dropped fliers denouncing the Austrian government.[58] Further reports in September said that the Tyrolean border was to be patrolled by companies of the Tyrolean alpine hunting regiment, two companies of the Viennese infantry regiment and three police aircraft.[59] In addition to these security measures, the

Tagespost frequently reported cases of denaturalization in the wake of a law passed on 16 August 1933 that stripped Austrians of their citizenship if they fled to Germany.[60] Although prevented from criticizing the Austrian government directly under the press laws introduced that year, the newspaper could still protest indirectly through stories of Nazis being hounded by Austrian authorities.

The newspaper's sympathy for Nazi refugees was most striking in the *Tagespost*'s coverage of Austrian National Socialists fleeing into Yugoslavia in the wake of Dollfuss's assassination in July 1934. Five days after the putsch, on 30 July, the *Tagespost* reported that Yugoslavian police had arrested several hundred Austrian refugees on the border and were interning them in camps in Varaždin, Bjelovar and Slavonska Požega.[61] Further reports in August described the relief efforts of the Yugoslavian Red Cross, which had transported about two hundred of the refugees from their temporary accommodation in a primary school to abandoned barracks in the Varaždin area.[62] The exact number of Nazi refugees interned in the camps was initially thought to be more than 1,000, according to the Austrian and German foreign ministries, but Austrian police authorities later estimated there were up to 3,000, which probably included those who lived outside the main camps with relatives and acquaintances, as well as returnees to Austria and later arrivals in November.[63]

Coverage of the National Socialist refugees in Yugoslavia intensified in early September and October. The *Tagespost* reported on 4 September that Chancellor Schuschnigg had dismissed rumours of an Austrian Legion being formed among National Socialists in Yugoslavia.[64] A feature article on the refugees filed two days later from a Viennese government organ, *Die Wiener Zeitung* (suggesting the government had greater insight into the refugee situation than Chancellor Schuschnigg was admitting), described the daily living conditions in the camps at Varaždin and Maribor and gave a picture of a sophisticated camp system run largely by the refugees themselves with curfews and monetary and food distributions.[65] Several descriptions, for example of Austrian mothers travelling by train to visit their children in the camps, evoked sympathetic tones while carefully avoiding all references to the political reasons for asylum.[66] Subsequent coverage in October focused on the humanitarian needs of the refugees: one report said that 40 women and some children were also in the camp at Varaždin and other reports suggested there were 60 women and 70 children among one transport of refugees being taken to Lipič because of overcrowding in the Varaždin camp.[67] The Varaždin camp included a separate camp for the unmarried female companions of the refugees, the so-called *Hitlermädellager*, and it was not uncommon for wives and children of refugees to follow their husbands and fathers to the camps by declaring themselves refugees once they arrived by train over the Yugoslavian border.[68] However, the *Tagespost* reported only the details concerning the humanitarian plight of the refugees and did not elaborate on the political motivations of either the men or the women. Finally, on 30 November, the *Tagespost* reported that the majority of the refugees had been transported to Germany while approximately eighty had chosen to return to Austria.[69]

Stories about interned refugees and concerned relatives held particular importance for Styrian readers, who may have had first-hand knowledge of the border crossings and the plight of National Socialists from Styria and Carinthia. The *Tagespost* was diligent in its task of supplying local news to its readers both in the refugee reports throughout 1934 and in many other reports on border incidents, such as shootings and illegal crossings on the Styrian border.[70] However, the human-interest appeal of these stories was a smokescreen for the newspaper's real sympathies for National Socialism. The *Tagespost* paid fleeting attention to Social Democrats who fled to Czechoslovakia after the civil war in February 1934. Where there was newspaper coverage of Austrian émigrés in Czechoslovakia and the Soviet Union, the emphasis in the narrative was on illegal migration, arrests, deportations, claims of espionage and expulsion.[71] Moreover, the newspaper referred to Social Democrats as 'emigrants', while the Austrian Nazis in Yugoslavia were cast sympathetically as political refugees.

The *Wiener Neueste Nachrichten* also included reports on the Austrian Nazis fleeing into Germany. One report on 31 August 1933 said that six armed National Socialist refugees crossing over the Bavarian border in Upper Austria had shot at a customs control officer on the border.[72] The report's detached tone, and its reference to the Nazis' weaponry and violence, was consistent with the *Wiener Neueste Nachrichten*'s abhorrence of terrorism in the wake of Dollfuss's assassination. However, coverage of Nazi refugees in the Viennese organ was not as prominent or as sustained as the reports in the *Tagespost*. We can interpret these reports in the light of what we already know about both newspapers' attitudes towards National Socialism. As we saw in Chapter 4, the *Tagespost* wore its Nazi sympathies on its sleeve, whereas the Viennese organ was more cautious and, at times, inclined to regard National Socialists as usurping the political clout of other German-nationalists in Austria. Given that the *Wiener Neueste Nachrichten* and its chief editor, Mauthe, advocated a German-nationalist opposition front in which National Socialists would play an important but not exclusive role, the scant attention paid to the Nazi emigration from Austria may indicate the newspaper's dismissive attitude towards party radicals. Stories about Nazi border crossings carried greater ideological significance than they would at first suggest and illustrate the complex relationship between German-nationalists and National Socialists in the interwar period.

Francoist refugees from Spain

The newspapers' ideological rendering of refugees was further evident during the Spanish Civil War with the reports of Germans and Austrians fleeing Spain in 1936. The German and Austrian expatriates in Spain were mainly members of the Spanish business community and were sympathetic to Franco and the Nationalist rebels.[73] Others were long-term residents or had married Spaniards. Towards the end of July, the *Tagespost* focused its attention on the plight of stranded German and Austrian refugees. The newspaper reported that several hundred German refugees from Spain had been transported by British and French warships to France and then by train to Germany where the German government had pledged 50,000 marks in emergency relief for the refugees.[74] On 3 August, the *Tagespost* reported that 70 Austrian refugees, including 25 locals from Graz, had arrived at the Innsbruck train station to be greeted by government officials.[75] More news of Austrian refugees continued throughout August and a report in January 1937 said that a total of 490 Austrians had fled Spain in 1936, according to official migration statistics.[76]

It was significant that these reports coincided with the resumption of diplomatic relations between Austria and Germany following the July Agreement of 1936. As we saw in Chapter 2, the *Tagespost* was one of five Austrian newspapers permitted to circulate in Germany under the terms of the Gentlemen's Agreement. The *Tagespost*'s proximity to the Nazi propaganda machine explains why, on 18 August 1936, it published an extract from the National Socialist newspaper, *Der Angriff*, which sought to discredit the Spanish republicans who had fled to France and Britain in the wake of Franco coming to power.[77] 'If the leader of the front slaughters hostages like cattle and then escapes over the border into a neighbour country, then there can be no more discussion about the application of international terms.' Rather, the Nazi organ argued, 'Political refugees always have the right to asylum; but murderers and mass killers must also grasp the full force of the law if, as in Spain, they think they can whitewash their bloody deeds with the colour of a questionable conscience.'[78] This extract from *Der Angriff* was published barely one month after Austrian Nazis had succeeded in assassinating Dollfuss, further evidence that the *Tagespost* condoned terror and violence if it advanced the cause of National Socialism. The *Tagespost* endorsed the Nazi organ's assertion that only legitimate political refugees (National Socialists) be accorded international protection, while other 'murderers' and 'mass killers' (presumably, socialists and communists) were liable to receive 'the full force of the law'. In short, the *Tagepost* agreed with the editors of the Nazi organ that governments had a legal mandate to enact wilful revenge and indiscriminate punishment on the enemies of fascism and nationalism, whether in Spain, Germany or Austria.

The *Wiener Neueste Nachrichten* also portrayed the Spanish republicans as pillagers and murderers in its reports of German and Austrian refugees fleeing Spain in 1936. These stories graphically reported the persecution, violence and terror directed against political and national opponents of the Spanish Republican Guard. Reports told of German-owned houses and businesses in Barcelona being raided and set alight.[79] The newspaper focused on personal stories of escape in the reports of Austrian refugee transports from Spain throughout August. An interview with one man who had married and settled in Spain recounted his evacuation by ship to France, where he stayed in a camp before journeying by three-day train to Austria.[80] More personal stories followed in a front-page article about the arrival of the first transport of Austrian refugees from Madrid. The article mentioned the names and professions of some and told the story of an elderly woman who had lived in Spain for sixty years, whose nursing home residence had been burnt down by communists leaving her homeless.[81] These stories were personal in the same way that the *Tagespost*'s coverage of Styrian Nazis fleeing to Yugoslavia was intended to appeal to local knowledge and associations with the people connected to the events.

In Salzburg, too, images of the refugees from Spain were local and personal. Reports in the *Salzburger Volksblatt* described the humanitarian assistance given by 'national Spain' to the elderly and children fleeing their villages in the war zone. The refugees had been told the nationalists would gouge out the eyes of the men, but instead they found shelter and warm food, as the girls in Falangist uniforms served soup and watched the children.[82] Salzburg's Archbishop Waitz (who had succeeded Rieder in 1934) announced that 3 September 1936 would be a day of mourning in the whole archdiocese with the faithful instructed in a pastoral letter to attend silent holy masses and pray to the saints for those who had lost their homes and loved ones.[83] Stories of 'national Spain' assisting poor villagers and refugees returning to their home countries, and of Austrian Catholics praying for the victims of the terror, contrasted with the stark factual reports of Jewish refugees attempting to flee Germany in 1933.

German Catholic refugees

One group of refugees in Austria who went unmentioned in the German-nationalist press were Catholics from Nazi Germany. Whereas Catholics from Spain were deemed refugees for their national credentials, Catholics from Germany were not, at least in the eyes of German-nationalists who wished to elevate nation above confession. However, unlike communists, Catholics could not be denigrated in the German-nationalist press because of the 1933 censorship law prohibiting offences against the religious beliefs of Austrians. Yet the newspapers' silence was also further indication of German-nationalists' uneasy relationship with Catholics. On the one hand, there was common support for pan-Germanism and a hesitation on the part of the newspapers to offend Catholics who sympathized with National Socialists, but on the other hand, the newspapers regarded the Church as an obstacle to German unity.

For the Austrofascist government, however, the arrival in Austria of German Catholic refugees vindicated its opposition to National Socialism. Many of the refugees were prominent journalists, academics, theologians and leaders of youth organizations, who had contacts abroad and were well positioned to participate in international efforts to oppose Hitler's regime.[84] In Austria, they found work more easily than their Jewish counterparts, often in academic posts, and they had a wider support base in general through parochial networks. This support was formalized in January 1936 through the creation of a Caritas aid agency for Catholic refugees under the auspices of the Archdiocese of Vienna.[85]

One of the most prominent German Catholic refugees in Austria during this period was Dietrich von Hildebrand (1889–1977). After the Nazis introduced a law on 7 April 1933 excluding non-Aryans from holding public offices, Hildebrand was forced to retire as Professor of Philosophy at the University of Munich because his grandmother had been Jewish. He came to Austria in September 1933 after Dollfuss promised that any Catholic professor who had left Germany would find a job in Austria. He was appointed to the theological faculty at the University of Salzburg in February 1934 and was made professor of philosophy at Vienna at the end of 1934, which automatically granted him Austrian citizenship. In December 1933, with Dollfuss's financial support, Hildebrand founded the weekly journal, *Der Christliche Ständestaat*, which aligned itself with the Austrofascist government's opposition to National Socialism.[86] The journal's chief editor, Klaus Dohrn, a journalist and relative of Hildebrand who had also immigrated to Austria in 1933, concentrated the journal's main political themes on Germany, the issue of Nazism's defeat, opposition to communism, and the preservation of Austrian independence.[87] It was especially critical of Nazi organs in Germany and Nazi-sympathizing newspapers in Austria, including the *Wiener Neueste Nachrichten*.[88]

Yet even supporters of the Austrofascist state, such as Hildebrand and Dohrn, were subjected to official surveillance if they engaged in political activities that were directed against Nazi Germany. Following the July

Agreement, Hildebrand and Dohrn faced growing criticism from within the ranks of both the Austrofascist state and the Catholic Church over their opposition to the Nazi regime. The *Christliche Ständestaat* was placed under surveillance by the *Heimatdienst* propaganda bureau and Dohrn's telephone calls were monitored between 1936 and 1937.[89] As well as being chief editor on Hildebrand's journal, Dohrn had been an outspoken advocate for a 'third way' between Nazism and communism. In June 1936, he had established the Young German Catholics' Circle (*Ring deutscher Jungkatholiken*) and the following year he founded the German Front Against the Hitler Regime (*Deutsche Front gegen das Hitler System*), which aimed to bring together all non-communist German exile groups into a common opposition front against Hitler. He was forced to disband the German Front, however, under pressure from both the Austrian authorities and the Vatican. Catholic bishops and Vatican officials had expressed concern that this opposition movement would unleash a renewed propaganda war against the Church under the guise of a struggle against 'political Catholicism'. In April 1937, Hildebrand left the editorship of the *Christliche Ständestaat* under pressure from the Austrian government to do so because of his criticism towards Nazi Germany.[90]

Another prominent German Catholic exile in Austria, Hubertus Prinz zu Löwenstein (1906–1984), was not only an opponent of the Nazis, but also a critic of the Austrofascist government's suppression of the workers' movement. Löwenstein had been leader of the German Republican Youth Movement until Hitler dissolved it in 1933, and had begun a promising career as a political writer. As a consequence of his speech at a pre-election meeting of the Catholic Centre Party in February 1933, Nazi storm troopers had searched his house, prompting him and his wife to leave their home in Berlin for the relative peace of Tyrol, where he had spent his childhood at his family estate. In his 1942 memoir, *On Borrowed Peace*, Löwenstein writes that he had not anticipated staying longer than a few weeks in Austria: 'I was not in exile. We were leaving Germany only for a while, until the end of the present terror.'[91] Löwenstein stayed at his base in Tyrol, while continuing his work as a political writer for Austria's liberal press. He made many and varied contacts with public figures in Austria, including Schuschnigg; Cardinal Innitzer; Social Democratic leaders, Julius Deutsch and Otto Bauer; as well as the leader of the Christian Social Workers' Movement, Leopold Kunschak. His interest in and support for the Austrian labour movement led him, while in England in February 1934, to send a telegram to Dollfuss undersigned by sixty members of the British Upper and Lower Houses, protesting against the murders of workers in the February civil war.[92] His political campaign against Nazi Germany was largely carried out abroad in England and America. In 1934, he co-founded the

American Guild for German Cultural Freedom, a representative body of German intellectuals abroad that offered scholarships to support German writers-in-exile. He also proposed the formation of a Youth League of Nations and published his first book, *The Tragedy of a Nation: Germany, 1918–1934*. However, the frequent threats against Löwenstein's and his family's life from underground Nazis in Tyrol made it increasingly difficult for him to continue this political opposition from his Austrian base. His isolated outpost in rural Austria, close to the German border, exacerbated his sense of vulnerability. The murder in August 1933 of the German-Jewish author, Theodor Lessing, by Nazi storm troopers who had been smuggled illegally into Czechoslovakia by local sympathizers, was a stark reminder to Löwenstein that exile was not a guarantee of protection from Nazis.[93]

Unlike Hildebrand and Dohrn, Löwenstein did not remain in Austria after the July Agreement, which would otherwise have prevented his continuing political opposition to the Nazis. When his German passport expired at the end of 1934, Löwenstein was personally granted Czechoslovakian citizenship by Foreign Minister Eduard Beneš, allowing him to continue travelling overseas and, after 1935, immigrate to America. With a secure existence and an international passport, he was more fortunate than most of his contemporaries. After the *Anschluss*, for example, he was able to use his connection with Beneš, by then president of Czechoslovakia, to arrange a Czech passport for his journalist friend, Richard Bermann, to escape from Austria to France via Czechoslovakia.[94]

The examples of Hildebrand, Dohrn and Löwenstein are the most prominent of the wider community of German Catholic refugees in Austria after 1933. Although their prominence also means they are less representative, the German Catholic community as a whole, nonetheless, found broader acceptance in Austria than socialists, communists and Jews and received material and moral support through friends, colleagues and parishioners.[95] However, these individuals also faced professional and political isolation in Austria if they spoke out too loudly against the Nazi state. If they had fled Hitler once already in 1933, they were likely to leave again after *Anschluss*, which both Hildebrand and Dohrn did, fleeing first to Czechoslovakia and eventually, during the war, to America.[96]

Fortress Austria

With pressure mounting on German refugees to desist from public criticisms of Nazi Germany following the July Agreement in 1936, the Austrian government meanwhile had quietly been negotiating the terms of a new immigration law that could regulate and control the entry of foreigners into Austria, including German citizens. The proposal was a shift away from the 1929 law, which had directly invoked imperial decrees on deportation and the rights of municipal and provincial governments to authorize entry and residency in a town or province. The new federal law, on the other hand, was intended to allow the government to obtain data about foreigners in the country and to categorize them into different groups for the purpose of closer surveillance by way of a population index and identity cards for every person residing in Austria. Although the legislation in Austria was eventually rejected because of a lack of finances, it points, firstly, to a shift towards greater state control over the population and, secondly, to the relationship between Austrofascist functionaries and their counterparts in Italy as we have already seen for the legislation on press and propaganda. Official debates about the proposed legislation reveal the dual aims of Austrian policy makers to facilitate greater surveillance of the population, and to reduce the number of Jews in Austria either through restricting immigration or by precluding Jews already residing in Austria from being naturalized.

While studies of population management in fascist regimes and so-called liberal democracies have examined eugenics and pronatalism, migration and citizenship policies have so far received less attention for the interwar period.[97] In the case of Fascist Italy, Carl Ipsen has argued that population politics were characterized by a range of measures spanning nuptiality, fertility, mortality, emigration and internal migration: the Fascist Deputy, Gaetano Zingali, explicitly referred to 'this famous demographic quintet' in a speech to parliament in 1929.[98] By exploring these multiple fronts of Mussolini's 'demographic battle', Ipsen extends the debate beyond Mussolini's 'battle for births' to include a spectrum of policies that the regime itself saw as part of a larger battle to create 'a new Fascist society'.[99] In Austria, the legislation was aimed at controlling immigration into the country, unlike Italy where the focus was on restricting emigration and controlling internal migration. Nonetheless, the convergence of different strands of population management in both the Italian and the Austrian case illustrates the value of transnational studies of fascism.[100]

Work on the legislation for a population index began in Austria in 1935, six years after the Italian state had introduced its own population index in 1929. A series of measures aimed at halting emigration in Italy (in contrast to previous liberal policies) had already begun following the introduction of the Public Security Law in November 1926, which made all Italian passports invalid. Less than a year later, strict eligibility criteria for new passports were introduced and in 1930, fines and penalties were introduced for assisting or engaging in clandestine emigration. Repatriation taxes were removed to encourage return migration of Italians working abroad and terminology was changed to reflect the regime's new priority of bringing Italian workers home. The formerly named General Emigration Commission (CGE), the government department responsible for Italian emigration, was renamed the General Directorship of Italians Abroad (DGIE) after Mussolini declared the word 'emigrant' defunct. The regime also sought to discourage migration to cities by providing housing and transport for rural workers to work on state projects and subsidizing charities that assisted state programmes of internal migration.[101]

Dovetailing with these measures in migration, the Italian state sought to create centralized systems of demographic data through its Central Statistics Institute of the Kingdom of Italy (ISTAT) as well as through specialist university courses. Zingali declared in his 1929 speech that in Fascist Italy 'not only men, but also statistical data, have become dynamic, almost as if following with the same insistent rhythm the course of these glorious times'.[102] Upon its creation in 1926, ISTAT gained control over all demographic statistics except for migration, which came under the jurisdiction of the government migration agencies – the CGE/DGIE for emigration from Italy; the Commission for Migration and Colonization (CMC); and the Permanent Committee for Internal Migration (CPMI) for migration within Italy. Municipal population registers, which had collated and stored data on internal migration since 1862, were also used as official agencies for migration statistics. When individuals arrived in a new municipality, or *commune*, they would be registered and their record was cancelled when they left the commune. In addition to arrivals and cancellations, the population registers also recorded births, deaths and marriages. However, legislation introduced in Italy in 1929 brought these population registers under the authority of ISTAT and municipalities were required to hand over their annual population registers to ISTAT. Any irregularity in the records, for instance omitting to report a birth or change of residence, was a punishable offence. Since most records of births, deaths and marriages were held in local parishes, the 1929 law effectively made parish activities subject to state surveillance and control, which strictly speaking was a violation of the Lateran Accords regulating church-state relations.[103]

The centralizing powers of ISTAT were constrained, however, by the fact that responsibility for data collection and collation still lay at the municipal level with the mayor. Nor did ISTAT have access to full data on clandestine migration to the cities, which Mussolini sought initially to discourage through the colonization projects and later banned in 1939. This limitation was a bone of contention for Italy's leading demographer in the Fascist period and president of ISTAT, Corrado Gini, who wanted to give more power to his organization by employing state-trained statisticians, rather than local authorities, to collect data for the 1931 census.[104] The Interior Ministry rejected Gini's proposal, but that does not imply its lack of reception among Fascist policy makers; it simply indicates a lack of financial and human resources in Italy during the years of consolidating power.

Despite its inability to achieve the kind of expansion of state powers that functionaries like Gini wished for, Italy was still a model of population management. Poland and Hungary also centralized their demographic systems in the 1930s and we can assume that demographers in those countries were also following closely the legislative changes in 1929 in Italy.[105] Given that Gini was already renowned in international demographic circles for his cyclical theory of population growth, his proposal in 1931 for a more professional approach to census data would have been well received by his peers elsewhere.[106]

Italy's influence on Austrofascist policy makers is evident in the legislation for a population index drafted by the Federal Council for Culture, which also created the legislation on the press chamber.[107] The Council met to discuss the proposal in September 1935. Minister Lenz, acting as Speaker on this occasion, referred directly to Italy's 1929 law and recommended in line with Italy that state inspectors be appointed to oversee the registration process and the various registry offices.[108] The parallels with Italy can also be seen from the Austrian proposal to include a compulsory identification card (*Erkennungskarte*) to be issued to every person over the age of eighteen, modelled on the Italian *Carta d'identità*. The Austrian card was to function as a domestic passport and would include the person's photograph, address, date of birth, nationality and occupation. Like in Italy, the purpose of the identity cards was to help individuals to better identify with the state by reminding them of their social obligations to the state: work and loyalty to one's country of birth. They were also intended for use for a range of other identification purposes still in process.[109] The new law was to take effect from 1 November 1935.[110]

However, there was one important difference between the Italian and the Austrian models that highlights the racial 'front' in Austria's demographic battle, one not witnessed in Italy until after the Axis pact between Mussolini and Hitler in 1935 and Italy's invasion of Ethiopia in 1936. Whereas in Italy individuals and families were registered separately, the Austrian population index was to include details about an individual's family on the same index card. During the Council debates, Lenz pointed out that the inclusion of an individual's family details was intentionally designed to require Austrian citizens to declare any business and family links outside Austria.[111] The concern that some Austrian citizens were supporting family members who were not citizens was directed at former refugees who had arrived during the First World War and who had been ineligible for Austrian citizenship under the new laws created after the empire's collapse, as we saw earlier in this chapter. The proposal to include family members on the population index was thus intended to force registrants to declare their non-Austrian relatives to the authorities.

The anti-Semitism of Austria's population index was further evident in the Council's discussions on administrative codes for non-permanent residents in Austria. Individuals who registered in a place where they did not have fixed residency were to have their identity cards stamped with a 'V' for vagabond. This category included not only 'tramps', one Council member observed, but also those performers and artists who only stayed in one place for two months, a remark which drew the mirth of other Council members.[112] Apparently what struck the ministers as funny were the many prominent Jewish theatre directors, actors and other performers who had come to Austria from Germany since 1933, often staying only for the annual summer season of the Salzburg Festival before immigrating to America, and who were the butt of many anti-Semitic jibes during the Festival. The Festival season had just ended, but now a more sinister joke was to be played on them as the Council moved to stamp an 'ST' – abbreviated from 'Stichtag' or expiration date – on their identification cards.[113]

The government did not mention Jews in the legislation, but the implication was that certain foreigners in Austria were 'undesirable'. In his opening remarks to introduce the immigration bill, Lenz placed Austria's need for a population index in the broader European context by claiming that industrial change and the economic crisis had transformed Europe from a 'culture of settling' to a 'culture of migrating'. Austria was 'the state of least resistance against socially undesirable elements' and for this reason it had been necessary to include foreigners as well as Austrian citizens in the population index. The increased numbers of stateless people had become an 'international affliction' on the Austrian state due to the reluctance or unwillingness of Austria's neighbours to take in former Austrian citizens who were now stateless.[114] This was a view shared by the highest state functionaries: the Interior Minister, Emil Fey, welcomed the new legislation as a way to centralize the long-standing practice of a municipal registration system, which Fey claimed had led to many discrepancies between local records and also had allowed the 'non-Austrians' to stay out of the authorities' clutches.[115]

At the same time that government ministers were debating the details of the new legislation, the German-nationalist press fixated on the theme of border security throughout Europe and in Austria. Continuing its earlier coverage of Jewish refugees in Europe, the *Tagespost* shifted focus from border crossings to border blocks. Reports in 1935 and 1936 emphasized the need to protect countries from foreigners who disrupted law and order. In February 1935, for example, the *Tagespost* reported that the Dutch government was planning to erect an internment camp for foreigners who were 'endangering the public order and safety'.[116] In the evening edition that day, the newspaper said that fighting had broken out in a French internment camp in Toulouse among German Saarland refugees who had fled over the border following the return of the Saar region to Germany.[117] Reports from Czechoslovakia described the government's crackdown on illegal immigration and the expulsion of German 'emigrants' who did not have proof of identity. An article in May 1935 said that twenty-five German emigrants, some without documents and some whose identity papers were under suspicion, had been arrested in Prague. The report also alleged that a number of the emigrants had already been deported three times and had re-entered under different names with different papers.[118] A later report mentioned that twelve emigrants had been arrested following a quarter-annual police swoop on foreigners living in Prague.[119] In July, the *Tagespost* reported that the Czechoslovak government had passed a new amendment to its earlier Alien Act, requiring foreigners to obtain a residence permit within thirty days unless they had been living continuously in Czechoslovakia since October 1918 or had sought citizenship during that time.[120] Reports in October 1935 said that Belgium had also intensified its border surveillance.[121]

These somewhat nebulous stories of European border security with their sensational headlines – 'New fortress ramparts in heart of Europe', 'Belgium reinforces border guard' – depicted a contemporary immigration crisis in Europe.[122] They also provided a wider context within which to address similar questions of surveillance, internment and deportation of foreigners in Austria. In June 1936, the *Tagespost* reflected on the historical dimensions of this debate in a series of articles that examined the causes of and international responses to migratory patterns of Europeans in the medieval and modern period. The newspaper concluded that present-day restrictions on immigration were due to the worldwide economic depression, which had forced all countries 'to reduce the previously wide opening of the gates to quite a small crack'.[123] For the editors of the *Tagespost*, immigration controls were seemingly an economic necessity and served as a corrective to previously generous policies of unchecked immigration, an argument that reiterated Fey's remarks the previous year.

By the end of 1937, opinion makers across the political spectrum were calling for an immigration law that would restrict the arrival and long-term residency of Jewish immigrants in Austria. The government did not need to single out Jews as the target of its proposed legislation: it already had its own press organs – as well as German-nationalist ones – to address the immigration debate publicly in more explicit anti-Semitic language.

'Austria should belong above all to the Austrians'

German-nationalists were staunch defenders of the government's tougher controls on immigration and residency in Austria. In Graz, the *Tagespost* editors framed the immigration debate as an issue of foreign labour, inferring that nearly all foreign workers in Austria were Jews. An editorial on 16 February 1937 claimed that as many foreigners had gained employment in Vienna in 1936 as Austrians had been looking for work. According to the editorial, the statistics showed the failure of the 1925 Domestic Workforce Protection Act to prevent foreigners gaining employment at the expense of Austrian citizens. It alleged that foreigners exploited the Austrian economy by taking the profits outside the country, enabling the families of these foreigners to seek passage to Austria at the expense and exploitation of Austrian families. 'It is, in the long term, an intolerable disparity when, on the one hand, there are nearly one and a half thousand unemployed, each with as many as two or three family members, whose dire need for subsistence is a noticeable strain on the economy, and an equal number of foreign workers on the other hand, who profit from the same economy.' Moreover, the editors claimed, 'a considerable fraction of the earnings of these foreigners does not even stay in Austria but instead is sent off to the family members who still temporarily remain back home.'[124]

Editors of the rival Christian Social organ in Styria, the *Grazer Volksblatt*, also played the foreign labour card, claiming that foreign workers in Austria were taking jobs from unemployed Austrians and citing Carinthia as an example with 11,000 foreign workers and 15,000 'native' Austrians out of work.[125] Interestingly, the issue of foreign workers never surfaced in the ministerial discussions about the new legislation. While the government was pondering the merit of the Italian laws and veiling their anti-Semitism behind remarks about a 'culture of settling', Styrian editors were distilling the debate in terms with which local readers could readily identify – jobs for 'native' Austrians.

Newspapers also reminded their readers of the burden Austria had already borne during the Great War by conflating two different groups of refugees into one ostensible flood of unwanted Jewish immigration. The *Tagespost* described the 'foreigners' as belonging 'almost entirely to a certain group of political émigrés', who had settled in Vienna 'albeit partly for different reasons then'. 'This influx', the newspaper said, 'which was by no means always wanted, as it later painfully became apparent, came from the East. Now it is coming from the West.'[126] The *Wiener Neueste*

Nachrichten drew similar parallels between the wartime and post-1933 immigration. A front-page editorial on 17 December 1937 suggested that Austria was an attractive destination for German Jewish refugees because they had relatives in Vienna and that attempts by the Austrian authorities to restrict immigration would be impossible due to the well-organized, clandestine smuggling groups who provided false identity papers for the refugees. Estimating that between 100 and 150 people arrived without passports each month and found lodging and black-market work in Austria, the editors sounded a clarion call for tighter controls on Jewish immigration: 'Protect our borders and our country from a new flood of *Ostjüdische*!'[127] Two days later, the newspaper published a letter to the editor affirming the editorial's view that it 'is the uncontested right of the state to ban or control immigration . . . Austria needs neither the labour nor the financial ownership of the Eastern European Jews.'[128] A notice in the newspaper for a public lecture series on 'The Foreign Guest in Austria' indicated that there were very likely more than a few anti-immigration activists among both readers and editors alike.[129]

By the beginning of 1938, government and German-nationalist newspapers reacted to a potential new wave of Jewish immigration from Romania by demanding tighter laws on immigration in Austria. The fear that Romanian Jews would soon arrive in Austria, following the election in December 1937 of Octavian Goga as prime minister, reached proportions of hysteria in the Austrian press.[130] The *Tagespost* declared that it was 'the duty of the state to put a stop [to immigration] before Austria is at the mercy of a new flood of foreigners.'[131] The morning and evening editions of the *Wiener Neueste Nachrichten* ran headline stories on the eve of 1938 calling for a border block (*Grenzsperre*) against the *Ostjuden*. 'Austria needs an immigration law that takes into account the changing circumstances and protects the native population from the invasion of a locust swarm from the East', the editors declared on 31 December 1937.[132] Articles in January alleged that Romanian Jews had already fled Romania for safe haven in Austria and its neighbouring countries. On 3 January, the *Tagespost* reported that a group of Romanian Jews had been denied entry into Austria by border guards on the Hungarian border and that similar border blocks had already been carried out by Yugoslavian and Hungarian authorities.[133] On 5 January, the *Wiener Neueste Nachrichten* said that Austrian border authorities had already deported a number of Romanian Jews, who had been visiting relatives or receiving medical treatment in Austria.[134] In Styria, the *Grazer Volksblatt* alleged that the Romanian government intended to deport 500,000 Jews.[135] By the end of the month, editors of the *Wiener Neueste Nachrichten* were claiming to have sighted Romanian Jews already in Vienna, just three days after the Romanian government had decreed that a quarter of its one million Jews would be stripped of their citizenship.[136]

Aside from their sensationalism, these articles had an important func-tion in perpetuating a stereotype of Jews as illegal immigrants. The article on 5 January underscored a recurring stereotype in the German-nationalist press that Jewish immigrants were well connected to the wider Jewish community and that they had no civic allegiances other than for personal gain, which explained why allegedly they would seek medical treatment in a foreign country. This stereotype was further evident in a caricature of Austria's border block against Romanian Jews, showing a map of Central Europe with a physical barricade erected along Austria's border with Hungary and Yugoslavia. Behind the barricade stood a white-collar worker, a farmer, a border police officer, a blue-collar worker and a Jew, dressed in Orthodox garb. The Jew was the only figure waving a welcome to the Romanian Jews on the other side of the border. The others stood, arms crossed, defending their economic interests against the Romanian Jews, who had fled Goga's clenched iron fist punching out of the map and carried backpacks labelled 'business projects', 'honest goods' and 'foreign currencies'. One of the Romanian Jews was attempting to lift the barricade with his hands, while the caption read in dialect: 'Well, off you go straight on back, mind; we already have enough of your kind!'[137] Later describing the reactions of the Lower Austrian Farmers' League and the Christian

„Ja, wer kommerlt denn doda?" —
„Mir kemmen vom Goga!" —

„Jetzt fohrts aber g'schwind z'rud,
Solcherne ham mir schon g'nug!"

German Railway Union to Jewish immigration, the newspaper concluded that, on the question of Jewish asylum in Austria, 'the middle class, the farmer and the worker are all of the same opinion.'[138] The cartoon graphically illustrated the effect of that cross-class border block against Jews.

While the Viennese newspaper based its anti-refugee politics on a supposedly unilateral opposition to refugees that crossed political and social boundaries in Austria, the *Tagespost* in Graz exploited the refugee issue for political gain over the outlawed Social Democrats. In an editorial on 12 January, the newspaper argued that Austria had a right to protect its own citizens against those who abused its system of fairness and 'hospitality'. The editorial spoke on behalf of the 'native population', whose objections to immigration, in the eyes of the newspaper at least, had long gone unheard. Referring to Vienna's Social Democratic municipal government in the 1920s, the *Tagespost* implied that the previous criteria for granting citizenship to Jews had been a political tactic to increase electoral appeal, 'since the freshly baked Austrian citizen immediately became the esteemed Mr Voter'. The editorial explained that Austria could no longer afford to accept immigrants in the country while so many 'fellow countrymen' remained on unemployment benefits, and was quick to defend its position as being patriotically concerned for Austrians.

> Hospitality is certainly a wonderful thing, and we wish that nothing should happen now or in the future that could damage our well-earned reputation. During and immediately after the war we were hospitable, even if perhaps not always from the same motives, when the great migration from the East of the old Monarchy brought us so many unwanted visitors, we were hospitable when a while ago some people in Poland found the ground under their feet to be too hot or even just too unsafe, and we have been hospitable with almost conspicuous zeal when the political upheaval in the German Reich brought many to search for another means of earning a living and a different business environment. We still want to remain the most hospitable country in Europe. But sooner or later comes a day when charity must begin at home and the concern for one's own existence is more pressing than what is often called humanitarianism, which tells everyone to share with everyone . . . It is not a contradiction of such a worthy tradition to say that *this Austria should belong above all to the Austrians*. Neither are we of the view that the most recent political development in Romania could pose such an overwhelming danger to us that it needs to be countered by special emergency regulations. But we wholeheartedly welcome the opportunity afforded by these events of dealing with the entire complex of problems pertaining to regulation and control of foreigners by means of a new Alien Act or, to keep to the official interpretation, to speed up the implementation of measures that have been planned for a long time. And we make a special request that the law be so carefully formulated that someone who, shall we

say, has the right contacts, cannot straight away slip through loopholes again.[139]

Here the newspaper constructed Austria's state borders through this appeal to protect Austrian citizens from 'foreigners', embodied in the stereotype of Jewish immigrants, who could 'slip through' a legal system because of their belonging to an underworld of forgery and assisted passage.

Even outside observers like *The Times* correspondent in Vienna, Douglas Reed, noted the problem of taking in Jewish refugees. He reported that Austria had 'been flooded with immigrants from Germany and Poland, a fair proportion of whom have criminal records' and predicted that 'a closer scrutiny is inevitable sooner or later'. He defended these sentiments as having 'nothing to do with anti-Semitism' and stated that the 'bulk of opinion in Austria' agreed with the views expressed in both the govern-ment and German-nationalist press. Reed's broad-brush strokes painted a sympathetic picture abroad that the Austrian authorities could scarcely have hoped for as vindication for their brand of population politics.[140]

When the Federal Council for Culture met in February 1938 to discuss amendments to the original 1935 law, Lenz again made reference to the problem of stateless people in Austria. He stated that while deporting stateless people from Austria would be possible in theory, in practice Aus-tria's neighbouring countries were not prepared to accept them and neither were they obligated to under international law if the deportees were not citizens of those countries. He also noted the ease with which these state-less people had so far been able to acquire identity cards stating their nationality without the information being thoroughly checked. Therefore he recommended to the Council that the identity cards be only a secondary identification of nationality, and that there be another more rigorous system to document a person's national status.[141]

At the same time that the Council was legislating for a population index in 1935, the Austrian Migration Office was drafting a new Alien Act to regulate foreign permits in Austria. The legislation underwent three revi-sions over an eighteen-month period but, like the legislation for a popula-tion index, was never fully implemented before the *Anschluss*. In the final stages of negotiation, the Interior Ministry conceded that a system of indexing all 290,000 foreigners in Austria was too costly an exercise and settled instead on a register for those who had arrived in Austria since 1 January 1933.[142] Nonetheless, the Alien Act and the population index and card system are significant because they reveal the full extent to which Austria's politicians were ready to mobilize the state's powers to curb what they perceived was a wave of uncontrolled immigration. If left unchecked, they believed that another population movement could potentially open the floodgates to more desperate and destitute refugees, genuine or otherwise.

Population policies in Austria, as in Italy, were 'audacious in their aspirations but modest in their accomplishments' constrained as they were by the economic crisis in the 1930s.[143] That the law was a reflection neither of escalating immigration into Austria, nor of a widespread concern about job security among the general workforce, has been shown already at the beginning of this chapter. But when we consider the extent and detail of Austrian legislation for a population index, we can see that what took more than seven years for the Italian Fascists to put in place required less than three in Austria and pre-dated by a few years Nazi Germany's first population registration in 1938 and introduction of a national card index in 1939.[144] The system of identity codes and population registries was certainly not unique to fascist regimes in the interwar years: in France, Britain, Belgium and Holland – as well as further a field in the United States and Australia – attempts to regulate the entry and residency of foreigners were a feature of protectionist labour policies against foreign workers and, in some cases, were a racialized response to the 'problem' of minorities after the war.[145] But it was in fascist states that the legislation rapidly extended beyond economic protectionism and minority laws to encompass the wider political and social spheres of citizens' everyday lives – from one's own place of baptism and marriage, residency and position of employment, to that of one's relatives. Even the act of registration was no longer just a parochial affair with state-appointed inspectors poised to swoop on any inconsistencies in the paperwork and report back to the central authorities.

Unlike the question of minorities, the immigration issue was never framed explicitly in terms of Austria as a German state with German-speaking citizens and public institutions by either the German-nationalist press or the Austrofascist state. The emphasis was instead on Austria 'for the Austrians'; in other words, ownership of Austria's territorial and public space. It was not necessary to draw specifically on ethnic criteria, such as language or religion, in those instances where Austria's state and institutional borders were in question. It sufficed for both German-nationalists and Austrofascists to represent the Jew as the single threat to these borders, without actually referring to the Jew as an ethnic Other. An ethnic discourse was still visible in the references to German farmers, in the stereotyping of the Romanian Jews, and in the stories of German and Austrian refugees from Spain, for example. A more discreet ethnic discourse was also evident in the ideological rendering of the true refugee in Europe: Nazis were homeland heroes, while Jews were likened to locusts, stripped of any humanity. However, the language of Austrians living in Austria, standing in solidarity against foreign immigrants, showed how the construction of *Austrian* borders was premised on a belief in Austria's identity as a German state. The immediate concern of both the German-nationalist press and the Austrofascist state in articulating a pan-German identity lay with a defence of Austria's state borders in the first instance, and only in the last instance with the larger projection of a national community beyond those borders.

Notes

1 The republic remained officially known as 'German-Austria' until the Allies insisted at the Paris Peace Conference in 1919 that the prefix 'German' be dropped.

2 For a discussion of this term, see Gerald Stourzh, 'Ethnic Attribution in Late Imperial Austria: Good Intentions, Evil Consequences', in Timms and Robertson (eds), *The Habsburg Legacy*, p. 79. Edward Timms has defined *Heimatrecht* as the 'right of domicile'. See Timms, 'Citizenship and "Heimatrecht" ', p. 158. Michael John's analysis of the term takes into account the pre-1918 criteria for residency and welfare, according to which *Heimatrecht* was traditionally defined for citizens of the Austro-Hungarian Empire. See Michael John and Albert Lichtblau, *Schmelztiegl Wien – einst und jetzt: Zur Geschichte und Gegenwart von Zuwanderung und Minderheiten* (Vienna: Böhlau, 1990), p. 13.

3 Margarete Grandner, 'Staatsbürger und Ausländer: Zum Umgang Österreichs mit den jüdischen Flüchtlinge nach 1918', in Heiss and Rathkolb (eds), *Asylland Wider Willen*, p. 62; Timms, 'Citizenship and "Heimatrecht" ', p. 161.

4 Hoffmann-Holter, 'Abreisendmachung', pp. 155–56.

5 Grandner, 'Staatsbürger und Ausländer', pp. 71–75. See also Edward Timms, 'The Kraus-Bekessy Controversy in Interwar Vienna', in Robert S. Wistrich (ed.), *Austrians and Jews in the Twentieth Century: From Franz Joseph to Waldheim* (New York: St Martin's Press, 1992), pp. 192–93.

6 Hoffmann-Holter, 'Abreisendmachung', pp. 229–34.

7 Timms, 'Citizenship and "Heimatrecht" ', pp. 161–62.

8 Stourzh, 'Ethnic Attribution in Late Imperial Austria', p. 80. Stourzh's rendering of the term '*Zugehörigkeit*' in English as 'attribution' rather than the usual and more subjective translation of 'belonging', is intended to convey the arbitrary nature of its definitional use and application in a legal and administrative context. See ibid., p. 68.

9 Hoffmann-Holter, 'Abreisendmachung', pp. 225–26, 246–57.

10 Stourzh, 'Ethnic Attribution in Late Imperial Austria'.

11 Illigasch, 'Migration aus und nach Österreich in der Zwischenkriegszeit', p. 14; John, ' "We Do Not Even Possess Ourselves" ', p. 47.

12 Illigasch, 'Migration aus und nach Österreich in der Zwischenkriegszeit', p. 14.

13 Andreas Fahrmeir, 'Nineteenth-Century German Citizenships: A Reconsideration', *Historical Journal* 40, 3 (1997): 721–52. Fahrmeir's argument counters the established thesis of Rogers Brubaker, who distinguishes between German and French nineteenth-century notions of nationhood based on descent (*jus sanguinis*) (German) and birth and residence in the nation's territory (*jus solis*) (French). See Rogers Brubaker, *Citizenship and Nationhood in France and Germany* (Cambridge, MA: Harvard University Press, 1992).

14 Dieter Gosewinkel, ' "Unerwünschte Elemente": Einwanderung und Einbürgerung der Juden in Deutschland 1848–1933', *Tel Aviver Jahrbuch für deutsche Geschichte* 27 (1998), pp. 97–104.

15 See, for example, Heinz Fassmann and Rainer Münz, *Einwanderungsland Österreich? Historische Migrationsmuster, aktuelle Trends und politische Massnahmen* (Vienna: Jugend & Volk, 1995); Heinz Fassmann, 'Der Wandel der Bevölkerungs- und Sozialstruktur in der Ersten Republik', in Emmerich Tálos, et al. (eds), *Handbuch des politischen Systems Österreichs: Erste Republik 1918–1933* (Vienna: Manz, 1995).

16 Illigasch, 'Migration aus und nach Österreich in der Zwischenkriegszeit', pp. 6, 18–19.

17 Marrus, *The Unwanted*, pp. 12–13.

18 Heiss, 'Ausländer, Flüchtlinge, Bolshewiken', pp. 92–96.

19 Alja Rachmanova, *Milchfrau in Ottakring: Tagebuch aus den dreissiger Jahren*, 2nd edn (Vienna: Amalthea, 1999). See also Dietmar Grieser, *Wien, Wahlheimat der Genies* (Munich: Amalthea, 1994), pp. 60–66.

20 Dietmar Grieser, 'Foreword' in Rachmanova, *Milchfrau in Ottakring*, pp. 12–13. Rachmanova was Orthodox.

21 By 1926, there was a total of 9.5 million refugees in Europe. Most of these refugee populations were clustered in Eastern European countries, such as Poland and Ukraine, where ongoing territorial disputes created precarious conditions for the permanent settlement of uprooted nationalities. For example, in 1923, Poland had already repatriated an estimated 703,250 people and was expecting a further 300,000 refugees. See Marrus, *The Unwanted*, pp. 51–52, 58.

22 Belgium and Holland introduced protective laws as a reaction against the open asylum policies after the First World War when foreign workers were recruited to make up the labour shortfall from massive wartime losses. In France, where more than 1.5 million foreign workers had arrived by 1928, a law for the 'protection of national manpower' was introduced in 1926 to regulate the type and duration of work permits. The law had the immediate effect of reducing the number of foreign workers arriving annually in France from 162,000 in 1926 to 64,000 in 1927. See Heiss, 'Ausländer, Flüchtlinge, Bolshewiken', pp. 91–92; Jeanne Singer-Kérel, 'Foreign Workers in France, 1891–1936', *Ethnic and Racial Studies* 14, 3 (1991), p. 287.

23 Oliver Rathkolb, 'Asyl- und Transitland 1933–1938?', in Heiss and Rathkolb (eds), *Asylland Wider Willen*, p. 111; John, ' "We Do Not Even Possess Ourselves" ', p. 47.

24 Rathkolb, 'Asyl- und Transitland', p. 111; John, 'Identity and Ethnicity in Austria', p. 47.
25 Between 1925 and 1930, the statistics record only the numbers of immigration permits (*Zuzugsbewillingungen*), but from 1931, the figures show only work permits (*Arbeitsbewillingungen*). The number of immigration visas between 1925 and 1930 was 35,056 and there were 48,385 work visas issued between 1931 and 1937. Since the statistical handbooks specified the gender and profession of the recipients of both types of permits, we can assume that the work permits simply replaced the earlier immigration permits. See Illigasch, 'Migration aus und nach Österreich in der Zwischenkriegszeit', pp. 19–20. For emigration outside Europe, see ibid., p. 9 (Table 2).
26 Rathkolb, 'Asyl- und Transitland', pp. 109–11; Heiss, 'Ausländer, Flüchtlinge, Bolshewiken', pp. 96, 99.
27 Rathkolb, 'Asyl- und Transitland', p. 109; Edmondson, *The Heimwehr and Austrian Politics*, p. 176; Wandruszka, 'Das "nationale" Lager', p. 286.
28 *Tagespost*, 10 February 1933, p. 1.
29 *Tagespost*, 11 February 1933, p. 3.
30 *Reichspost*, 11 February 1933, cited in Rathkolb, 'Asyl- und Transitland', p. 113.
31 *Tagespost*, 1 March 1933, p. 3.
32 *Tagespost*, 1 March 1933 (Abendblatt), p. 1.
33 Rathkolb, 'Asyl- und Transitland', p. 113.
34 *Tagespost*, 3 June 1933 (Abendblatt), p. 1.
35 *Tagespost*, 1 September 1933 (Abendblatt), pp. 1–2.
36 Rathkolb, 'Asyl- und Transitland', p. 114.
37 Marrus, *The Unwanted*, pp. 161–65; Klaus Mammach, 'Deutsche Emigration in Österreich 1933–1938', *Bulletin des Arbeitskreises "Zweiter Weltkrieg"* 1–4 (1988), pp. 194–95.
38 Illigasch, 'Migration aus und nach Österreich in der Zwischenkriegszeit', p. 19.
39 Ursula Seeber, 'Österreich als Exil 1933 bis 1938', in Ursula Seeber (ed.), *Asyl Wider Willen: Exil in Österreich 1933 bis 1938* (Vienna: Picus, 2003), pp. 8–9. Rathkolb estimates more conservatively that the number of Jewish refugees supported by charities in the same period was at least 2,500. See Rathkolb, 'Asyl- und Transitland', p. 115.
40 Mammach, 'Deutsche Emigration in Österreich 1933–1938', p. 195.
41 *Tagespost*, 3 April 1933 (Abendblatt), p. 2; 10 April 1933 (Abendblatt), p. 2.
42 *Tagespost*, 5 April 1933 (Abendblatt), p. 6.
43 *Tagespost* 25 August 1933 (Abendblatt), p. 2; 26 August 1933 (Abendblatt), p. 2.
44 *Tagespost*, 1 December 1933, p. 3; 1 December 1933 (Abendblatt), p. 1.
45 Marrus, *The Unwanted*, p. 137.
46 Claudena M. Skran, *Refugees in Inter-War Europe: The Emergence of a Regime* (Oxford: Clarendon, 1995), p. 50. See also Caron, *Uneasy Asylum*, pp. 14–15.
47 Marrus, *The Unwanted*, p. 130.
48 *Wiener Neueste Nachrichten*, 12 July 1933, p. 3.

49 *Wiener Neueste Nachrichten*, 20 December 1934, pp. 1–2.
50 *Wiener Neueste Nachrichten*, 29 November 1933, p. 2.
51 *Wiener Neueste Nachrichten*, 5 January 1934, p. 3.
52 *Wiener Neueste Nachrichten*, 24 January 1934, p. 3.
53 *Wiener Neueste Nachrichten*, 22 February 1934, p. 1.
54 See *Wiener Neueste Nachrichten-Bilder*, 6 May 1934, pp. 2–4, in Chapter 5.
55 Caron, *Uneasy Asylum*, p. 40.
56 For reports of border arrests see, for example, *Tagespost*, 4 August 1933, p. 2. For reports of Austrian Nazis and smuggler sympathizers, see *Tagespost*, 31 August 1933, p. 2; 11 October 1933 (Abendblatt), p. 1; 19 October 1933, p. 2.
57 See *Tagespost*, 16 July 1933, p. 2; 17 July 1933 (Abendblatt), p. 1.
58 *Tagespost*, 26 July 1933, p. 1.
59 *Tagespost*, 5 September 1933 (Abendblatt), p. 1; 6 September 1933, p. 2. See also a report on Carinthia's border control, 9 September 1933 (Abendblatt), p. 1.
60 See *Tagespost*, 24 September 1933, p. 3; 5 October 1933, p. 2; 3 December 1933, p. 2.
61 *Tagespost*, 30 July 1934 (Abendblatt), p. 3.
62 *Tagespost*, 11 August 1934, p. 4; 17 August 1934 (Abendblatt), p. 1; 24 August 1934, p. 2; 29 August 1934 (Abendblatt), p. 1.
63 Dušan Necak, *Die österreichische Legion II: Nationalsozialistische Flüchtlinge in Jugoslawien nach dem misslungenen Putsch vom 25. Juli 1934*, trans. Franci Zwitter (Vienna: Böhlau, 1996), pp. 34–41.
64 *Tagespost*, 4 September 1934 (Abendblatt), p. 1.
65 *Tagespost*, 6 September 1934 (Abendblatt), pp. 2–3. A police commissioner's report in the Carinthian town of Villach, dated 30 August 1934, noted that Nazi SS members among the 1,100 refugees in Varaždin were acting as camp police, holding morning roll-call and enforcing evening curfew. A later report revealed a tightly administered daily schedule in the camp that included physical exercises and political and military instruction. See Necak, *Die österreichische Legion II*, p. 105.
66 *Tagespost*, 6 September 1934 (Abendblatt), pp. 2–3.
67 *Tagespost*, 8 October 1934 (Abendblatt), p. 2; 24 October 1934, p. 2.
68 Necak, *Die österreichische Legion II*, pp. 71–76.
69 *Tagespost*, 30 November 1934, p. 3.
70 See, for example, *Tagespost*, 7 December 1935 (Abendblatt), p. 3; 3 November 1936, p. 3. Other reports in 1934 told of returned émigrés, customs checks at the Yugoslav border and deportations from Yugoslavia into neighbouring Hungary. See *Tagespost*, 17 October 1934 (Abendblatt), p. 5; 19 May 1936 (Abendblatt), p. 2; 6 December 1934 (Abendblatt), p. 2.
71 See, for example, *Tagespost*, 10 March 1934, p. 2; 11 June 1937 (Abendblatt), p. 1; 10 August 1937, p. 2.
72 *Wiener Neueste Nachrichten*, 31 August 1933, p. 5.
73 Martin Blinkhorn, *Democracy and Civil War in Spain 1931–1939* (London: Routledge, 1988), pp. 36, 48.

74 *Tagespost*, 28 July 1936, p. 3. The British and French governments evacuated thousands of Spanish refugees fleeing anti-clerical violence and republican attacks. See Marrus, *The Unwanted*, p. 190.
75 *Tagespost*, 3 August 1936 (Abendblatt), p. 2.
76 *Tagespost*, 13 January 1937, pp. 3–4. For reports on Austrian refugees in August 1936, see *Tagespost*, 4 August 1936, p. 2; 5 August 1936, p. 2; 11 August 1936, p. 2; 12 August 1936, p. 2 and 14 August 1936, p. 2.
77 The numbers of republican refugees reached into hundreds of thousands as Franco's military regime took hold. By April 1939, 450,000 Spanish soldiers and civilians had escaped to France. About half of these refugees were eventually repatriated to Spain, some 20,000 found asylum in Mexico, a small number went to the Soviet Union and thousands of remaining Spaniards enlisted in the French army, suffering the same fate as the French under Nazi occupation. See Marrus, *The Unwanted*, pp. 191–94.
78 *Tagespost*, 18 August 1936 (Abendblatt), p. 2.
79 See, for example, *Wiener Neueste Nachrichten*, 28 July 1936, p. 2; 11 August 1936, p. 1.
80 *Wiener Neueste Nachrichten*, 7 August 1936, p. 2.
81 *Wiener Neueste Nachrichten*, 11 August 1936, p. 1.
82 ÖStA/AdR, BKA/BPD, Carton 36, *Salzburger Volksblatt*, 21 October 1937.
83 ÖStA/AdR, BKA/BPD, Carton 8, *Reichspost*, 3 September 1936.
84 Werner Röder, 'The Political Exiles: Their Policies and Their Contribution to Post-war Reconstruction', in *Biographisches Handbuch der deutschsprachigen Emigration nach 1933* (Munich: K.G. Saur, 1980), pp. xxix–xxx.
85 Seeber, 'Österreich als Exil 1933 bis 1938', p. 9; Peter Stuiber, 'Chronik des deutschen Exils in Österreich', in Seeber (ed.), *Asyl Wider Willen*, p. 118.
86 Ebneth, *Die österreichische Wochenschrift*, pp. 2, 8, 38–40.
87 Mammach, 'Deutsche Emigration in Österreich 1933–1938', pp. 199–200.
88 Ebneth, *Die österreichische Wochenschrift*, pp. 86–87.
89 An article by a former German Nazi in the *Christliche Ständestaat* in May 1936 attracted the attention of *Heimatdienst* officials. See ÖStA/AdR, BKA/HD, Carton 9, Zeitungsausschnitte 1936.
90 Ebneth, *Die österreichische Wochenschrift*, pp. 55, 197–98, 202, 207, 215–16. See also Mammach, 'Deutsche Emigration in Österreich 1933–1938', pp. 200, 207; Stuiber, 'Chronik des deutschen Exils in Österreich', p. 118.
91 Prinz Hubertus Löwenstein, *On Borrowed Peace* (London: Faber & Faber, 1943), p. 7. The original American edition was published in 1942. See also Mammach, 'Deutsche Emigration in Österreich 1933–1938', p. 199. Löwenstein had been born into the German and English aristocracy and had grown up at Schloss Schönworth in Tyrol. In 1933, he purchased NeuMatzen Castle near Brixlegg, where he and his wife, brother and servants lived prior to 1935.
92 Mammach, 'Deutsche Emigration in Österreich 1933–1938', p. 199.
93 Löwenstein, *On Borrowed Peace*, p. 21.
94 Ibid.

95 There are no estimates for German Catholic refugees, given the notorious difficulty in accounting for political immigration. Neither Mammach's nor Illigasch's figures for German immigration to Austria give any clue about the breakdown into socialist, communist, Jewish, Catholic or otherwise.

96 Hildebrand immigrated to America via Czechoslovakia, Italy, Switzerland, France, Spain, Portugal and Brazil; Dohrn travelled via Czechoslovakia, then France, Spain and Portugal. He later immigrated to Switzerland from America. See Christina Kleiser, 'Biografien', in Seeber (ed.), *Asyl Wider Willen*, pp. 97, 100.

97 Studies of European population policies have mostly focused on Western Europe. See, for example, Maria Sophia Quine, *Population Politics in Twentieth Century Europe: Fascist Dictatorships and Liberal Democracies* (London: Routledge, 1996). More recently scholarship has branched out to include Central and Eastern European regimes. See Turda and Weindling (eds), *'Blood and Homeland'*.

98 Cited in Carl Ipsen, *Dictating Demography* (Cambridge: Cambridge University Press, 1996), p. 88.

99 See Ipsen's review of his own book in 'Population Policy in the Age of Fascism: Observations on Recent Literature', *Population and Development Review* 24, 3 (1998), p. 591.

100 Transnational studies have shown recently that the Italian state institutionalized racial theories and practices after 1935 not only in Italian colonies in Africa, but also later in Italian-occupied Slovenia, Dalmatia and the Ionian islands, including the establishment of a concentration camp for 7,000 Slovenes. These state policies followed the 'punitive expeditions' that the Fascist militia had already carried out in Jewish quarters in Tripoli, Florence and Padua in the early phase of Fascist rule before 1926 and again in 1934 and 1936. See Reichardt and Nolzen (eds), *Faschismus in Italien und Deutschland*, pp. 20–22.

101 While these new policies were partially a reaction to international restrictions on migration, they cannot be seen solely in terms of a pragmatic response to external pressures since the United States – the country with the highest intake of Italian emigrants – introduced its immigration quotas in 1921 and again in 1924, some years before the laws on passports and internal migration were enacted in Italy. Rather, as Ipsen states, placed in the broader context of Italy's 'demographic quintet', Italian migration policy 'came on the heels – and as an integral part – of the general move towards totalitarian social control initiated in January 1925'. Ipsen, *Dictating Demography*, pp. 50–65, quotation p. 65.

102 Ibid., pp. 82, 88.

103 Ibid., pp. 92–100, 196.

104 Ibid., pp. 64, 100, 118, 197.

105 On Poland and Hungary, see Paul Weindling, 'Fascism and Population in Comparative European Perspective', *Population and Development Review* 14,

Supplement: Population and Resources in Western Intellectual Traditions (1988), p. 104.

106 Gini's theory, first presented at an international conference in Trieste in 1911, built on other pre-war demographic theories that emphasized environmental factors, rather than Social Darwinian ideas, in explaining the rise and fall of fertility. Gini developed the idea of differential fertility by which different classes in a nation reproduce at different rates. See Ipsen, *Dictating Demography*, pp. 45–46, 221–28.

107 See Chapter 2.

108 ÖStA/AdR, 04R106/1, Protokolle der Bundeskulturrat, vol. 1, 18th Session, 18 September 1935.

109 Ibid.

110 *Wiener Neueste Nachrichten*, 20 September 1935; *Reichspost*, 30 October 1935.

111 ÖStA/AdR, 04R106/1, Protokolle der Bundeskulturrat, vol. 1, 18th Session, 18 September 1935.

112 Ibid.

113 Ibid.

114 Ibid.

115 *Neue Freie Presse*, 25 September 1935, p. 4.

116 *Tagespost*, 15 February 1935, p. 2.

117 *Tagespost*, 15 February 1935 (Abendblatt), p. 2. Until 1935, the Saarland had been under the administration of the League of Nations and had been an important haven for political refugees from Nazi Germany. See Marrus, *The Unwanted*, p. 133.

118 *Tagespost*, 7 May 1935, p. 2.

119 *Tagespost*, 19 January 1936, p. 2.

120 *Tagespost*, 10 July 1935 (Abendblatt), p. 2.

121 *Tagespost*, 15 October 1936, p. 1.

122 The headlines were from the above reports in December 1934 and October 1936.

123 *Tagespost*, 21 June 1936, pp. 17–18; 19 July 1936, p. 13.

124 *Tagespost*, 16 February 1937 (Abendblatt), p. 1.

125 *Grazer Volksblatt*, 1 January 1938, p. 3; 27 January 1938, p. 6.

126 *Tagespost*, 16 February 1937 (Abendblatt), p. 1.

127 *Wiener Neueste Nachrichten*, 17 December 1937, pp. 1–2.

128 *Wiener Neueste Nachrichten*, 19 December 1937, p. 4.

129 *Wiener Neueste Nachrichten*, 17 March 1936, p. 4.

130 Although King Carol dismissed Goga in January 1938, the Romanian monarch himself publicly advocated the emigration of the Jews. See Marrus, *The Unwanted*, pp. 143–45.

131 *Tagespost*, 31 December 1937, pp. 1–2.

132 *Wiener Neueste Nachrichten*, 31 December 1937, pp. 1–2.

133 *Tagespost*, 3 January 1938 (Abendblatt), p. 2.

134 *Wiener Neueste Nachrichten*, 5 January 1938 (Abendblatt), p. 1.

135 *Grazer Volksblatt*, 15 January 1938 (Mittag), p. 2.

136 *Wiener Neueste Nachrichten*, 25 January 1938, p. 1. See also Rathkolb, 'Asyl- und Transitland', p. 119.

137 *Wiener Neueste Nachrichten*, 7 January 1938, p. 1.

138 *Wiener Neueste Nachrichten*, 1 February 1938, p. 1; 8 February 1938, p. 1.

139 *Tagespost*, 12 January 1938, p. 1. My emphasis in italics.

140 Cited in Clare, *Last Waltz in Vienna*, p. 158.

141 ÖStA/AdR, 04R106/4, Protokolle der Bundeskulturrat, vol. 4, 47th Session, 3 February 1938.

142 Rathkolb, 'Asyl- und Transitland', pp. 117–19.

143 Ipsen, *Dictating Demography*, p. 90.

144 Weindling, 'Fascism and Population in Comparative European Perspective', p. 110.

145 In France, for example, where more than 1.5 million foreign workers had arrived by 1928, a law for the 'protection of national manpower' was introduced in 1926 to regulate the type and duration of work permits. The law had the immediate effect of reducing the number of foreign workers arriving annually in France from 162,000 in 1926 to 64,000 in 1927. See Singer-Kérel, 'Foreign Workers in France, 1891–1936', p. 287. Moreover, France had also introduced it own system of identity cards with codes for various degrees of 'Frenchness' in Alsace-Lorraine in 1919. See Tara Zahra, 'The "Minority Problem" and National Classification in the French and Czechoslovak Borderlands', *Contemporary European History* 17, 2 (2008): 137–65.

Conclusion

This book has shown that Austria was already a fascist state before the Nazi takeover in 1938. It has demonstrated that the achievements of the Austrofascists and their visions for a new state and a new citizenry were entangled with the fascist visions and achievements in Italy and Germany. At the same time, I have argued that the creation of a fascist state in Austria was also entangled with the construction of a pan-German identity in the aftermath of empire. Austrofascists drew on past tropes and practices of nationalism in Austria-Hungary and repackaged them for a new era of state building. Where German-speakers in the empire had been exhorted to perform their civic duty by preaching German values and raising German children in the multinational state, German-speakers in the new Austria were instructed to think, act, speak and pray as an example to their fellow Germans in the Reich and in neighbouring countries. As will have become apparent, this one-upmanship against Reich Germans was always expressed in fraternal terms and had a second purpose of Germanizing minorities in the Austrian state. Austrofascists can therefore be seen both as state builders and nation builders, seeking to defend and legitimize Austria against the incursions of the Nazi state while mythologizing and racializing differences between Germans and non-Germans within Austria.

One of the recurring questions in fascism studies, from the first comparative approaches in the 1960s to the debates about 'generic fascism' in the 1990s, has been how to define regimes that appear to be fascist on the outside but lack a core ideology or structure that stands up to the comparison with Italy and Germany. The emerging transnational histories seemingly make that comparative approach redundant as the nation-state no longer serves as our only point of reference; it is the extent to which cross-national ideas and policies shaped the regimes in interwar Europe that is important. Ironically – and perhaps prophetically – one of the leading authorities on twentieth-century Austria who has contributed most to the notion that Austria was an example of an authoritarian regime trying to keep up with its fascist neighbours, Bruce Pauley, wrote in 1976 that Austria's 'geographic position exposed it to the crosscurrents of both Italian and German forms of fascism and made Austria a kind of microcosm of European fascism'[1] If indeed it was a 'microcosm' of fascism precisely due to the impact of both Italian and German fascism on the country's leaders and public institutions, then the Austrian regime was hardly in the shadow of fascism. Rather, it was directly placed within a larger process of fascistization sweeping across Europe in the interwar years. My case studies of Austria's press and propaganda, minority politics, religion and immigration demonstrated how Austrofascism extended beyond the boundaries of the Austrian state and across the channels of international diplomacy, regional transcultural networks and confessional and population politics in the 1930s.

My book argues that Austrians in the 1930s imagined themselves both as members of the wider German-speaking community in Central Europe, and as citizens of a German Austrian state. Chapter 1 showed that the universal and particular expressions of pan-German identity were present throughout modern Austrian history from the Habsburg era to the interwar years of the First Republic and the Austrofascist state. I have argued that the conventional Anglophone usage of the term 'pan-Germanism' is restricted to the radical groups that, in Austria at least, were never numerically or politically dominant before 1938. I contend, further, that these pan-German discourses not only encapsulated both the local and universal elements of national identity, but also deployed both ethnic and civic terms which enabled Austrians to think of themselves as part of a national community linked by language and ethnicity, and as citizens who had ownership over the national community's public spaces. My definition of pan-Germanism as both a political and cultural idea of nationhood thus reaches beyond conventional definitions to encompass both the particular regional and local expressions of German identity and the universal idea of a wider German-speaking community in Central Europe.

My definition of pan-Germanism also invites us to move beyond one of the enduring orthodoxies of twentieth-century Austrian historiography, that Austrians were always and everywhere firmly fixed to their particular political-cultural milieux, be it conservative Catholic, social democratic or right-wing nationalist. But pan-Germanism often united the competing liberal, German-nationalist, Christian Social, Social Democratic, Austrofascist and National Socialist groups. The points of convergence (as well as contestation) between and within political-cultural milieux explain why, for example, Christian Socials had much in common with German-nationalists in the empire over the issues of language ordinances in Bohemia or public funding for bilingual schools in Styria. The competing pan-German discourses also explain why German-nationalists were split into so many factions before the First World War. They also explain some of the anomalies of the interwar period: why, for example, Social Democrats (especially those on the Right, such as Renner, and even a doctrinaire Austro-Marxist like Bauer) were not able to shed their Greater German vision of German socialism and articulate a separate Austrian identity prior to 1938. The cross-milieu cooperation of provincial Christian Social and German-nationalist elites in supporting and planning for the Salzburg Festival, which I described in Chapter 3, is another exception to the *Lager* theory that can be explained in terms of a mutually inclusive pan-German identity.

My focus on the German-nationalist press has revealed the dynamics of this cross-milieu cooperation between local elites, government functionaries, minority communities (both within and outside Austria) and international representatives of the arts, the Catholic Church, and European interwar politics. My book has shown that the relationship between the Austrofascist state and the German-nationalist press was complex and characterized by multiple local associational and cultural networks. I have argued that German-nationalists were not uniform in their beliefs or in their attitudes towards National Socialists. Nor were all German-nationalists biding their time waiting for the Nazis to take over their country, as if they knew it to be imminent. We have seen that some German-nationalists had already adapted their concept of the national community to the Nazi vision before 1938, while some were more reluctant after 1933 to abandon their earlier dreams of a Greater German empire in which Austrians had a central part to play. Others, like Glaser, chose the path of expediency and complied with a regime they did not want, while maintaining ideological and political consent for National Socialism. The lines of compliance and consent, which I traced in my case study of Salzburg, make it difficult for us to draw broad conclusions about the extent of cooperation or distance between German-nationalists and Austrofascists. Rather, I have argued that we must assess this relationship at the level of individual and local compliance and consent. My case studies illustrate how, in Graz, Keil could appease the Styrian Fatherland Front authorities and, at the same time, give press coverage to Nazi refugees in Yugoslavia, while, in Salzburg, Glaser maintained close contact with federal press authorities in Vienna and was a trusted confidant of the highest Austrofascist authority in the province.

The symmetry between German-nationalists and Austrofascists was most conspicuous in their attitudes towards Czech agricultural workers, their intolerance of the Slovene language in Austrian public institutions and their shared commitment to Germanizing Austria. The reaction of German-nationalists to the alleged 'Czechification' of the Austrian borderlands (discussed in Chapter 4) is a classic illustration of German-Czech rivalries reappearing in a historically contested public space. The evidence that German-nationalists in Salzburg as well as local Austrofascist functionaries in Lower Austria asserted ownership over this border space using a combination of ethnic and civic discourses, underscores my argument that pan-Germanism was not a clear-cut example of 'ethnic' nationalism. In the same way, German-nationalists combined an ethnic dissimilationist discourse with a civic voluntarist discourse to imply that Slovenes who sent their children to Slovene schools in Yugoslavia, who then returned to Austria as Slovene nationalists to set up schools and write for the Slovene newspaper, violated the civic standards of a German-language education and press in Austria. They also maintained that the well-funded private Czech schools undermined Austria's public school system and signified the Czech minority's belonging to Czechoslovakia instead of the Austrian state. That this rhetoric of German ownership of Austria was shared by Austrofascist policy makers – who deemed even the 'good Croats' a threat to national identity in the New Austria – indicates how closely German-nationalists followed the designs of the Austrofascist state. Conversely, Austrofascist leaders relied on an army of national activists in the borderlands to act as rank and file members of the government's new auxiliary body for minority politics – the ÖVVA. Former Nazis, choirboys, women's committees and state youth leaders in the ÖJV banded together to raise money for and support the government initiatives among the Sudeten Germans in Czechoslovakia and along Austria's own linguistic frontier in southern Carinthia and Lower and Upper Austria.

Anti-Semitism was a further salient example of how German-nationalists and Austrofascists consistently agreed over the need for the Austrian state to be protected from an invasion of illegal, foreign (and mostly Jewish) immigrants. Chapters 5 and 6 revealed German-nationalists' support for the state's laws on policing the borders and regulating foreigners' rights to live in Austria. On the question of Jews in Austria, the often surprising alliances between Zionists and government ministers in the highest echelon of Austrofascist politics, or between Catholic theologians and German-nationalist editors, indicate the complexity of anti-Semitism in Austria. As with pan-Germanism, support for one design of citizenship or national community could be found on all sides of politics. At the same time, state leaders could not always rely on the support of church dignitaries on issues of race politics, just as the outspoken remarks of an Austrian cardinal on the Nazi abuses of German clergy might have been a little disconcerting for Austrian politicians pursuing *rapprochement* with Hitler. Rather than see anti-Semitism as a perennial disease affecting the population from school children up to the highest clerical authority, I have attempted to analyse the construction of an anti-Semitic stereotype in Austria within a particular context in the 1930s. My case studies of the German-nationalist press also uncovered some surprising evidence of immunity to anti-Semitism where local relations with Jewish leaders and cultural figures were linked to the preservation of economic and political fortunes.

The campaign for a new immigration bill in Austria was also predicated on the image of foreign Jews marauding the state's public resources. That this campaign in the German-nationalist press and the legislative chambers of the Austrofascist state was carried out in the preceding months and weeks before *Anschluss* further demonstrates that German-nationalists and Austrofascists were more preoccupied with maintaining the ethnic and civic boundaries of the Austrian state than the question of Austro-German relations. Moreover, the population policies of the Austrofascist state showed how far Austria had been exposed to the 'crosscurrents' from Fascist Italy and Nazi Germany and the extent to which Austrian policy choices were grounded in Italian and German models of population management, irrespective of how successful those models had proven to be. Whereas the question of who was a Jew in Austria and which ethnic background could preclude a person from contributing to public life had a longer genealogy in national politics in the empire, the question of who could reside in Austria was mired in the population politics of Fascist and Nazi statisticians in the interwar period.

My book shows that Austrofascist population politics – encompassing the state's racial legislation, Germanizing policies and the creeping legislation that sought to restrict the movements of the population and declare them members of the nation on a stamped piece – needs to be placed in a larger context of European right-wing efforts to remake states and citizens on multiple levels. Austrofascists and their supporters in education, the press and on the borders were single-minded in their efforts to forge new citizens in the New Austria. Placing the Austrian case within this broader comparative and transnational context, historians are better equipped to resolve the process-versus-outcomes dichotomy of fascism because instead of measuring words against deeds in a vacuum, we can return both the visions and the actions of Austrian politicians and opinion makers to mainstream accounts of European projects for modernizing states and citizens.

Notes

1 Bruce Pauley, 'A Case Study in Fascism: The Styrian *Heimatschutz* and Austrian National Socialism', *Austrian History Yearbook* 12/13 (1976/77), p. 251.

Bibliography

Archives

Österreichische Staatsarchiv/Archiv der Republik, Vienna
Archiv der Stadt Salzburg, Salzburg
Forschungszentrum für historische Minderheiten, Vienna

Newspapers

Grazer Tagespost
Grazer Volksblatt
Reichspost
Salzburger Volksblatt
Wiener Neueste Nachrichten

Other primary sources

Allgemeiner Deutscher Katholikentag Wien 1933, 7. bis 12. September 1933 (Vienna: Verlag des Katholikentagcomitees, 1934).

Bauer, Otto, 'The Nationalities Question and Social Democracy (1907)', in Omar Dahbour and Micheline R. Ishay (eds), *The Nationalism Reader* (Atlantic Highlands: Humanities Press, 1995).

Clare, George, *Last Waltz in Vienna: The Destruction of a Family 1842–1942* (London: Pan Books, 1982).

'Das "Linzer Programm" der Sozialdemokratischen Arbeiterpartei Österreichs, 1926', in Albert Kadan and Anton Pelinka (eds), *Die Grundsatzprogramme der österreichischen Parteien: Dokumente und Analyse* (St Pölten: Niederösterreichisches Pressehaus, 1979).

'Das Programm der Christlichsozialen Partei, 1926', in Albert Kadan and Anton Pelinka (eds), *Die Grundsatzprogramme der österreichischen Parteien: Dokumente und Analyse* (St Pölten: Niederösterreichisches Pressehaus, 1979).

'Das "Salzburger Programm" der Grossdeutschen Volkspartei, 1920', in Klaus Berchtold (ed.), *Österreichische Parteiprogramme, 1868–1966* (Vienna: Verlag für Geschichte und Politik, 1967).

Dell, Robert, 'The Corruption of the French Press', *Current History* 35 (1931): 193–97.

Dubrovic, Milan, *Veruntreute Geschichte: Die Wiener Salons und Literatencafes* (Berlin: Aufbau Taschenbuch, 2001[Vienna: Paul Tsolnay, 1985]).

Festführer zum Allgemeinen Deutschen Katholikentag in Wien (Vienna: Pressekomitees des Katholikentages, 1933).

Franckenstein, Sir George, *Facts and Figures of My Life* (London: Cassell, 1939).

Funder, Friedrich, *Als Österreich den Sturm bestand: Aus der Ersten in die Zweite Republik* (Vienna: Herold, 1957).

Funder, Friedrich, *Vom Gestern ins Heute: Aus dem Kaiserreich in die Republik* (Vienna: Herold, 1971).

Hartmann, Mitzi, *Austria Still Lives* (London: Michael Joseph, 1938).

Hock, Stefan, 'Vienna Life', *Contemporary Review*, 151, 1 (Jan–June 1937): 476–84.

Löwenstein, Prinz Hubertus, *On Borrowed Peace* (London: Faber & Faber, 1943).

Murdoch, Nina, *Tyrolean June: A Summer Holiday in Austrian Tyrol* (London: Harrap, 1936).

Rachmanova, Alja, *Milchfrau in Ottakring: Tagebuch aus den dreissiger Jahren*, 2nd edn (Vienna: Amalthea, 1999).

Roth, Joseph, *Juden auf Wanderschaft*, 7th edn (Cologne: Kiepenhauer and Witsch, 2000).

Schuschnigg, Kurt, *Im Kampf gegen Hitler: Die Überwindung der Anschlussidee* (Vienna: Fritz Molden, 1969).

Seton-Watson, R.W., 'Europe and the Austrian Problem', *International Affairs* 15, 3 (May–June 1936): 327–50.

Steinwender, Leonhard, *Christus im Konzentrationslager: Wege der Gnade und Opfers* (Salzburg: Otto Müller, 1946).

Secondary literature

Albrecht, Catherine, 'The Bohemian Question', in Mark Cornwall (ed.), *The Last Years of Austria-Hungary: A Multinational Experiment in Early Twentieth-century Europe* (Exeter: University of Exeter Press, 2002).

Allen, James Smith, *In the Public Eye: A History of Reading in Modern France, 1800–1940* (Princeton: Princeton University Press, 1991).

Ardelt, Rudolf G. (ed.), *Salzburger Quellenbuch: Von der Monarchie bis zum Anschluss* (Salzburg: Schriftenreihe des Landespressebüros, 1985).

Arendt, Hannah, *The Origins of Totalitarianism*, 2nd edn (London: Allen & Unwin, 1958).

Aschacher, Nora, 'Die Presse der Steiermark von 1918 – 31 July 1955' (PhD dissertation, University of Vienna, 1972).

Aschheim, Stephen E., *Brothers and Strangers: The East European Jews in German and German Jewish Consciousness, 1800–1923* (Madison: University of Wisconsin Press, 1982).

Bachhiesl, Christian, *Der Fall Josef Streck: Ein Sträfling, sein Professor und die Erforschung der Persönlichkeit* (Vienna: Lit, 2006).

Bandhauer-Schöffmann, Irene, 'Der "Christliche Ständestaat" als Männerstaat? Frauen- und Geschlechterpolitik im Austrofaschismus', in Emmerich Tálos and Wolfgang Neugebauer (eds), *Austrofaschismus: Politik–Ökonomie–Kultur 1933–1938*, 5th rev. edn (Vienna: Lit, 2005).

Bandhauer-Schöffmann, Irene, 'Gottgewollte Geschlechterdifferenzen', in Brigitte Lehmann (ed.), *Dass die Frau zur Frau erzogen wird: Frauenpolitik und Ständestaat* (Vienna: Löcker, 2008).

Barker, Thomas M., *The Slovene Minority of Carinthia* (Boulder: Columbia University Press, 1984).

Bärnthaler, Irmgard, 'Geschichte und Organisation der Vaterländische Front: Ein Beitrag zum Verständnis totalitärer Organisation' (PhD dissertation, University of Vienna, 1964).

Beniston, Judith, 'Cultural Politics in the First Republic: Hans Brečka and the "Kunststelle für christliche Volksbildung"', in Judith Beniston and Ritchie Robertson (eds), *Catholicism and Austrian Culture* (Edinburgh: Edinburgh University Press, 1999).

Berchtold, Klaus (ed.), *Österreichische Parteiprogramme, 1868–1966* (Vienna: Verlag für Geschichte und Politik, 1967).

Berkley, George E., *Vienna and its Jews: The Tragedy of Success 1880s–1980s* (Cambridge, MA: Abt Books, 1988).

Blinkhorn, Martin, *Democracy and Civil War in Spain 1931–1939* (London: Routledge, 1988).

Bluhm, William T., *Building an Austrian Nation: The Political Integration of a Western State* (New Haven: Yale University Press, 1973).

Borut, Jacob, 'Antisemitism in Tourist Facilities in Weimar Germany', *Yad Vashem Studies* 28 (2000): 7–50.

Bosworth, R.J.B., *Mussolini's Italy: Life under the Dictatorship* (London: Penguin, 2005).

Botz, Gerhard, *Gewalt in der Politik: Attentate, Zusammenstösse, Putschversuche, Unruhen in Österreich 1918 bis 1938*, 2nd edn (Munich: Wilhelm Fink, 1983).

Botz, Gerhard, 'The Short- and Long-term Effects of the Authoritarian Regime and of Nazism in Austria: The Burden of a "Second Dictatorship"', in Jerzy Borejsza and Klaus Ziemer (eds), *Totalitarian and Authoritarian Regimes in Europe: Legacies and Lessons from the Twentieth Century* (New York: Berghahn, 2006).

Botz, Gerhard, 'Varieties of Fascism in Austria: Introduction', in Stein Ugelvik Larsen, Bernt Hagtvet and Jan Petter Myklebust (eds), *Who Were the Fascists? Social Roots of European Fascism* (Bergen: Universitetsforlaget, 1980).

Boyer, John S., *Political Radicalism in Late Imperial Vienna: Origins of the Christian Social Movement 1848–1897* (Chicago: University of Chicago Press, 1981).

Brandeis, Marie, *Wir kamen von anderswo: Interviewbuch mit Tschechen und Slowaken in Österreich* (Prague: KLP, 2003).

Brauer, Fay, 'Commercial Spies and Cultural Invaders: The French Press, *Pénétration Pacifique* and Xenophobic Nationalism in the Shadow of War', in Malcolm

Gee and Tim Kirk (eds), *Printed Matters: Printing, Publishing and Urban Culture in Europe in the Modern Period* (Aldershot: Ashgate, 2002).

Breuilly, John, *Nationalism and the State*, 2nd edn (Manchester: Manchester University Press, 1993).

Brook-Shepherd, Gordon, *The Austrians: A Thousand-Year Odyssey* (London: HarperCollins, 1996).

Brousek, Karl M., *Wien und seine Tschechen: Integration und Assimilation einer Minderheit im 20. Jahrhundert* (Munich: Oldenbourg, 1980).

Brubaker, Rogers, *Citizenship and Nationhood in France and Germany* (Cambridge, MA: Harvard University Press, 1992).

Bukey, Evan Burr, *Hitler's Hometown: Linz, Austria, 1908–1945* (Bloomington: Indiana University Press, 1986).

Bullock, Malcolm, *Austria 1918–1938: A Study in Failure* (London: Macmillan, 1939).

Burleigh, Michael, *Germany Turns Eastward: A Study of* Ostforschung *in the Third Reich* (Cambridge: Cambridge University Press, 1988).

Busch, Brigitta, 'Shifting Political and Cultural Borders: Language and Identity in the Border Region of Austria and Slovenia', *European Studies* 19 (2003): 125–44.

Caron, Vicki, *Uneasy Asylum: France and the Jewish Refugee Crisis, 1933–1942* (Stanford: Stanford University Press, 1999).

Carr, William, 'The Unification of Germany', in John Breuilly (ed.), *The State of Germany: The National Idea in the Making, Unmaking and Remaking of a Modern Nation-state* (London: Longman, 1992).

Carsten, F.L., *Fascist Movements in Austria: From Schönerer to Hitler* (London: Sage, 1977).

Carsten, F.L., *The Rise of Fascism*, 2nd edn (London: Batsford, 1980).

Cohen, Deborah and Maureen O'Connor (eds), *Comparison and History: Europe in Cross-National Perspective* (New York: Routledge, 2004).

Cole, T.J., 'Constructing the "Jew", Writing the Holocaust: Hungary 1925–40', *Patterns of Prejudice* 33, 3 (1999): 19–27.

Cornwall, Mark, ' "A Leap into Ice-Cold Water": The Manoeuvres of the Henlein Movement in Czechoslovakia, 1933–1938', in Mark Cornwall and R.J.W. Evans (eds), *Czechoslovakia in a Nationalist and Fascist Europe 1918–1948* (Oxford: Oxford University Press, 2007).

Cornwall, Mark, 'News, Rumour and the Control of Information in Austria-Hungary, 1914–1918', *History* 77, 249 (1992): 50–64.

Cornwall, Mark, 'The Struggle on the Czech–German Language Border, 1880–1940', *English Historical Review* 109, 433 (1994): 914–51.

Cornwall, Mark, *The Undermining of Austria-Hungary: The Battle for Hearts and Minds* (New York: St Martins, 2000).

Cornwall, Mark and R.J.W. Evans (eds), *Czechoslovakia in a Nationalist and Fascist Europe 1918–1948* (Oxford: Oxford University Press, 2007).

Csoklich, Fritz, 'Presse und Rundfunk', in Erika Weinzierl and Kurt Skalnik (eds), *Österreich 1918–1938: Geschichte der Ersten Republik*, vol. 2 (Graz: Styria, 1983).

Dachs, Herbert, ' "Austrofaschismus" und Schule: Ein Instrumentalisierungsversuch', in Emmerich Tálos and Wolfgang Neugebauer (eds), *Austrofaschismus: Politik–Ökonomie–Kultur 1933–1938*, 5th rev. edn (Vienna: Lit, 2005).

Dachs, Herbert, 'Das Parteiensystem', in Emmerich Tálos, Herbert Dachs, Ernst Hanisch and Anton Staudinger (eds), *Handbuch des politischen Systems Österreichs: Erste Republik 1918–1933* (Vienna: Manz, 1995).

de Grazia, Victoria, *The Culture of Consent: Mass Organization of Leisure in Fascist Italy* (Cambridge: Cambridge University Press, 1981).

de Grazia, Victoria, *How Fascism Ruled Women: Italy, 1922–1945* (Berkeley: University of California Press, 1992).

Diament, Alfred, *Austrian Catholics and the First Republic: Democracy, Capitalism and the Social Order, 1918–1934* (Princeton: Princeton University Press, 1960).

Dostal, Thomas, 'Die Grossdeutsche Volkspartei', in Emmerich Tálos, Herbert Dachs, Ernst Hanisch and Anton Staudinger (eds), *Handbuch des politischen Systems Österreichs: Erste Republik 1918–1933* (Vienna: Manz, 1995).

Drapac, Vesna, *Constructing Yugoslavia: A Transnational History* (Basingstoke: Palgrave Macmillan, 2010).

Drapac, Vesna, *War and Religion: Catholics in the Churches of Occupied Paris* (Washington, DC: Catholic University of America, 1998).

Duchowitsch, Wolfgang, 'Umgang mit "Schädlingen" und "schädlichen Auswüchsen": Zur Auslöschung der freien Medienstruktur im "Ständestaat" ', in Emmerich Tálos and Wolfgang Neugebauer (eds), *Austrofaschismus: Politik–Ökonomie–Kultur 1933–1938*, 5th rev. edn (Vienna: Lit, 2005).

Ebneth, Rudolf, *Die österreichische Wochenschrift 'Der Christliche Ständestaat': Deutsche Emigration in Österreich 1933–1938* (Mainz: Matthias-Grünewald, 1976).

Edmondson, C. Earl, *The Heimwehr and Austrian Politics, 1918–1936* (Athens: University of Georgia Press, 1978).

El Refaie, Elisabeth, 'Keeping the Truce? Austrian Press Politics between the "July Agreement" (1936) and the *Anschluss* (1938)', *German History* 20, 1 (2002): 44–66.

Embacher, Helga, 'Von Liberal zu National: Das Linzer Vereinswesen 1848–1938', *Historisches Jahrbuch der Stadt Linz* (1991): 41–110.

Esden-Tempska, Carla, 'Civic Education in Authoritarian Austria, 1934–38', *History of Education Quarterly* 30, 2 (1990): 187–211.

Fahrmeir, Andreas, 'Nineteenth-Century German Citizenships: A Reconsideration', *Historical Journal* 40, 3 (1997): 721–52.

Fassmann, Heinz, 'Der Wandel der Bevölkerungs- und Sozialstruktur in der Ersten Republik', in Emmerich Tálos, Herbert Dachs, Ernst Hanisch and Anton Staudinger (eds), *Handbuch des politischen Systems Österreichs: Erste Republik 1918–1933* (Vienna: Manz, 1995).

Fassmann, Heinz and Rainer Münz, *Einwanderungsland Österreich? Historische Migrationsmuster, aktuelle Trends und politische Massnahmen* (Vienna: Jugend & Volk, 1995).

Felder, Nicole, *Die historische Identität der österreichischen Bundesländer* (Innsbruck: Studien, 2002).

Fellner, Fritz, 'The Problem of the Austrian Nation after 1945', *Journal of Modern History* 60, 2 (1988): 264–89.

Fellner, Günter, 'Antisemitismus in Salzburg 1918–1938' (PhD dissertation, University of Salzburg, 1979).

Fellner, Günter, 'Judenfreundlichkeit, Judenfeindlichkeit: Spielarten in einem Fremdenverkehrsland', in Robert Kriechbaumer (ed.), *Der Geschmack der Vergänglichkeit: Jüdische Sommerfrische in Salzburg* (Vienna: Böhlau, 2002).

Fletcher, Roger, 'Karl Leuthner's Greater Germany: The Pre-1914 Pan-Germanism of an Austrian Socialist', *Canadian Review of Studies in Nationalism* 9, 1 (1982): 57–79.

Fletcher, Roger 'Socialist Nationalism in Central Europe before 1914: The Case of Karl Leuthner', *Canadian Journal of History* 17, 1 (1982): 27–57.

Fräss-Ehrfeld, Claudia, *Geschichte Kärntens* vol. 2, *Kärnten 1918–1920* (Klagenfurt: Heyn, 2000).

Freidenreich, Harriet Pass, *Jewish Politics in Vienna 1918–1938* (Bloomington: Indiana University Press, 1991).

Fritzsche, Peter, 'Readers, Browsers, Strangers, Spectators: Narrative Forms and Metropolitan Encounters in Twentieth-Century Berlin', in Malcolm Gee and Tim Kirk (eds), *Printed Matters: Printing, Publishing and Urban Culture in Europe in the Modern Period* (Aldershot: Ashgate, 2002).

Fritzsche, Peter, *Reading Berlin 1900* (Cambridge, MA: Harvard University Press, 1996).

Frölich-Steffen, Susanne, *Die österreichische Identität im Wandel* (Vienna: Braumüller, 2003).

Galassi, Stefania, *Pressepolitik im Faschismus: Das Verhältnis von Herrschaft und Presseordnung in Italien zwischen 1922 und 1940* (Stuttgart: Steiner, 2008).

Gallup, Stephen, *A History of the Salzburg Festival* (London: Weidenfeld & Nicolson, 1987).

Geary, Dick, *Hitler and Nazism*, 2nd edn (London and New York: Routledge, 2000).

Gee, Malcolm and Tim Kirk (eds), *Printed Matters: Printing, Publishing and Urban Culture in Europe in the Modern Period* (Aldershot: Ashgate, 2002).

Geehr, Richard S., *Karl Lueger: Mayor of Fin de Siècle Vienna* (Detroit: Wayne State University Press, 1990).

Gellott, Laura, *The Catholic Church and the Authoritarian Regime in Austria, 1933–1938* (New York: Garland, 1987).

Gellott, Laura, 'Defending Catholic Interests in the Christian State: The Role of Catholic Action in Austria, 1933–1938', *Catholic Historical Review* 74, 4 (1988): 571–89.

Gellott, Laura, 'Recent Writings on the Ständestaat, 1934–1938', *Austrian History Yearbook* 26 (1995): 207–38.

Gellott, Laura and Michael Phayer, 'Dissenting Voices: Catholic Women in Opposition to Fascism', *Journal of Contemporary History* 22, 1 (1987): 91–114.

Goldstein, Robert J., 'Freedom of the Press in Europe, 1815–1914', *Journalism Monographs* 80 (1983): 1–23.

Gosewinkel, Dieter, ' "Unerwünschte Elemente": Einwanderung und Einbürgerung der Juden in Deutschland 1848–1933', *Tel Aviver Jahrbuch für deutsche Geschichte* 27 (1998): 71–106.

Grandner, Margarete, 'Staatsbürger und Ausländer: Zum Umgang Österreichs mit den jüdischen Flüchtlinge nach 1918', in Gernot Heiss and Oliver Rathkolb (eds), *Asylland Wider Willen: Flüchtlinge im Europäischen Kontext seit 1914* (Vienna: Jugend & Volk, 1995).

Grieser, Dietmar, *Wien, Wahlheimat der Genies* (Munich: Amalthea, 1994).

Grillhofer, Claudia, 'Die Öffentlichkeitsarbeit wird "amtlich": Zur Geschichte der Wiener "Rathaus-Korrespondenz" in der Ersten Republik', in Wolfgang Duchkowitsch, Hannes Haas and Klaus Lojka (eds), *Kreativität aus der Krise: Konzepte zur gesellschaftlichen Kommunikation in der Ersten Republik* (Vienna: Literas, 1991).

Grunberger, Richard, *The 12–Year Reich: A Social History of Nazi Germany, 1933–1945* (New York: Holt, Rinehart, and Winston, 1971).

Haag, John, 'Heinrich von Srbik', in Kelly Boyd (ed.), *Encyclopedia of Historians and Historical Writing* (London: Fitzroy Dearborn, 1999).

Haag, John, 'Marginal Men and the Dream of the Reich: Eight Austrian National-Catholic Intellectuals, 1918–1938', in Stein Ugelvik Larsen, Bernt Hagtvet and Jan Petter Myklebust (eds), *Who Were the Fascists? Social Roots of European Fascism* (Bergen: Universitetsforlaget, 1980).

Haag, John, 'Othmar Spann and the Quest for a "True State" ', *Austrian History Yearbook* 12/13 (1976/77): 227–50.

Haas, Hanns, 'Staats- und Landesbewusstsein in der Ersten Republik', in Emmerich Tálos, Herbert Dachs, Ernst Hanisch and Anton Staudinger (eds), *Handbuch des politischen Systems Österreichs: Erste Republik 1918–1933* (Vienna: Manz, 1995).

Haas, Hanns and Karl Stuhlpfarrer, *Österreich und seine Slowenen* (Vienna: Löcker & Wögenstein, 1977).

Hanisch, *Gau der guten Nerven: Die nationalsozialistische Herrschaft in Salzburg 1938–1945* (Salzburg: Anton Pustet, 1997).

Hanisch, Ernst, *Der Lange Schatten des Staates: Österreichische Gesellschaftsgeschichte im 20. Jahrhundert* (Vienna: Ueberreuter, 1994).

Hanisch, Ernst, 'Der Politische Katholizismus als ideologischer Träger des "Austrofaschismus" ', in Emmerich Tálos and Wolfgang Neugebauer (eds), *Austrofaschismus: Politik–Ökonomie–Kultur 1933–1938*, 5th rev. edn (Vienna: Lit, 2005).

Hanisch, Ernst, 'Salzburg', in Erika Weinzierl and Kurt Skalnik (eds), *Österreich 1918–1938: Geschichte der Ersten Republik*, vol. 2 (Graz: Styria, 1983).

Hanisch, Ernst, 'Die Salzburger Presse in der Ersten Republik 1918–1938', *Mitteilungen der Gesellschaft für Salzburger Landeskunde* 128 (1988): 345–64.

Harris, Ruth, *Lourdes: Body and Spirit in the Secular Age* (New York: Allen Lane, 1999).

Harvey, Elizabeth, 'Pilgrimages to the "Bleeding Border": Gender and Rituals of Nationalist Protest in Germany, 1919–39', *Women's History Review* 9, 2 (2000): 201–29.

Harvey, Elizabeth, *Women and the Nazi East: Agents and Witnesses of Germanization* (New Haven: Yale University Press, 2003).

Haslinger, Adolf and Peter Mittermayr (eds), *Salzburger Kulturlexikon* (Salzburg: Residenz, 2001).

Hausjell, Fritz, *Journalisten für das Reich: Der Reichsverband der deutschen Presse in Österreich 1938–45* (Vienna: Verlag für Gesellschaftskritik, 1993).

Healy, Maureen, *Vienna and the Fall of the Habsburg Empire: Total War and Everyday Life in World War I* (Cambridge: Cambridge University Press, 2004).

Hecht, Dieter J., 'Jüdische Frauen im Austrofaschismus', in Brigitte Lehmann (ed.), *Dass die Frau zur Frau erzogen wird: Frauenpolitik und Ständestaat* (Vienna: Löcker, 2008).

Heiss, Gernot, 'Ausländer, Flüchtlinge, Bolshewiken: Aufenthalt und Asyl 1918–1933', in Gernot Heiss and Oliver Rathkolb (eds), *Asylland Wider Willen: Flüchtlinge im Europäischen Kontext seit 1914* (Vienna: Jugend & Volk, 1995).

Hoffmann, Robert, 'Gab es ein "Schönerianisches Milieu?" Versuch einer Kollektivbiographie von Mitgliedern des "Vereins der Salzburger Studenten in Wien"', in Ernst Bruckmüller, Ulrike Döcker, Hannes Stekl and Peter Urbanitsch (eds), *Bürgertum in der Habsburgermonarchie* (Vienna: Böhlau, 1990).

Hoffmann-Holter, Beatrix, '*Abreisendmachung': Jüdische Kriegsflüchtlinge in Wien 1914–1923* (Vienna: Böhlau, 1995).

Illigasch, Jürgen, 'Migration aus und nach Österreich in der Zwischenkriegszeit', *Zeitgeschichte* 26, 1 (1999): 5–27.

Ipsen, Carl, *Dictating Demography* (Cambridge: Cambridge University Press, 1996).

Ipsen, Carl, 'Population Policy in the Age of Fascism: Observations on Recent Literature', *Population and Development Review* 24, 3 (1998): 591.

Ivan, Franz, Helmut W. Lang and Heinz Pürer (eds), *200 Jahre Tageszeitungen in Österreich 1783–1983: Festschrift von Ausstellungskatalog* (Vienna: ÖNB, 1983).

Jagschitz, Gerhard, 'Die Nationalsozialistische Partei', in Emmerich Tálos, Herbert Dachs, Ernst Hanisch and Anton Staudinger (eds), *Handbuch des politischen Systems Österreichs: Erste Republik 1918–1933* (Vienna: Manz, 1995).

Jagschitz, Gerhard, 'Der österreichische Ständestaat 1934–1938', in Erika Weinzierl and Kurt Skalnik (eds), *Österreich 1918–1938: Geschichte der Ersten Republik*, vol. 1 (Graz: Styria, 1983).

Jagschitz, Gerhard, 'Die Presse in Österreich von 1918 bis 1945' in Heinz Pürer, Helmut W. Lang and Wolfgang Duchkowitsch (eds), *Die österreichische Tagespresse: Vergangenheit, Gegenwart, Zukunft. Ein Dokumentation von Vorträgen des Symposions "200 Jahre Tageszeitung in Österreich"* (Salzburg: Kuratorium für Journalistenausbildung, 1983).

Jagschitz, Gerhard, 'Zwischen Befriedung und Konfrontation: Zur Lage der NSDAP in Österreich 1934 bis 1936', in Ludwig Jedlicka and Rudolf Neck (eds), *Das Juliabkommen von 1936: Vorgeschichte, Hintergründe und Folgen* (Vienna: Verlag für Geschichte und Politik, 1977).

Jedlicka, Ludwig, 'The Austrian Heimwehr', *Journal of Contemporary History* 1, 1 (1966): 127–44.

Jedlicka, Ludwig and Rudolf Neck (eds), *Das Juliabkommen von 1936: Vorgeschichte, Hintergründe und Folgen* (Vienna: Verlag für Geschichte und Politik, 1977).

Jelavich, Barbara, *Modern Austria: Empire to Republic* (Cambridge: Cambridge University Press, 1987).

Jenkins, Brian (ed.), *France in the Era of Fascism: Essays on the French Authoritarian Right* (New York: Berghahn, 2005).

John, Michael, 'Angst, Kooperation und Widerstand: Die autochthonen Minderheiten Österreichs 1938–1945', *Zeitgeschichte* 17, 2 (1989): 66–89.

John, Michael, ' "We Do Not Even Possess Ourselves": On Identity and Ethnicity in Austria, 1880–1937', *Austrian History Yearbook* 30 (1999): 17–64.

John, Michael and Albert Lichtblau, *Schmelztiegl Wien – einst und jetzt: zur Geschichte und Gegenwart von Zuwanderung und Minderheiten* (Vienna: Böhlau, 1990).

Judson, Pieter M., *Exclusive Revolutionaries: Liberal Politics, Social Experience and National Identity in the Austrian Empire* (Ann Arbor: University of Michigan Press, 1996).

Judson, Pieter M., *Guardians of the Nation: Activists on the Language Frontiers of Imperial Austria* (Cambridge, MA: Harvard University Press, 2006).

Judson, Pieter M., 'Nationalizing Rural Landscapes in Cisleithania, 1880–1914', in Nancy M. Wingfield (ed.), *Creating the Other: Ethnic Conflict and Nationalism in Habsburg Central Europe* (New York: Berghahn, 2003).

Judson, Pieter M., ' "Not Another Square Foot!" German Liberalism and the Rhetoric of National Ownership in Nineteenth-Century Austria', *Austrian History Yearbook* 26 (1995): 83–97.

Kallis, Aristotle A., ' "Fascism", "Para-fascism" and "Fascistization": On the Similarities of Three Conceptual Categories', *European History Quarterly* 33, 2 (2003): 219–49.

Kammerhofer-Aggermann, Ulrike, 'Dirndl, Lederhose und Sommerfrischenidylle', in Robert Kriechbaumer (ed.), *Der Geschmack der Vergänglichkeit: Jüdische Sommerfrische in Salzburg* (Vienna: Böhlau, 2002).

Kann, Robert A., *A History of the Habsburg Empire 1526–1918* (Berkeley: University of California Press, 1974).

Kann, Robert A., *The Multinational Empire: Nationalism and National Reform in the Habsburg Monarchy 1848–1918*, vol. 1 (New York: Columbia University Press, 1950).

Karner, Stefan, *Die Steiermark im Dritten Reich 1938–1945: Aspekte ihrer politischen, wirtschaftlichen-sozialen und kulturellen Entwicklung* (Graz: Leykam, 1986).

Katzburg, Nathaniel, *Hungary and the Jews: Policy and Legislation, 1920–1943* (Ramat-Gan: Bar-Ilan University Press, 1981).

Kerekes, Lájos, *Abenddämmerung einer Demokratie: Mussolini, Gömbös und die Heimwehr* (Vienna: Europa, 1966).

Klamper, Elisabeth, 'Die Mühen der Wiederverchristlichung: Die Sakralkunst und die Rolle der Kirche während des Austrofaschismus', in Jan Tabor (ed.), *Kunst und Diktatur: Architektur, Bildhauerei und Malerei in Österreich, Deutschland, Italien und der Sowjetunion 1922–1956* (Baden: Grasl, 1994).

Kleiser, Christina, 'Biografien', in Ursula Seeber (ed.), *Asyl Wider Willen: Exil in Österreich 1933 bis 1938* (Vienna: Picus, 2003).

Klusacek, Christine and Kurt Stimmer, *Leopoldstadt* (Vienna: Kurt Mohl, 1978).

Königseder, Angelika, 'Antisemitismus 1935–1938', in Emmerich Tálos and Wolfgang Neugebauer (eds), *Austrofaschismus: Politik–Ökonomie–Kultur 1933–1938*, 5th rev. edn (Vienna: Lit, 2005).

Kriechbaumer, Robert (ed.), *Der Geschmack der Vergänglichkeit: Jüdische Sommerfrische in Salzburg* (Vienna: Böhlau, 2002).

Langewiesche, Dieter, 'Germany and the National Question in 1848', in John Breuilly (ed.), *The State of Germany: The National Idea in the Making, Unmaking and Remaking of a Modern Nation-state* (London: Longman, 1992).

Langewiesche, Dieter, *Zur Freiheit des Arbeiters: Bildungsbestrebungen und Freizeitgestaltung österreichischer Arbeiter im Kaiserreich und in der Ersten Republik* (Stuttgart: Klett-Cotta, 1980).

Lehnert, Detlef, 'Politisch-kulturelle Integrationsmilieus und Orientierungslager in einer polarisierten Massengesellschaft', in Emmerich Tálos, Herbert Dachs, Ernst Hanisch and Anton Staudinger (eds), *Handbuch des politischen Systems Österreichs: Erste Republik 1918–1933* (Vienna: Manz, 1995).

Lewis, Jill, 'Conservatives and Fascists in Austria, 1918–34', in Martin Blinkhorn (ed.), *Fascists and Conservatives: The Radical Right and the Establishment in Twentieth-century Europe* (London: Unwin Hyman, 1990).

Lewis, Jill, *Workers and Politics in Occupied Austria, 1945–55* (Manchester: Manchester University Press, 2007).

Lichtblau, Albert, ' "Ein Stück Paradies . . .": Jüdische Sommerfrischler in St Gilgen', in Robert Kriechbaumer (ed.), *Der Geschmack der Vergänglichkeit: Jüdische Sommerfrische in Salzburg* (Vienna: Böhlau, 2002).

Liebmann, Maximilian, *Theodor Innitzer und der Anschluss: Österreichs Kirche 1938* (Graz: Styria, 1988).

Liebscher, Daniela, 'Faschismus als Modell: Die faschistische *Opera Nazionale Dopolavoro* und die NS-Gemeinschaft "Kraft durch Freude" in der Zwischenkriegszeit', in Sven Reichardt and Armin Nolzen (eds), *Faschismus in Italien und Deutschland: Studien zu Transfer und Vergleich* (Göttingen: Wallstein, 2005).

Liulevicius, Vejas Gabriel, *War Land on the Eastern Front: Culture, National Identity, and German Occupation in World War I* (Cambridge: Cambridge University Press, 2000).

Lohrmann, Klaus, 'Vorgeschichte: Juden in Österreich vor 1867', in Gerhard Botz, Ivar Oxaal, Michael Pollak and Nina Scholz (eds), *Eine zerstörte Kultur: Jüdisches*

Leben und Antisemitismus in Wien seit dem 19. Jahrhundert (Vienna: Czernin, 2002).

Löscher, Monika, 'Eugenics and Catholicism in Interwar Austria', in Marius Turda and Paul J. Weindling (eds), *'Blood and Homeland': Eugenics and Racial Nationalism in Central and Southeast Europe, 1900–1940* (Budapest: Central European University Press, 2007).

Low, Alfred D., *The Anschluss Movement, 1931–1938, and the Great Powers* (Boulder: East European Monographs, 1985).

Low, Alfred D., 'Otto Bauer, Austro-Marxism, and the *Anschluss* Movement 1918–1938', *Canadian Review of Studies in Nationalism* 6, 1 (1979): 33–57.

Lüer, Andreas, 'Nationalismus in Christlichsozialen Programmen 1918–1933', *Zeitgeschichte* 14, 4 (1987): 147–66.

Maderthaner, Wolfgang, 'Legitimationsmuster des Austrofaschismus', in Wolfgang Maderthaner and Michaela Maier (eds), *'Der Führer bin ich selbst': Engelbert Dollfuss-Benito Mussolini Briefwechsel* (Vienna: Löcker, 2004).

Maderthaner, Wolfgang, and Michaela Maier (eds), *'Der Führer bin ich selbst': Engelbert Dollfuss-Benito Mussolini Briefwechsel* (Vienna: Löcker, 2004).

Malina, Peter, 'Berichte aus einem fernen Land? Die Berichterstattung der *Reichspost* über die Lage der Kirchen in Deutchland 1933', *Medien & Zeit* 5, 4 (1990): 11–17.

Mammach, Klaus, 'Deutsche Emigration in Österreich 1933–1938', *Bulletin des Arbeitskreises "Zweiter Weltkrieg"* 1–4 (1988): 194–209.

Mann, Michael, *Fascists* (Cambridge: Cambridge University Press, 2004).

Markovits, Andrei S., 'Peter Pulzer's Writing on Political Anti-Semitism and the Jewish Question in Germany and Austria: An Assessment', in Henning Tewes and Jonathan Wright (eds), *Liberalism, Anti-Semitism and Democracy: Essays in Honour of Peter Pulzer* (Oxford: Oxford University Press, 2001).

Marrus, Michael, *The Unwanted: European Refugees in the Twentieth Century* (Oxford: Oxford University Press, 1985).

Mayer, Jill E., ' "By Drip and By Drop": The Discourse of German Nationalism in the Press of Habsburg Austria. Salzburg, Styria, Vienna, 1877–1897' (PhD dissertation, University of Manitoba, 1993).

Melischek, Gabriele and Josef Seethaler (eds), *Die Wiener Tageszeitungen: Eine Dokumentation 1918–1938*, vol. 3 (Frankfurt am Main: Peter Lang, 1992).

Mitteilungen der Gesellschaft für Salzburger Landeskunde 101 (1961): 343–44.

Morgan, Philip, *Fascism in Europe, 1919–1945* (London: Routledge, 2003).

Necak, Dušan, *Die österreichische Legion II: Nationalsozialistische Flüchtlinge in Jugoslawien nach dem misslungenen Putsch vom 25. Juli 1934*, trans. Franci Zwitter (Vienna: Böhlau, 1996).

Neureitner, Gerlinde, 'Die Geschichte des *Salzburger Volksblattes* von 1870 bis 1942' (PhD dissertation, University of Salzburg, 1985).

Nord, Philip, *The Republican Moment: Struggles for Democracy in Nineteenth-Century France* (Cambridge, MA: Harvard University Press, 1995).

Olechowski, Richard, 'Schulpolitik', in Erika Weinzierl and Kurt Skalnik (eds), *Österreich 1918–1938: Geschichte der Ersten Republik*, vol. 2 (Graz: Styria, 1983).

Pauley, Bruce, 'A Case Study in Fascism: The Styrian *Heimatschutz* and Austrian National Socialism', *Austrian History Yearbook* 12/13 (1976/77): 251–73.

Pauley, Bruce, 'Fascism and the *Führerprinzip*: The Austrian Example', *Central European History* 12, 3 (1979): 272–96.

Pauley, Bruce, *From Prejudice to Persecution: A History of Austrian Anti-Semitism* (Chapel Hill: University of North Carolina Press, 1992).

Pauley, Bruce, *Hitler and the Forgotten Nazis: A History of Austrian National Socialism* (Chapel Hill: University of North Carolina Press, 1981).

Pauley, Bruce, 'Politischer Antisemitismus im Wien der Zwischenkriegszeit', in Gerhard Botz, Ivar Oxaal, Michael Pollak and Nina Scholz (eds), *Eine zerstörte Kultur: Jüdisches Leben und Antisemitismus in Wien seit dem 19. Jahrhundert* (Vienna: Czernin, 2002).

Paupié, Kurt, *Handbuch der Österreichischen Pressegeschichte, 1848–1959*, 2 vols (Vienna: Braumüller, 1960).

Paupié, Kurt, 'Das Pressewesen in Österreich 1918–1938', *Österreich in Geschichte und Literatur* 6, 4 (1962): 166–73.

Paxton, Robert, *The Anatomy of Fascism* (New York: Allen Lane, 2004).

Payne, Stanley G., *A History of Fascism, 1914–1945* (London: University College London Press, 1995).

Pegelow, Thomas, ' "German Jews", "National Jews", "Jewish Volk" or "Racial Jews"? The Constitution and Contestation of "Jewishness" in Newspapers of Nazi Germany, 1933–1938', *Central European History* 35, 2 (2002): 195–221.

Peniston-Bird, C.M., 'The Debate on Austrian National Identity in the First Republic, 1918–1938' (PhD dissertation, University of St Andrews, 1996).

Pfarrhofer, Hedwig, *Friedrich Funder: Ein Mann zwischen Gestern und Morgen* (Graz: Styria, 1978).

Phayer, Michael, *The Catholic Church and the Holocaust, 1930–1965* (Bloomington: Indiana University Press, 2000).

Pollard, John, 'Conservative Catholics and Italian Fascism: The Clerico-Fascists', in Martin Blinkhorn (ed.), *Fascists and Conservatives: The Radical Right and the Establishment in Twentieth-century Europe* (London: Unwin Hyman, 1990).

Potyka, Alexander, 'Ideologie und Tagesgeschehen für den "kleinen Mann": Das "Kleine Blatt" 1927–1934', in Wolfgang Duchkowitsch, Hannes Haas and Klaus Lojka (eds), *Kreativität aus der Krise: Konzepte zur gesellschaftlichen Kommunikation in der Ersten Republik* (Vienna: Literas, 1991).

Pridham, Geoffrey, *Hitler's Rise to Power: The Nazi Movement in Bavaria, 1923–1933* (London: Hart-Davis, MacGibbon, 1973).

Priestly, Tom, 'Denial of Ethnic Identity: The Political Manipulation of Beliefs about Language in Slovene Minority Areas of Austria and Hungary', *Slavic Review* 55, 2 (1996): 364–98.

Promitzer, Christian, 'The South Slavs in the Austrian Imagination: Serbs and Slovenes in the Changing View from German Nationalism to National

Socialism', in Nancy M. Wingfield (ed.), *Creating the Other: Ethnic Conflict and Nationalism in Habsburg Central Europe* (New York: Berghahn, 2003).

Pulzer, Peter, 'Der Erste Weltkrieg', in Steven M. Lowenstein, Paul Mendes-Flohr, Peter Pulzer and Monika Richarz (eds), *Deutsch-jüdische Geschichte in der Neuzeit*, vol. 3 (Munich: C.H. Beck, 1997).

Pulzer, Peter, 'Spezifische Momente und Spielarten des österreichischen und des Wiener Antisemitismus', in Gerhard Botz, Ivar Oxaal, Michael Pollak and Nina Scholz (eds), *Eine zerstörte Kultur: Jüdisches Leben und Antisemitismus in Wien seit dem 19. Jahrhundert* (Vienna: Czernin, 2002).

Quine, Maria Sophia, *Population Politics in Twentieth Century Europe: Fascist Dictatorships and Liberal Democracies* (London: Routledge, 1996).

Rath, R. John, 'History and Citizenship Training: An Austrian Example', *Journal of Modern History* 21, 3 (1949): 227–38.

Rath, R. John, 'Training for Citizenship, "Authoritarian" Austrian Style', *Journal of Central European Affairs* 3, 2 (1943): 121–46.

Rath, John and Carolyn W. Schum, 'The Dollfuss-Schuschnigg Regime: Fascist or Authoritarian?', in Stein Ugelvik Larsen, Bernt Hagtvet and Jan Petter Myklebust (eds), *Who Were the Fascists? Social Roots of European Fascism* (Bergen: Universitetsforlaget, 1980).

Rathkolb, Oliver, 'Asyl- und Transitland 1933–1938?', in Gernot Heiss and Oliver Rathkolb (eds), *Asylland Wider Willen: Flüchtlinge im Europäischen Kontext seit 1914* (Vienna: Jugend & Volk, 1995).

Reichardt, Sven and Armin Nolzen (eds), *Faschismus in Italien und Deutschland: Studien zu Transfer und Vergleich* (Göttingen: Wallstein, 2005).

Reimann, Viktor, *Innitzer: Kardinal zwischen Hitler und Rom*, rev. and expanded edn (Vienna: Amalthea, 1988).

Röder, Werner, 'The Political Exiles: Their Policies and Their Contribution to Postwar Reconstruction', in *Biographisches Handbuch der deutschsprachigen Emigration nach 1933* (Munich: K.G. Saur, 1980).

Rozenblit, Marsha L., 'Jewish Ethnicity in a New Nation-State: The Crisis of Identity in the Austrian Republic', in Michael Brenner and Derek J. Penslar (eds), *In Search of Jewish Communities: Jewish Identities in Germany and Austria 1918–1933* (Bloomington: Indiana University Press, 1998).

Rozenblit, Marsha L., *The Jews of Vienna, 1867–1914: Assimilation and Identity* (Albany: State University of New York Press, 1983).

Scheichl, Sigurd Paul, 'The Contexts and Nuances of Anti-Jewish Language: Were all the "Antisemites" Antisemites?', in Ivar Oxaal (ed.), *Jews, Antisemitism and Culture in Vienna* (London: Routledge and Kegan Paul, 1987).

Scheu, Friedrich, *Der Weg ins Ungewisse: Österreichs Schicksalskurve 1929–1938* (Vienna: Molden, 1972).

Schlag, Gerald, 'Die Kroaten im Burgenland 1918 bis 1945', in Stefan Geosits (ed.), *Die burgenländischen Kroaten im Wandel der Zeiten* (Vienna: Edition Tusch, 1986).

Schmied, Harald, ' "D'rum straff angezogen … den stahldrähtigen Maulkorb": Presse und Diktatur (1933–1938) am Beispiel der Steiermark' (MA dissertation, Karl-Franzens-University, 1996).

Schmied, Wieland, 'Die österreichische Malerei in den Zwischenkriegsjahren', in Erika Weinzierl and Kurt Skalnik (eds), *Österreich 1918–1938: Geschichte der Ersten Republik*, vol. 2 (Graz: Styria, 1983).

Schmolke, Michael, 'Katholische Journalistik in Österreich 1933–1938', *Medien & Zeit* 3, 4 (1988): 17–24.

Schmolke, Michael, 'Das Salzburger Medienwesen', in Heinz Dopsch and Hans Spatzenegger (eds), *Geschichte Salzburgs: Stadt und Land* (Salzburg: Anton Pustet, 1991).

Schorske, Carl E., 'Politics in a New Key: An Austrian Triptych', *Journal of Modern History* 39, 4 (1967): 343–86.

Seeber, Ursula, 'Österreich als Exil 1933 bis 1938', in Ursula Seeber (ed.), *Asyl Wider Willen: Exil in Österreich 1933 bis 1938* (Vienna: Picus, 2003).

Segar, Kenneth, 'Austria in the Thirties: Reality and Exemplum', in Kenneth Segar and John Warren (eds), *Austria in the Thirties: Culture and Politics* (Riverside, CA: Ariadne, 1991).

Seton-Watson, Hugh, 'Fascism, Right and Left', *Journal of Contemporary History* 1, 1 (1966): 183–97.

Singer-Kérel, Jeanne, 'Foreign Workers in France, 1891–1936', *Ethnic and Racial Studies* 14, 3 (1991): 279–93.

Skalnik, Kurt, 'Auf der Suche nach der Identität', in Erika Weinzierl and Kurt Skalnik (eds), *Österreich 1918–1938: Geschichte der Ersten Republik*, vol. 1 (Graz: Styria, 1983).

Skran, Claudena M., *Refugees in Inter-War Europe: The Emergence of a Regime* (Oxford: Clarendon, 1995).

Soucy, Robert, 'Fascism in France: Problematizing the Immunity Thesis', in Brian Jenkins (ed.), *France in the Era of Fascism: Essays on the French Authoritarian Right* (New York: Berghahn, 2005).

Staudinger, Anton, 'Austrofaschistische "Österreich"-Ideologie', in Emmerich Tálos and Wolfgang Neugebauer (eds), *Austrofaschismus: Politik–Ökonomie–Kultur 1933–1938*, 5th rev. edn (Vienna: Lit, 2005).

Staudinger, Anton, 'Katholischer Antisemitismus in der Ersten Republik', in Gerhard Botz, Ivar Oxaal, Michael Pollak and Nina Scholz (eds), *Eine zerstörte Kultur: Jüdisches Leben und Antisemitismus in Wien seit dem 19. Jahrhundert* (Vienna: Czernin, 2002).

Staudinger, Anton, 'Zur "Österreich"-Ideologie des Ständestaates', in Ludwig Jedlicka and Rudolf Neck (eds), *Das Juliabkommen von 1936: Vorgeschichte, Hintergründe und Folgen* (Vienna: Verlag für Geschichte und Politik, 1977).

Steigmann-Gall, Richard, *The Holy Reich: Nazi Conceptions of Christianity, 1919–1945* (Cambridge: Cambridge University Press, 2003).

Steinberg, Michael, *The Meaning of the Salzburg Festival: Austria as Theatre and Ideology, 1890–1938* (Ithaca: Cornell University Press, 1990).

Steinböck, Erwin, 'Kärnten', in Erika Weinzierl and Kurt Skalnik (eds), *Österreich 1918–1938: Geschichte der Ersten Republik*, vol. 2 (Graz: Styria, 1983).

Stourzh, Gerald, 'Erschütterung und Konsolidierung des Österreichbewusstseins: Vom Zusammenbruch der Monarchie zur Zweiten Republik', in Richard G.

Plaschka, Gerald Stourzh and Jan Paul Niederkorn (eds), *Was heisst Österreich? Inhalt und Umfang des Österreichbegriffs vom 10. Jahrhundert bis heute* (Vienna: Verlag der österreichischen Akademie der Wissenschaften, 1995).

Stourzh, Gerald, 'Ethnic Attribution in Late Imperial Austria: Good Intentions, Evil Consequences', in Edward Timms and Ritchie Robertson (eds), *The Habsburg Legacy: National Identity in Historical Perspective* (Edinburgh: Edinburgh University Press, 1994).

Stuiber Peter, 'Chronik des deutschen Exils in Österreich', in Ursula Seeber (ed.), *Asyl Wider Willen: Exil in Österreich 1933 bis 1938* (Vienna: Picus, 2003).

Suchy, Viktor (ed.), *Dichter zwischen den Zeiten: Festschrift für Rudolf Henz zum 80. Geburtstag* (Vienna: Braumüller, 1977).

Suval, Stanley, *The Anschluss Question in the Weimar Era: A Study of Nationalism in Germany and Austria 1918–32* (Baltimore: Johns Hopkins University Press, 1974).

Sweet, Paul R., 'The Historical Writing of Heinrich von Srbik', *History and Theory* 9, 1 (1970): 37–58.

Sweet, Paul R., 'Seipel's Views on *Anschluss* in 1928: An Unpublished Exchange of Letters', *Journal of Modern History* 19, 4 (1947): 320–23.

Szucsich, Franz, 'Das Vereinswesen der burgenländischen Kroaten', in Stefan Geosits (ed.), *Die burgenländischen Kroaten im Wandel der Zeiten* (Vienna: Edition Tusch, 1986).

Tálos, Emmerich, 'Das austrofaschistische Herrschaftssystem', in Emmerich Tálos and Wolfgang Neugebauer (eds), *Austrofaschismus: Politik–Ökonomie–Kultur 1933–1938*, 5th rev. edn (Vienna: Lit, 2005).

Tálos, Emmerich and Walter Manoschek, 'Aspekte der politischen Struktur des Austrofaschismus', in Emmerich Tálos and Wolfgang Neugebauer (eds), *Austrofaschismus: Politik–Ökonomie–Kultur 1933–1938*, 5th rev. edn (Vienna: Lit, 2005).

Taylor, A.J.P., *The Habsburg Monarchy, 1809–1918: A History of the Austrian Empire and Austria-Hungary*, Paperback edn (Chicago: University of Chicago Press, 1967).

Ther, Philipp, 'Beyond the Nation: The Relational Basis of a Comparative History of Germany and Europe', *Central European History* 36, 1 (2003): 45–73.

Thorpe, Julie, 'Austrofascism: Revisiting the "Authoritarian State" Forty Years On', *Journal of Contemporary History* 45, 2 (2010): 1–29.

Timms, Edward, 'Citizenship and "Heimatrecht" after the Treaty of Saint-Germain', in Edward Timms and Ritchie Robertson (eds), *The Habsburg Legacy: National Identity in Historical Perspective* (Edinburgh: Edinburgh University Press, 1994).

Timms, Edward, 'The Kraus-Bekessy Controversy in Interwar Vienna', in Robert S. Wistrich (ed.), *Austrians and Jews in the Twentieth Century: From Franz Joseph to Waldheim* (New York: St Martin's Press, 1992).

Turda, Marius and Paul J. Weindling (eds), *'Blood and Homeland': Eugenics and Racial Nationalism in Central and Southeast Europe, 1900–1940* (Budapest: Central European University Press, 2007).

Tweraser, Kurt, 'Carl Beurle and the Triumph of German Nationalism in Austria', *German Studies Review* 4, 3 (1981): 403–26.

von Klemperer, Klemens, *Ignaz Seipel: Christian Statesman in a Time of Crisis* (Princeton: Princeton University Press, 1972).

Vyleta, Daniel, 'Jewish Crimes and Misdemeanours: In Search of Jewish Criminality (Germany and Austria, 1890–1914)', *European History Quarterly* 35, 2 (2005): 299–325.

Waitzbauer, Harald, ' "San die Juden scho' furt?": Salzburg, die Festspiele und das jüdische Publikum', in Robert Kriechbaumer (ed.), *Der Geschmack der Vergänglichkeit: Jüdische Sommerfrische in Salzburg* (Vienna: Böhlau, 2002).

Waltraud, Jakob, *Salzburger Zeitungsgeschichte* (Salzburg: Schriftenreihe des Landespressebüros, 1979).

Wandruszka, Adam, 'Das "nationale" Lager', in Erika Weinzierl and Kurt Skalnik (eds), *Österreich 1918–1938: Geschichte der Ersten Republik*, vol. 1 (Graz: Styria, 1983).

Wandruszka, Adam, 'Österreichs politische Struktur: Die Entwicklung der Parteien und politischen Bewegungen', in Heinrich Benedikt (ed.), *Geschichte der Republik Österreich* (Vienna: Verlag für Geschichte und Politik, 1954).

Warren, John, ' "Weisse Strümpfe oder neue Kutten": Cultural Decline in Vienna in the 1930s', in Deborah Holmes and Lisa Silverman (eds), *Interwar Vienna: Culture Between Tradition and Modernity* (Rochester, NY: Camden House, 2009).

Weindling, Paul, *Epidemics and Genocide in Eastern Europe, 1890–1945* (Oxford: Oxford University Press, 2000).

Weindling, Paul, 'Fascism and Population in Comparative European Perspective', *Population and Development Review* 14, Supplement: Population and Resources in Western Intellectual Traditions (1988): 102–21.

Weinzierl, Erika and Kurt Skalnik (eds), *Österreich 1918–1938: Geschichte der Ersten Republik*, 2 vols (Graz: Styria, 1983).

Weissensteiner, Friedrich, *Der ungeliebte Staat: Österreich zwischen 1918 und 1938* (Vienna: ÖBV, 1990).

Westermann, Klaus, *Joseph Roth, Journalist: Eine Karriere 1915–1939* (Bonn: Bouvier, 1987).

Whiteside, Andrew G. 'The Germans as an Integrative Force in Imperial Austria: The Dilemma of Dominance', *Austrian History Yearbook* 3, 1 (1967): 157–200.

Whiteside, Andrew G., *The Socialism of Fools: Georg Ritter von Schönerer and Austrian Pan-Germanism* (Berkeley: University of California Press, 1975).

Wistrich, Robert S., *The Jews of Vienna in the Age of Franz Joseph* (Oxford: Oxford University Press, 1989).

Wood, Nathaniel D., 'Urban Self-Identification in East Central Europe before the Great War: The Case of Cracow', *East Central Europe/L'Europe du Centre-Est/ Eine wissenschaftliche Zeitung* 33, 1–2 (2006): 11–31.

Zeldin, Theodore, *France, 1848–1945*, vol. 2 (Oxford: Clarendon, 1977).

Zahra, Tara, *Kidnapped Souls: National Indifference and the Battle for Children in the Bohemian Lands, 1900–1948* (Ithaca: Cornell University Press, 2008).

Zahra, Tara, 'The "Minority Problem" and National Classification in the French and Czechoslovak Borderlands', *Contemporary European History* 17, 2 (2008): 137–65.

Zahra, Tara, 'Reclaiming Children for the Nation: Germanization, National Ascription and Democracy in the Bohemian Lands, 1900–1945', *Central European History* 37, 4 (2004): 501–43.

Zeps, Michael J., *Education and the Crisis of the First Republic* (Boulder: Eastern Europe Monographs, 1987).

Zimmer, Oliver, 'Boundary Mechanisms and Symbolic Resources: Towards a Process-Oriented Approach to National Identity', *Nations and Nationalism* 9, 2 (2003): 173–93.

Zimmer, Oliver, *Nationalism in Europe, 1890–1940* (Basingstoke: Palgrave Macmillan, 2003).

Zöllner, Erich, 'The Germans as an Integrating and Disintegrating Force', *Austrian History Yearbook* 3, 1 (1967): 201–33.

Zwitter, Fran, 'The Slovenes and the Habsburg Monarchy', *Austrian History Yearbook* 3, 2 (1967): 159–88.

Electronic sources

AEIOU, AEIOU Encyclopedia, www.aeiou.at/

Index